THE CITY WITHIN

BROOKLYN

THE CITY WITHIN

ALEX WEBB & REBECCA NORRIS WEBB

INTERVIEW BY SEAN CORCORAN

aperture

There seems almost no conceivable end
to Brooklyn . . . horizon beyond horizon
forever unfolded . . . street by street . . .

—

OVER THE PAST FIVE YEARS, Rebecca and I have been photographing Brooklyn, the borough we've called home for two decades. I've been photographing all over Brooklyn and focusing on, among other things, its tremendous cultural diversity— it's said that one in every eight US families had relatives come through Brooklyn at one time or another. So I've been exploring Mexican Brooklyn, Caribbean Brooklyn, Chinese Brooklyn, and other communities. It's a bit like what I've done for the past forty years—traveling to photograph a variety of cultures from around the world— except, instead of taking an airplane, I've been riding the subway. Meanwhile, Rebecca has been photographing the green heart of the borough: Prospect Park, Brooklyn Botanic Garden, and Green-Wood Cemetery. Originally a poet, she's also written about her walks through these green spaces near our home in Park Slope— and her own interior landscape. Together, her words and pictures create places where landscape and memory, history and reverie meet.

We're calling this book *The City Within* not only because Brooklyn was once its own city 120 years ago, although it now lies within the vast confines of New York City, but also because the green heart where Rebecca has photographed lies in the center of the borough. With millions of visitors each year, it's a kind of green city within the city within the city. Echoing this geography, Rebecca's lyrical text pieces and images inhabit the middle of the book.

Lastly, since Rebecca and I will be leaving our Park Slope neighborhood sometime in the next few years, we also see this book as the beginning of our farewell to Brooklyn.

—

ALEX WEBB

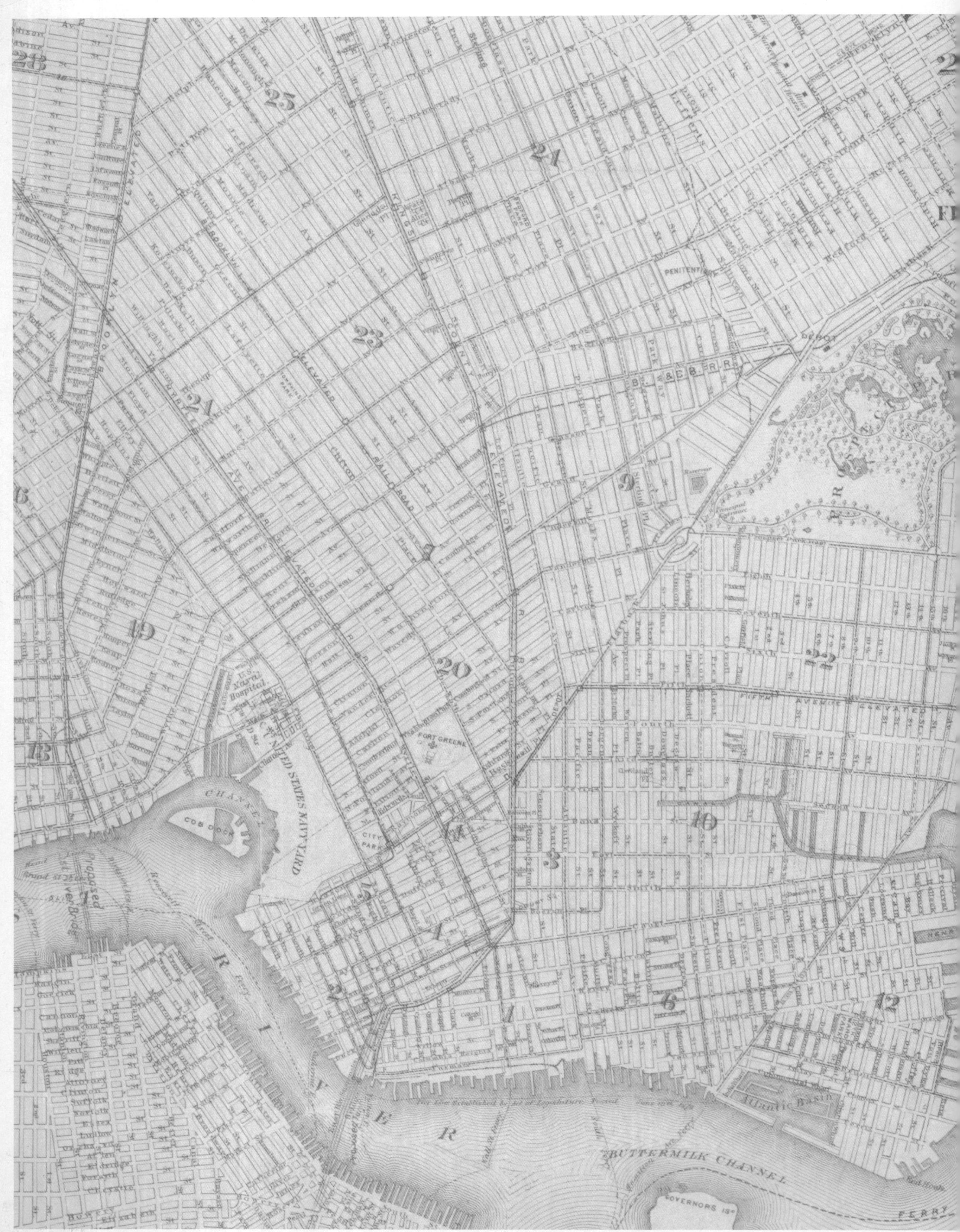

28
25
21
FL
PENITENTIARY
DEPOT
23
B.E. & E. R.R.
21
9
PROSPECT PARK
13
19
U.S. Naval Hospital
20
22
UNITED STATES NAVY YARD
FORT GREENE
CHANNEL
COB DOCK
13
FIFTH AVENUE ELEVATED
10
11
CITY PARK
3
EAST RIVER
24
8
22
1
6
12
Port Line Established by Act of Legislature Passed June 12th 1878
EAST RIVER
ATLANTIC BASIN
BUTTERMILK CHANNEL
GOVERNORS ISd
FERRY

I

ALEX WEBB

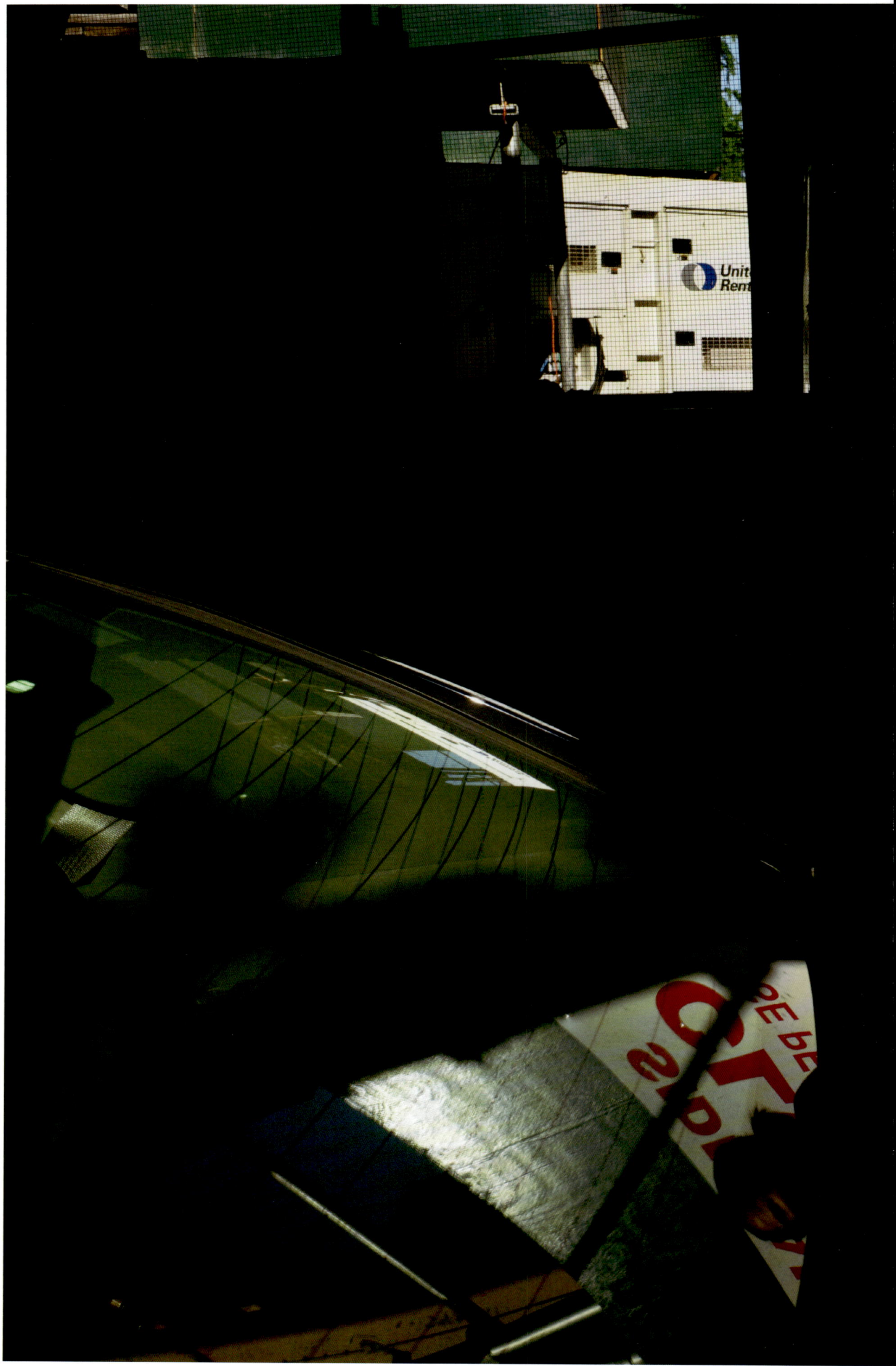

Unit
Rent

BROOKLYN HEIGHTS, 2014

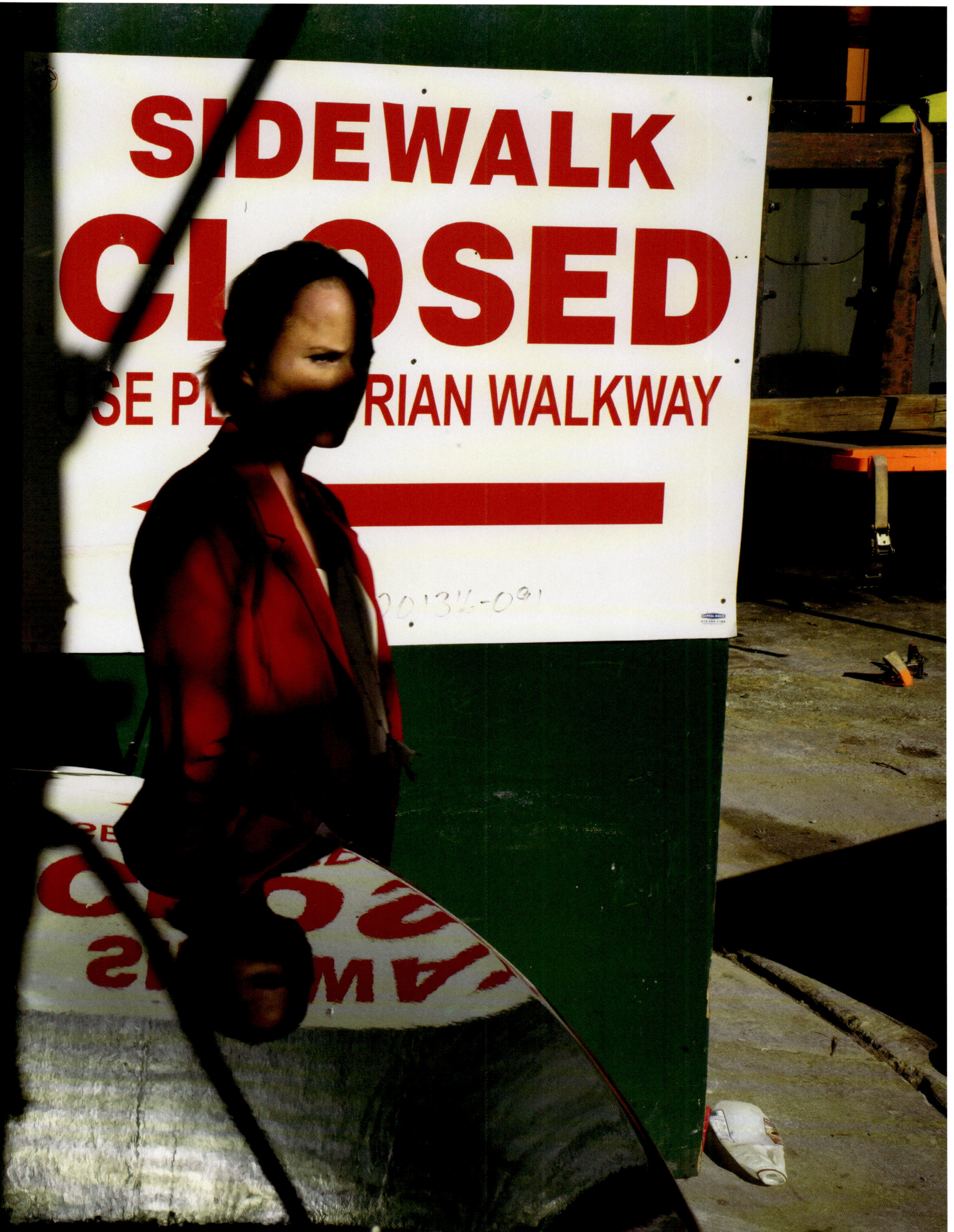

SIDEWALK
CLOSED
SE PEDESTRIAN WALKWAY

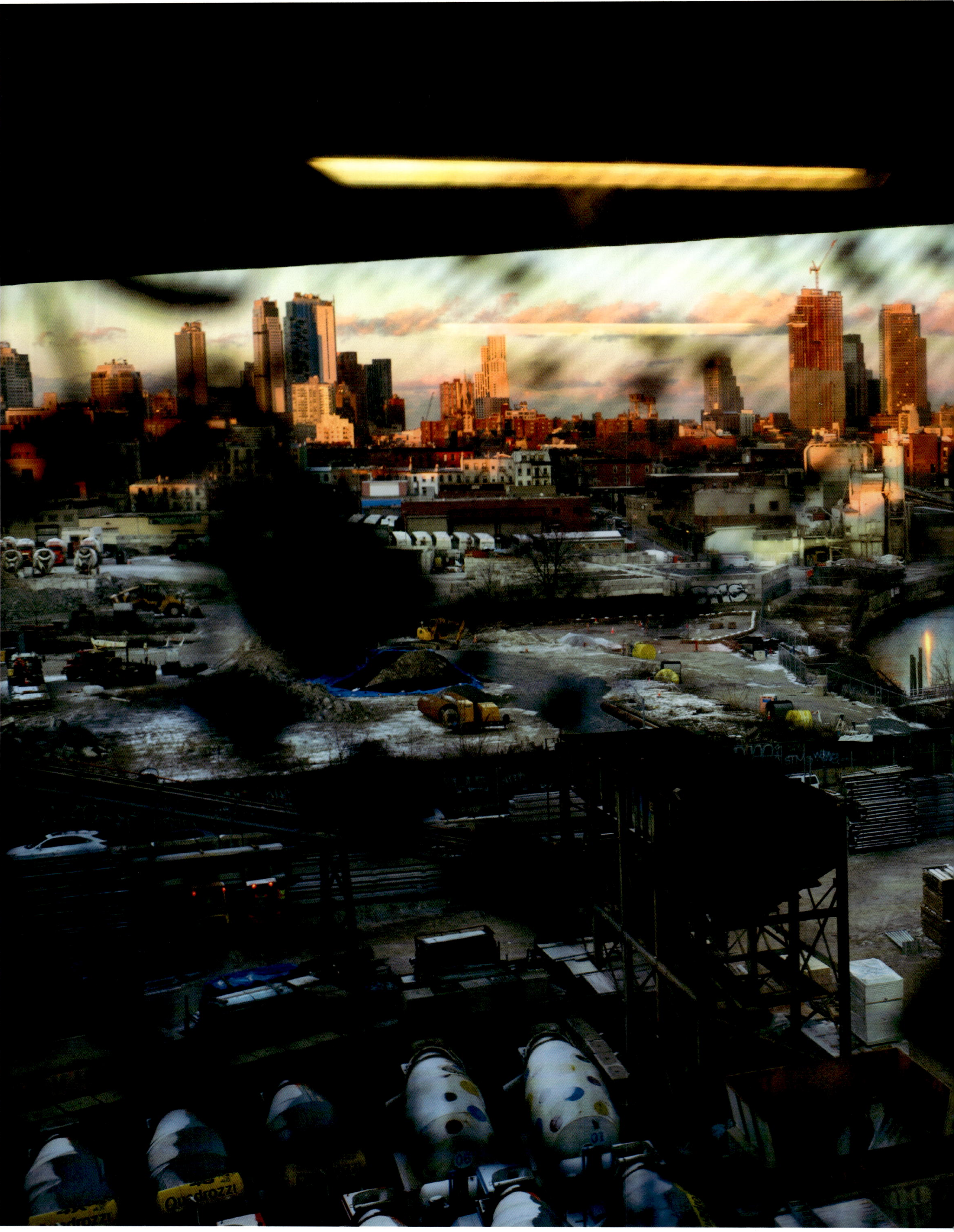

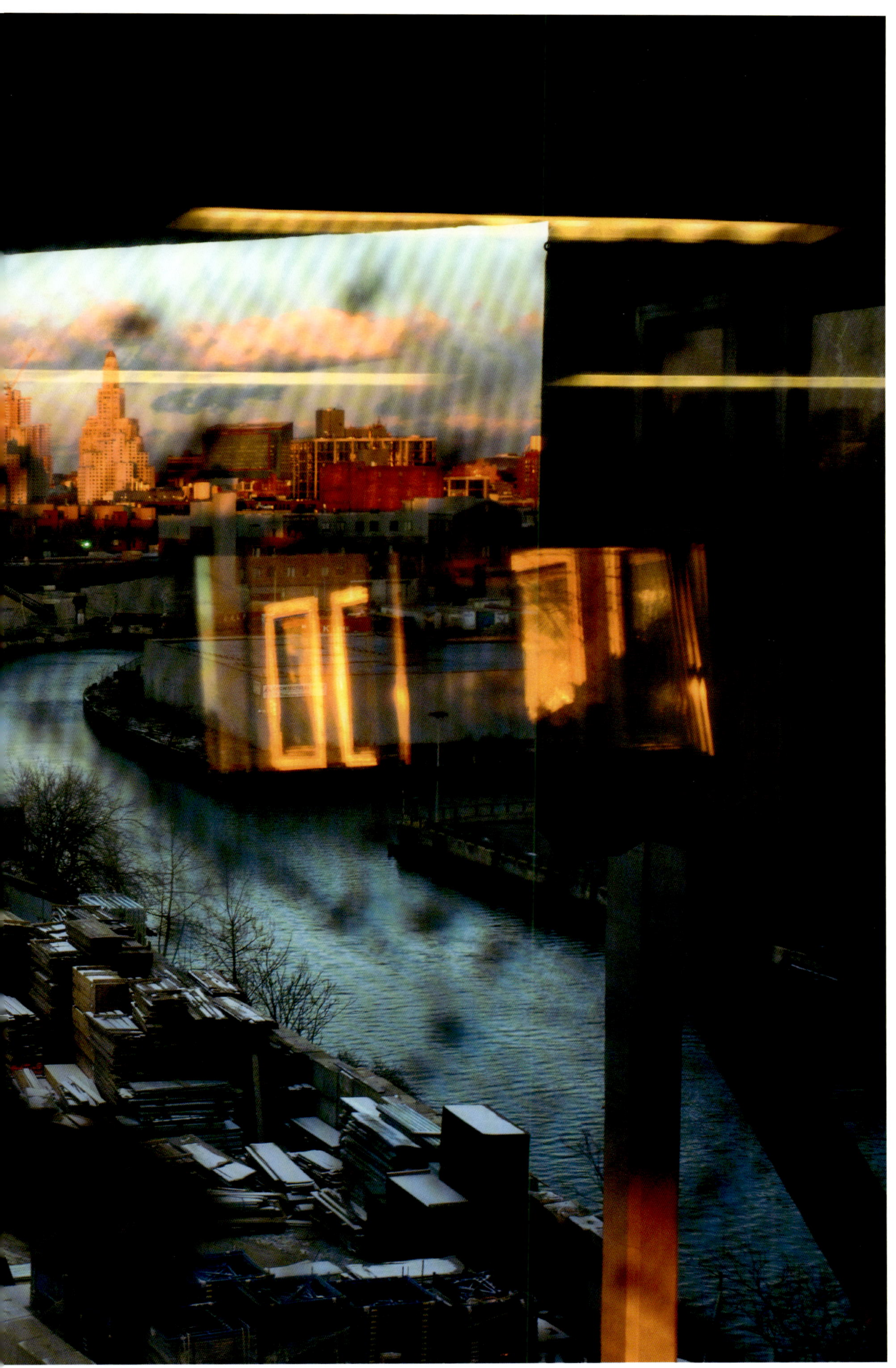

GOWANUS, 2016

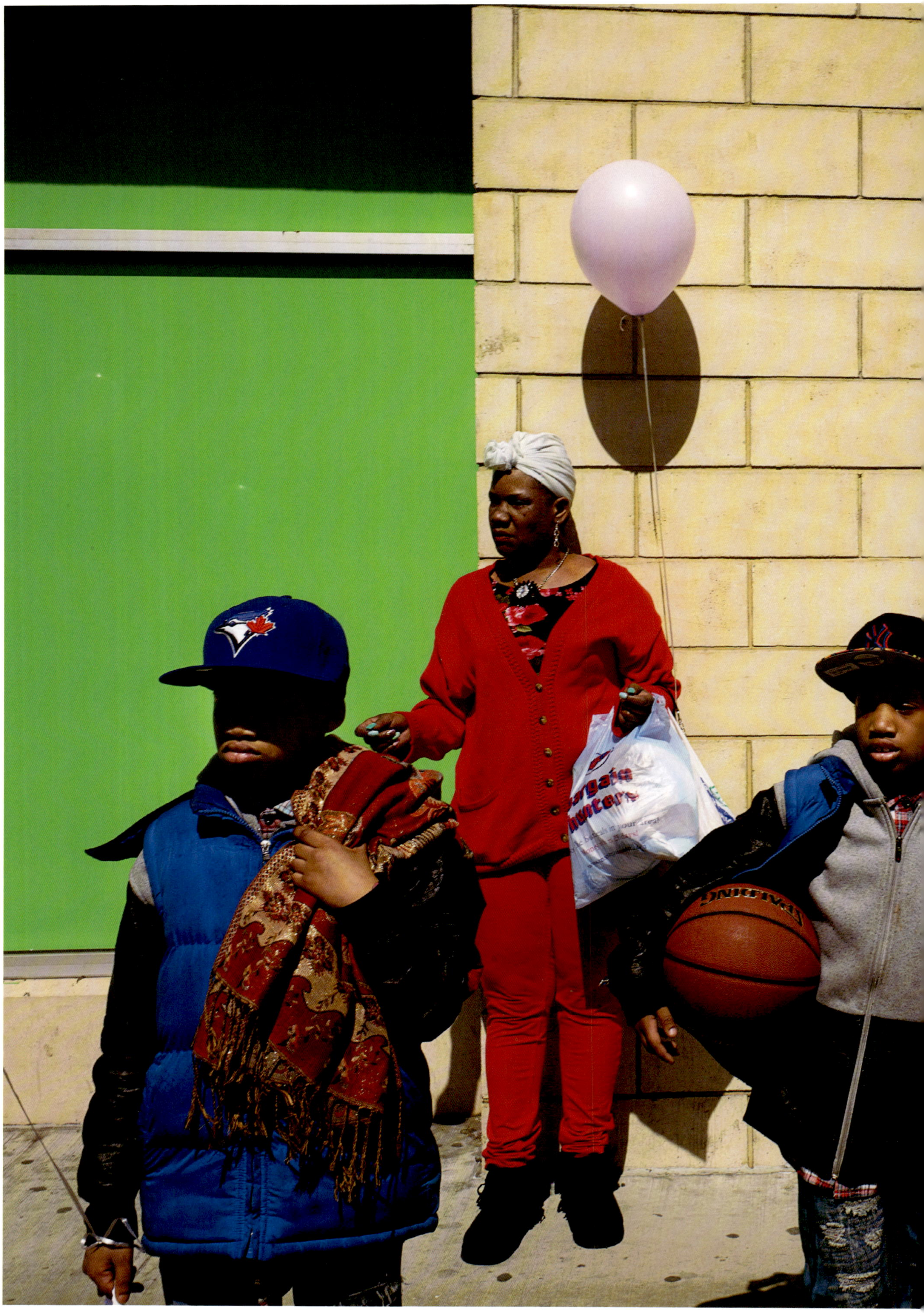

BROWNSVILLE, EASTER SUNDAY, 2016

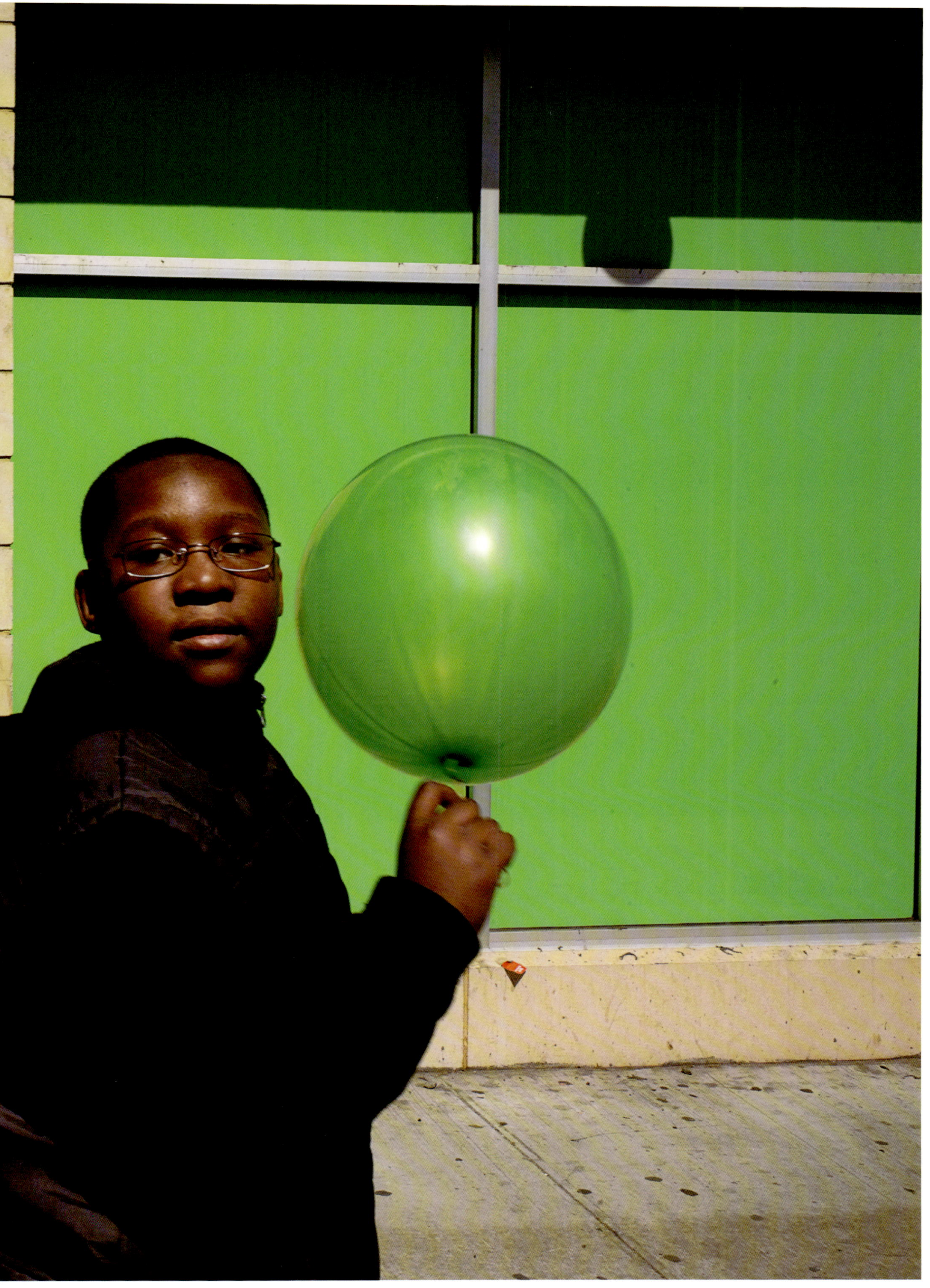

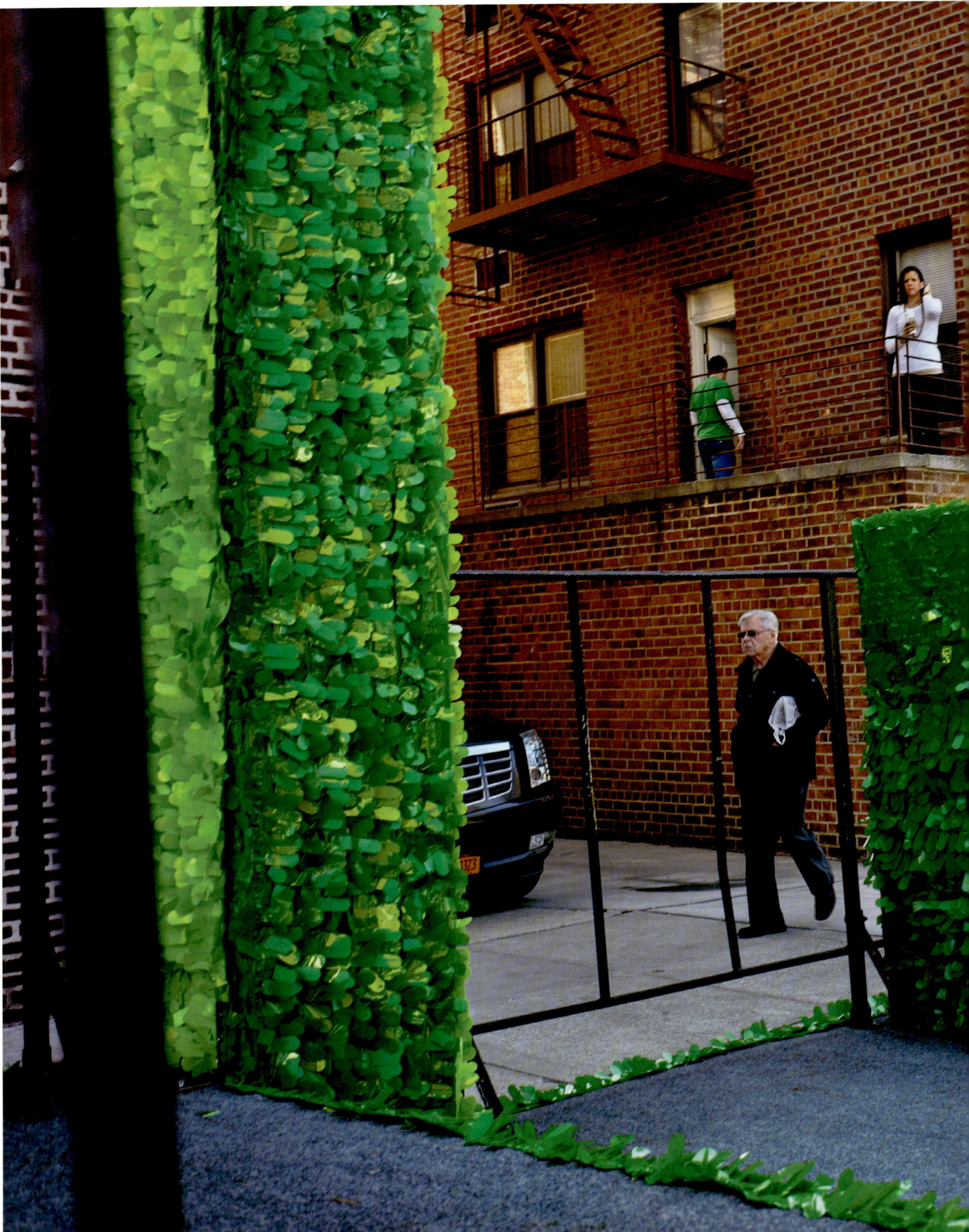

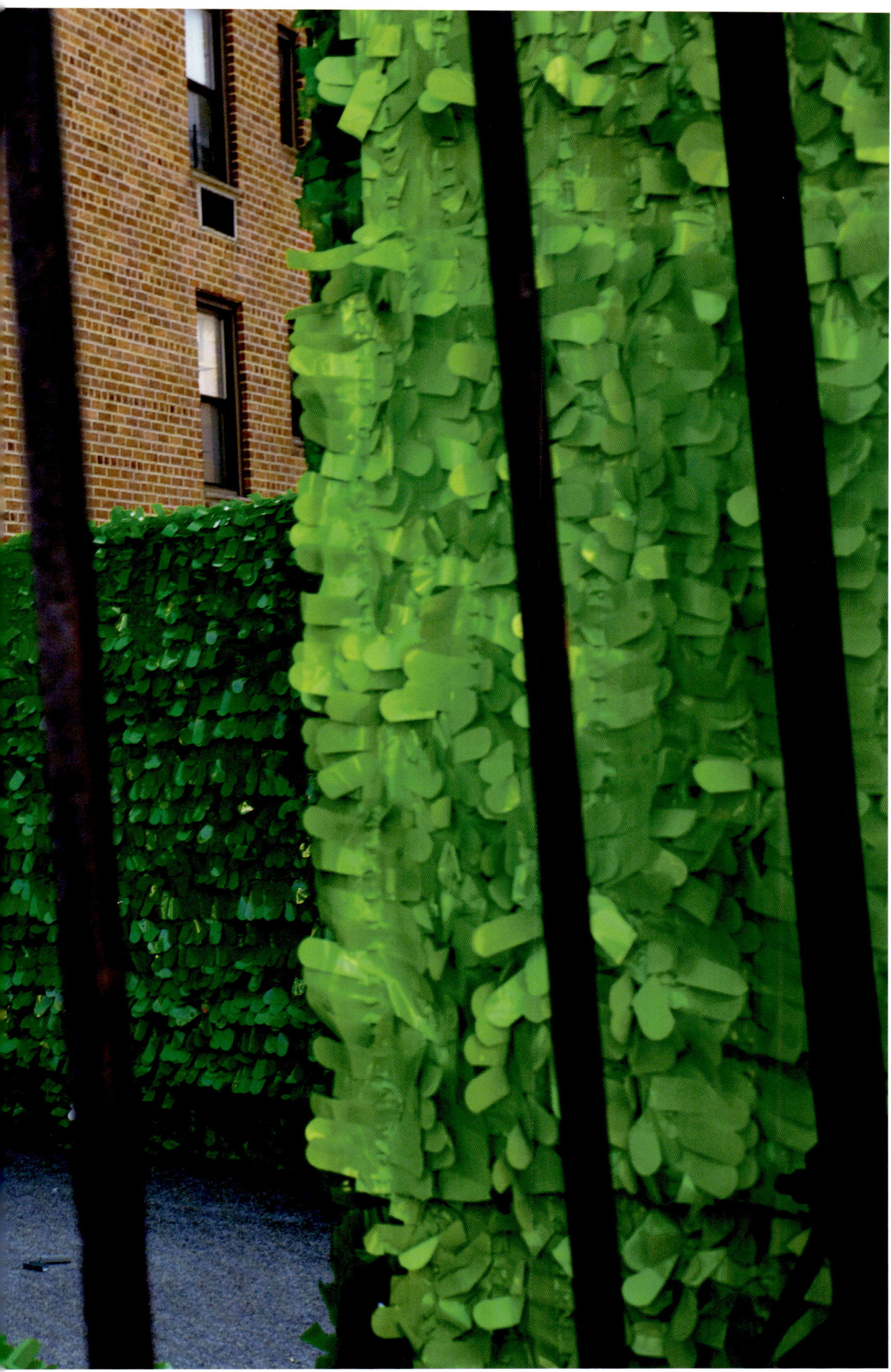

BAY RIDGE, SAINT PATRICK'S DAY, 2015

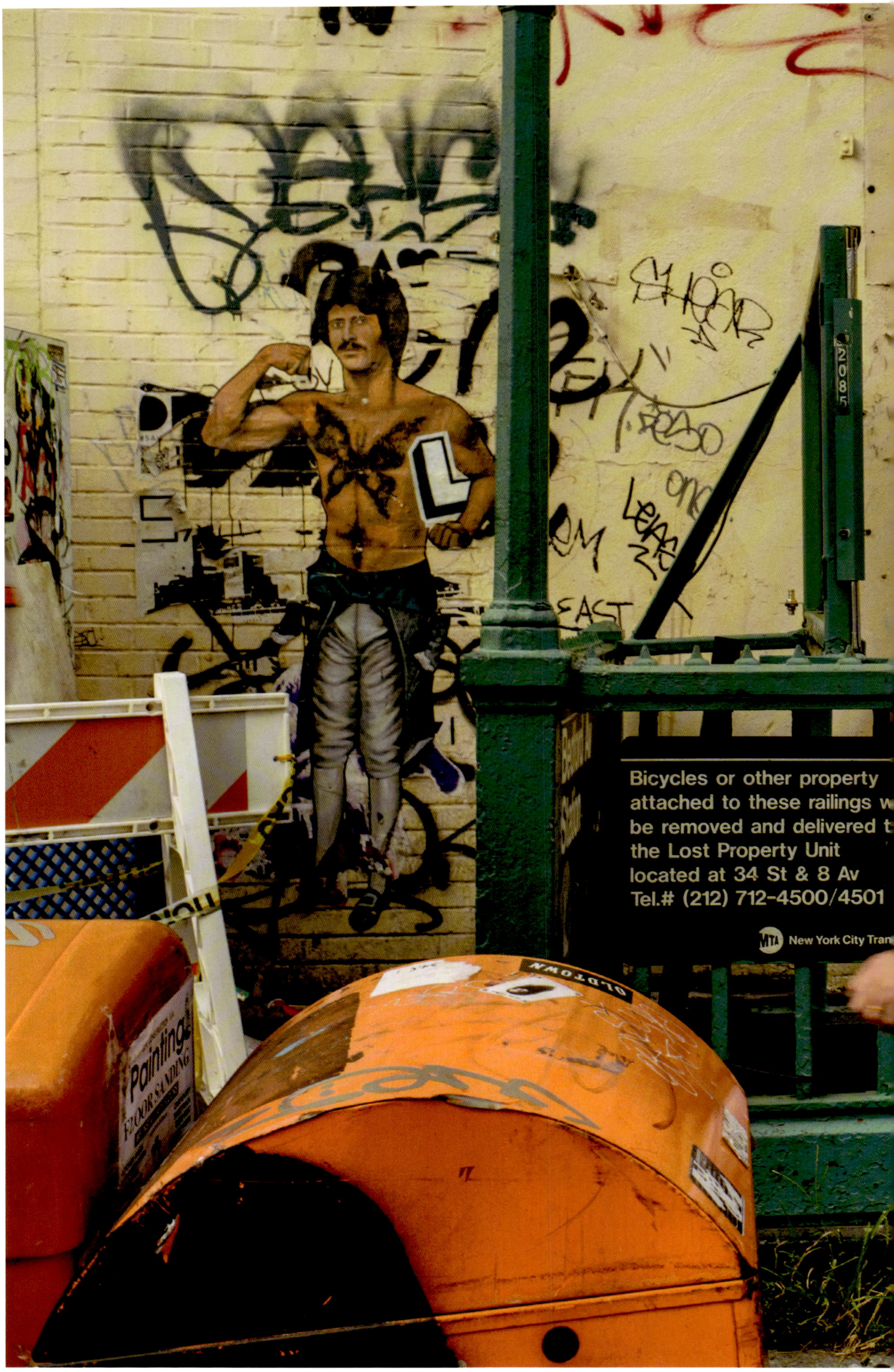

Bicycles or other property
attached to these railings w
be removed and delivered t
the Lost Property Unit
located at 34 St & 8 Av
Tel.# (212) 712-4500/4501
New York City Tran

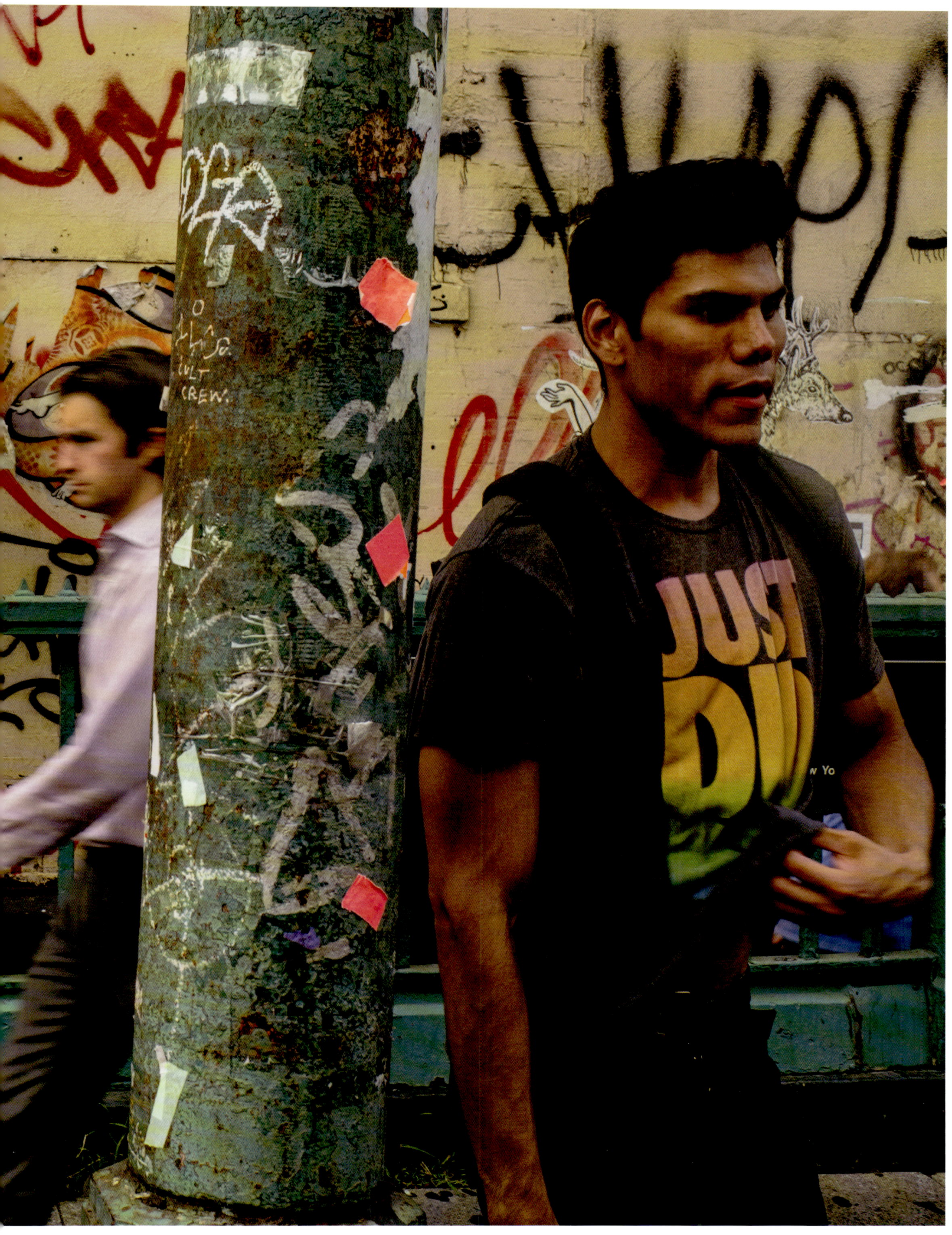

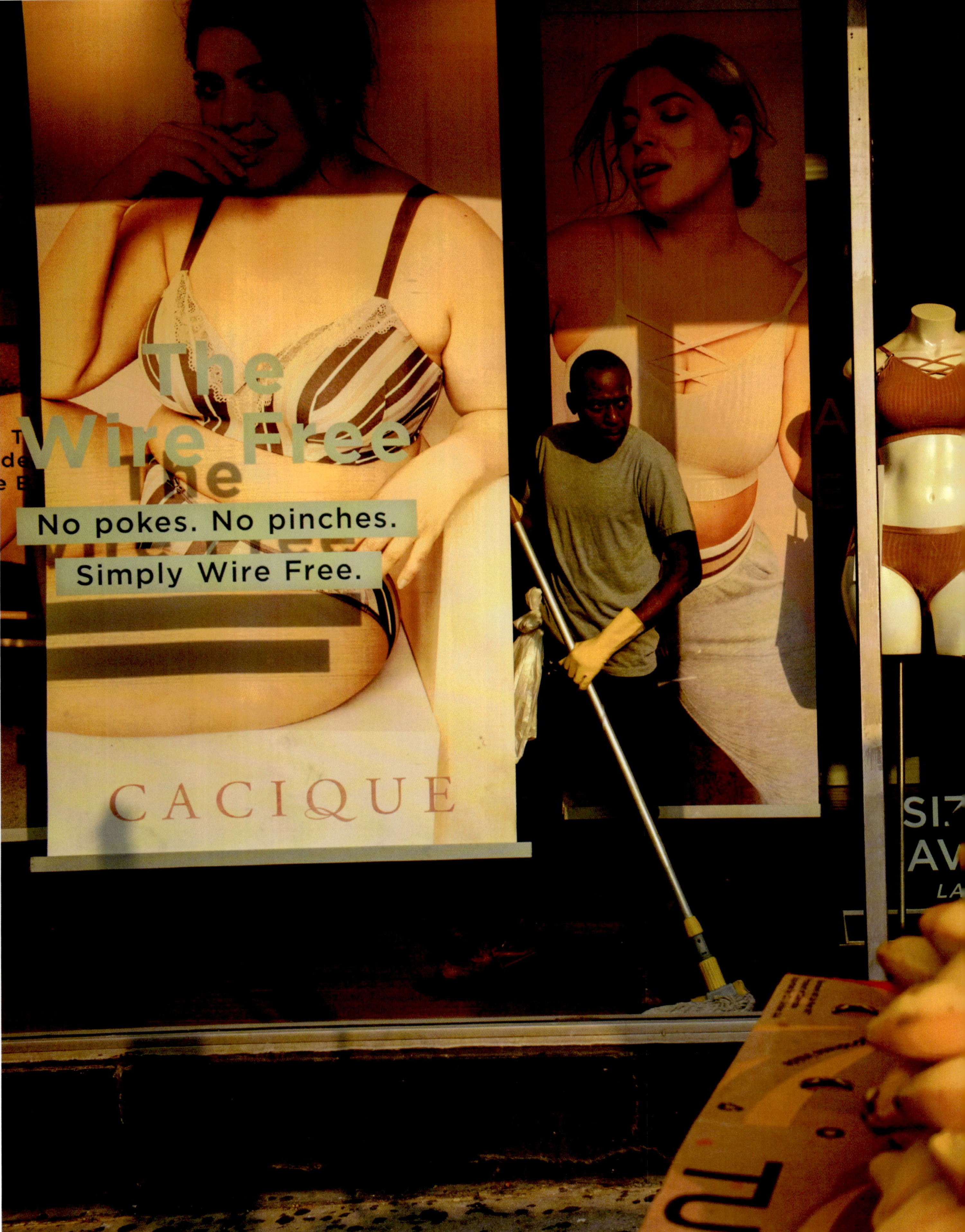

The
Wire Free
No pokes. No pinches.
Simply Wire Free.
CACIQUE

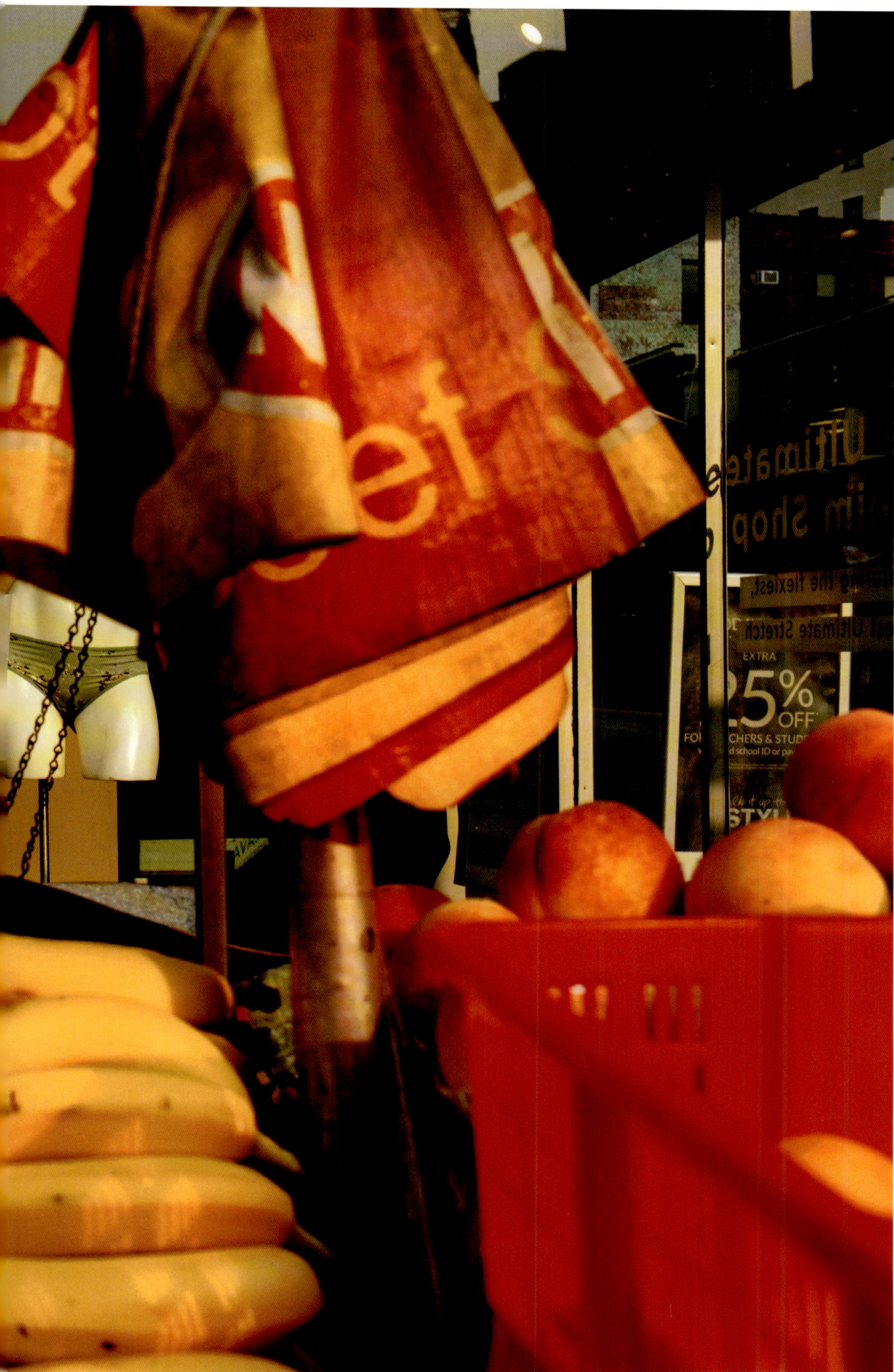
ef
Ultimate
im Shop
the flexiest,
Ultimate Stretch
EXTRA
25% OFF
FOR TEACHERS & STUDE
school ID or pa
STYLE

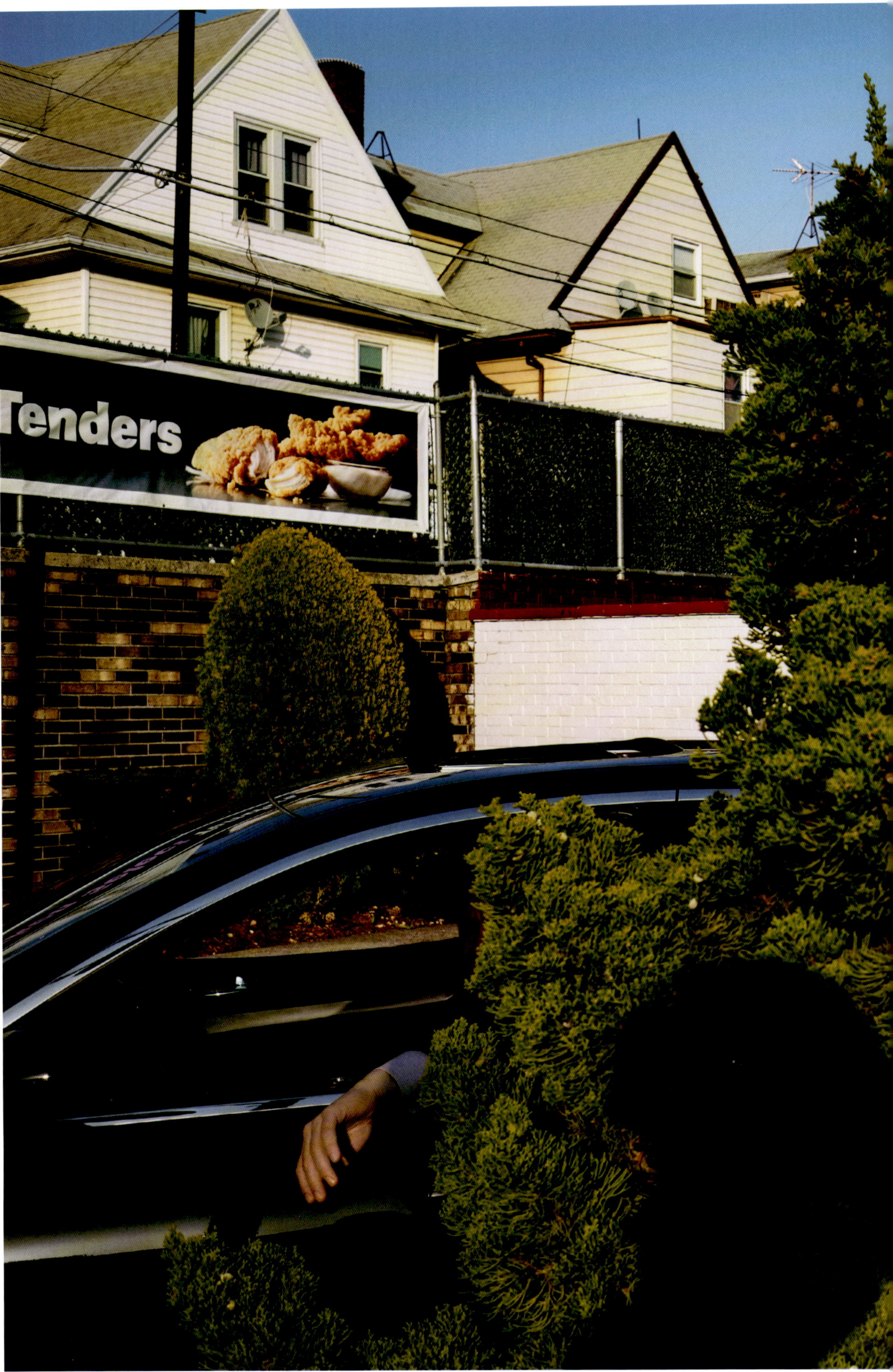
Tenders

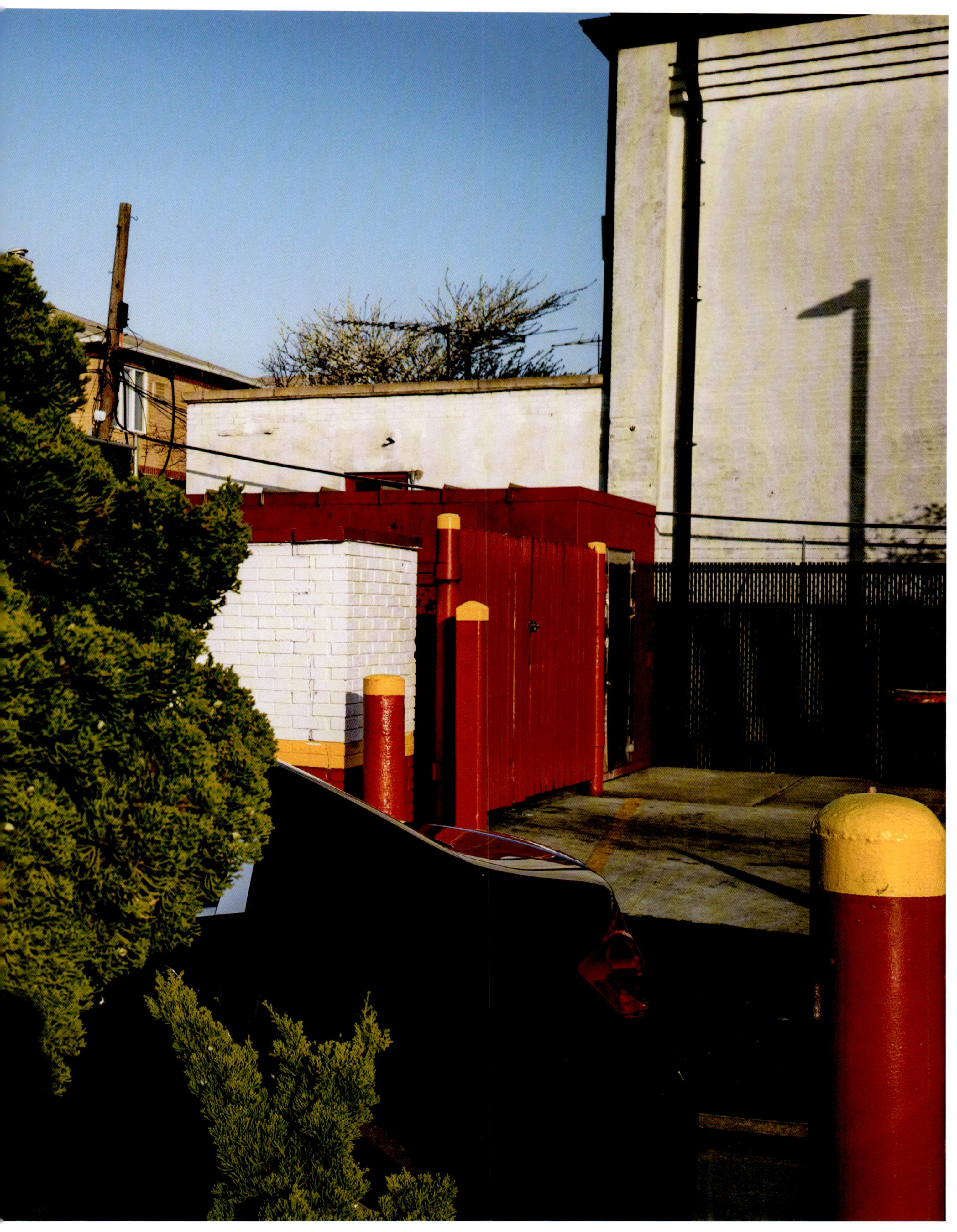

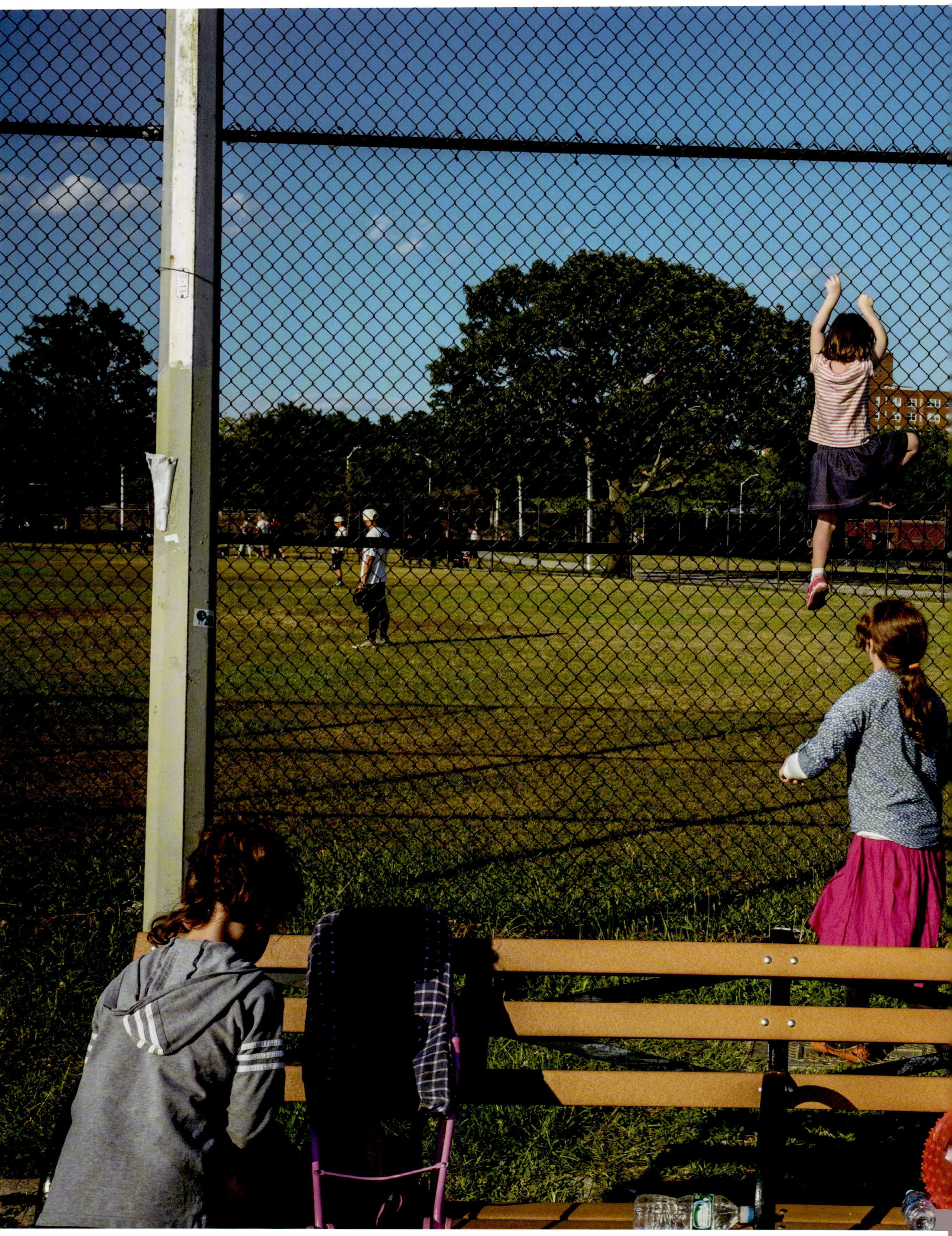

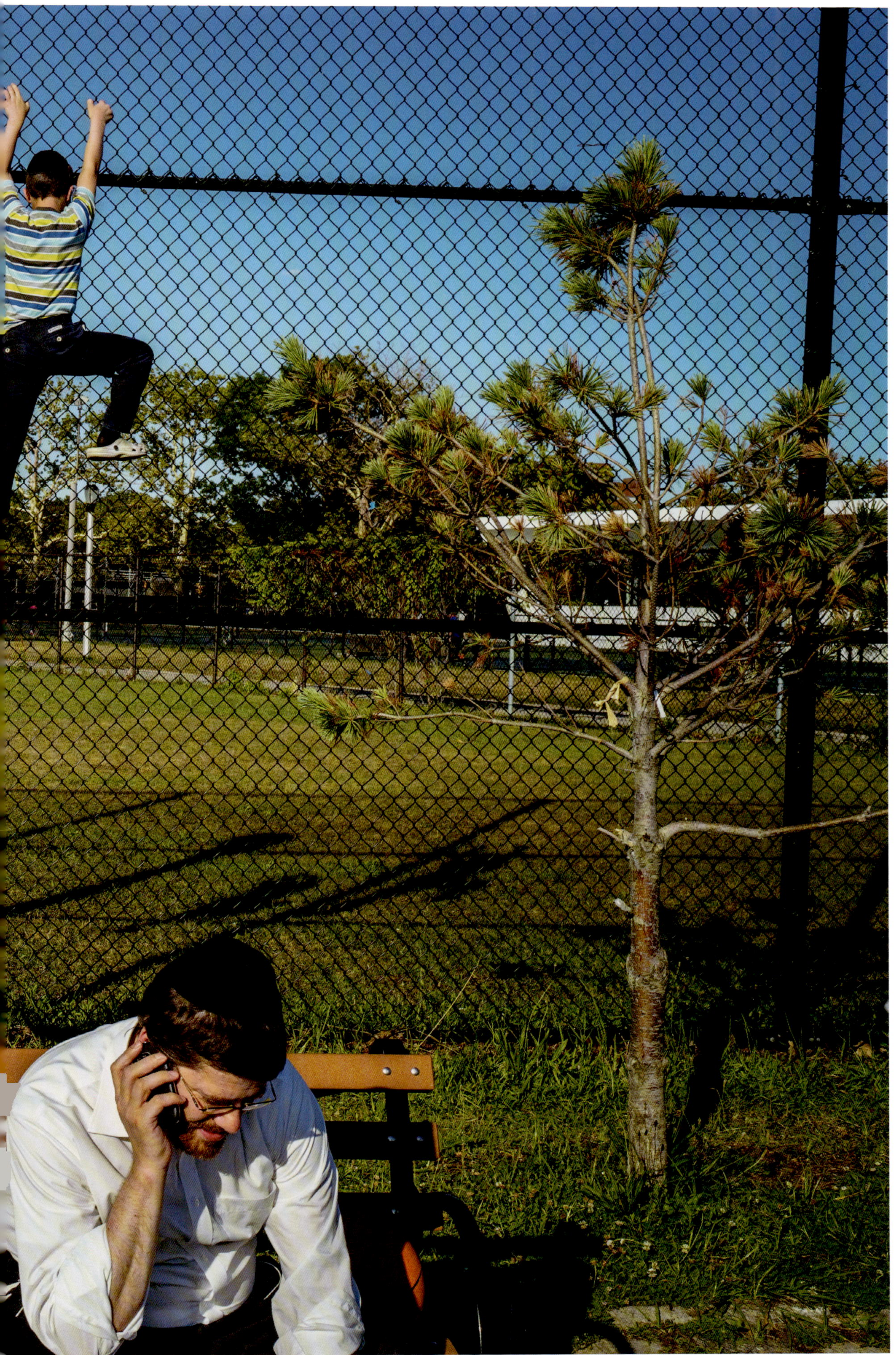

BATH BEACH, 2015

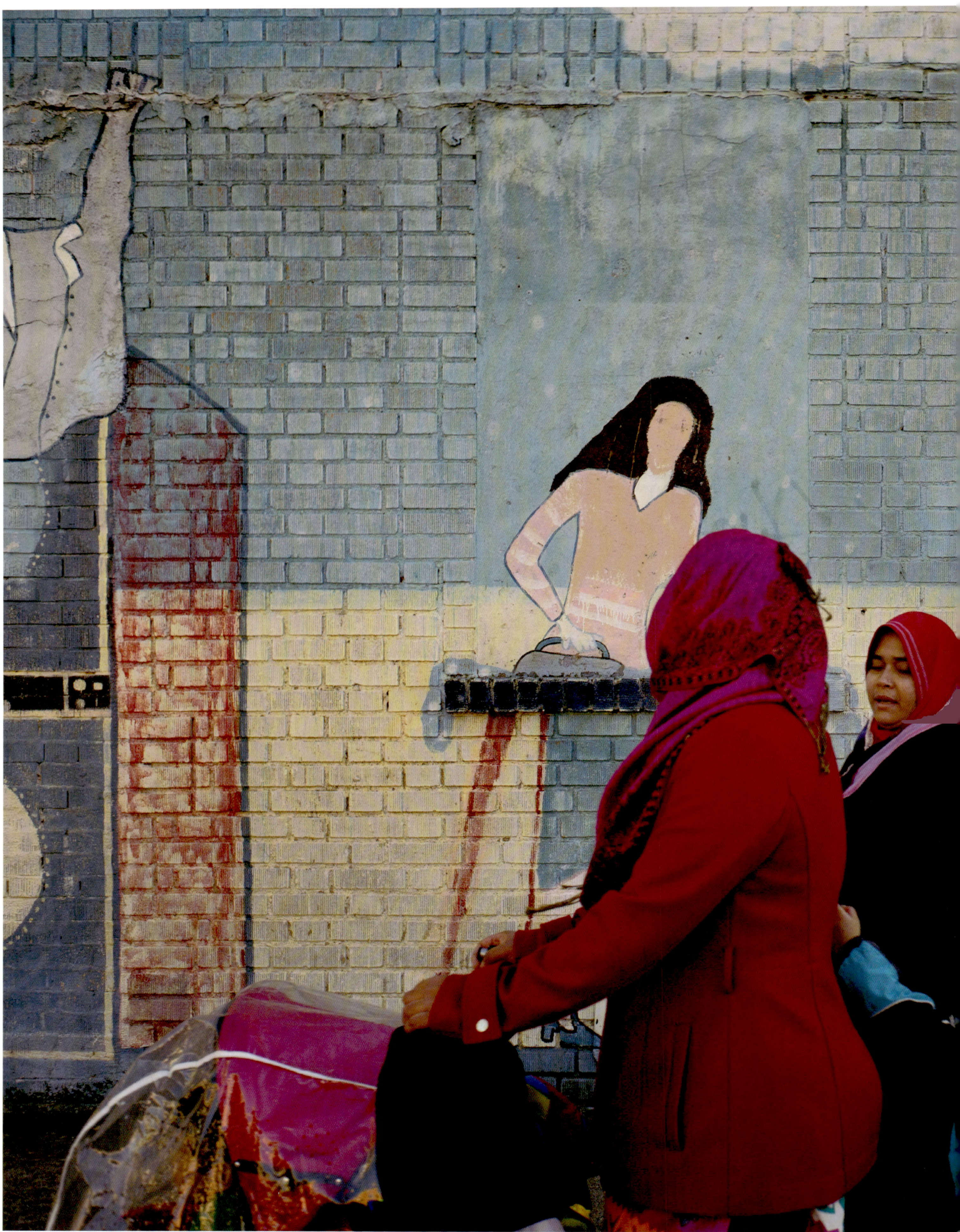

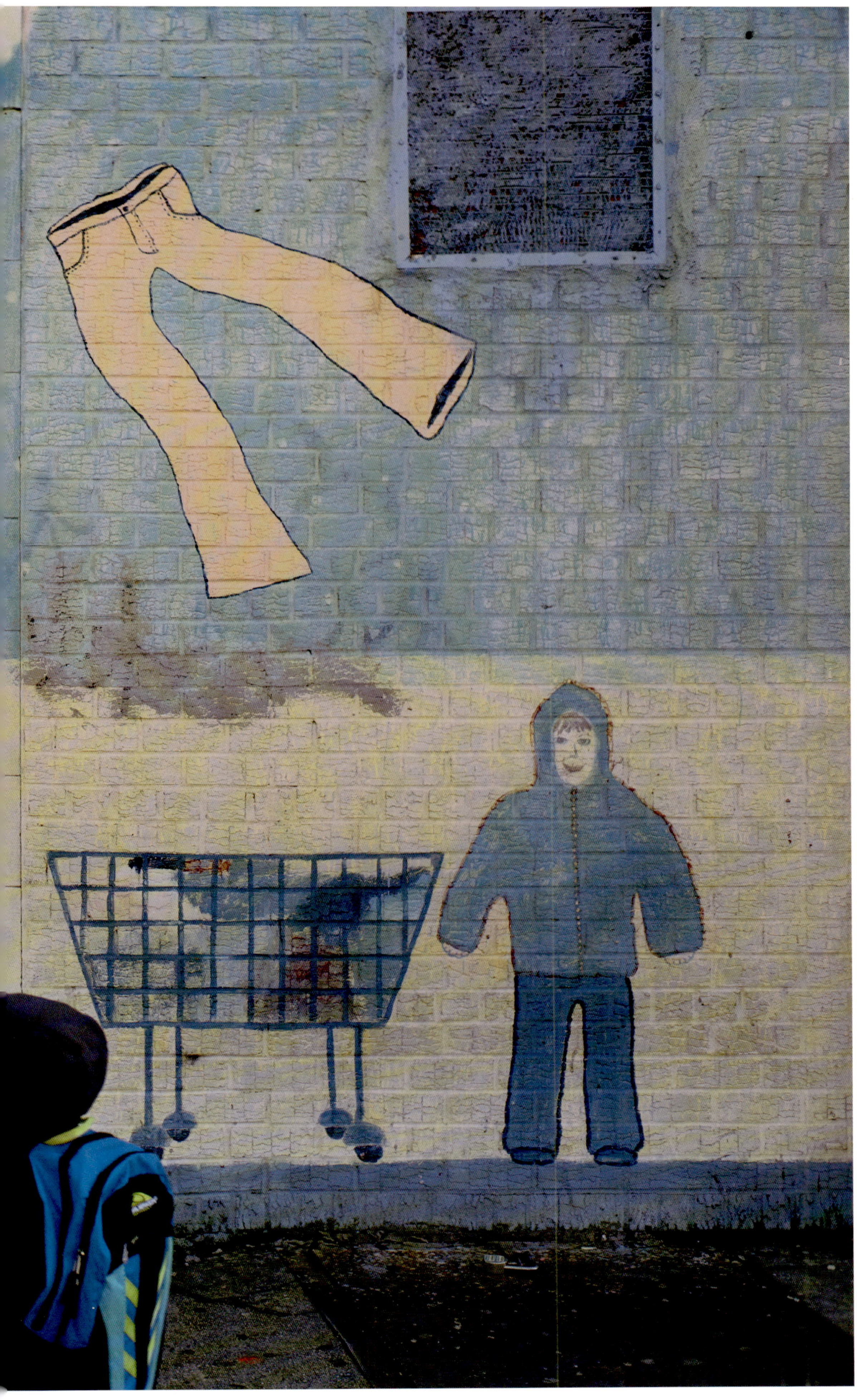

BOROUGH PARK, 2016

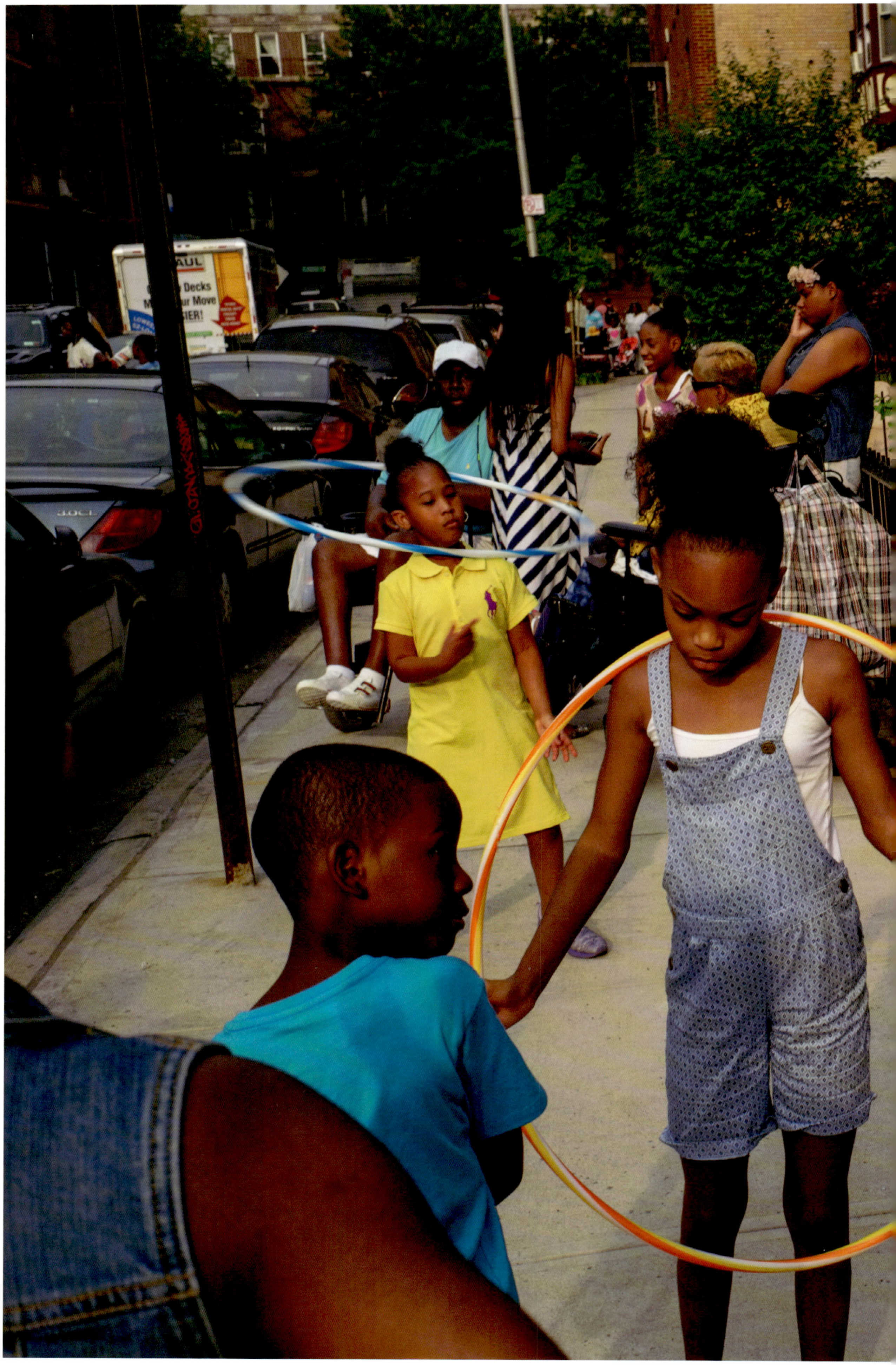

PROSPECT-LEFFERTS GARDENS, 2015

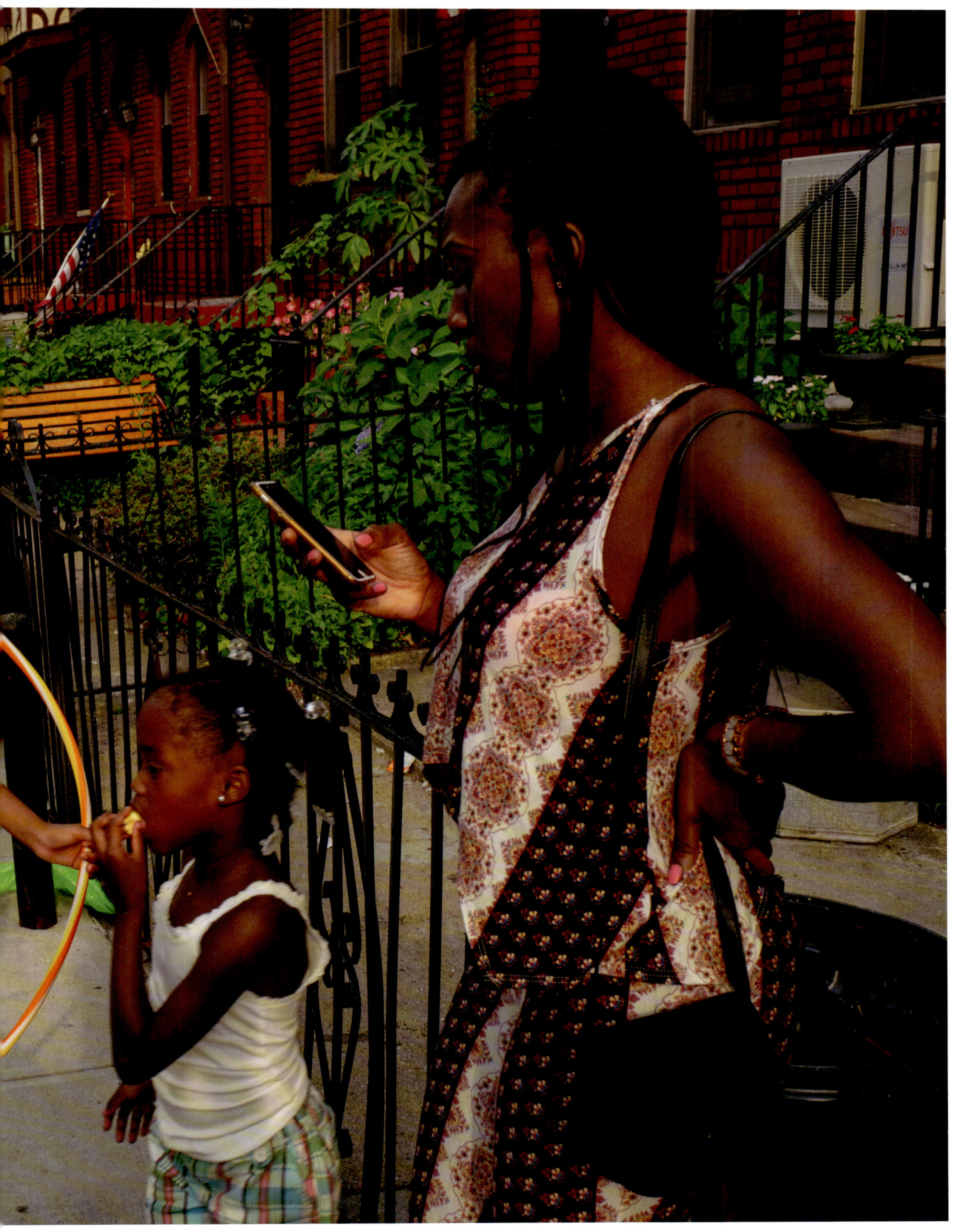

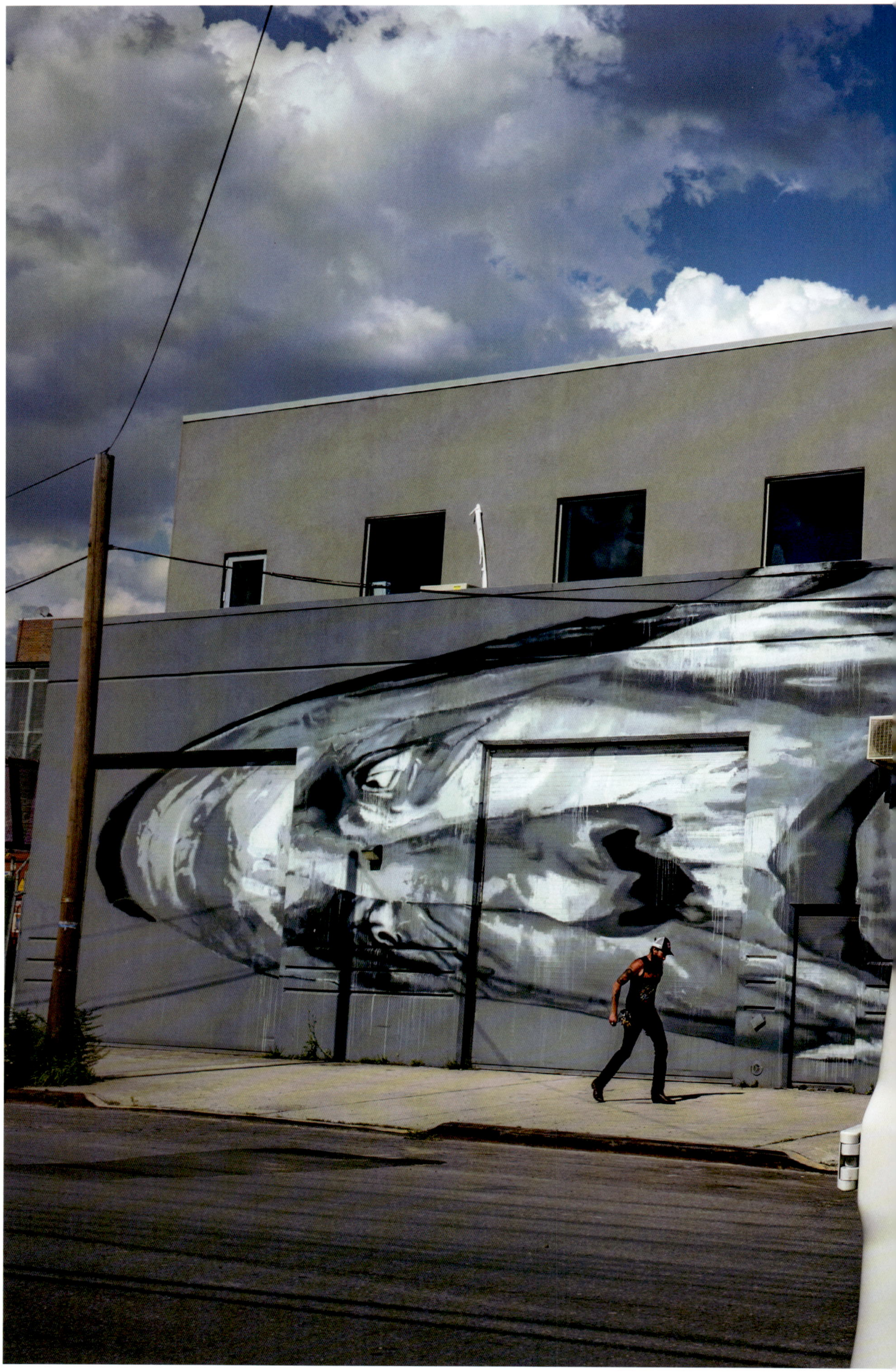

EAST WILLIAMSBURG, 2015

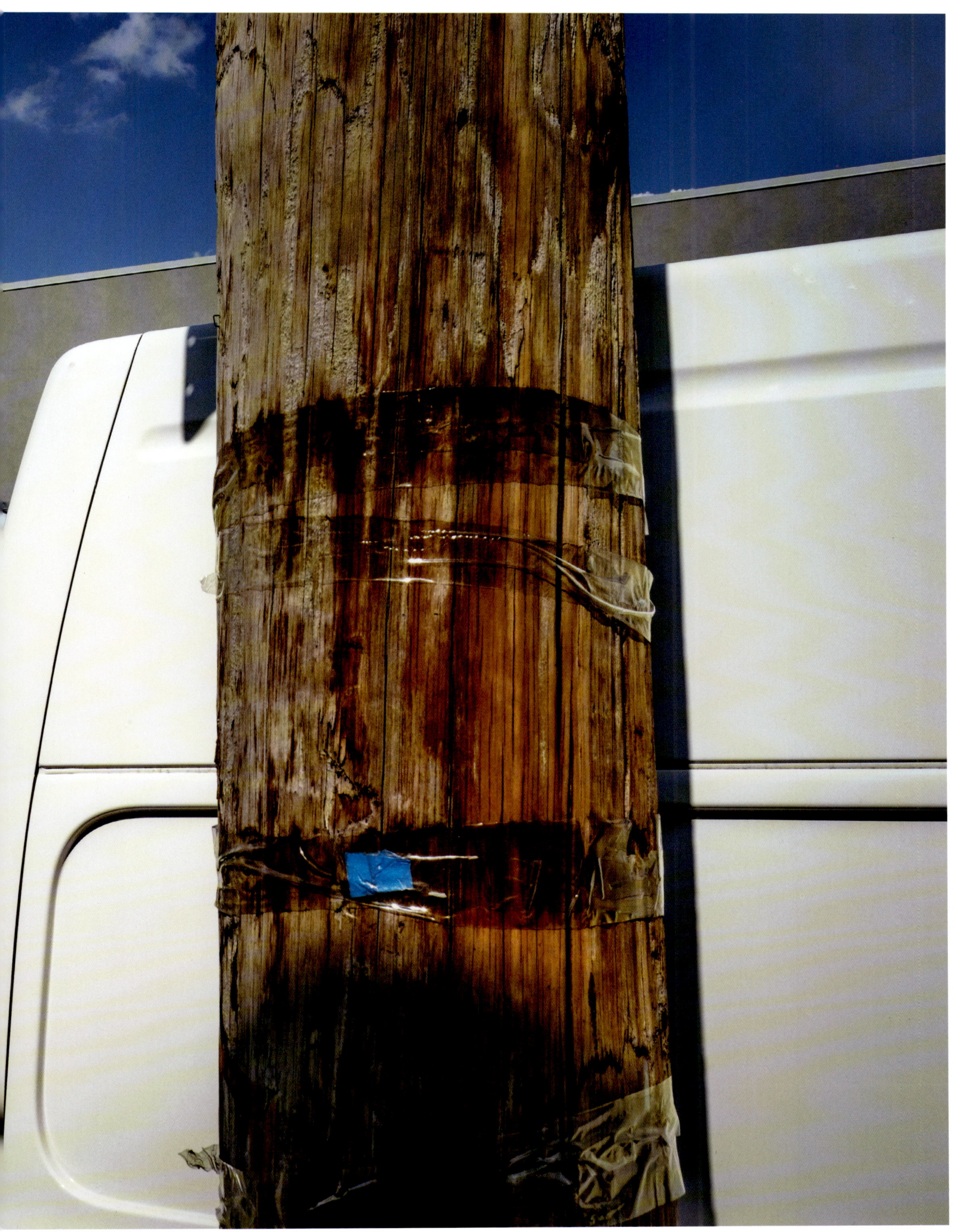

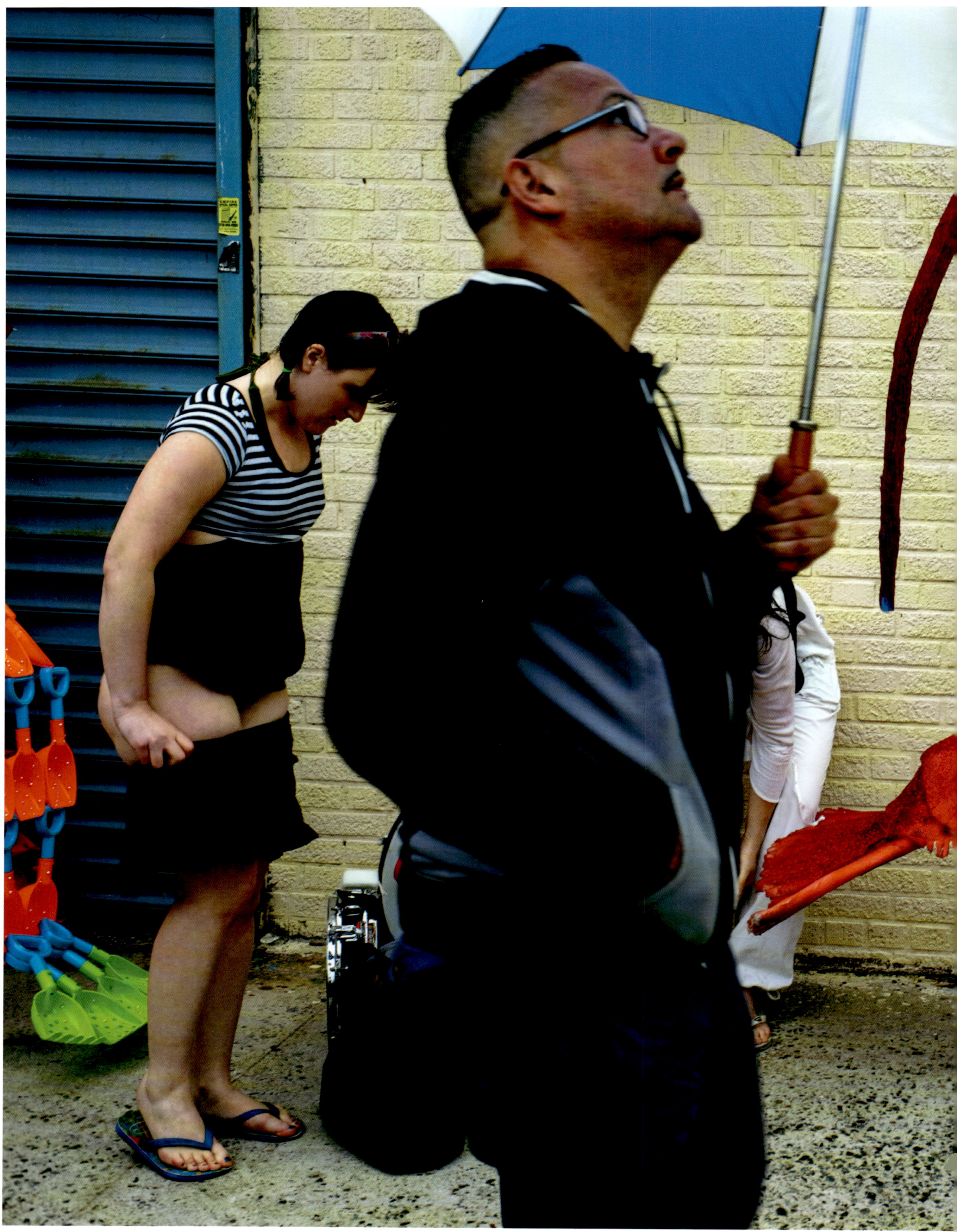

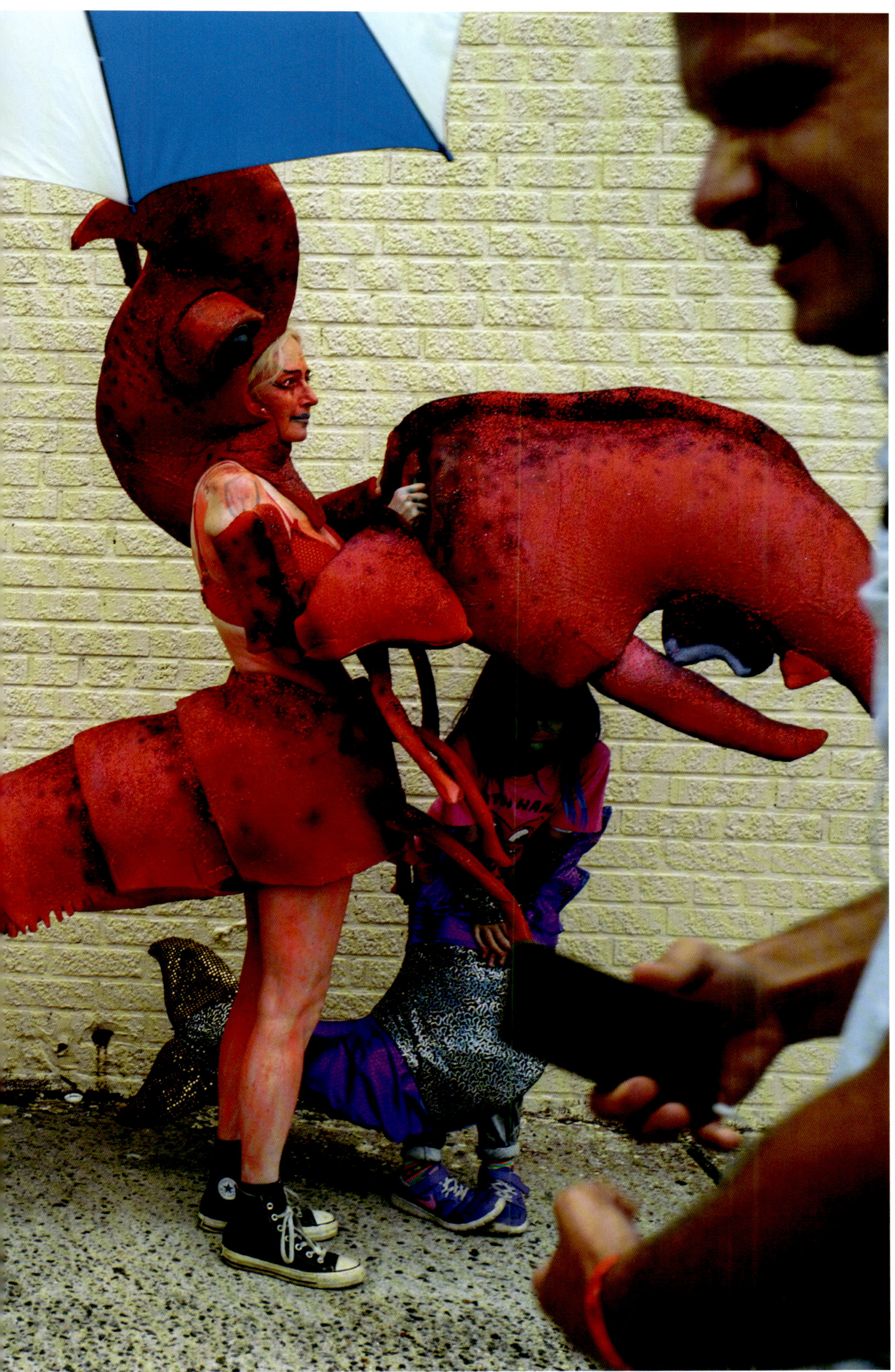

CONEY ISLAND, MERMAID PARADE, 2015

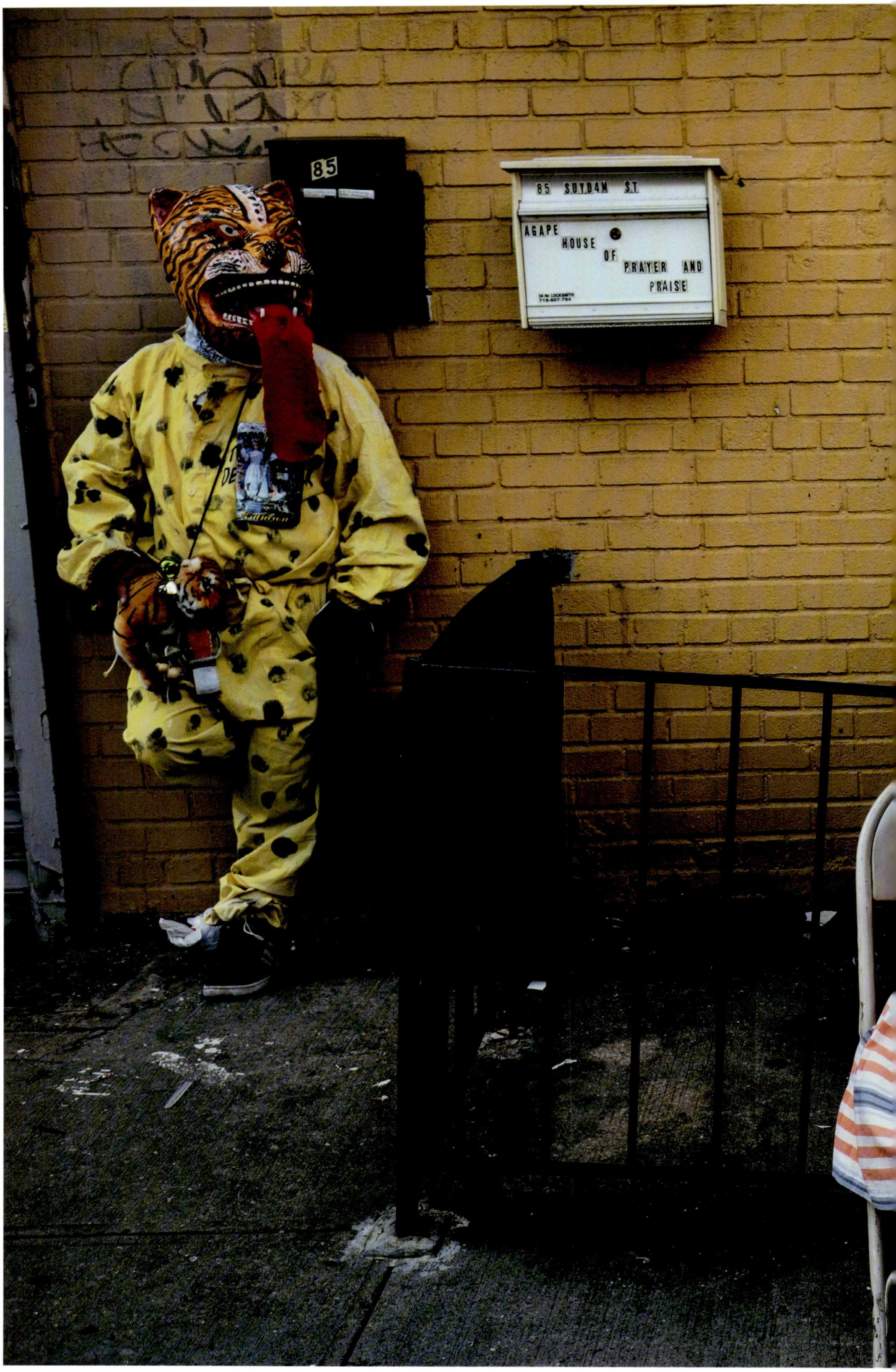

BUSHWICK, ASSUMPTION DAY, 2015

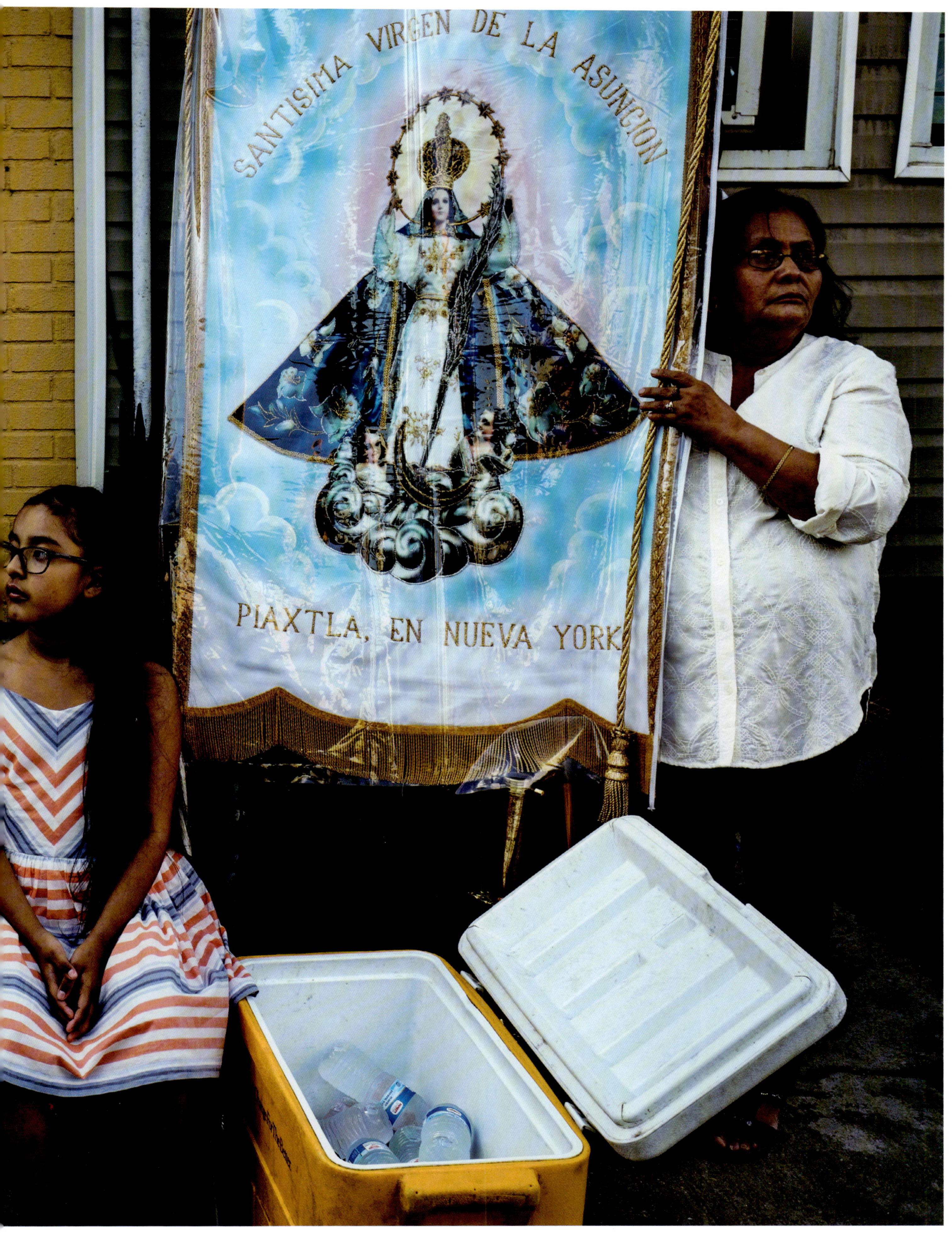

SANTISIMA VIRGEN DE LA ASUNCION
PIAXTLA, EN NUEVA YORK

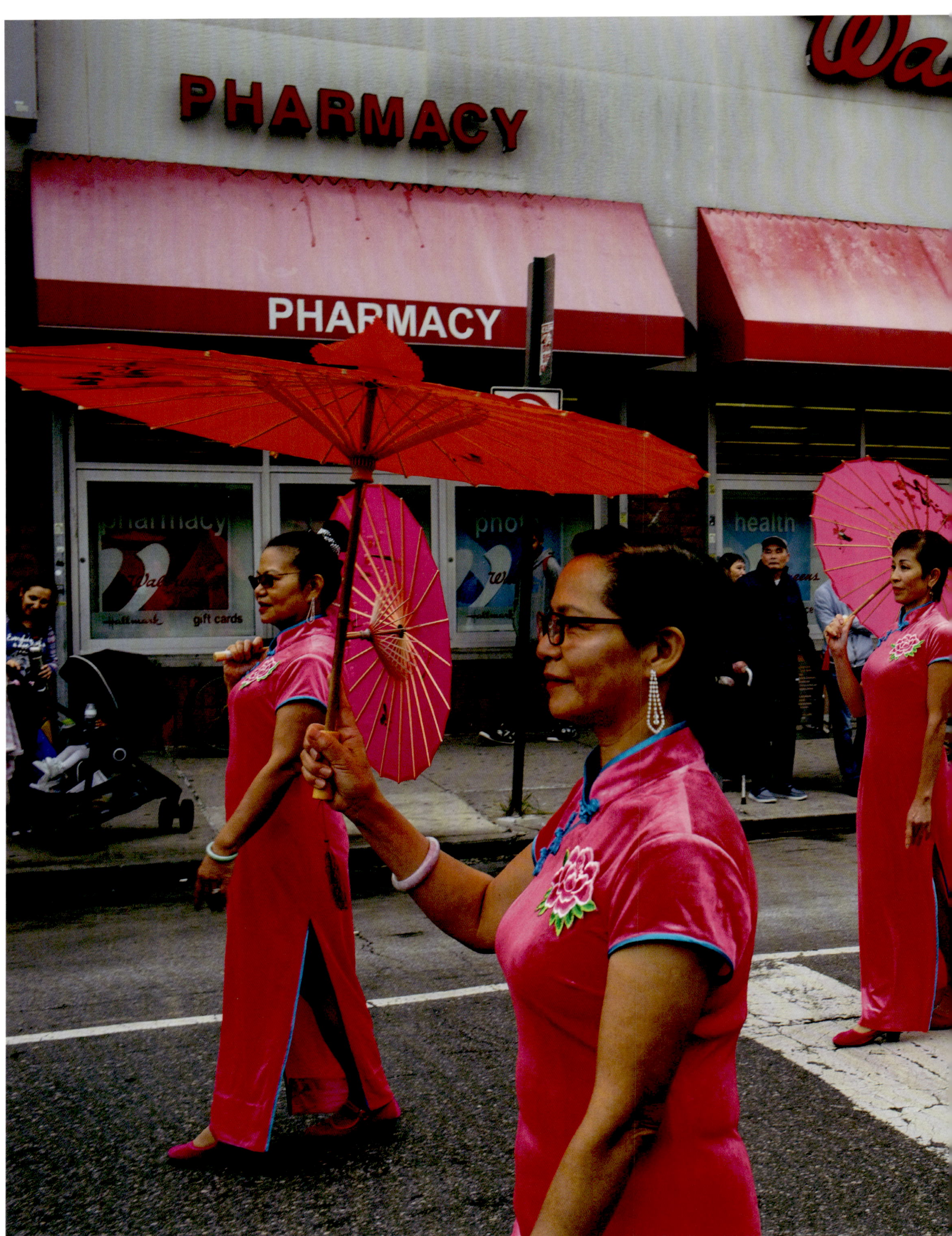
PHARMACY
Wa
PHARMACY
pharmacy
health
gift cards

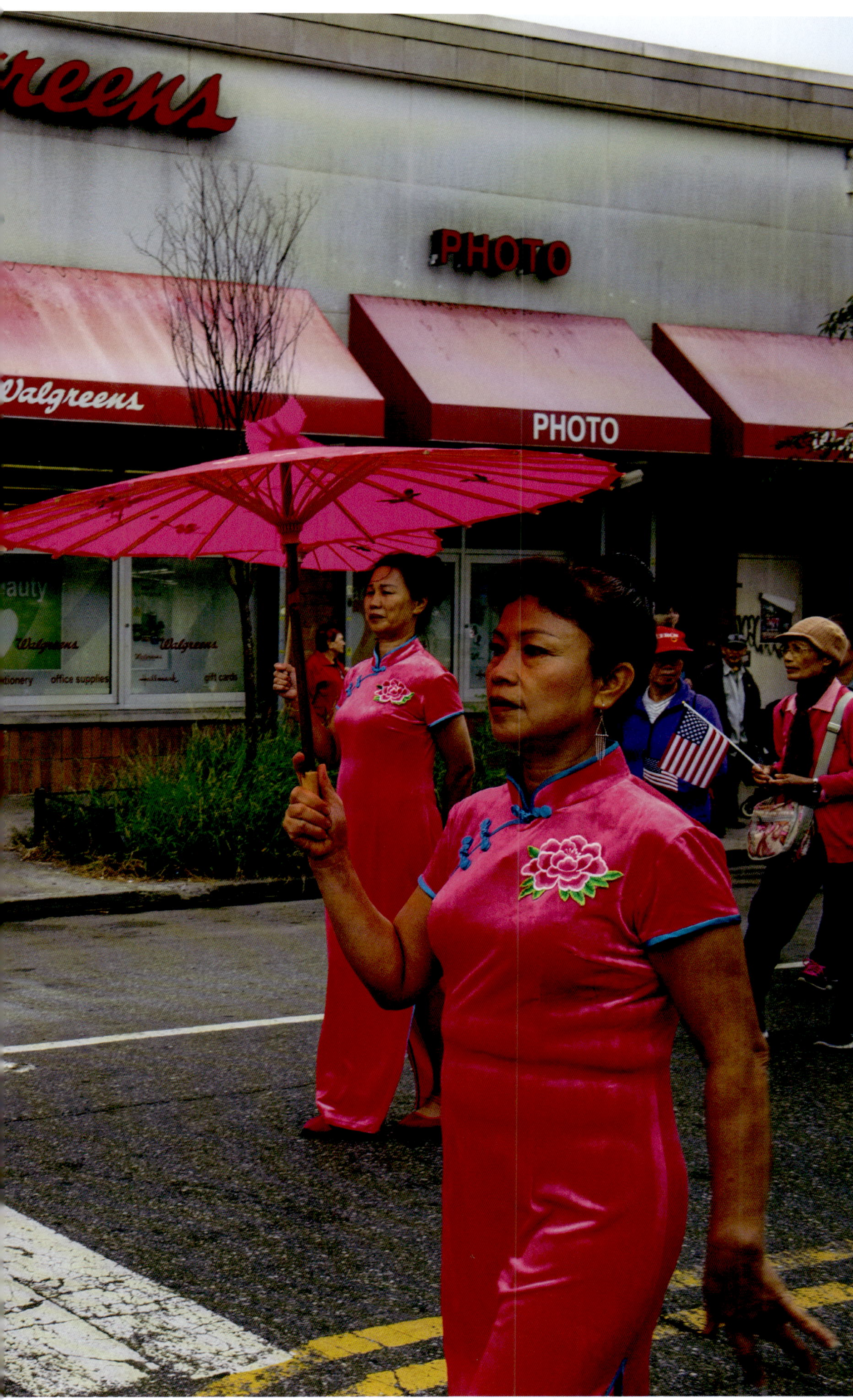

BENSONHURST, COLUMBUS DAY, 2018

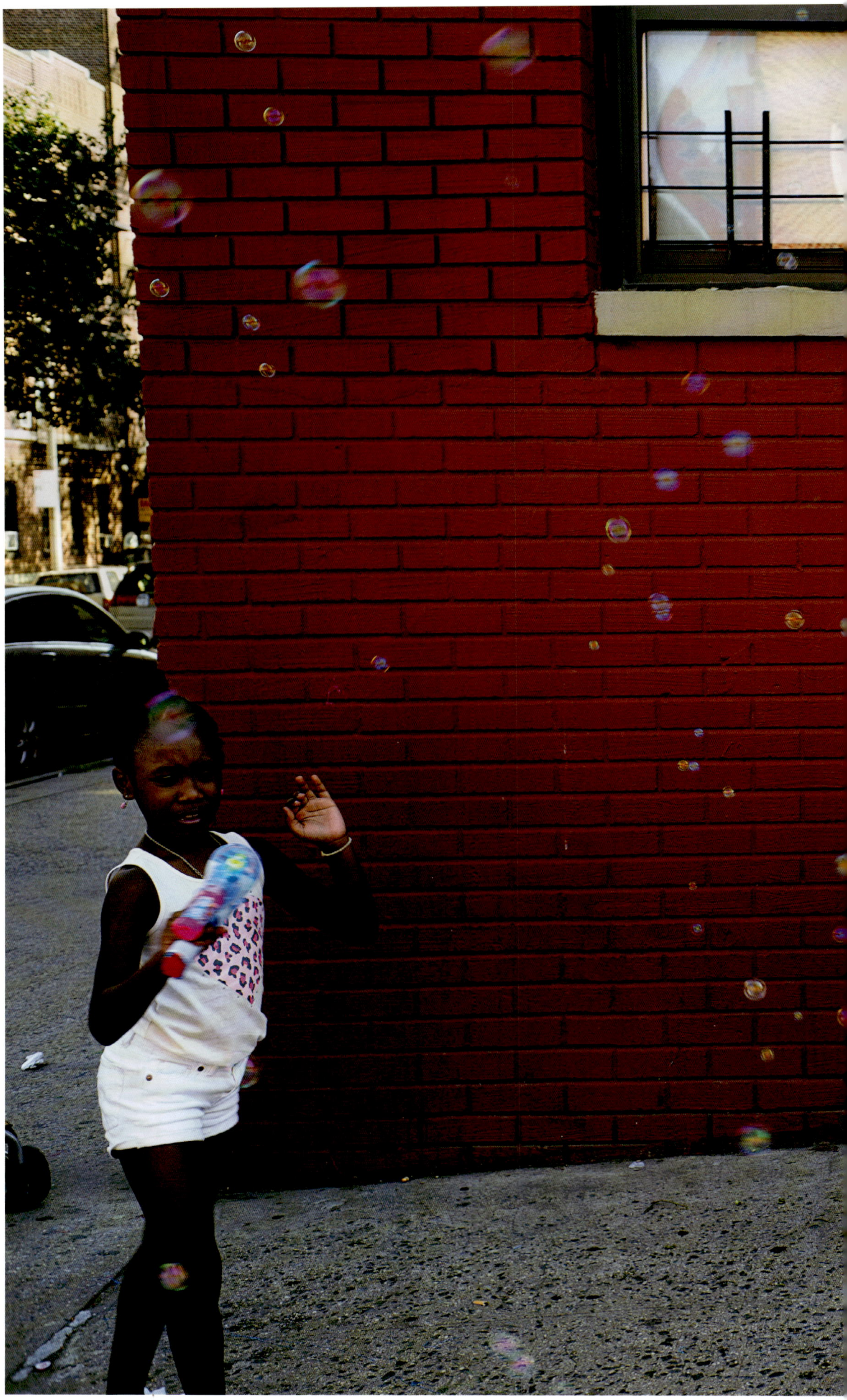

CROWN HEIGHTS, 2015

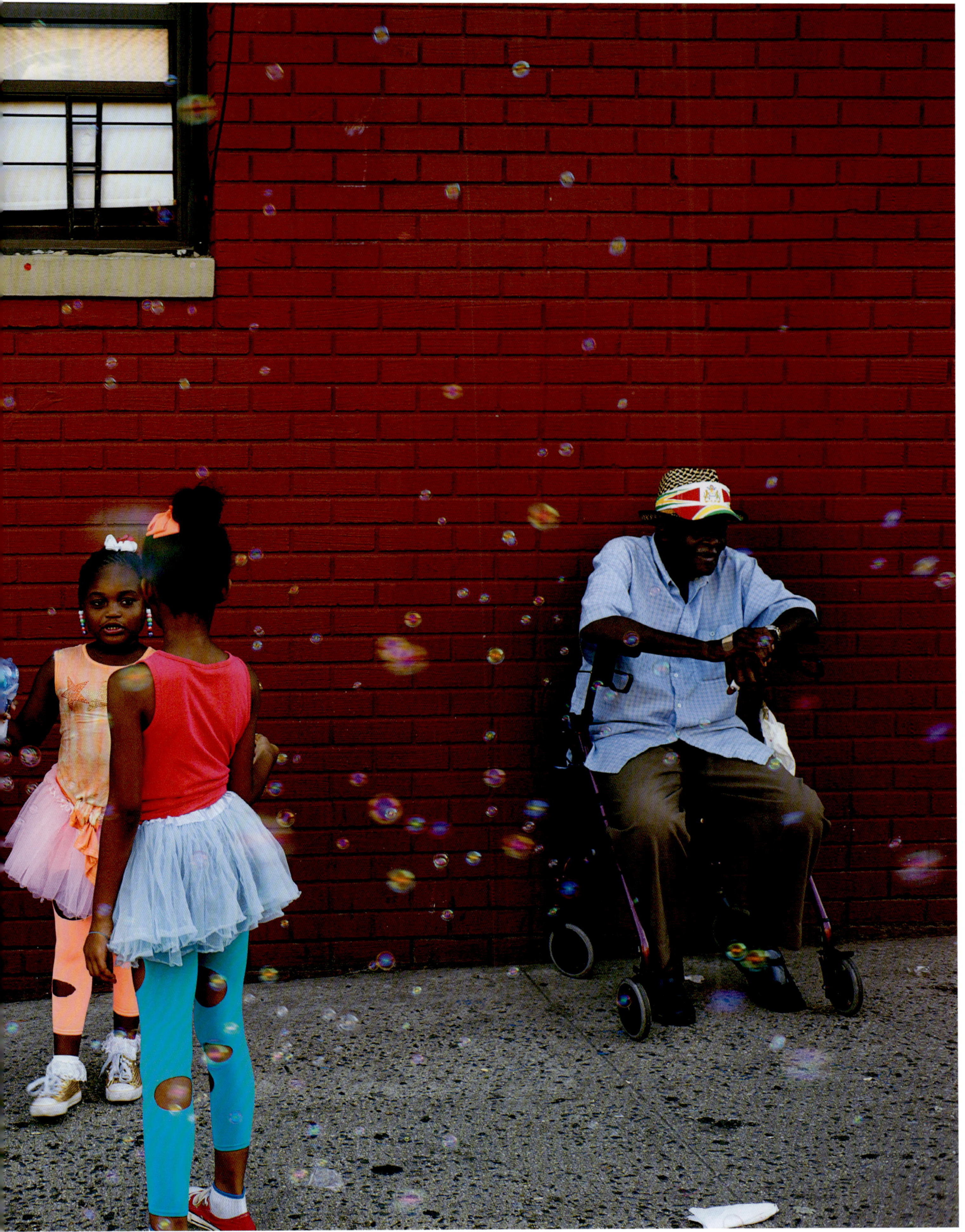

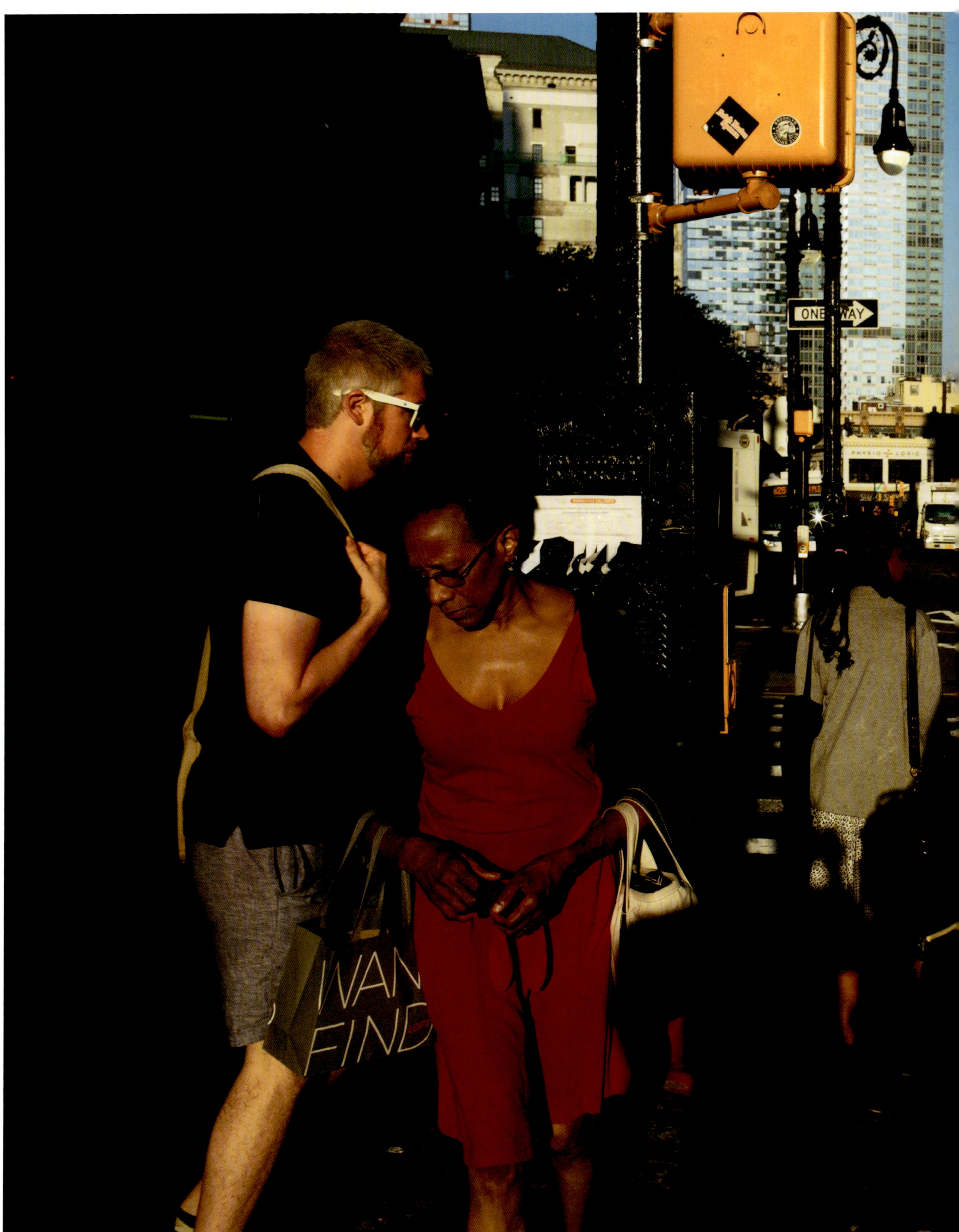

ONE WAY
PHYSIO LOGIC
WAN
FIND

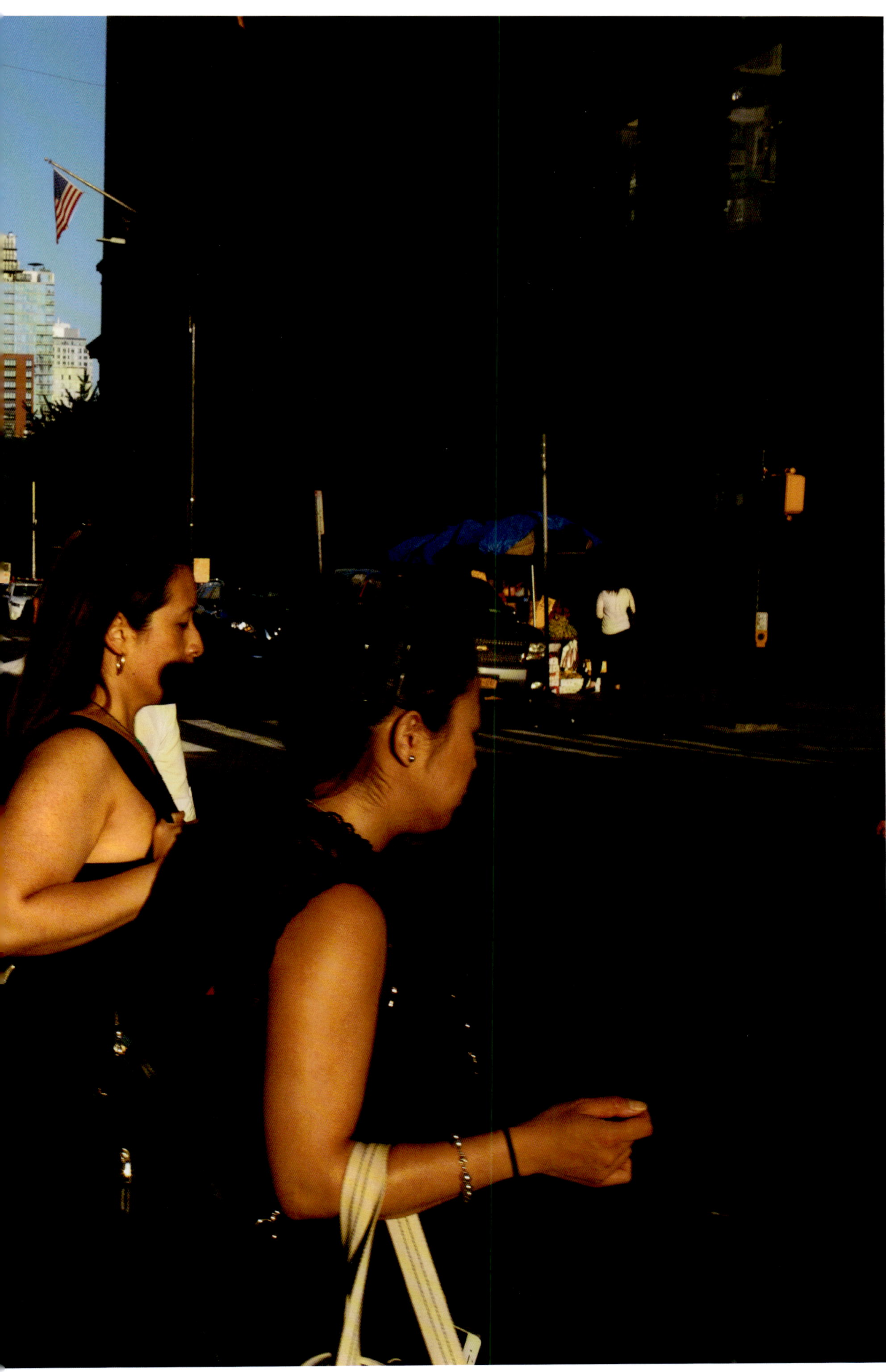

DOWNTOWN BROOKLYN, 2018

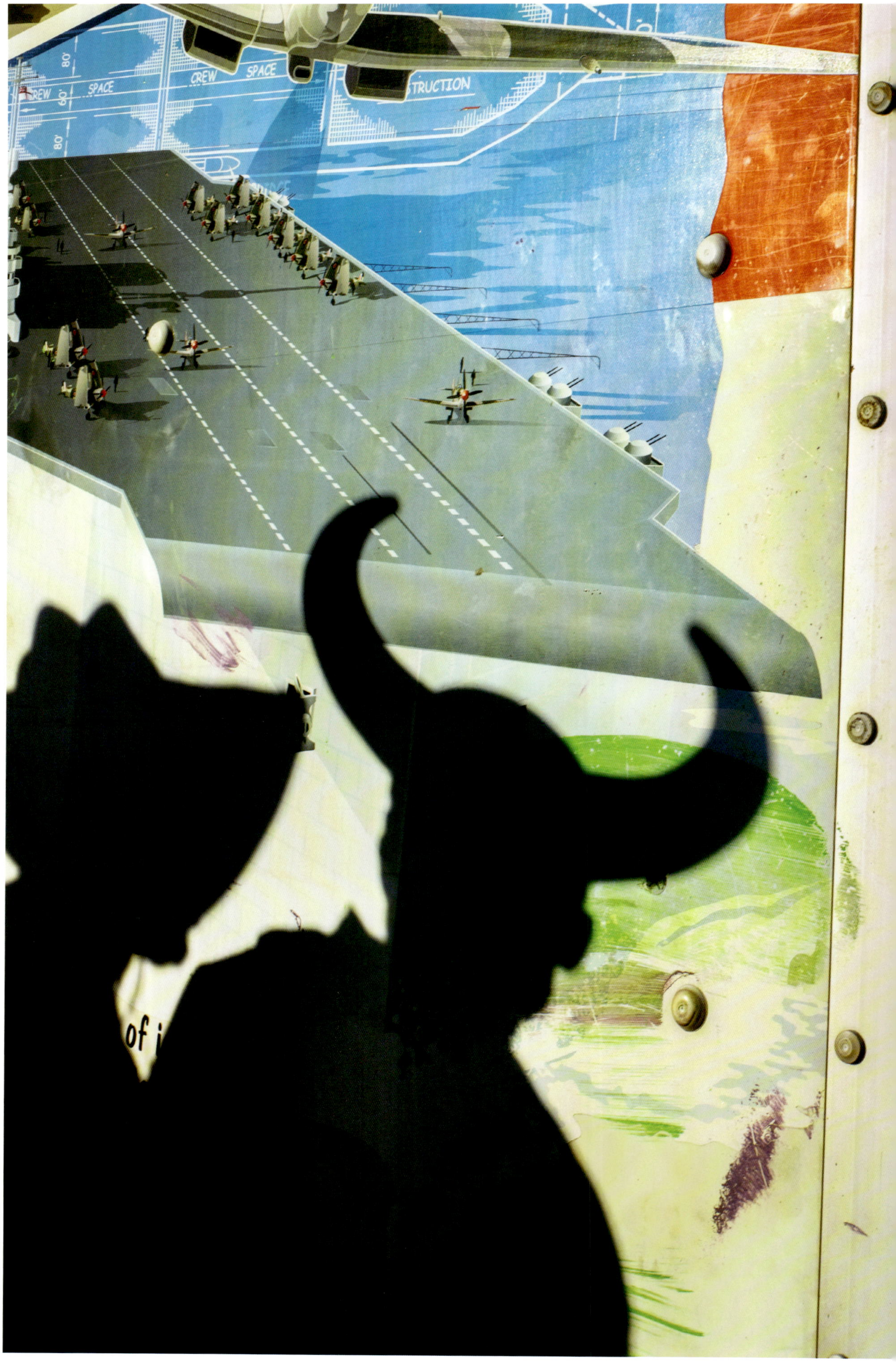

CREW SPACE
CREW SPACE
TRUCTION
of i

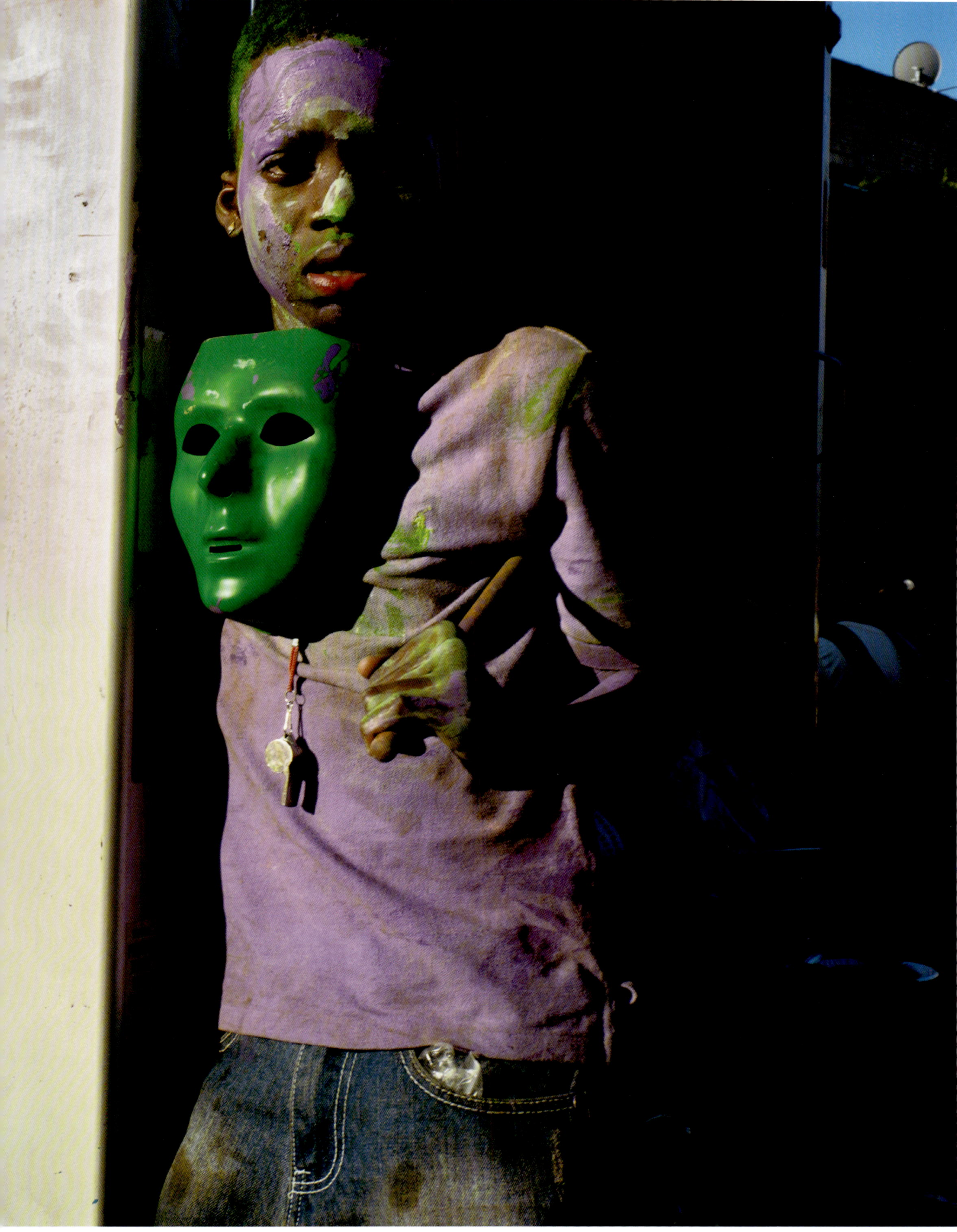

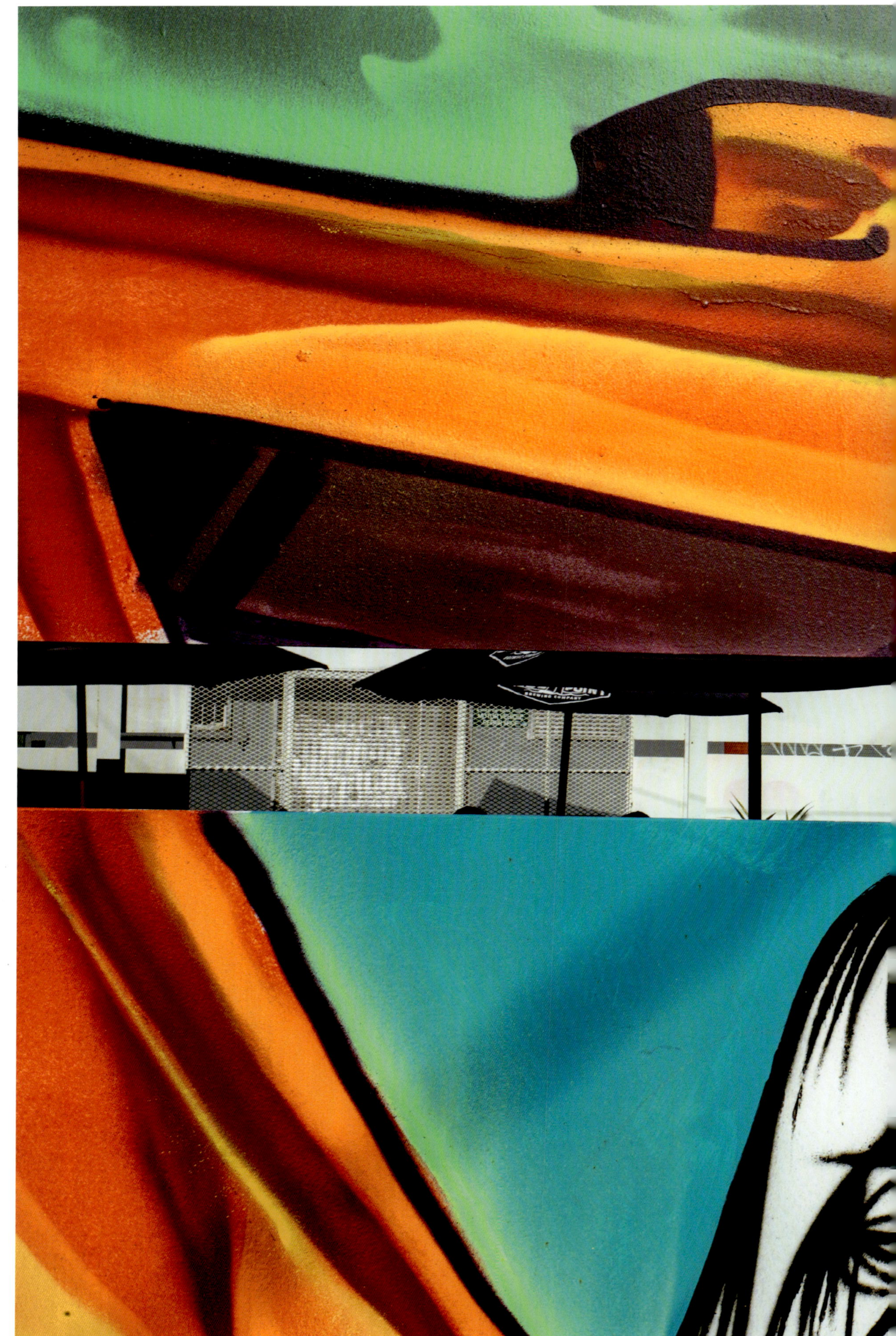

BUSHWICK, 2017

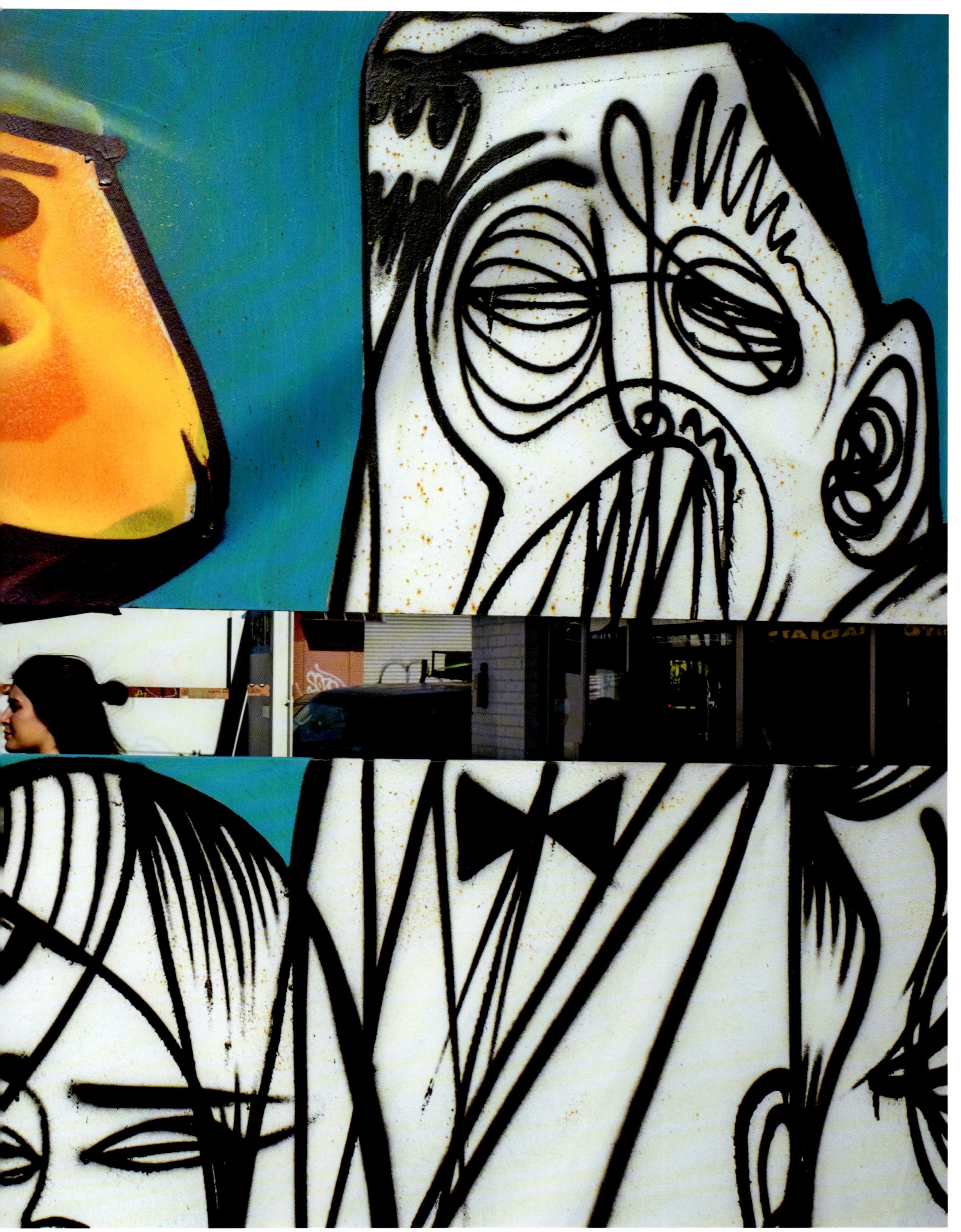

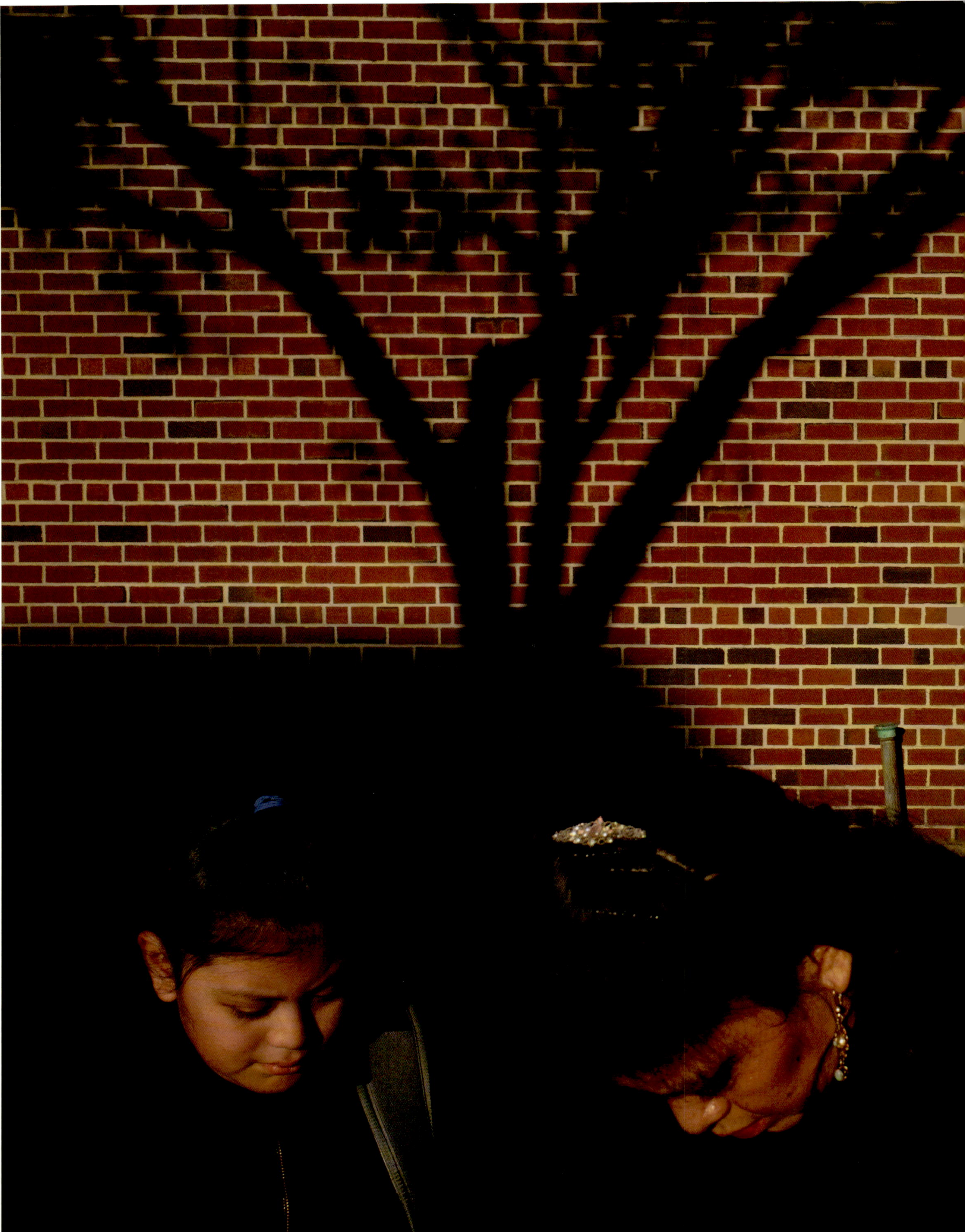

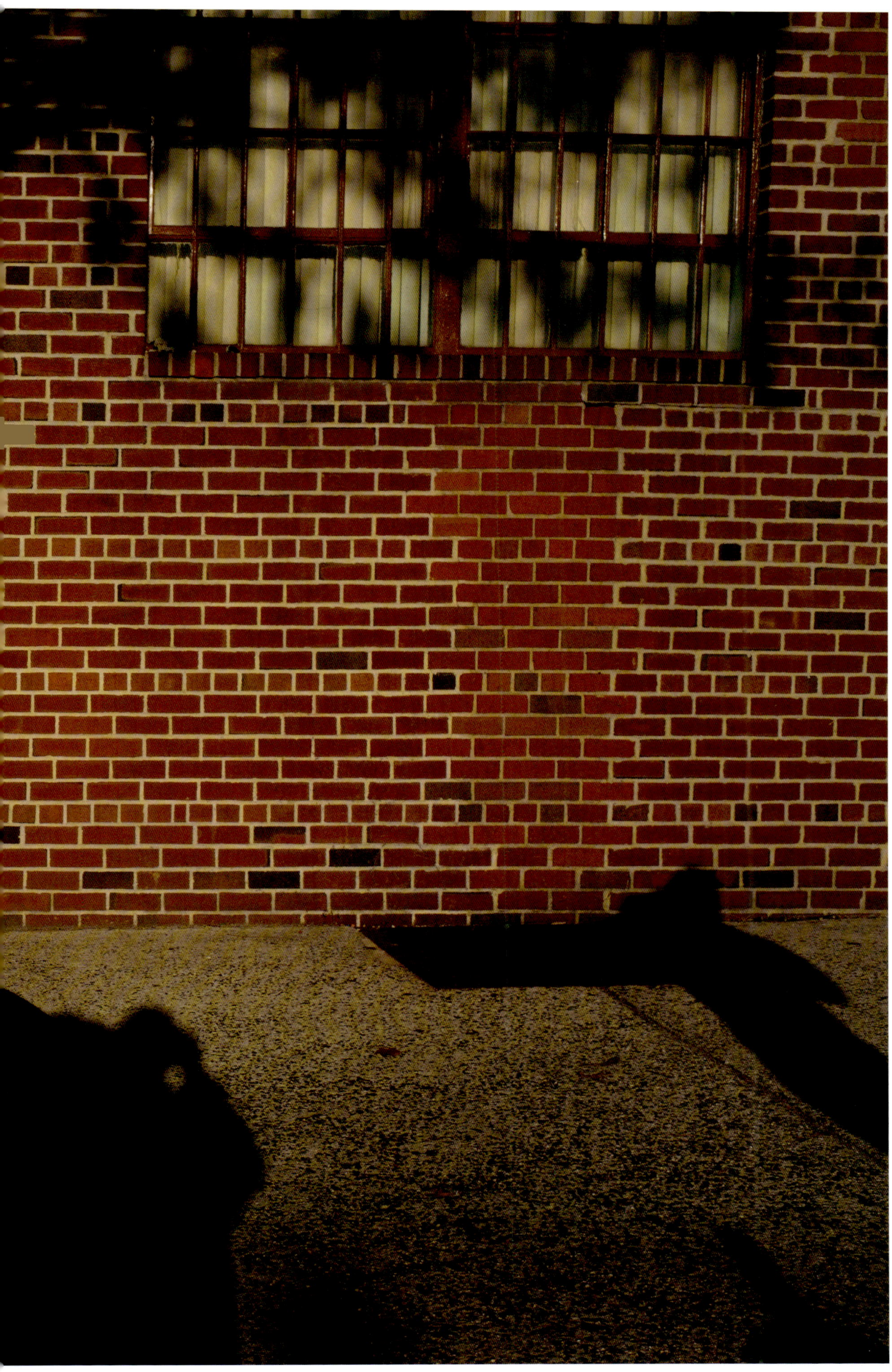

PARK SLOPE, 2015

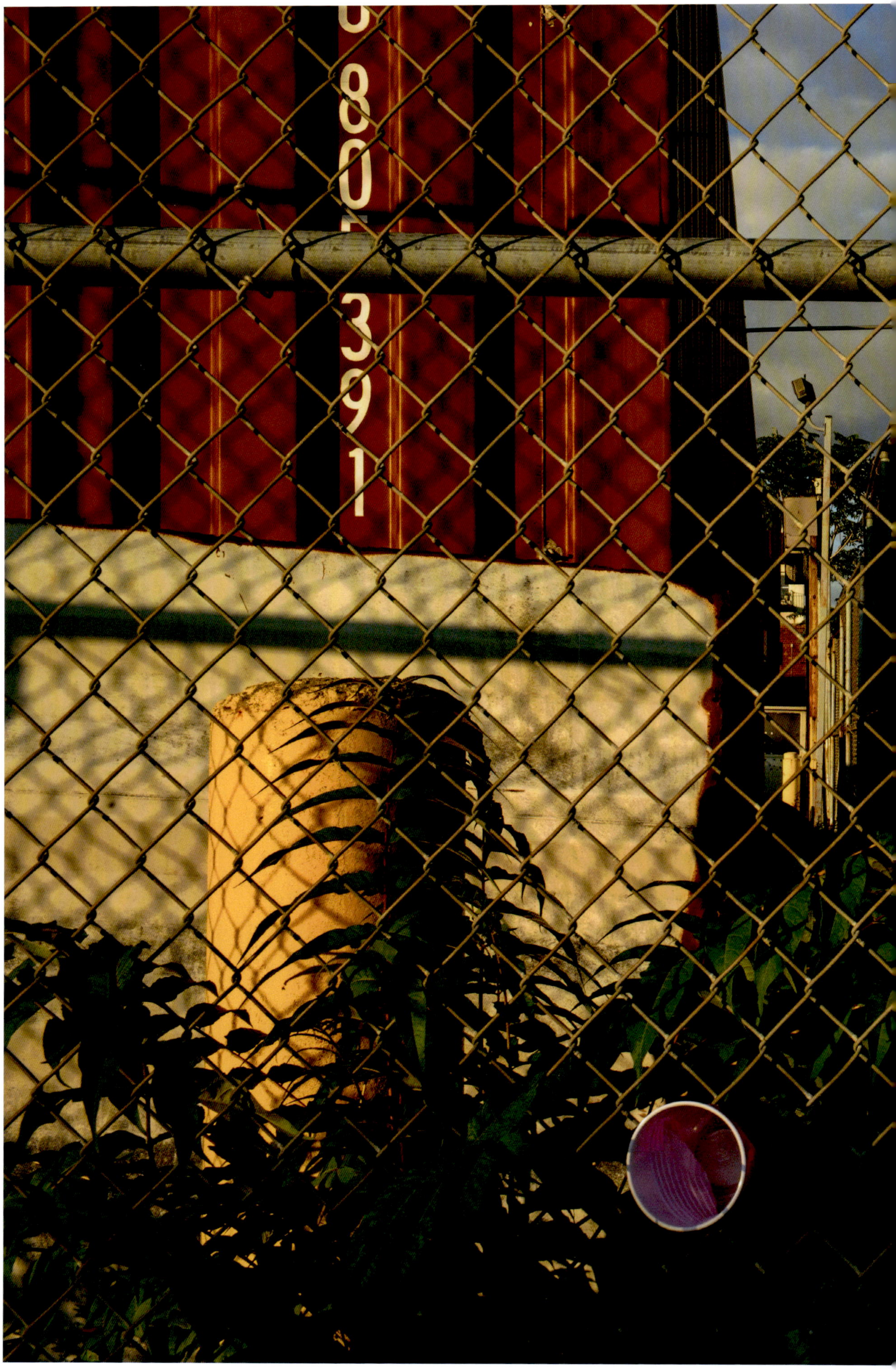

80
391

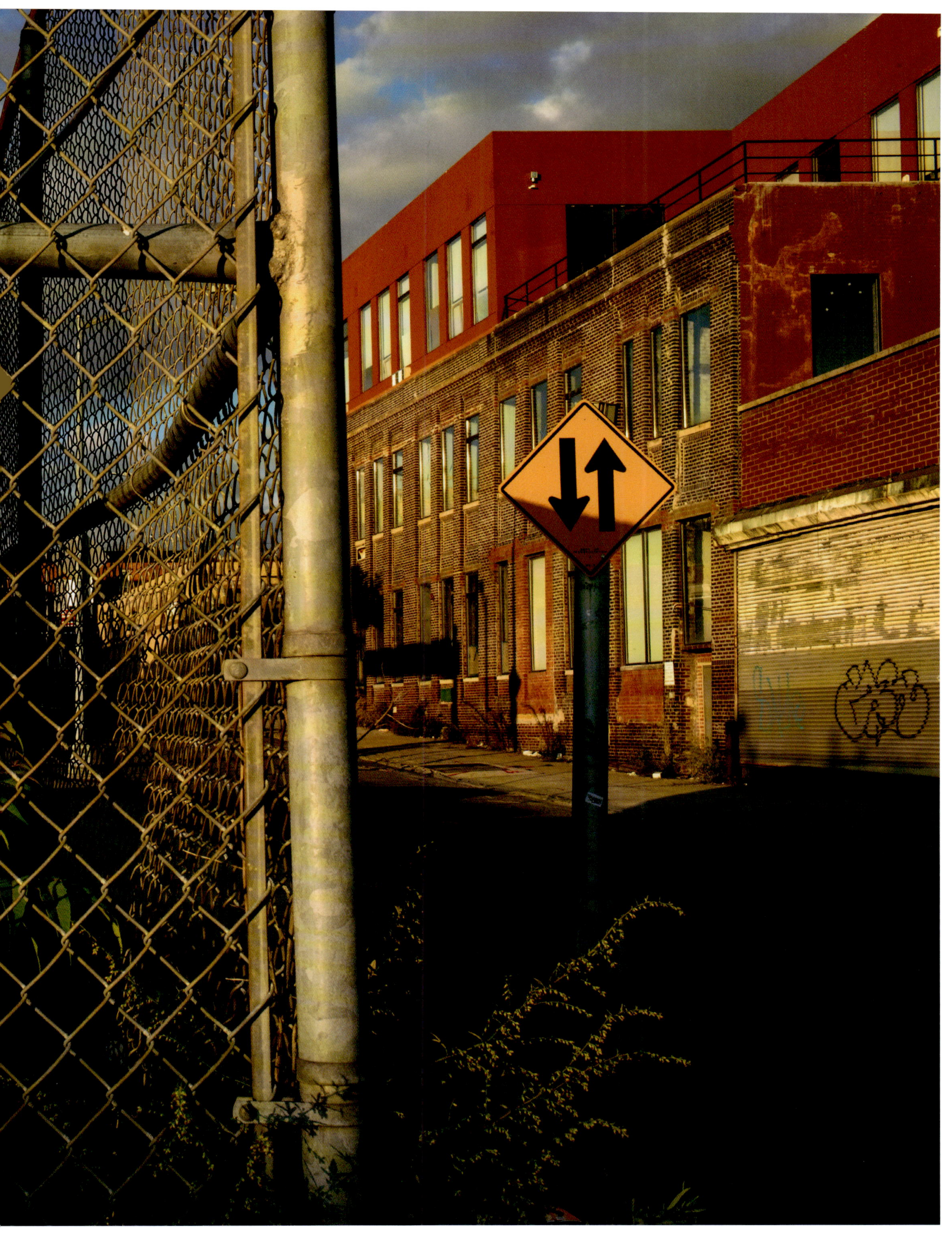

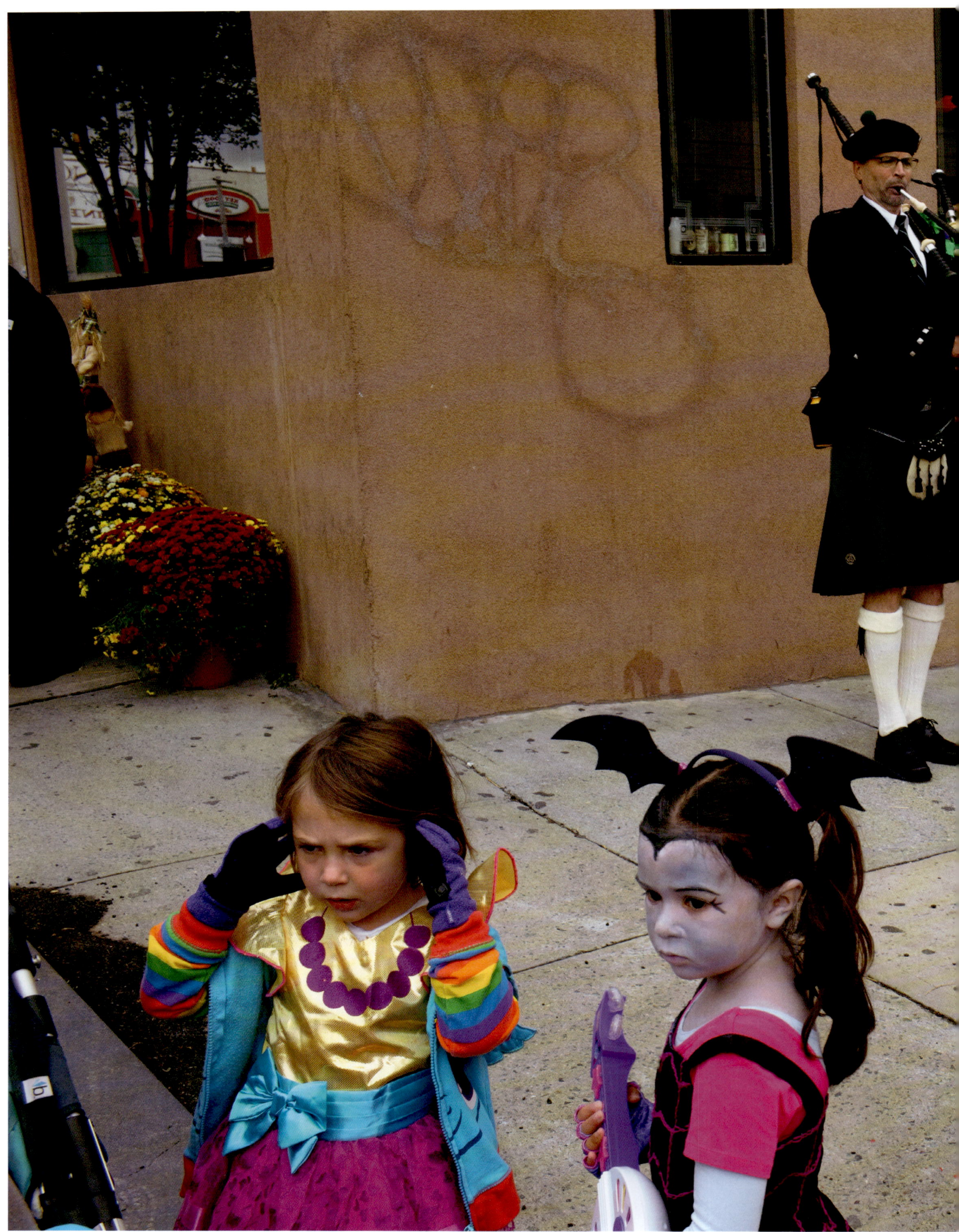

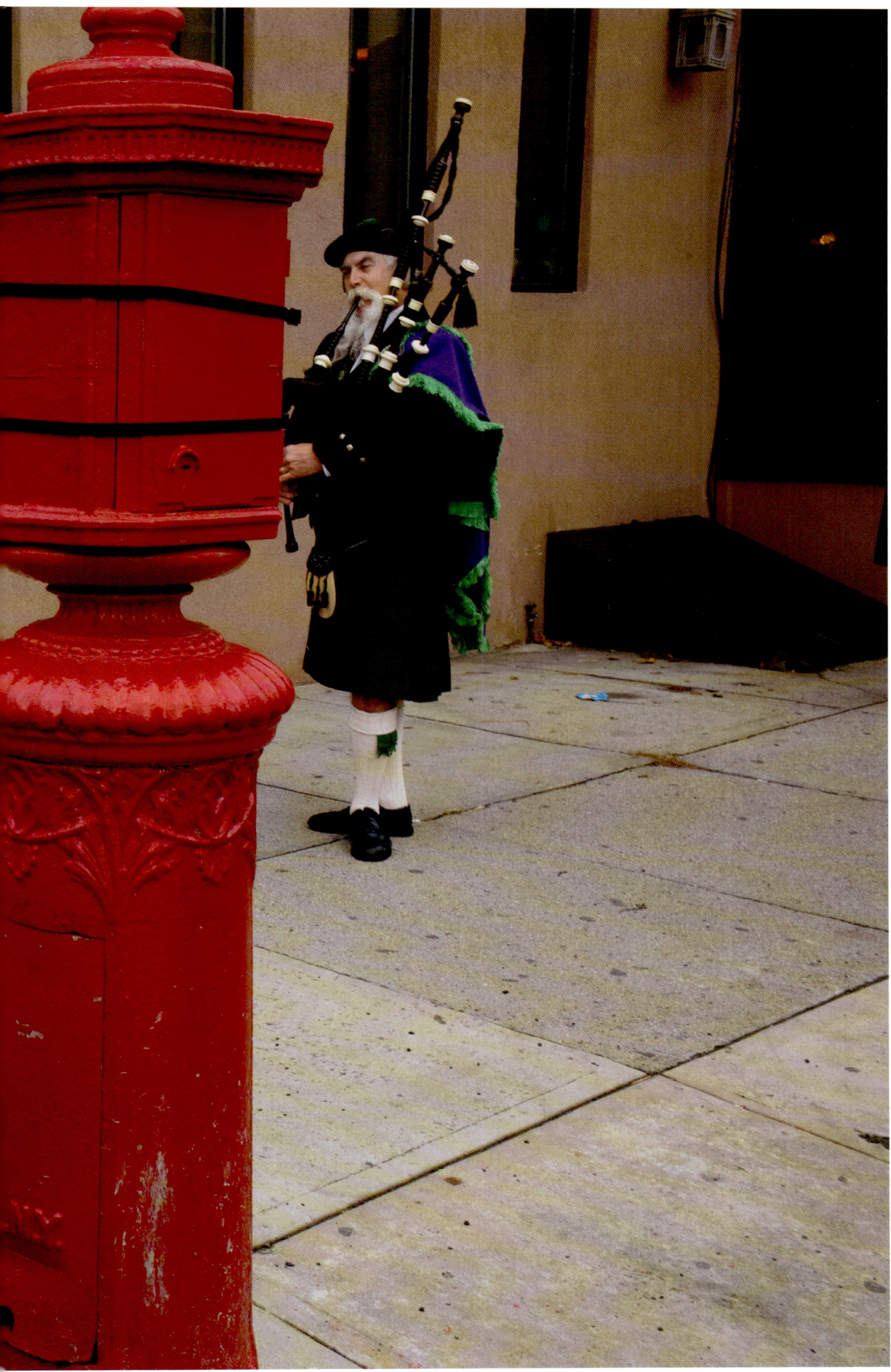

BAY RIDGE, RAGAMUFFIN PARADE, 2018

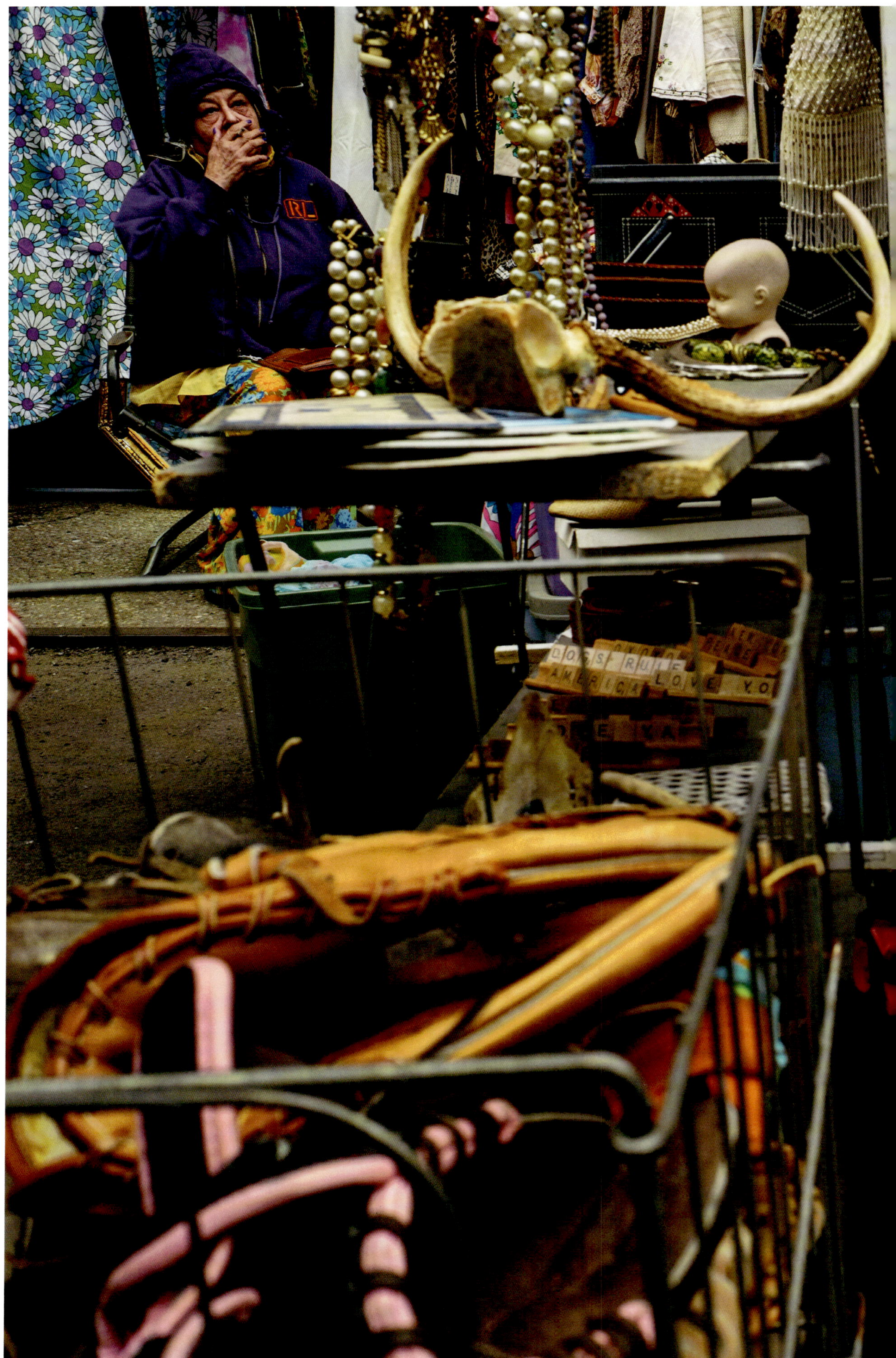

DUMBO, 2017

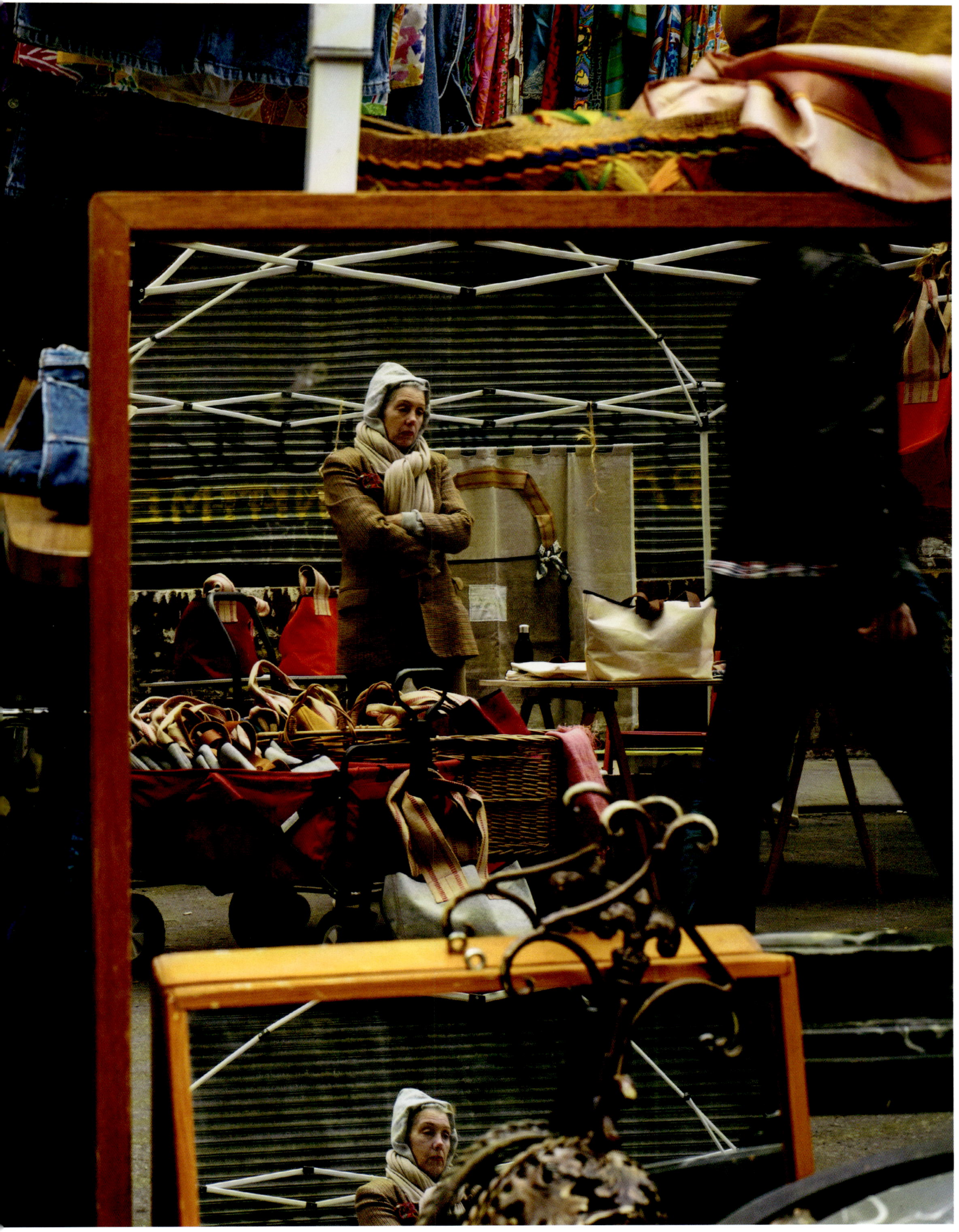

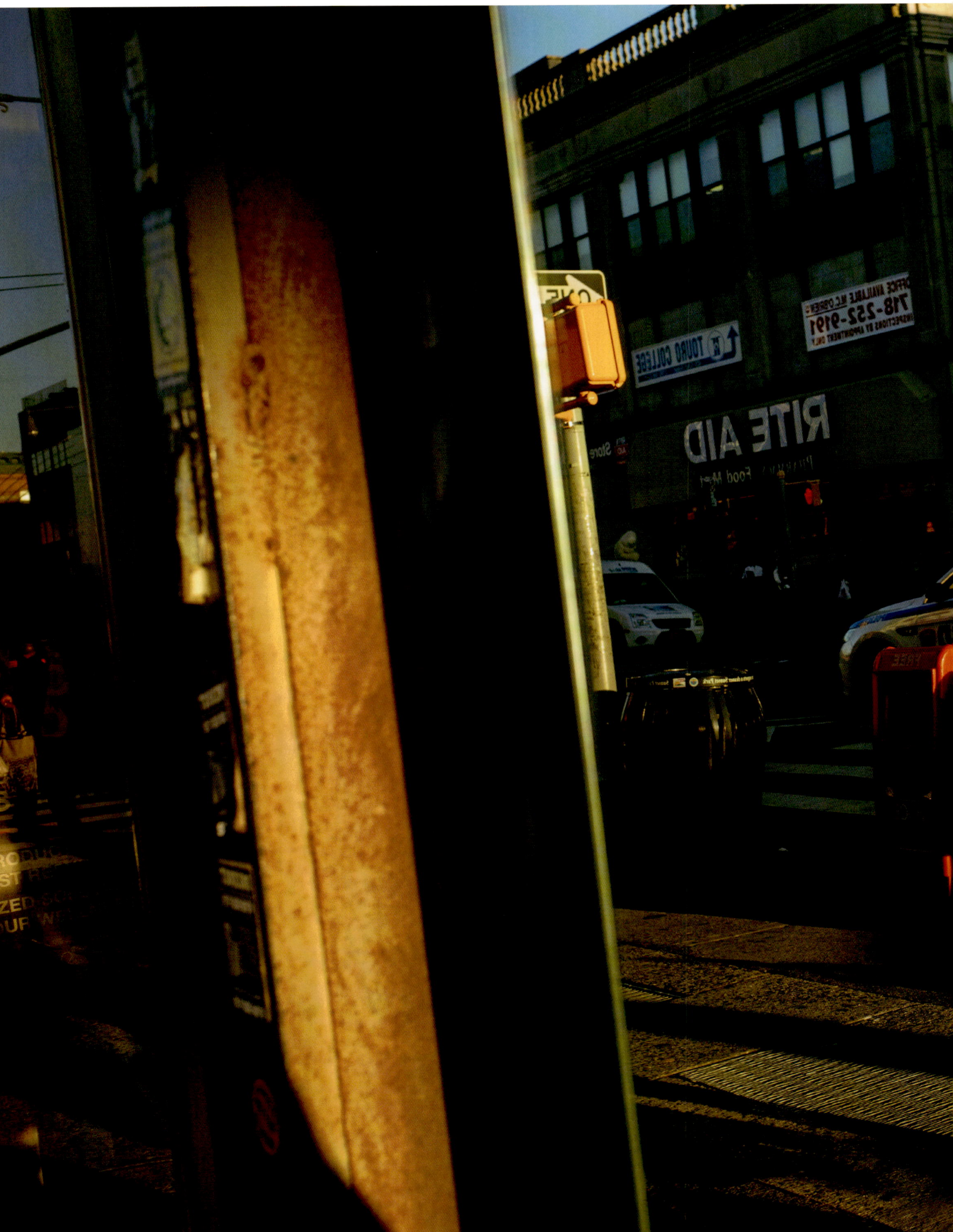
RITE AID
TOURO COLLEGE
718-252-9191
OFFICE AVAILABLE M/C OPEN
FREE

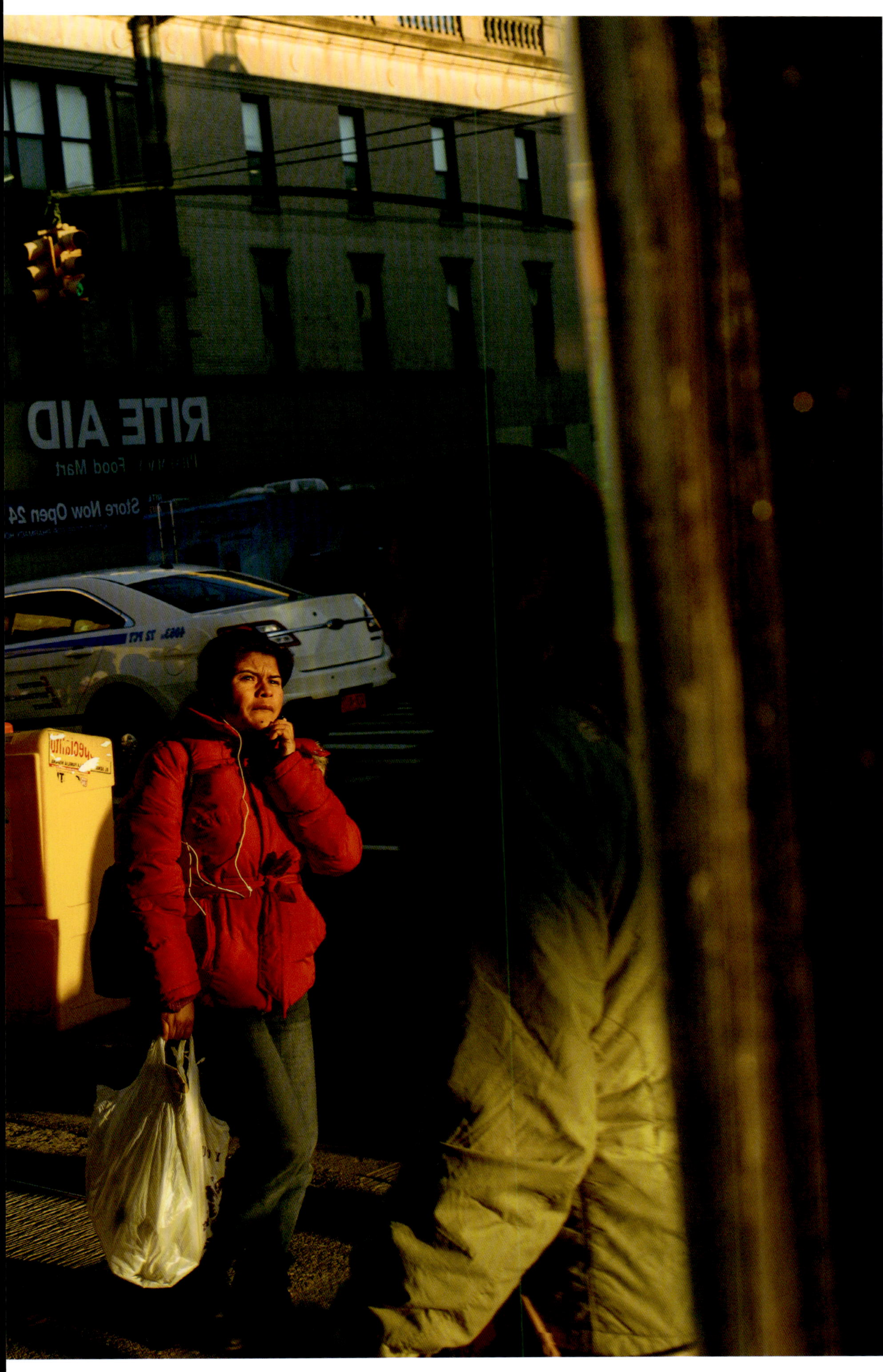

SUNSET PARK, 2014

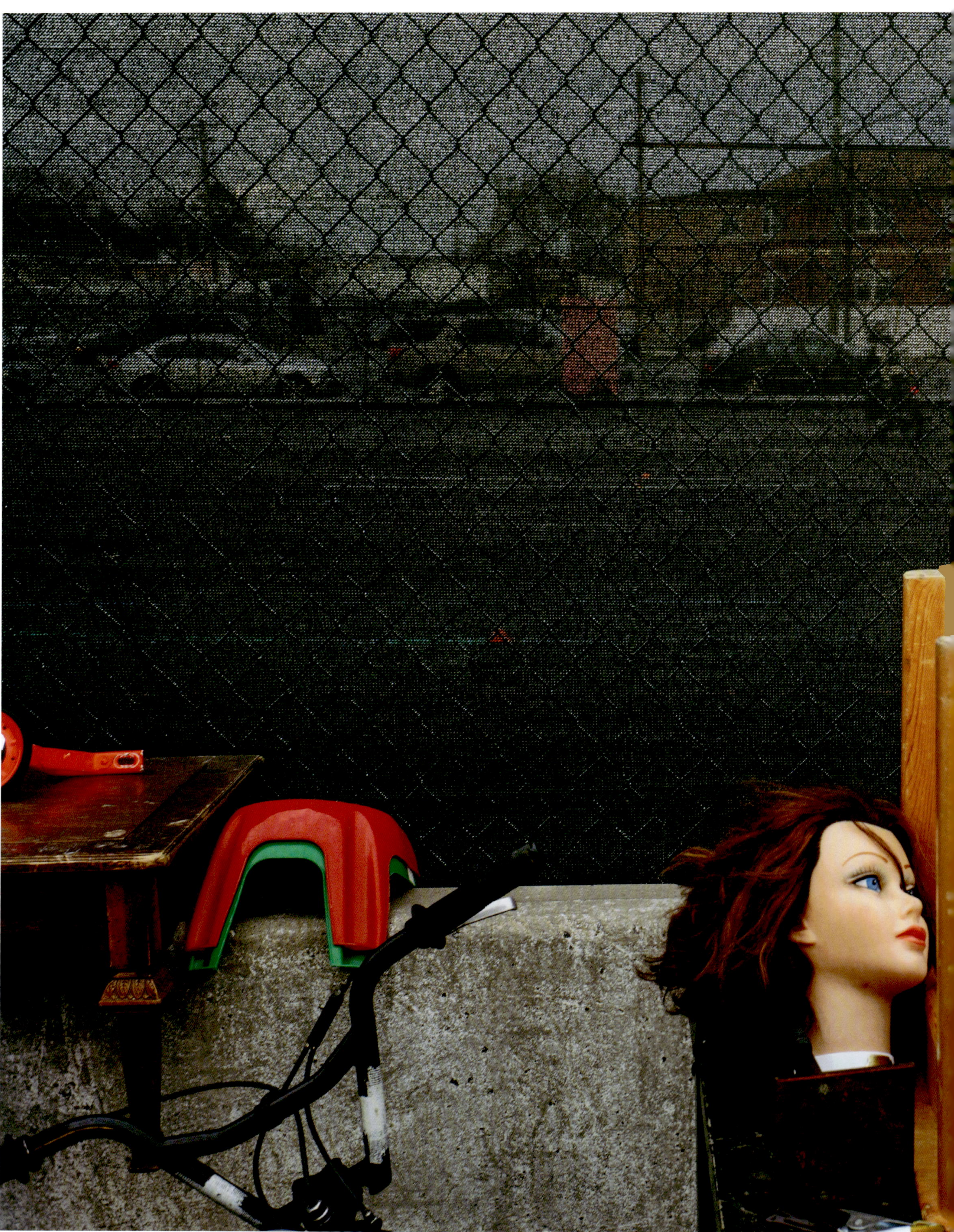

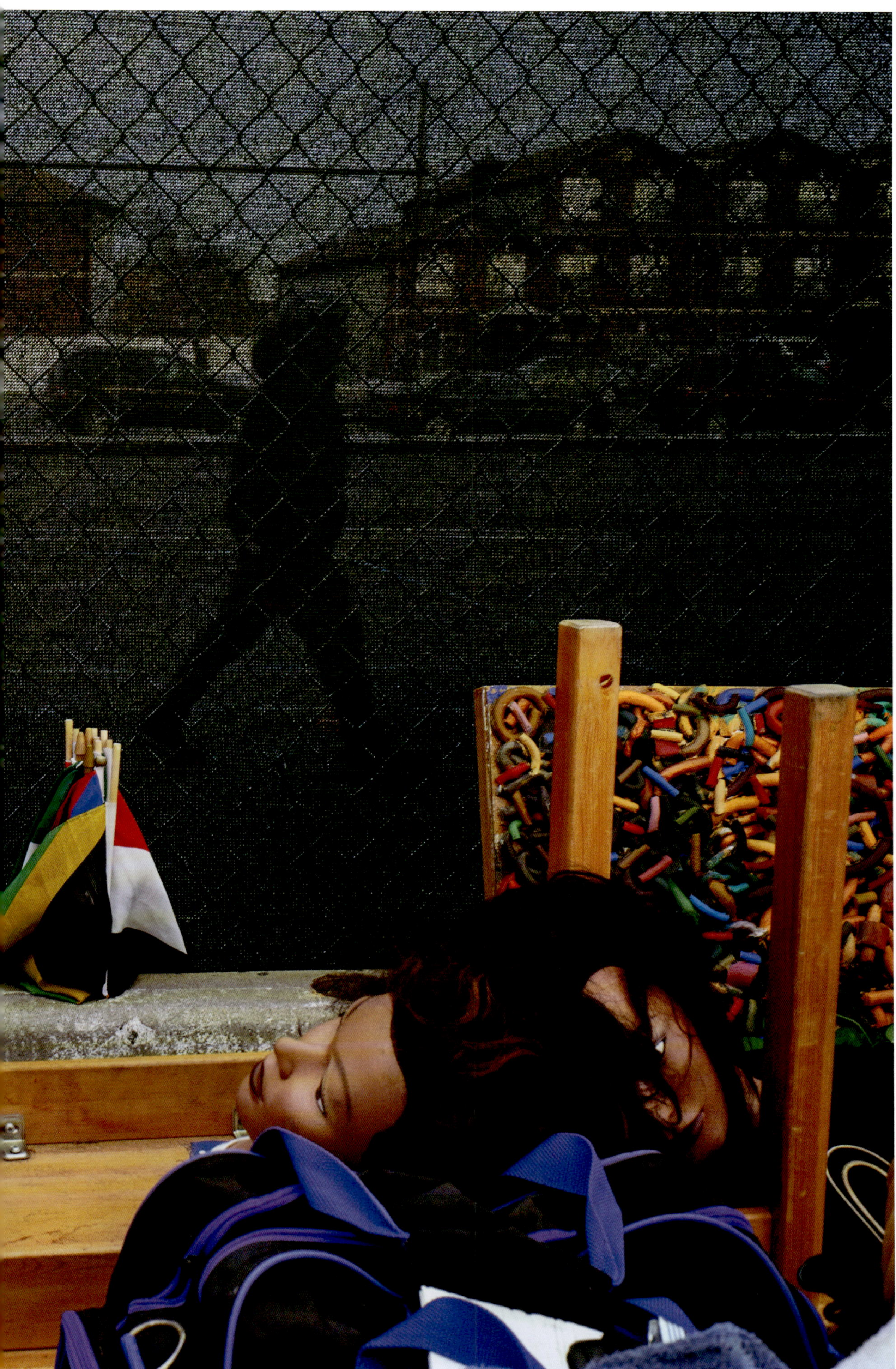

EAST NEW YORK, 2014

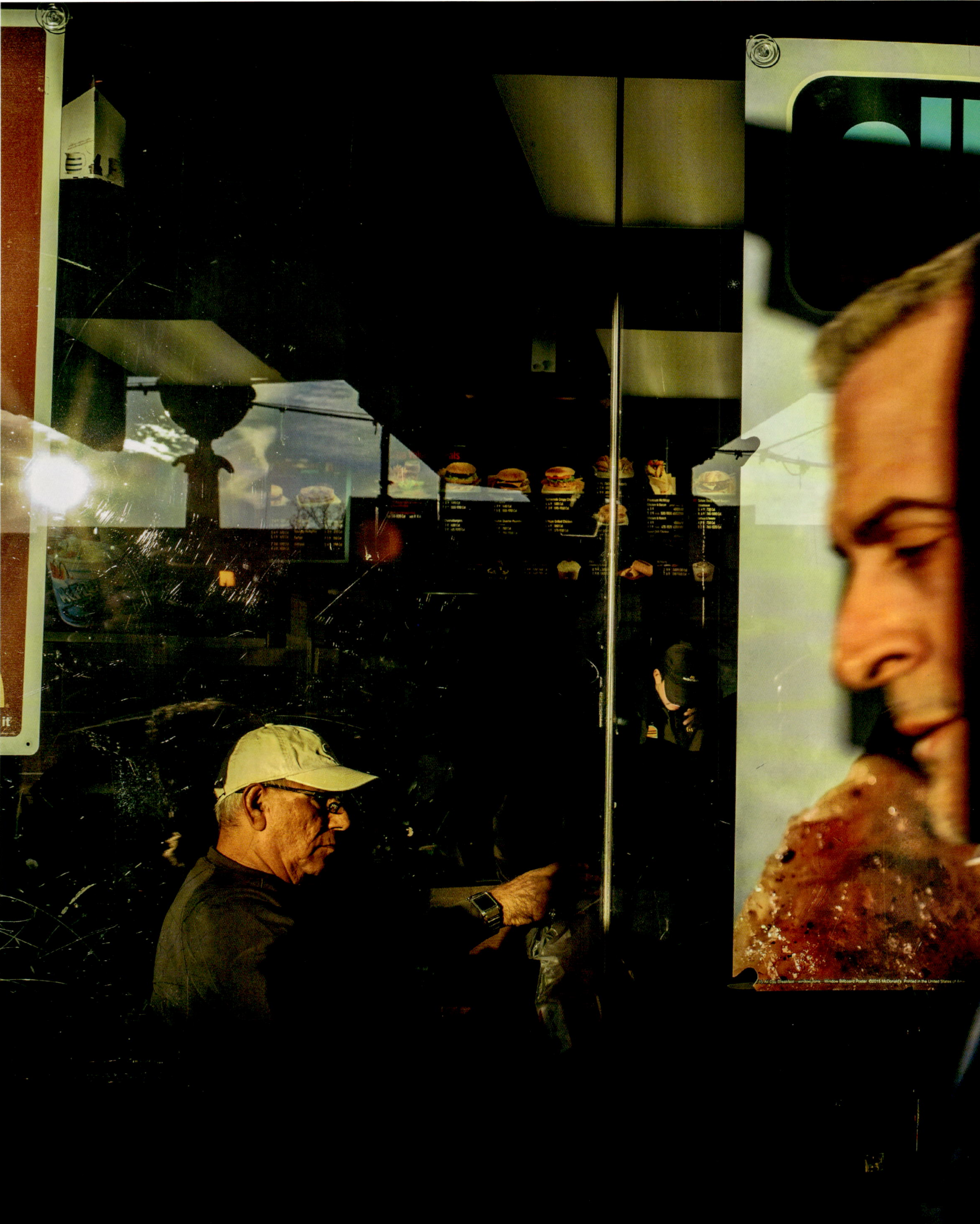

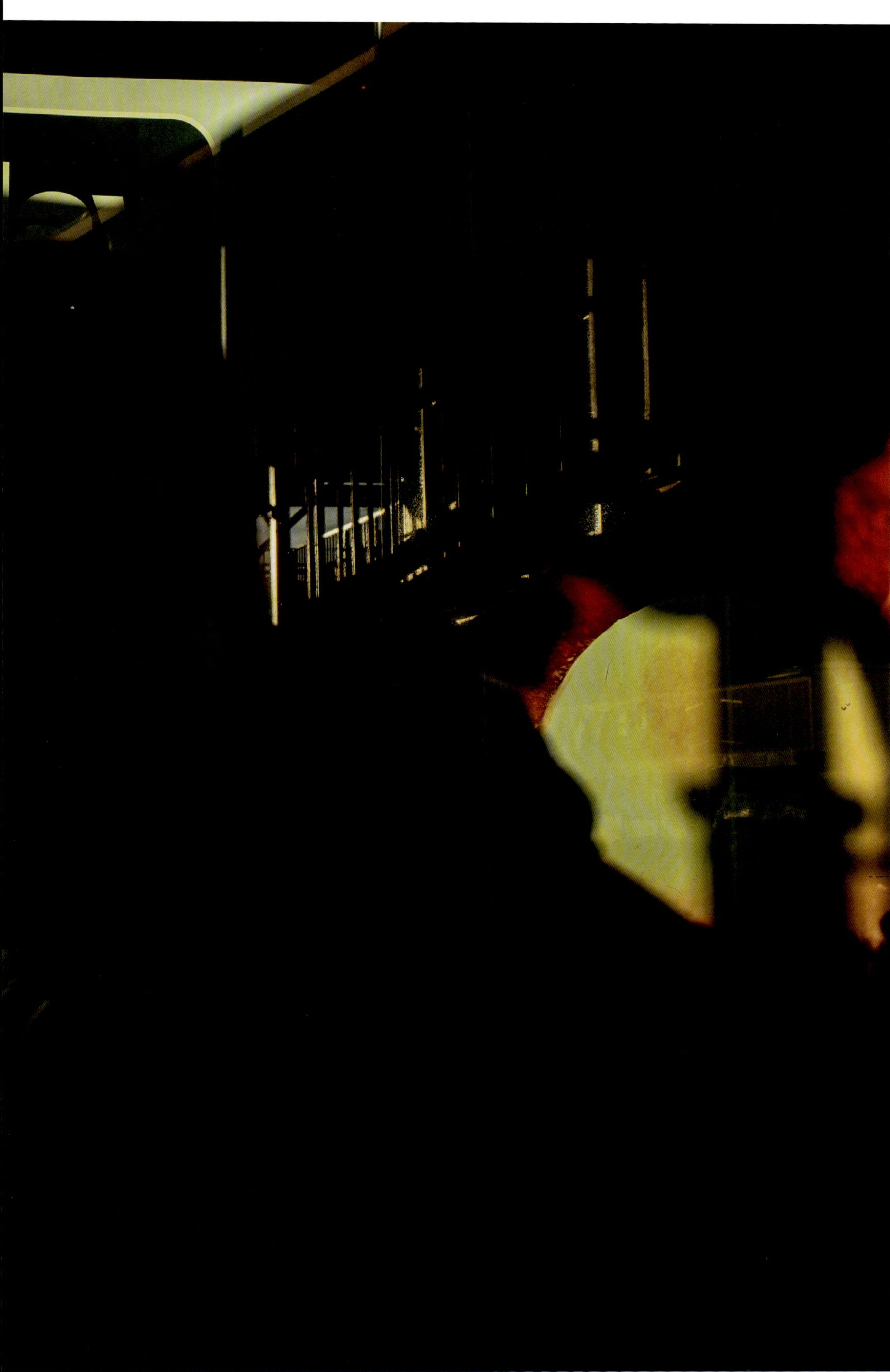

BENSONHURST, 2016

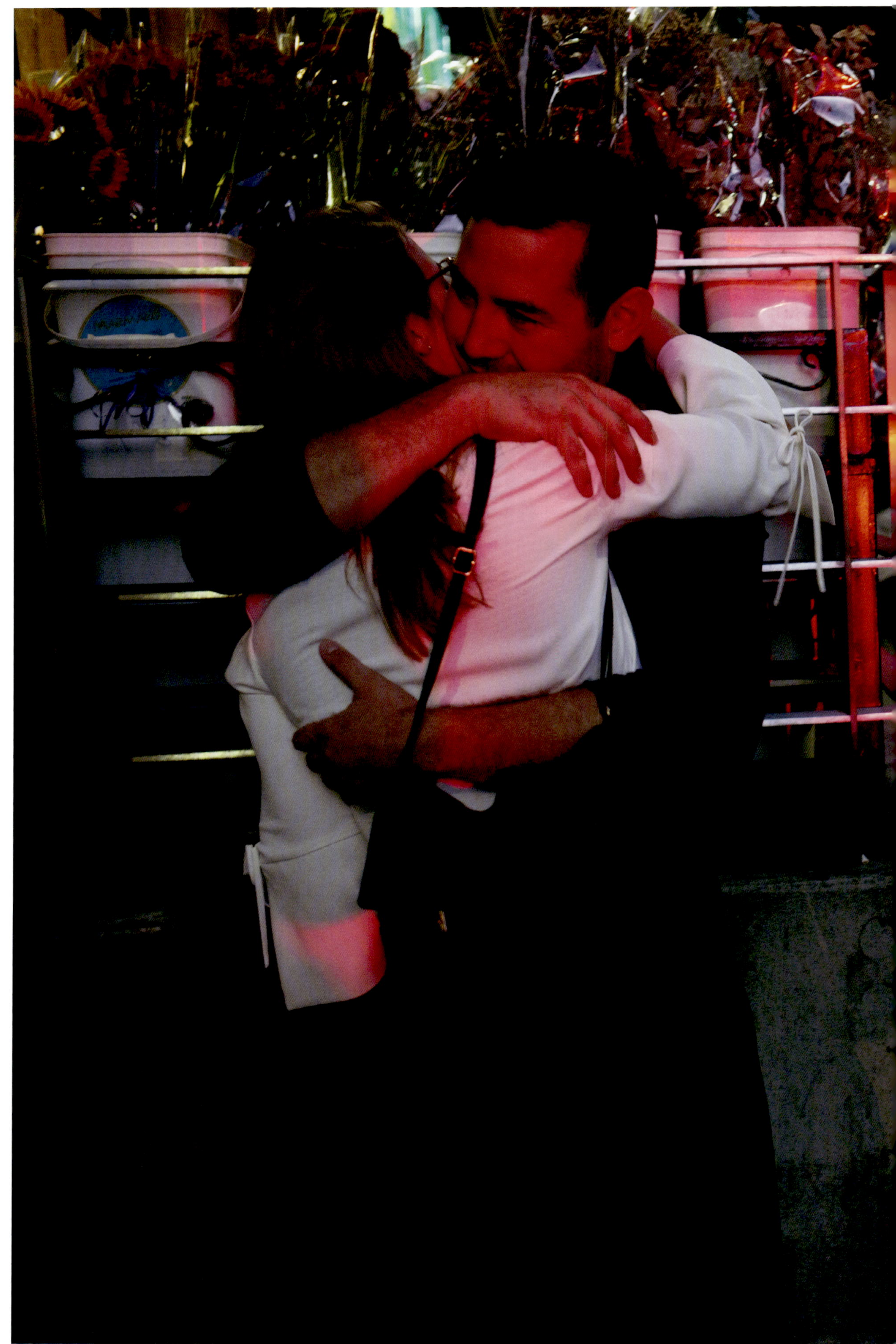

DUMBO, 2018

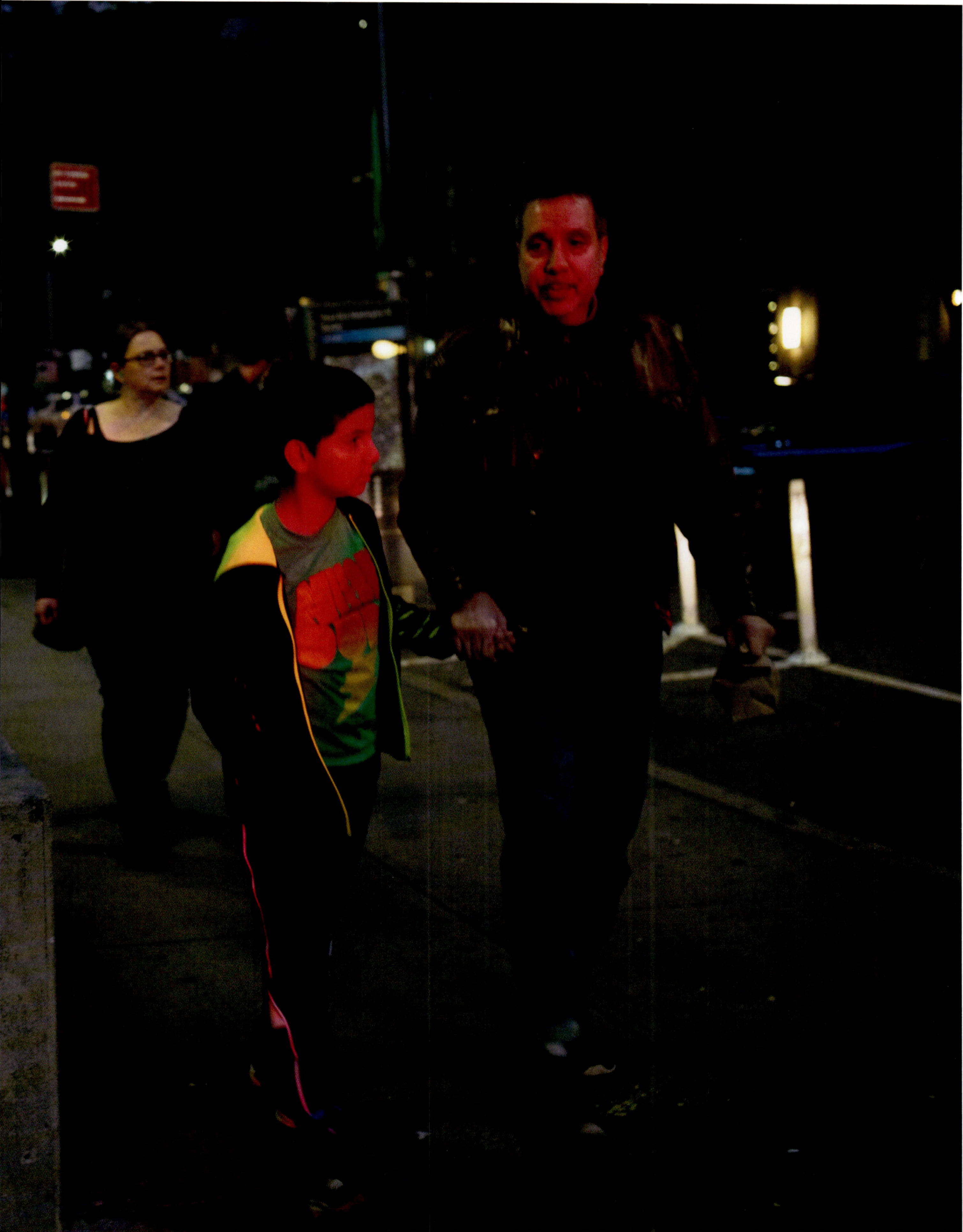

CONEY ISLAND, 2016

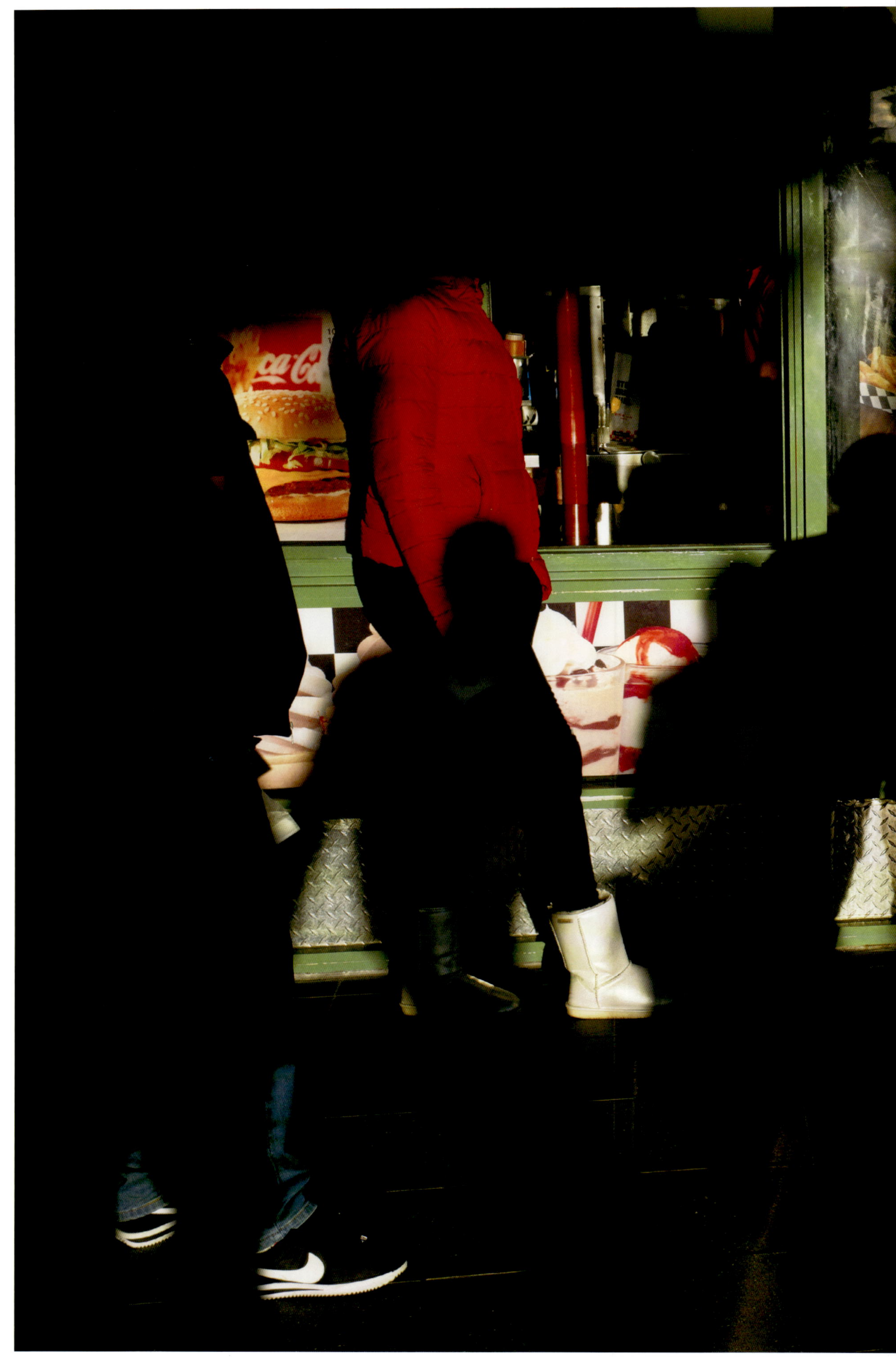

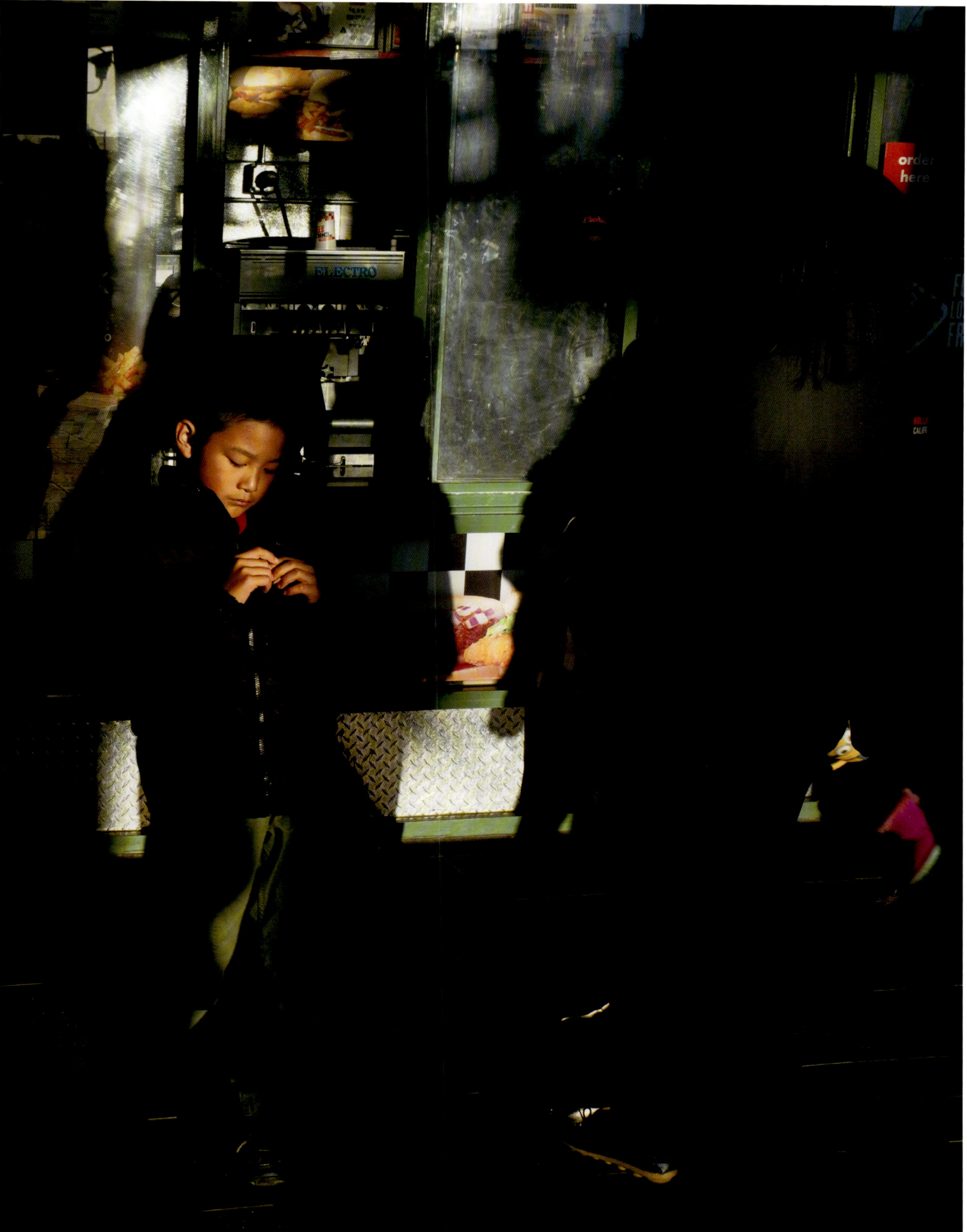

ELECTRO
order
here

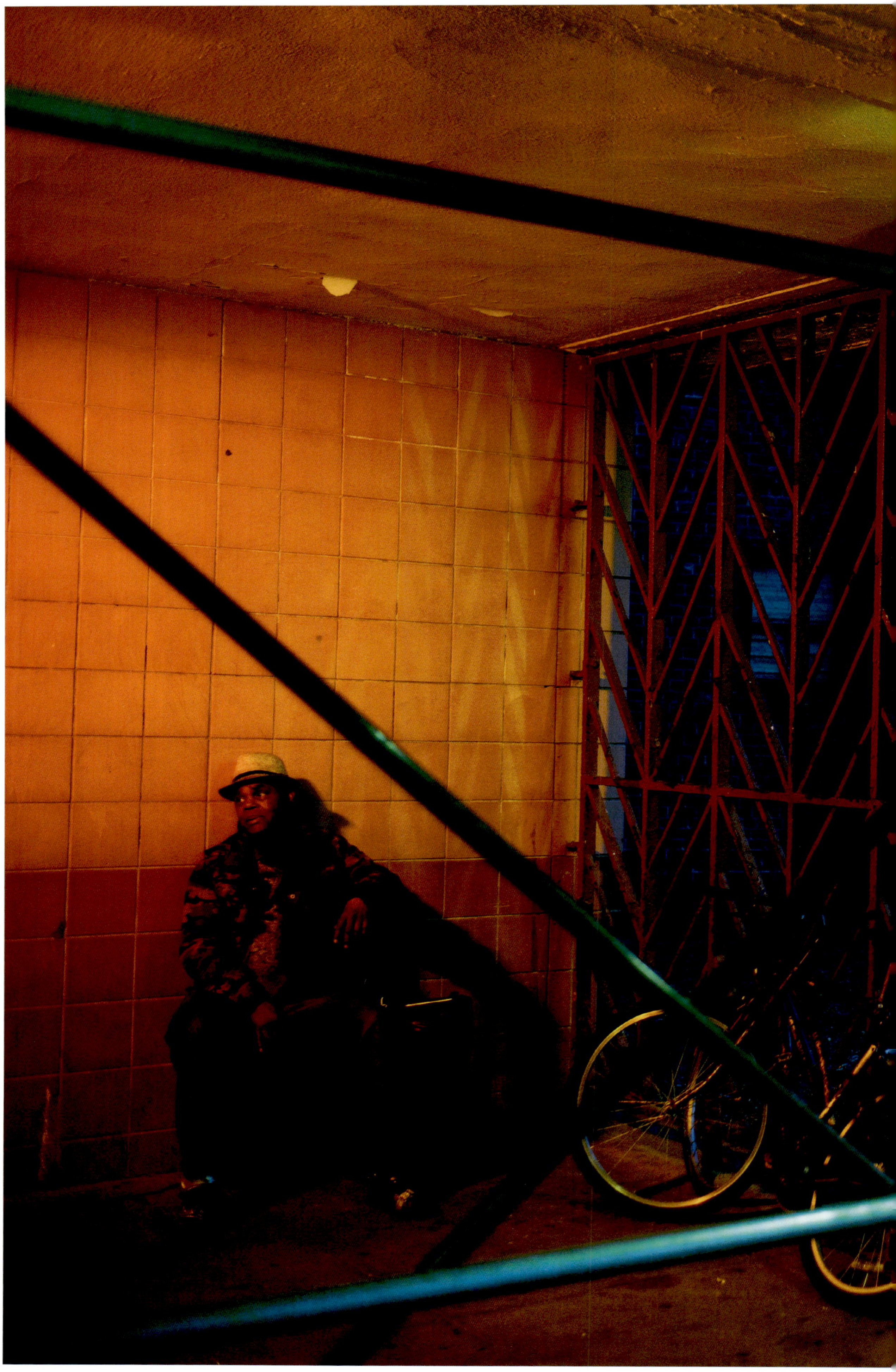

VINEGAR HILL, 2016

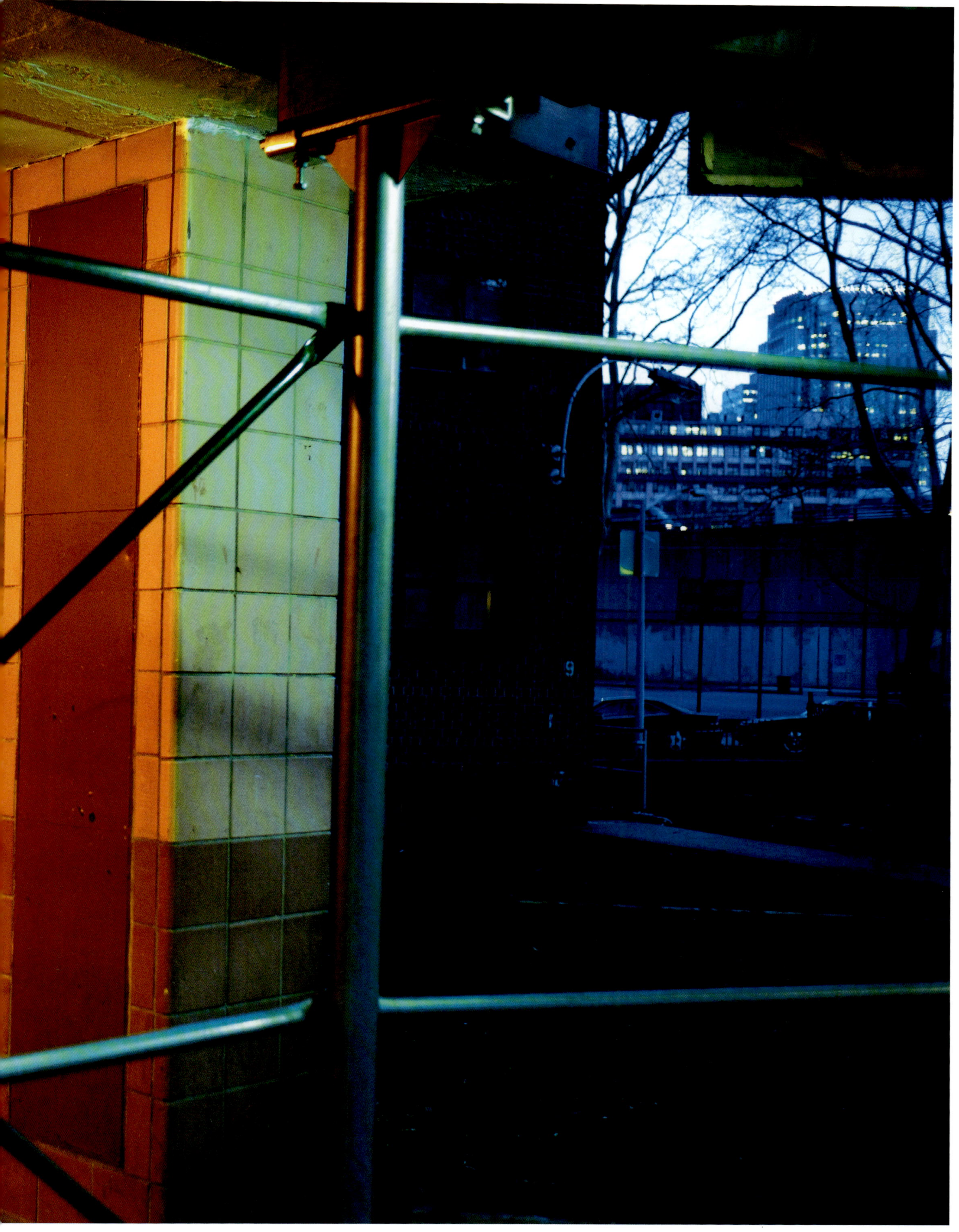

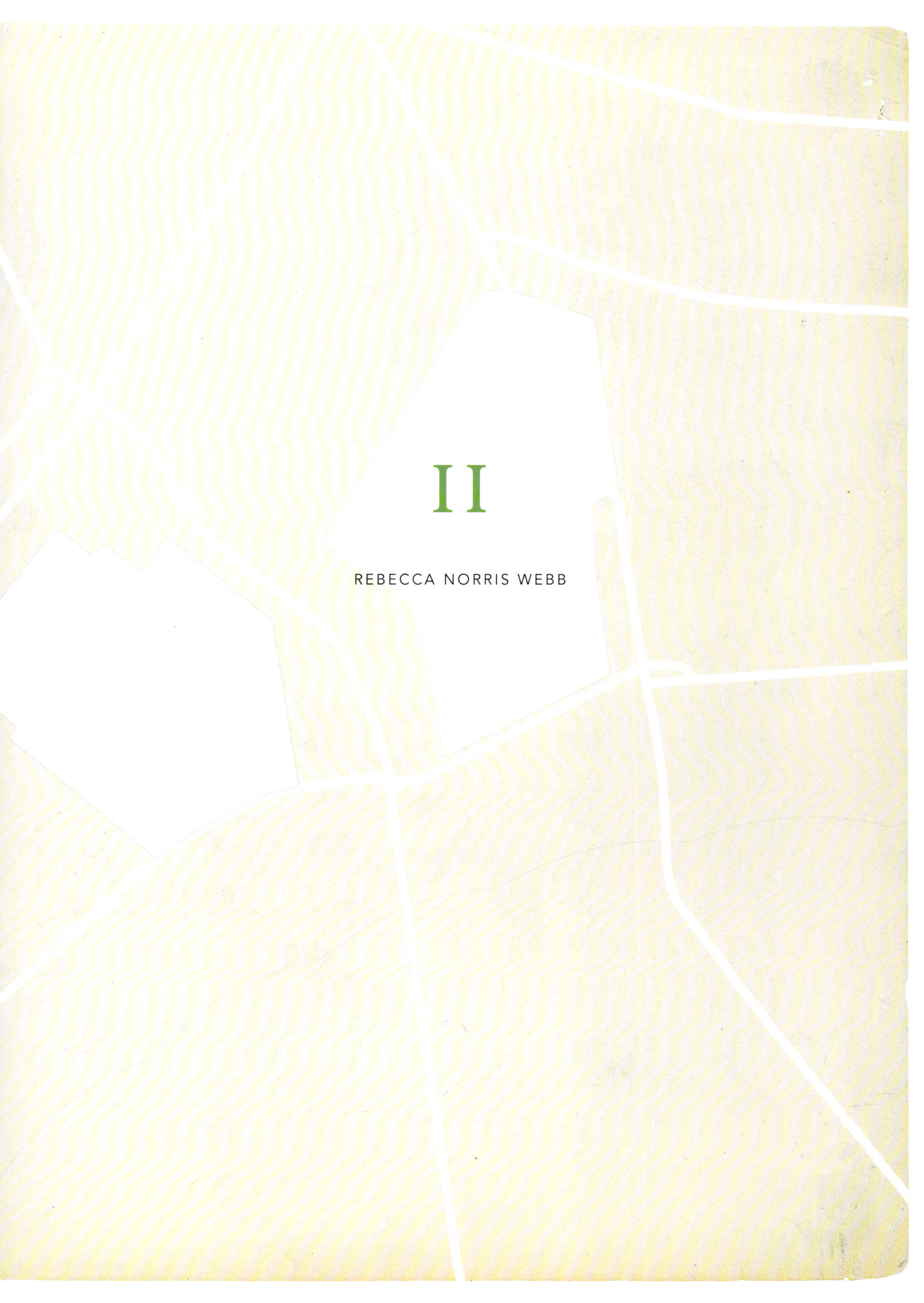
II

REBECCA NORRIS WEBB

FLYING AT NIGHT

Flying at night, we see the glow of the city where we live, Brooklyn,
this bioluminescence *of being numerous*—more than two and a half
million human beings inhabiting what was once forest and marshland.
Adrift in all that luminance, Prospect Park passes beneath us like a great
dark ship, built of ironwood, hornbeam, scarlet oak. In its wooden hold,
I know that we are home.

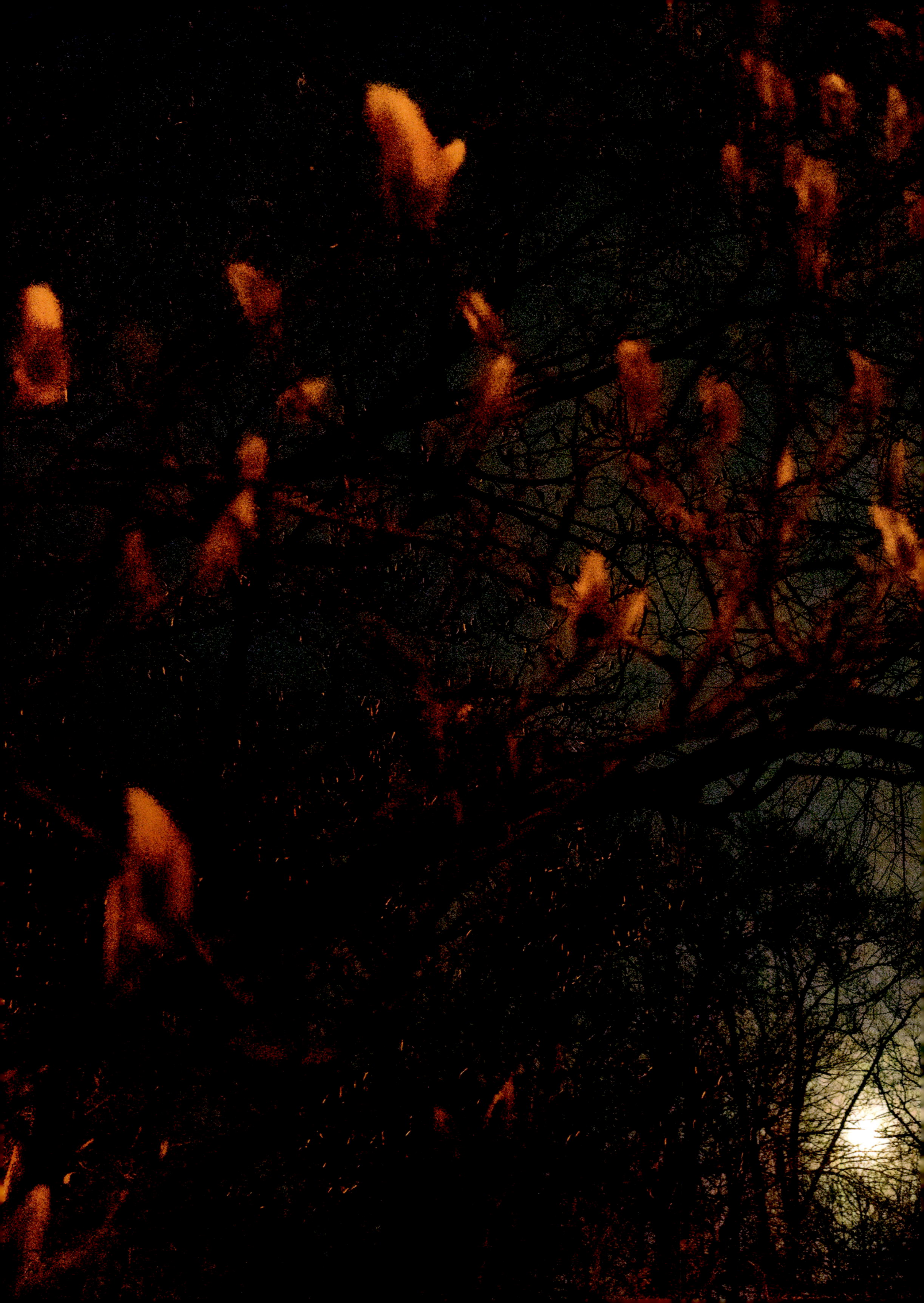

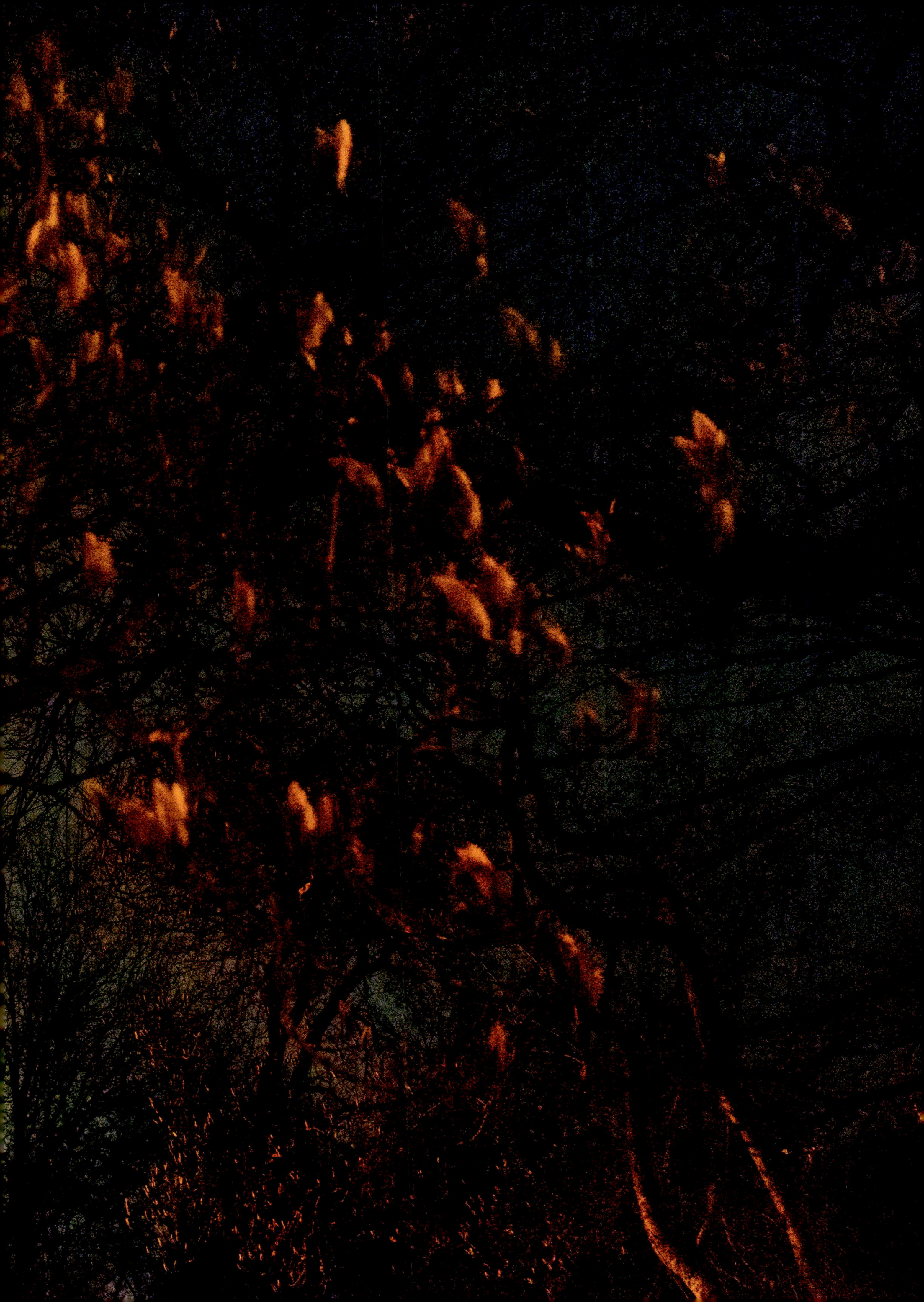

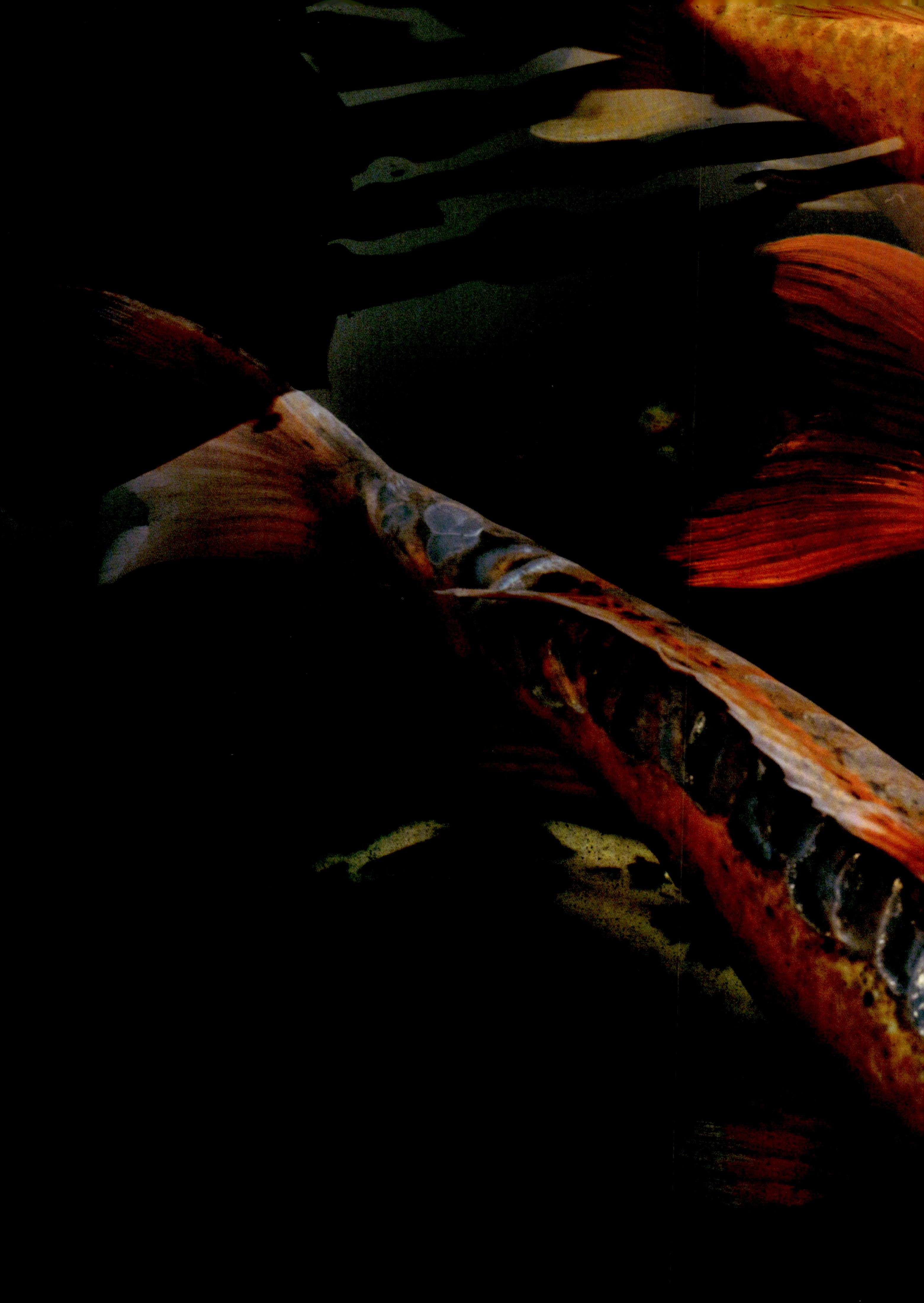

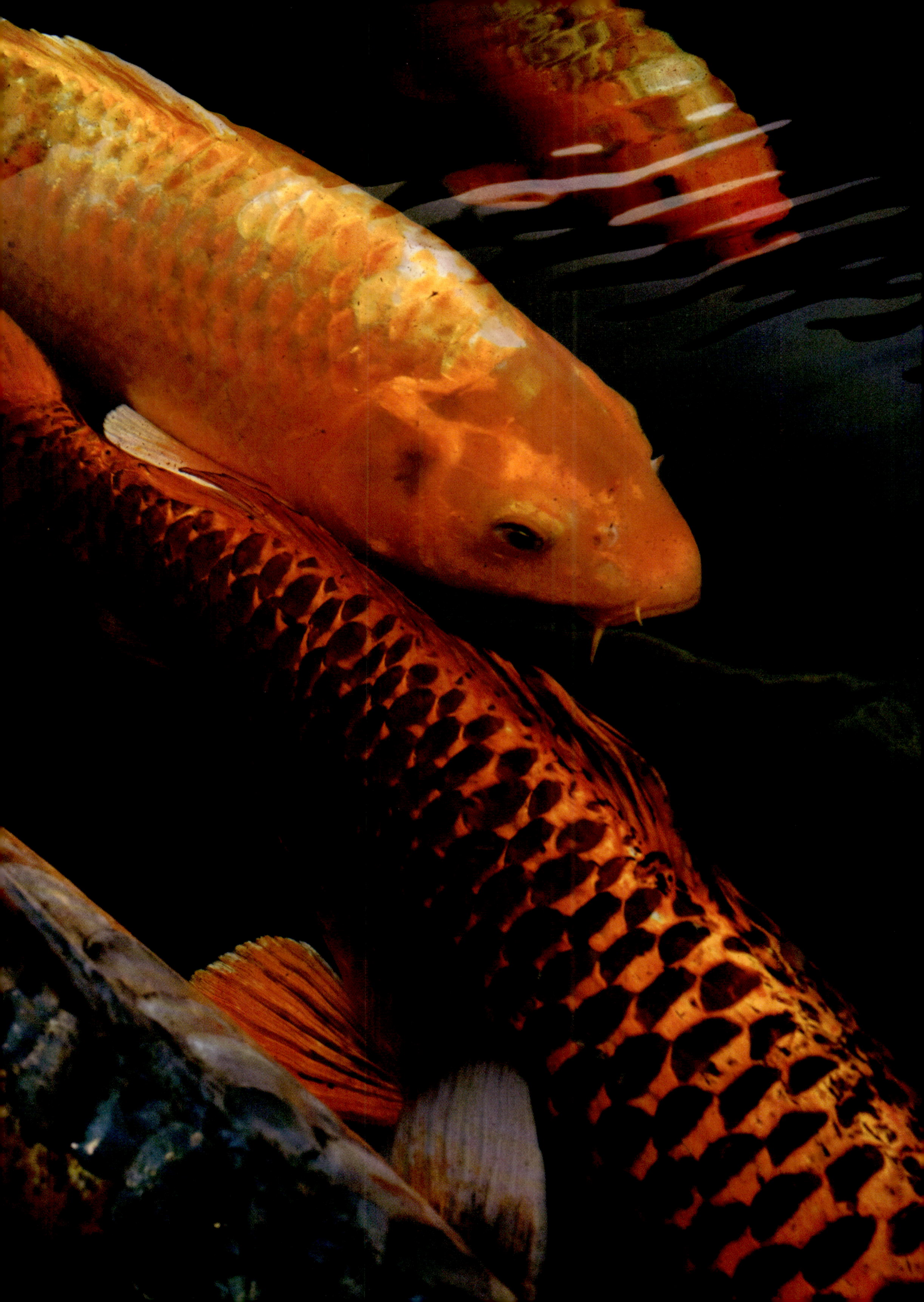

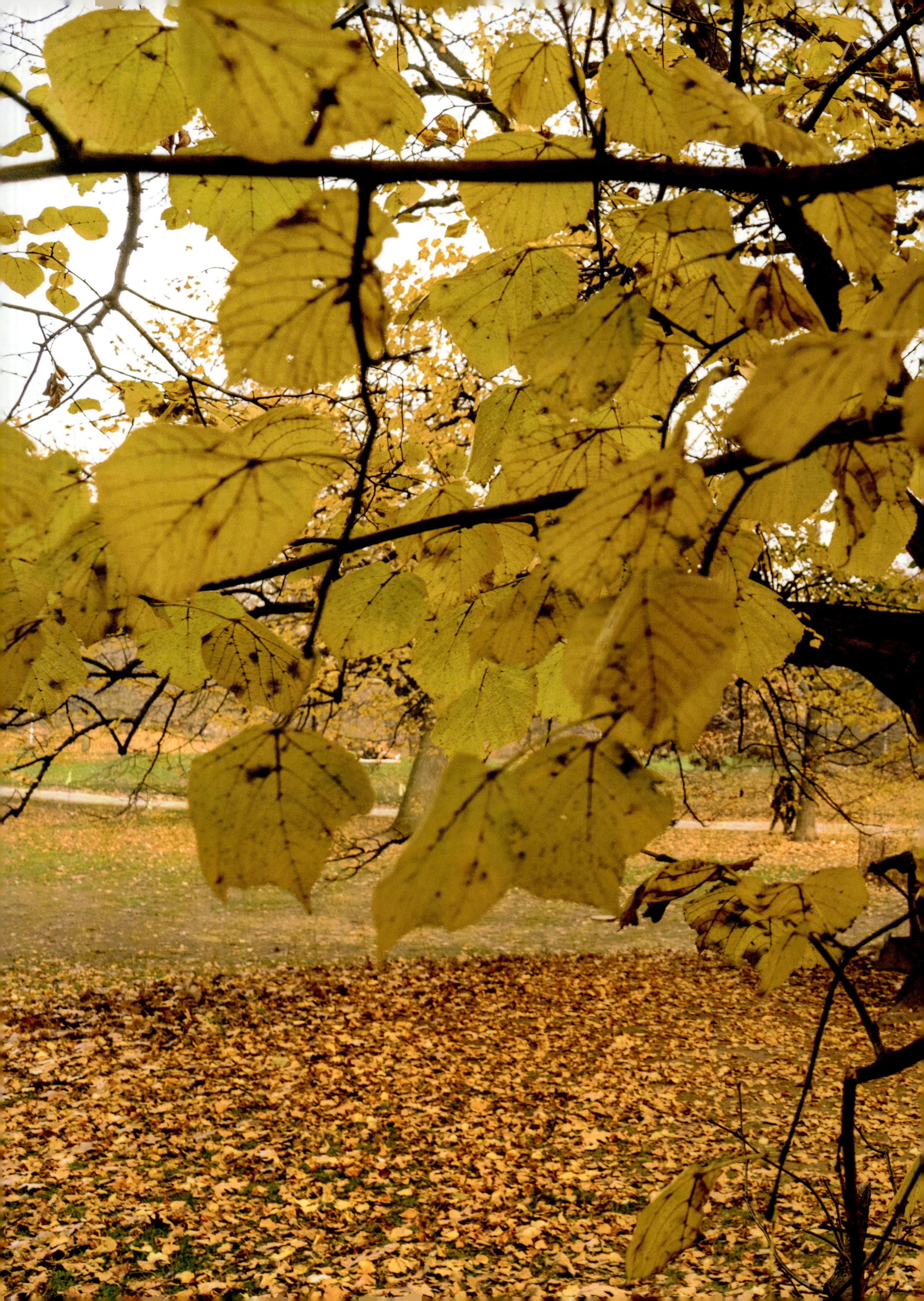

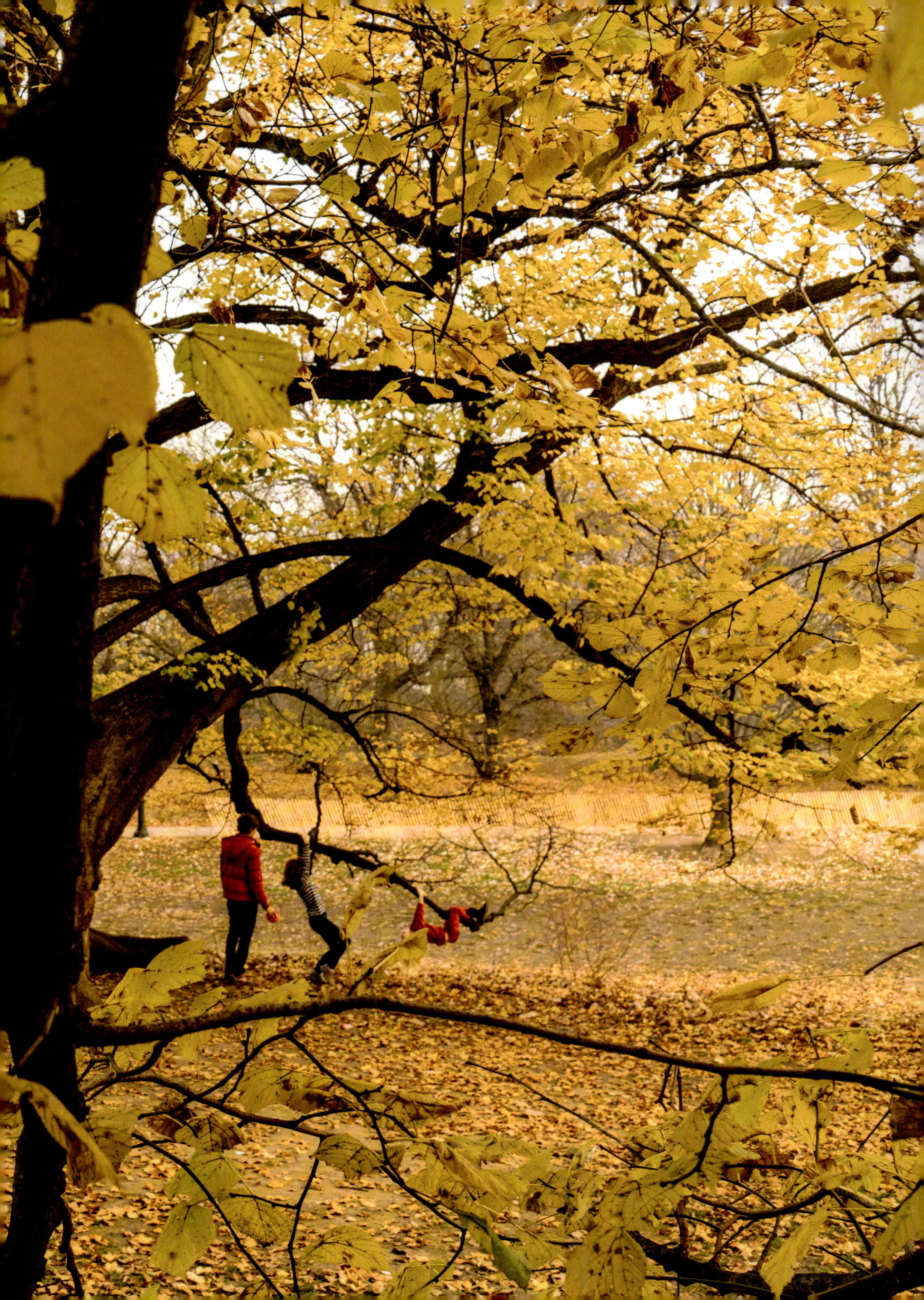

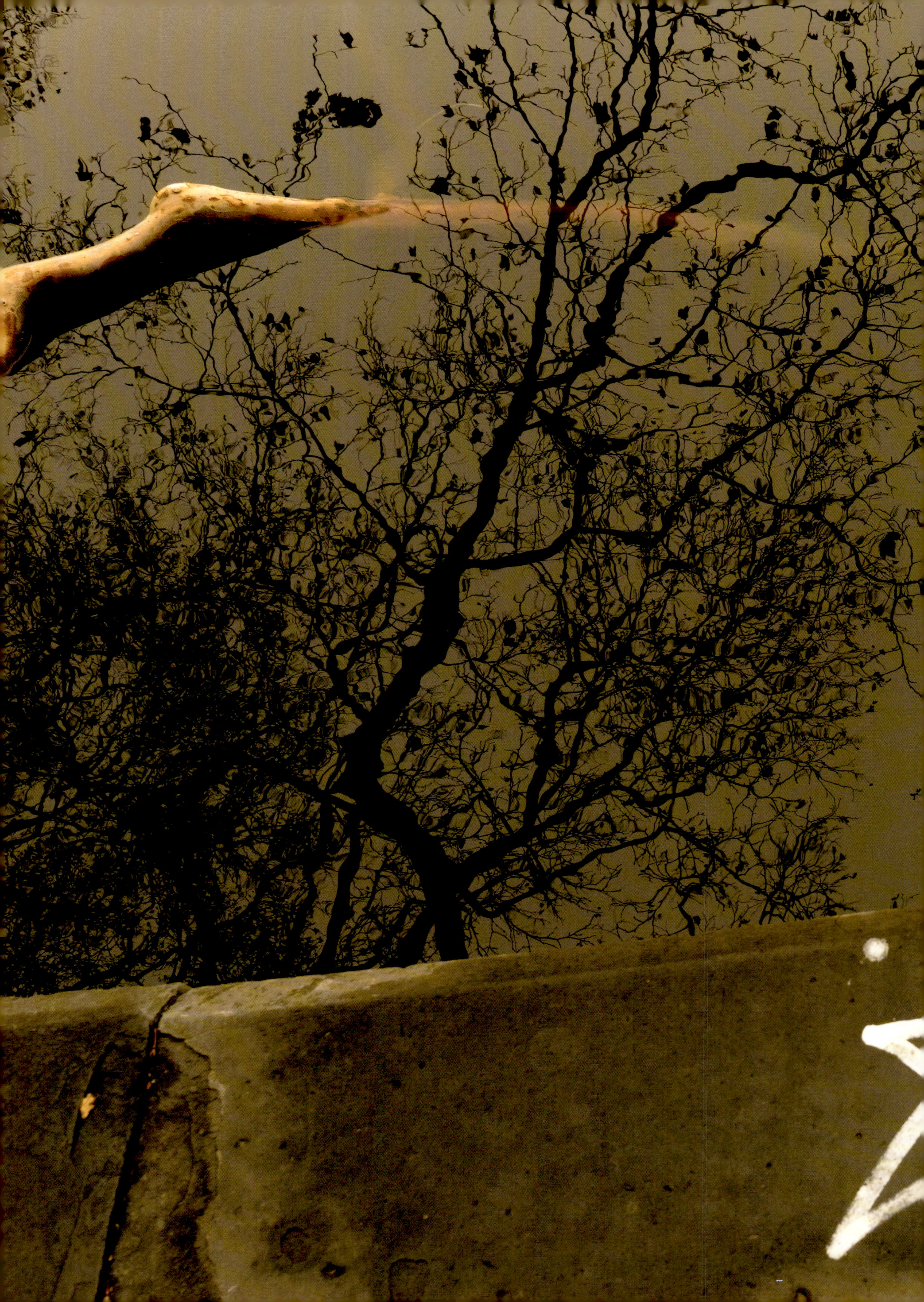

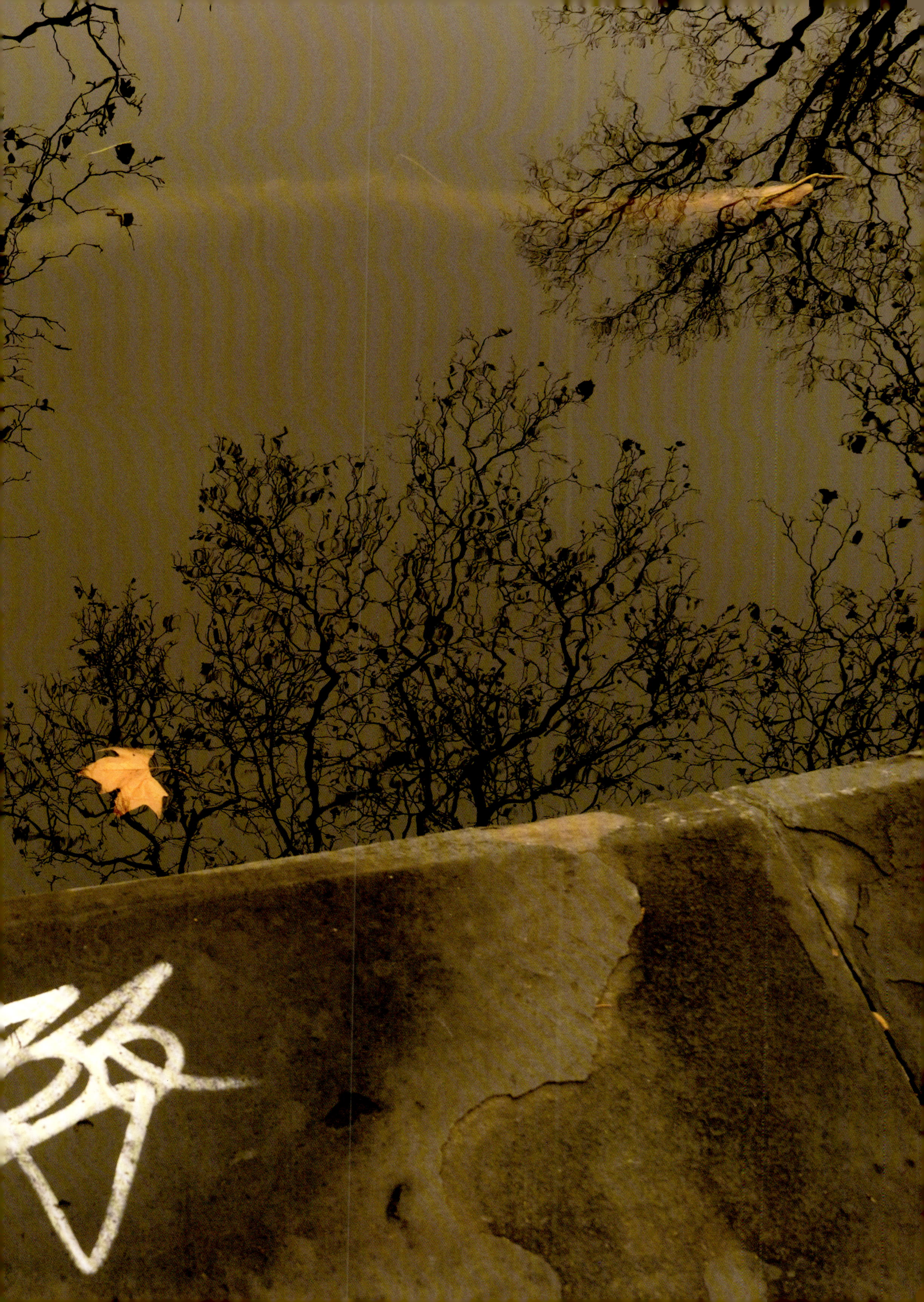

STAND OF ELM

There's a knoll not far from here. You can only get there by walking. In the
distance, yellow leaves signal that you're almost there. It's the twisted bodies
I come for, meandering like dark rivers in the air. How can you look away?
We're in the presence of survivors, after all, one of the last stands of American
elm, from millions lost to Dutch elm disease over the past century. How can you
not look up? (It's the crown that's infected first, a telltale brown.) For isn't looking
up, sometimes looking through? Beyond the canopy, can you see her, or at least
her gaze—the piercing eyes of Beatrice, or simply Bea, as she preferred to be called,
an early Dutch woman scientist? She saved so many by looking closely at each
dying body, until she could give the darkness a name. Is that how, years later,
she'd also survive the concentration camp in Indonesia during World War II,
and save her two sons, too?

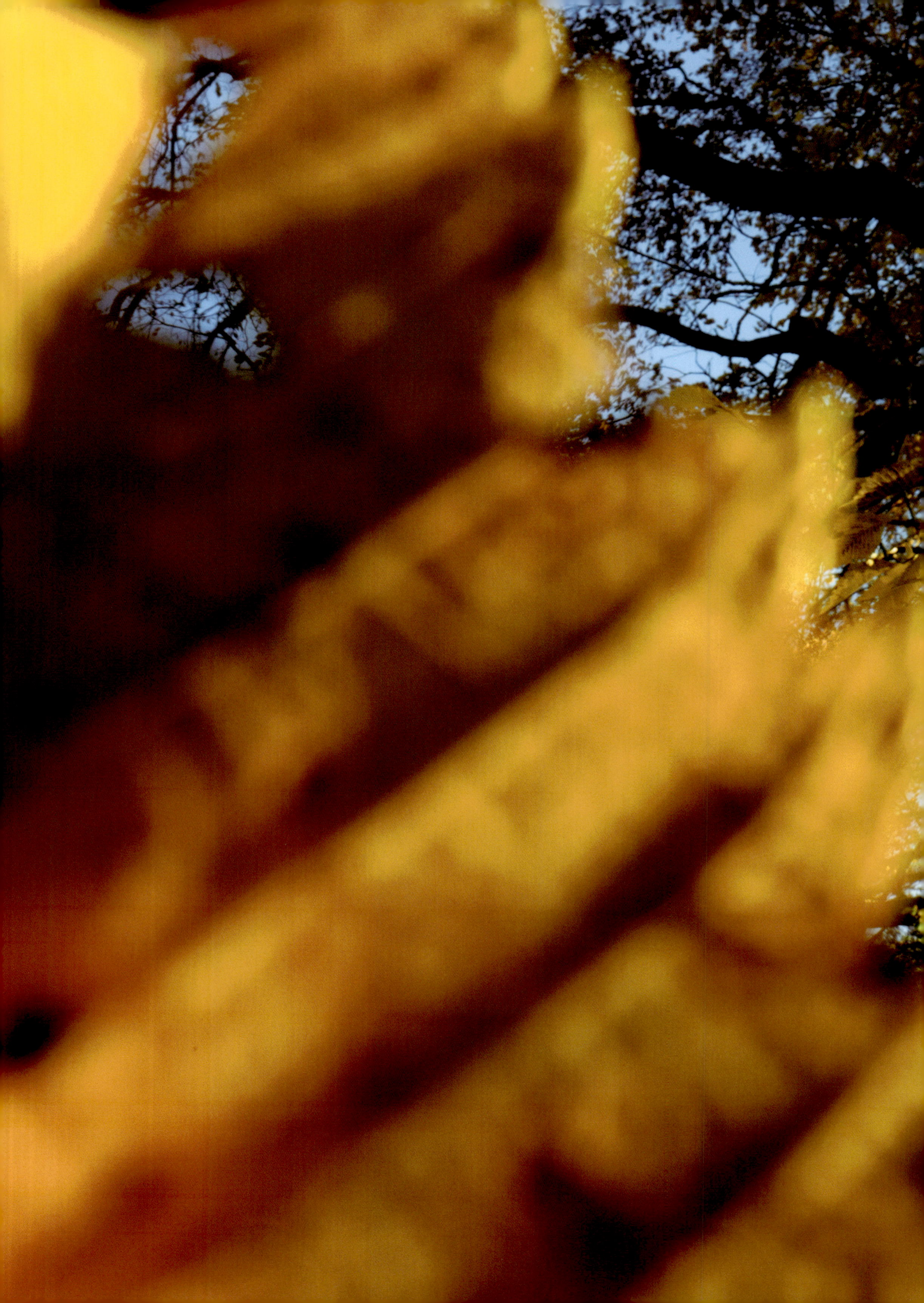

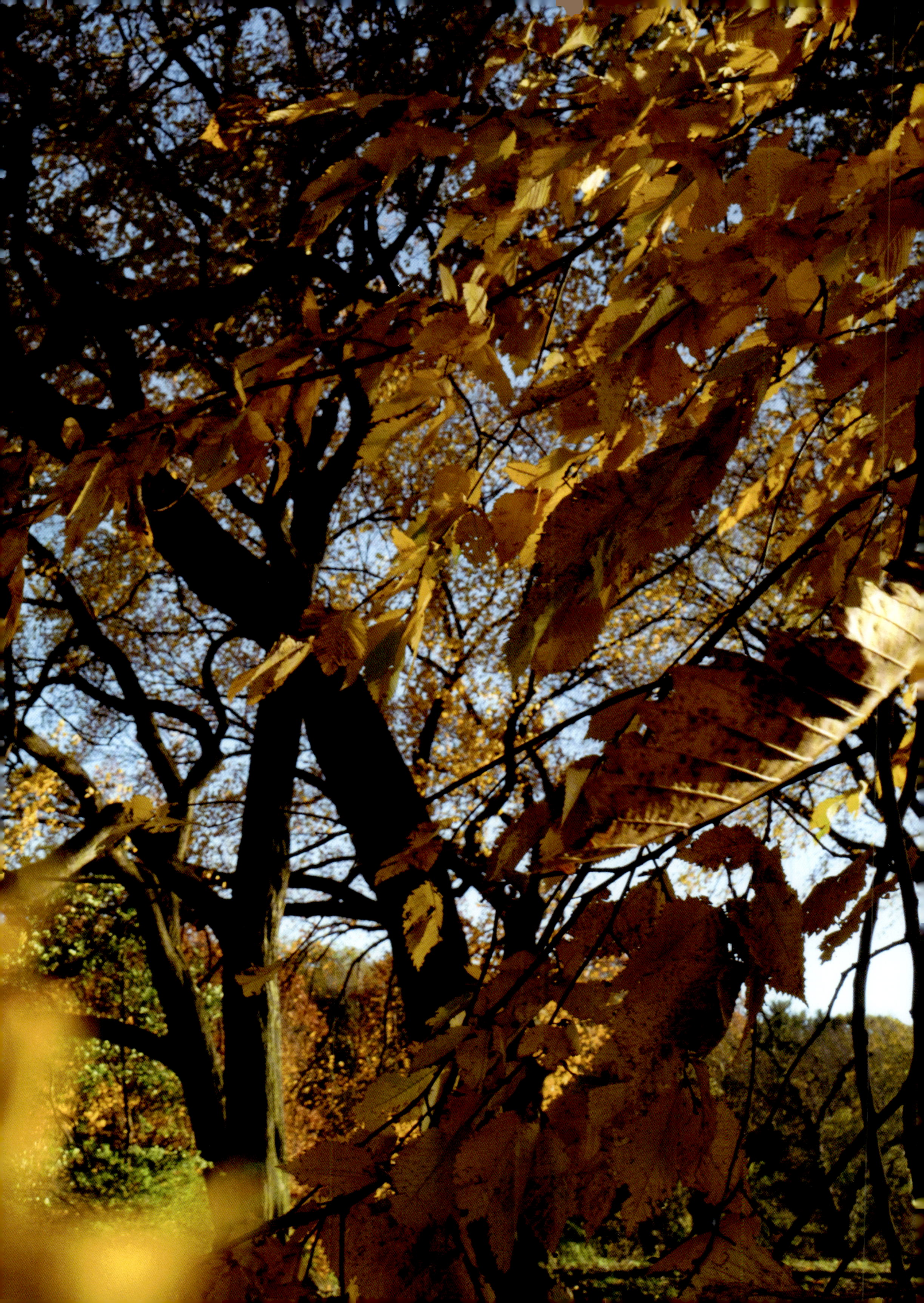

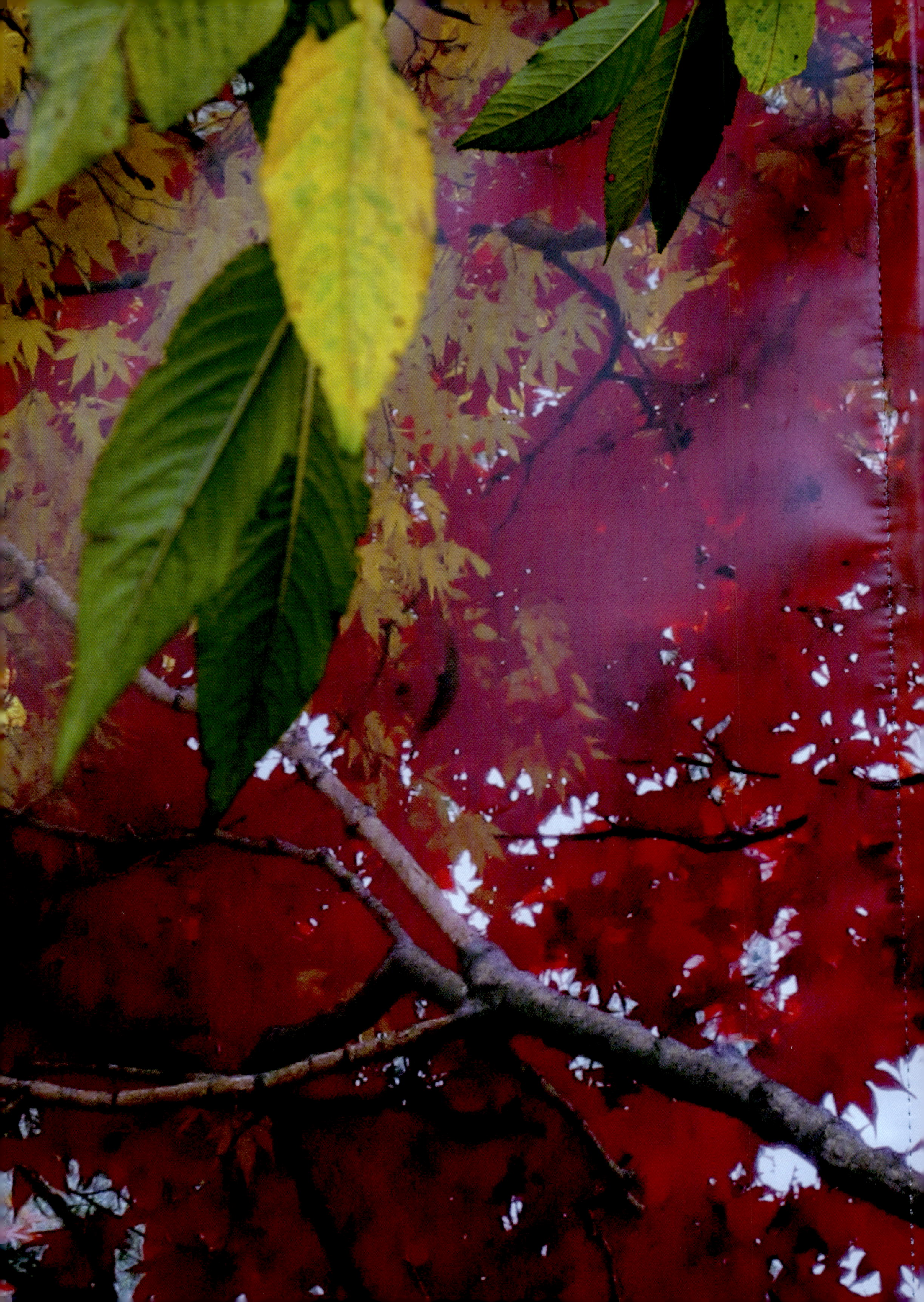

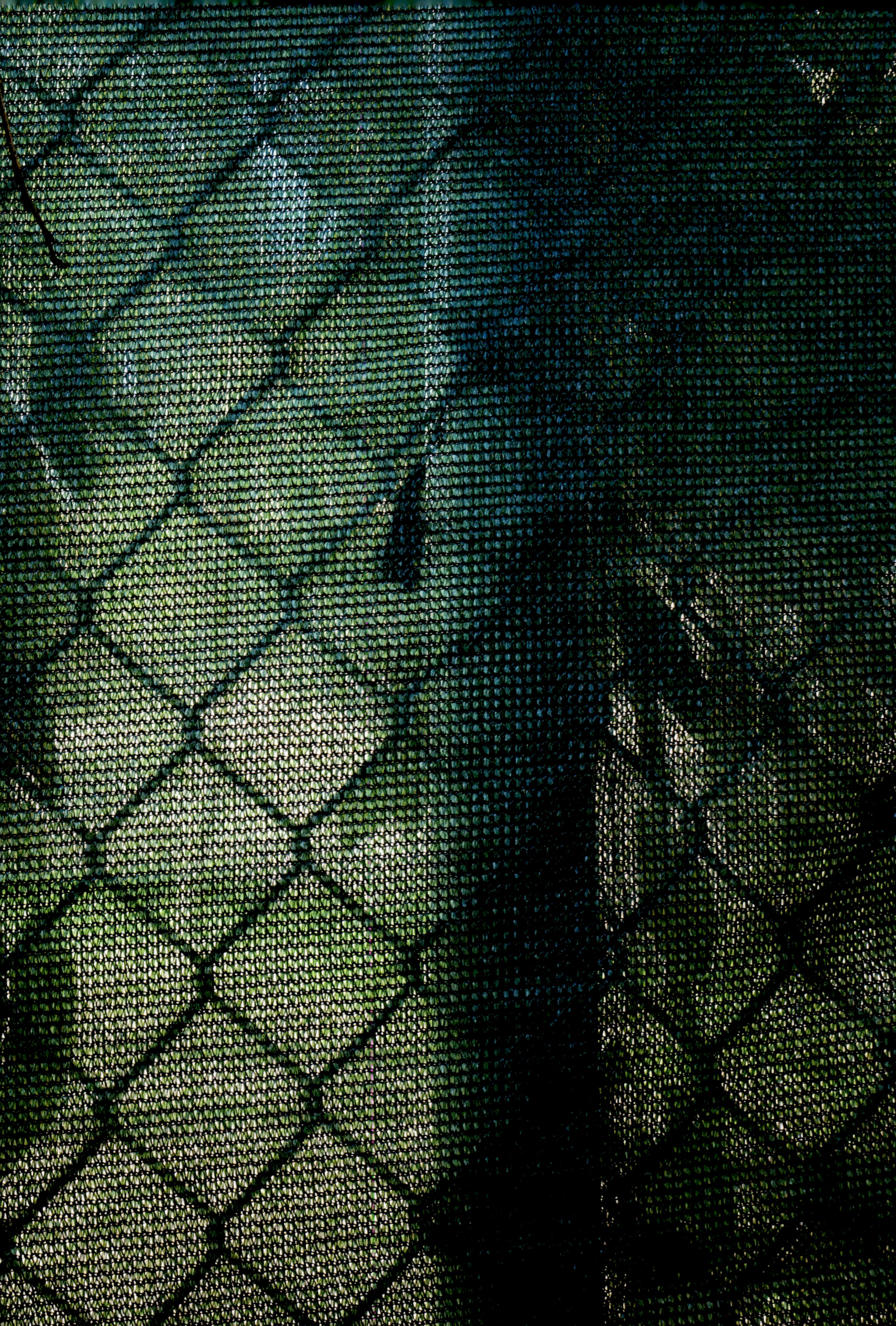

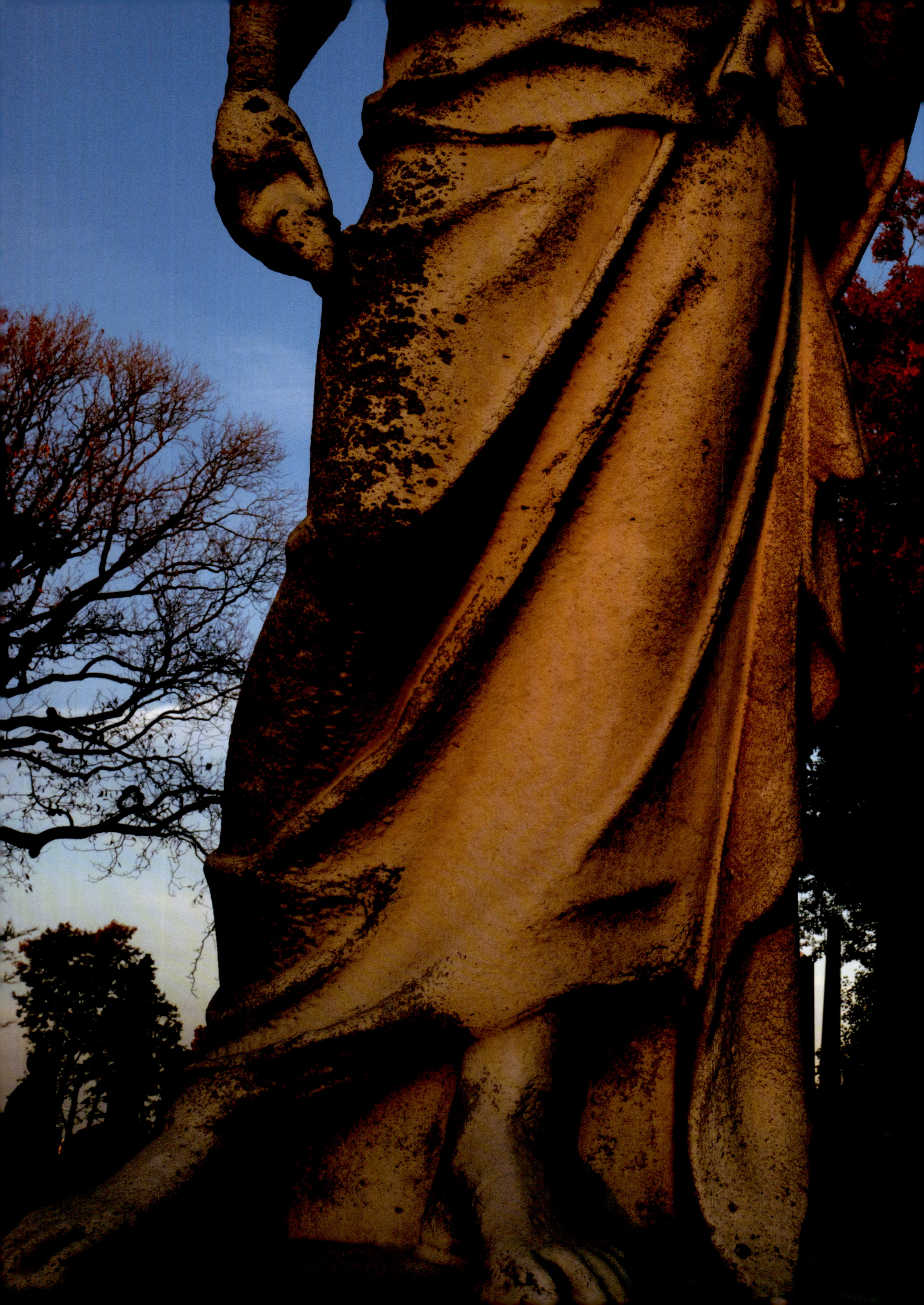

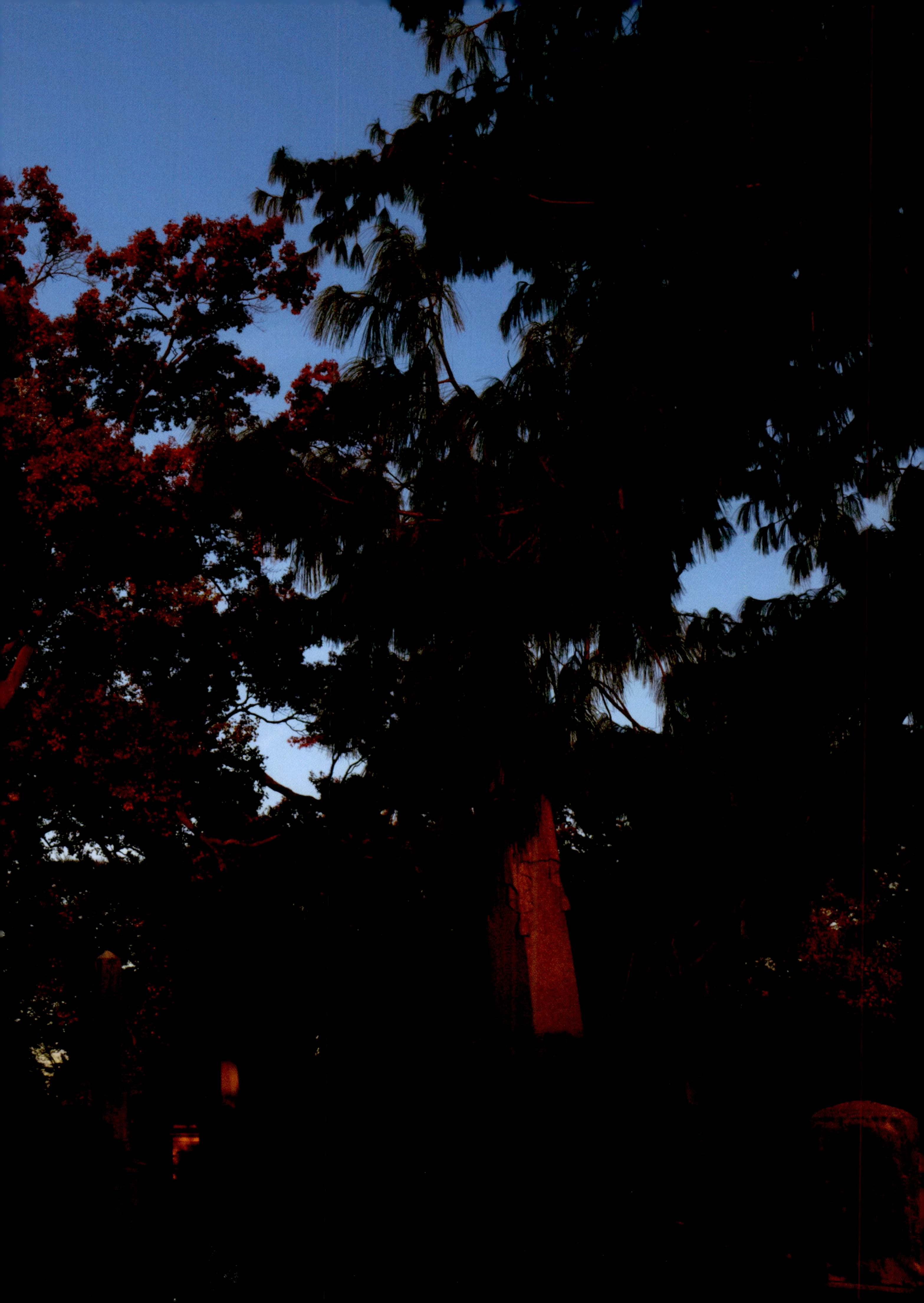

MUTE SWAN

For the past two months, I feel a curious need to be in the company of swans.
Mute swans that, it just so happens, aren't actually mute; something I love
about them. And such an otherworldly call—so hushed you have to lean into
the darkness to hear their plaintive, countertenor cry. Last light, I watch their
seven bodies drift closer. Why are they calling to me? Perhaps it's because I
know too much about them: those hauntingly beautiful swan songs before
death are nothing but sheer myth. Or is it the fact that two people I love
are dying so quietly, that each time they call, I hear between their words
that same baroque minor key?

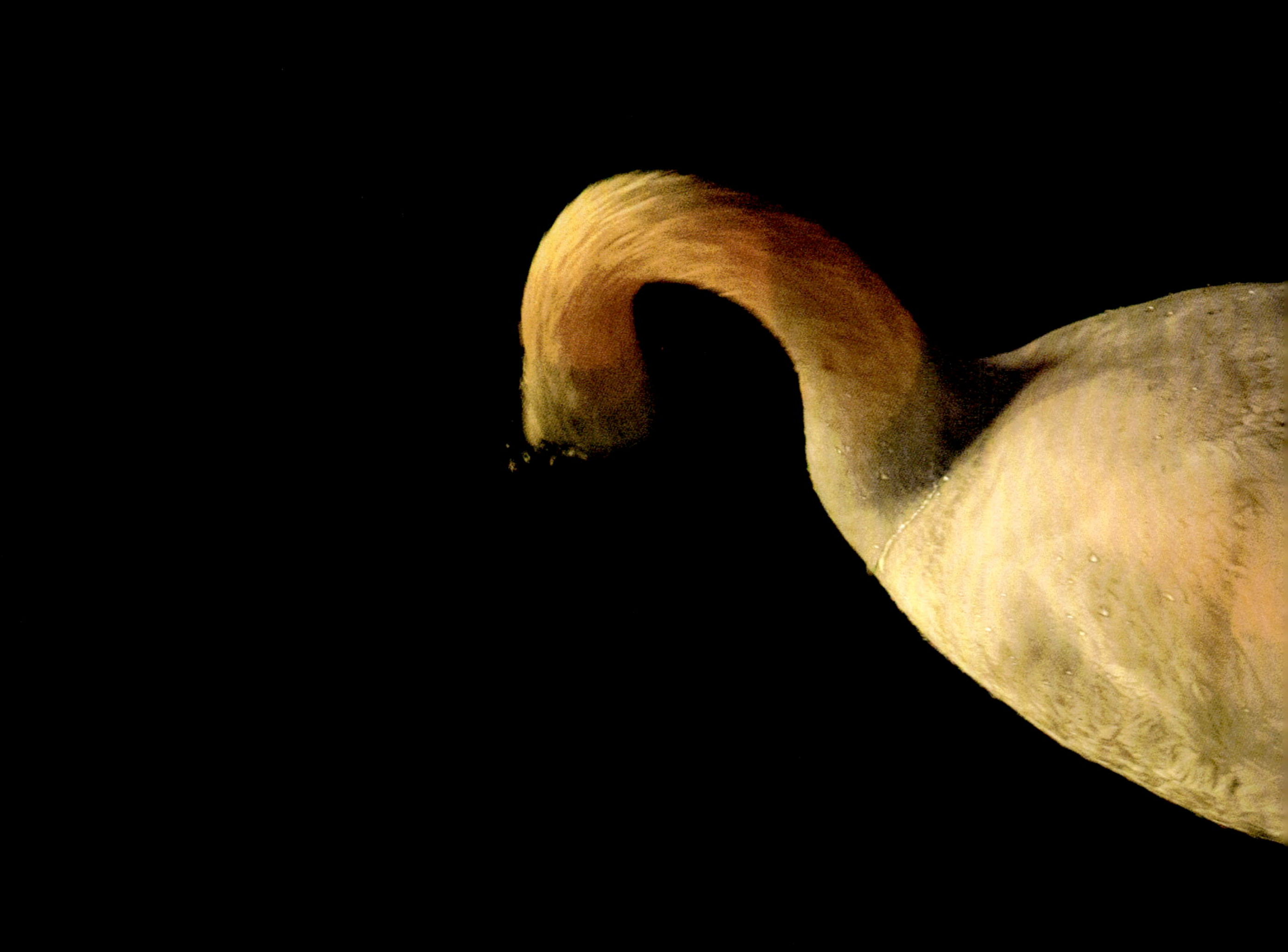

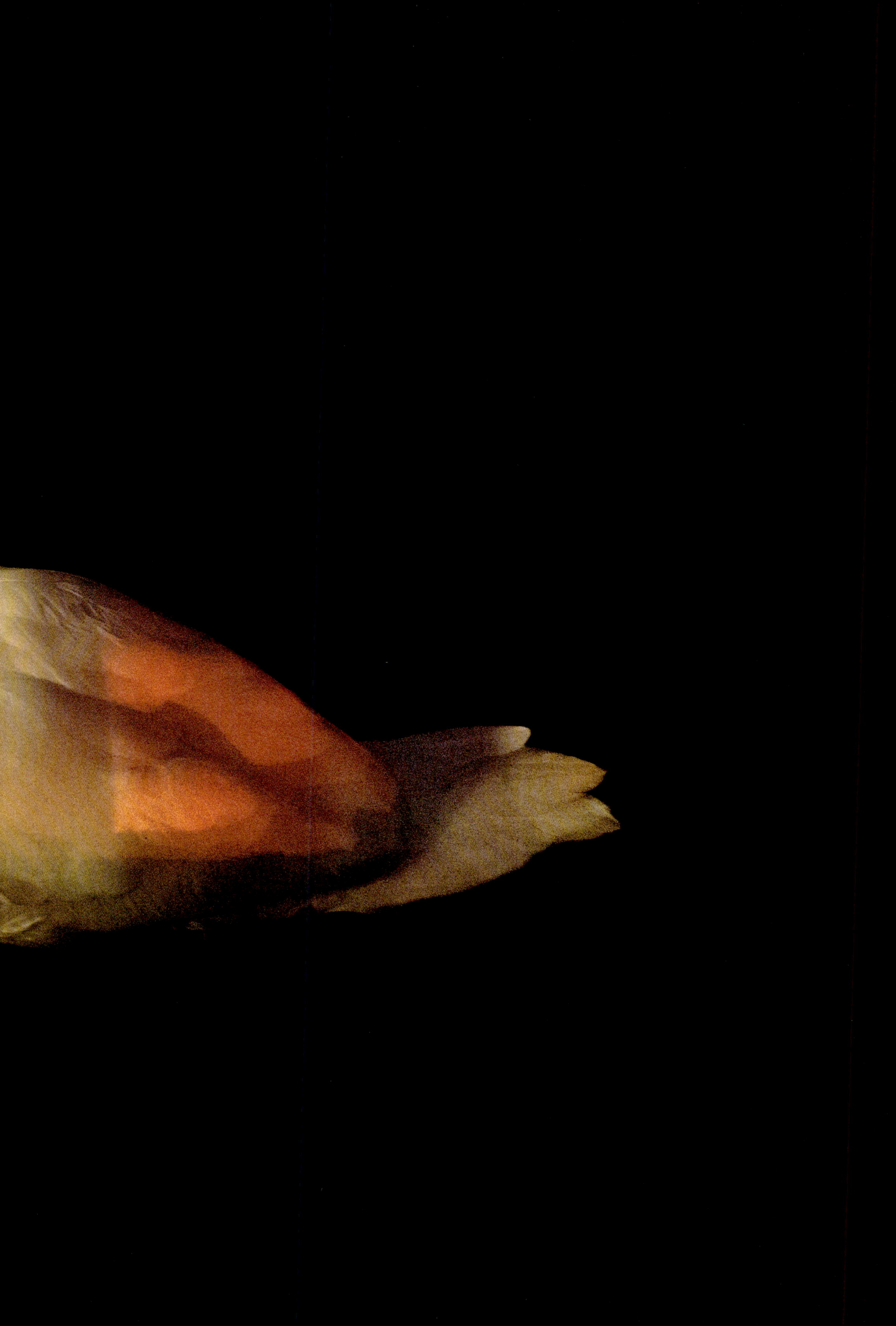

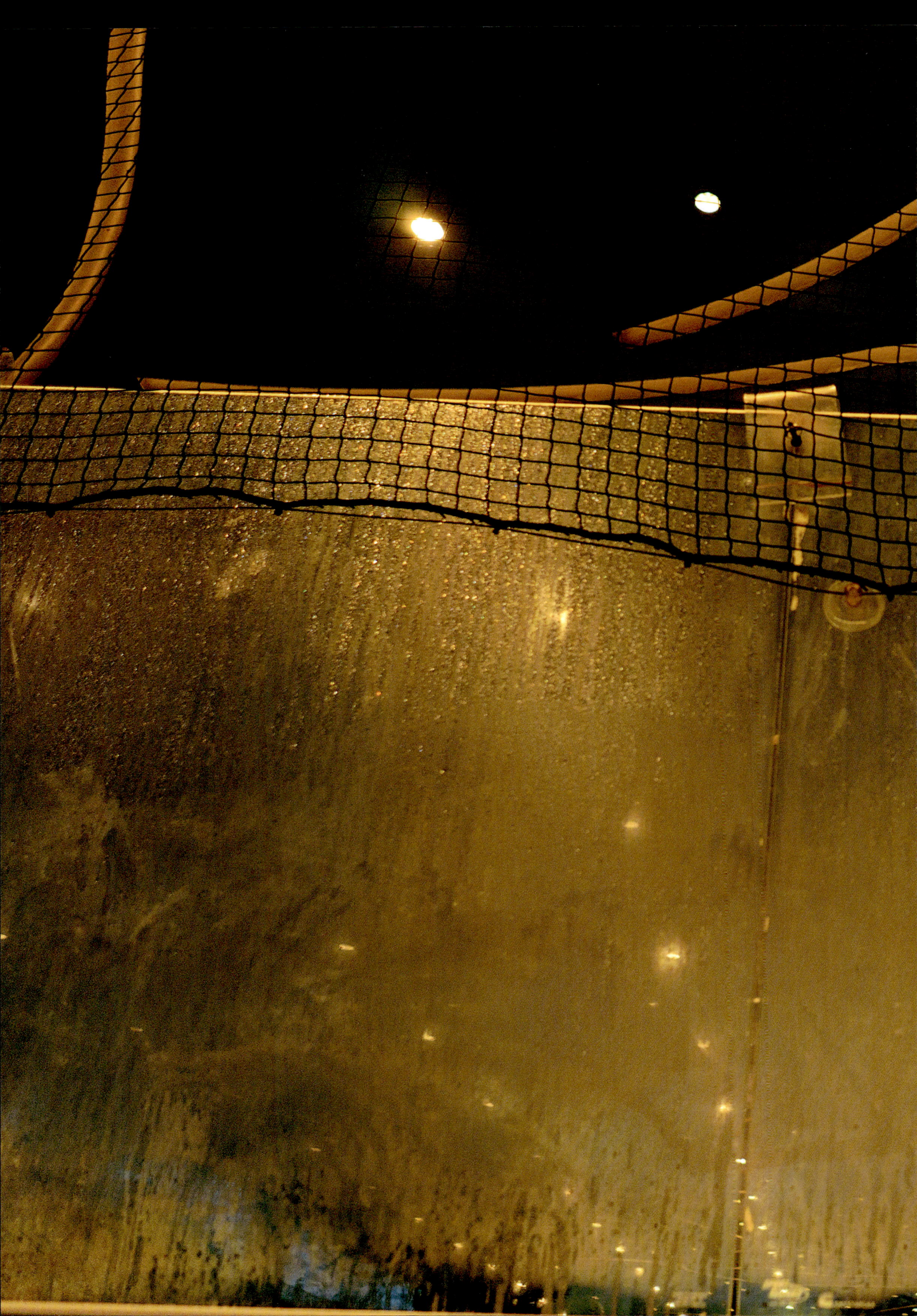

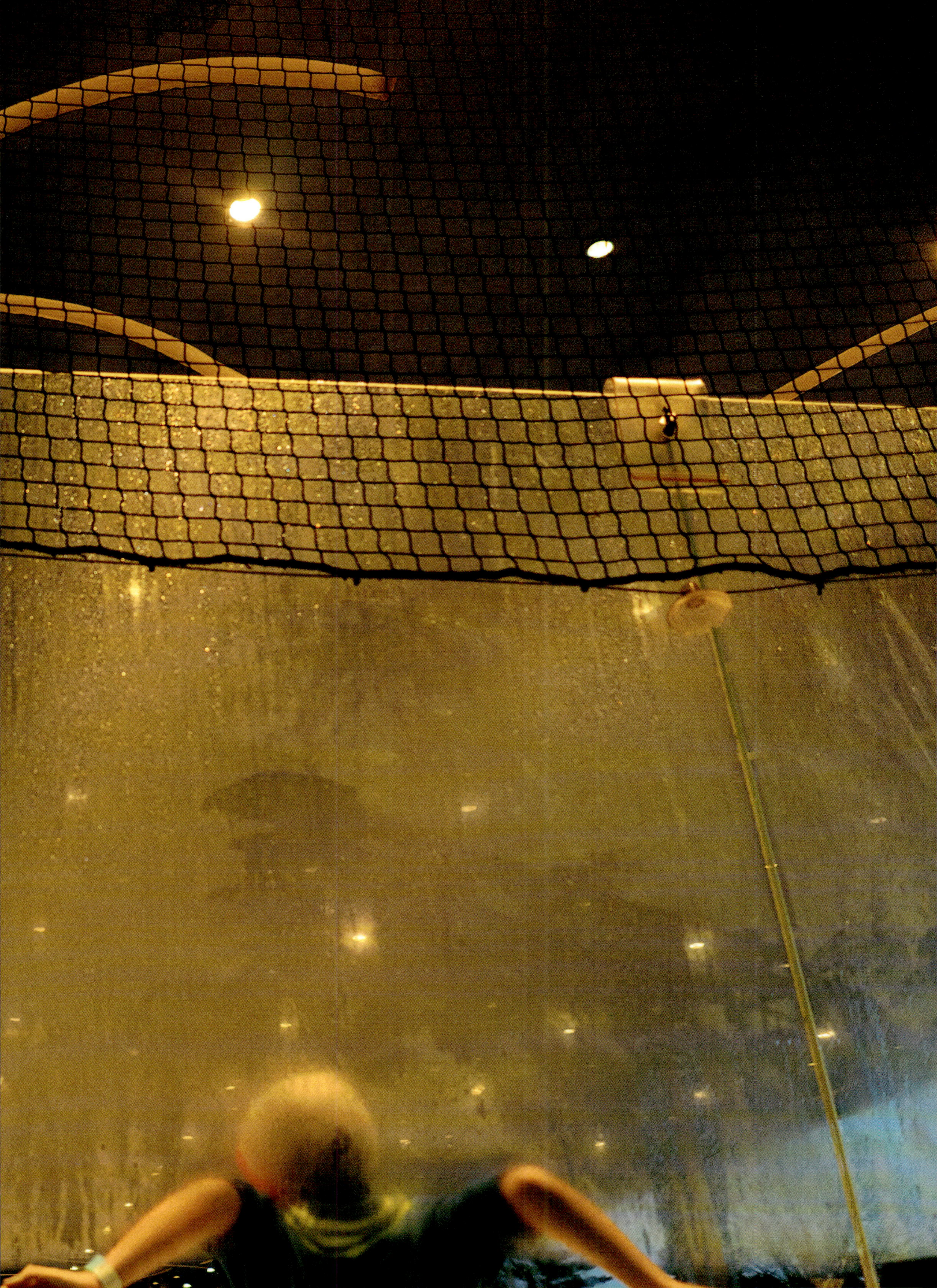

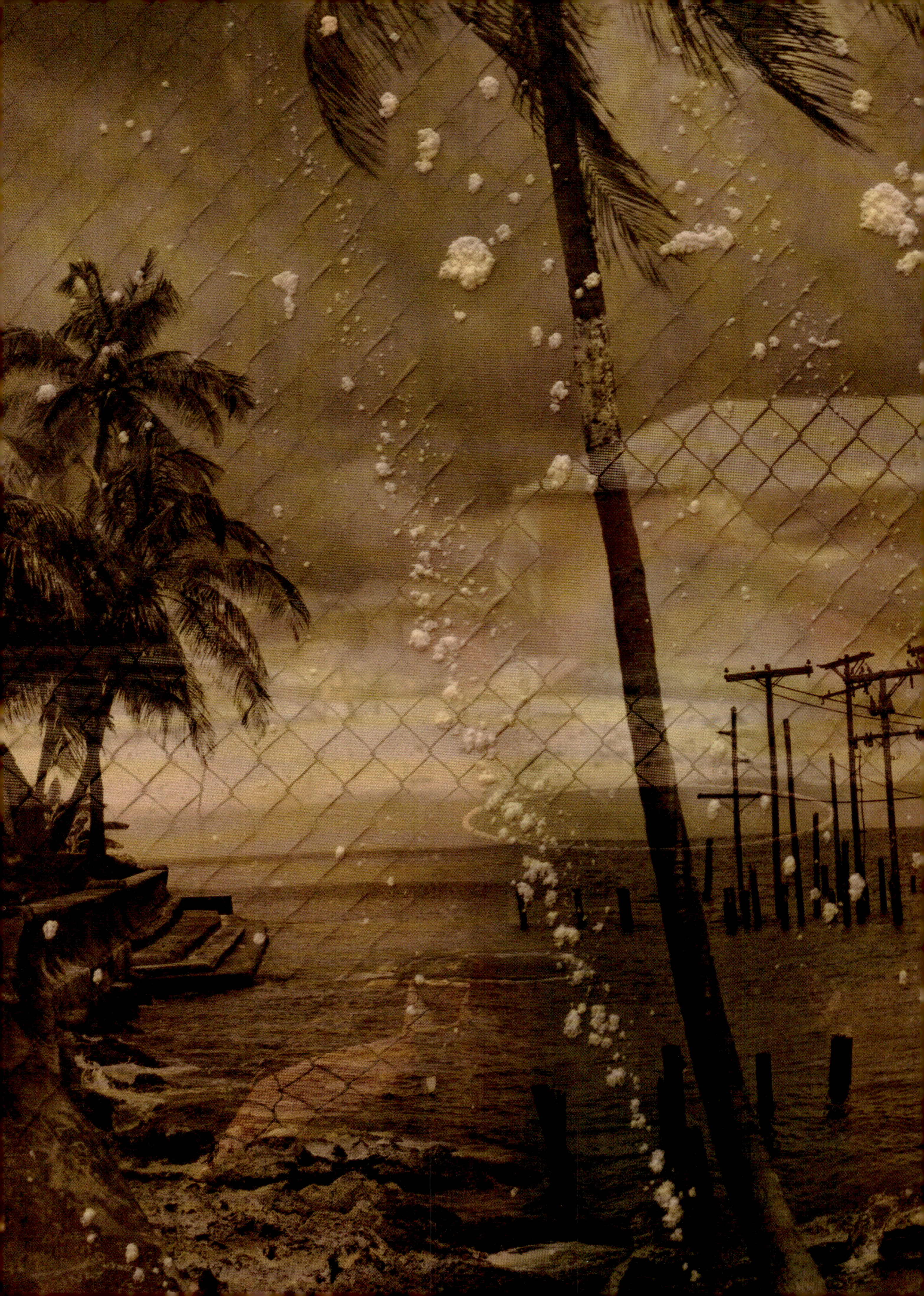

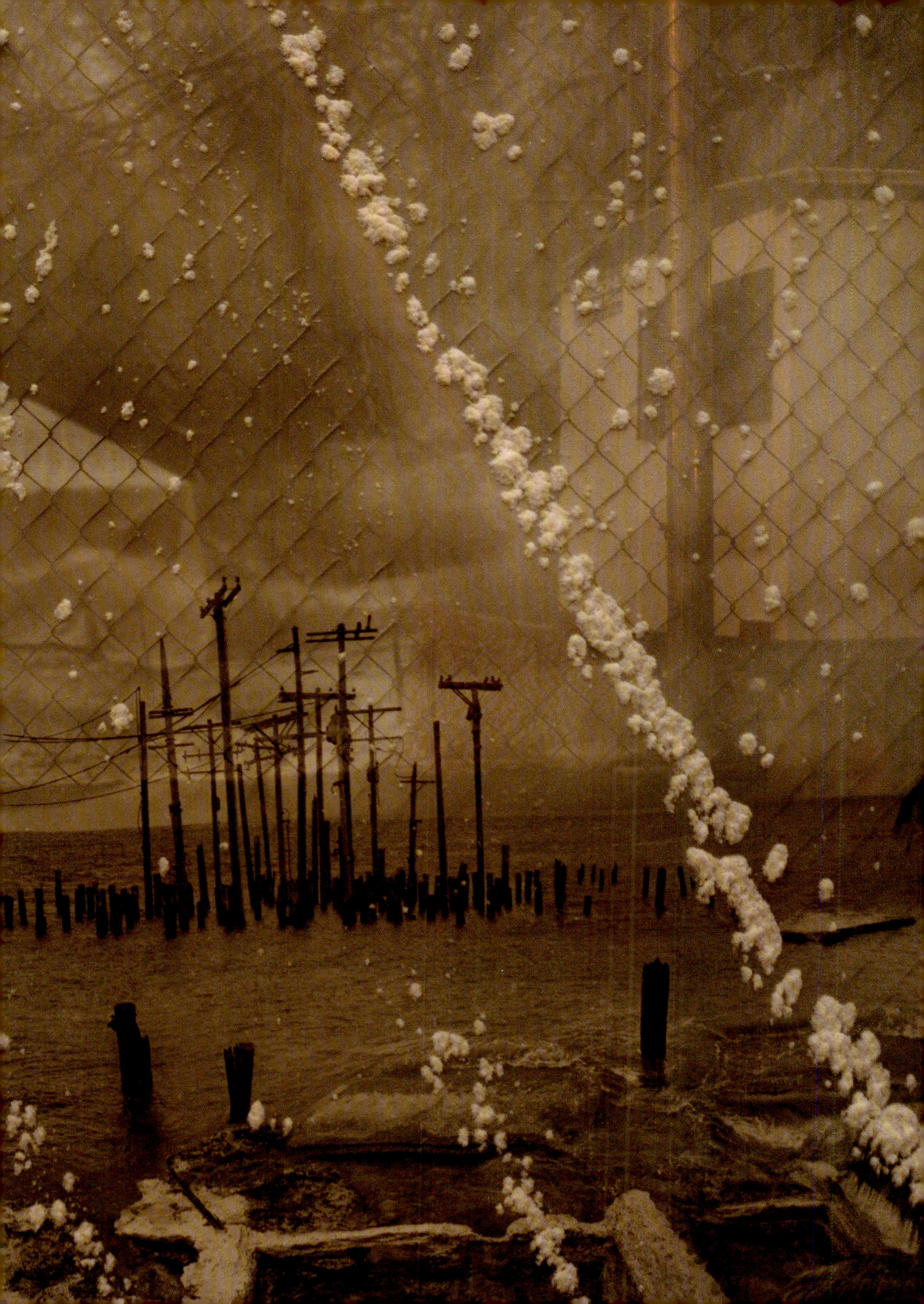

WINTER STORM

In this eerie yellow light, it seems the snow will never end. Hard to focus when the fingers are so cold. I keep thinking about those Canada geese—hundreds of wings folding under the unbearable weight of snow. How lightly they float, now, across Prospect Lake, like some half-remembered longing. How do any of us, for that matter, find our way? One January traveling alone across the South Dakota prairie, I remember waking—half dreaming at three a.m.—and opening my motel room door to a blizzard of geese, blown off course by an unexpected snow. Head bowed against this icy wind, I wonder how many of us now—this moment in Brooklyn— find ourselves inhabiting two worlds at once?

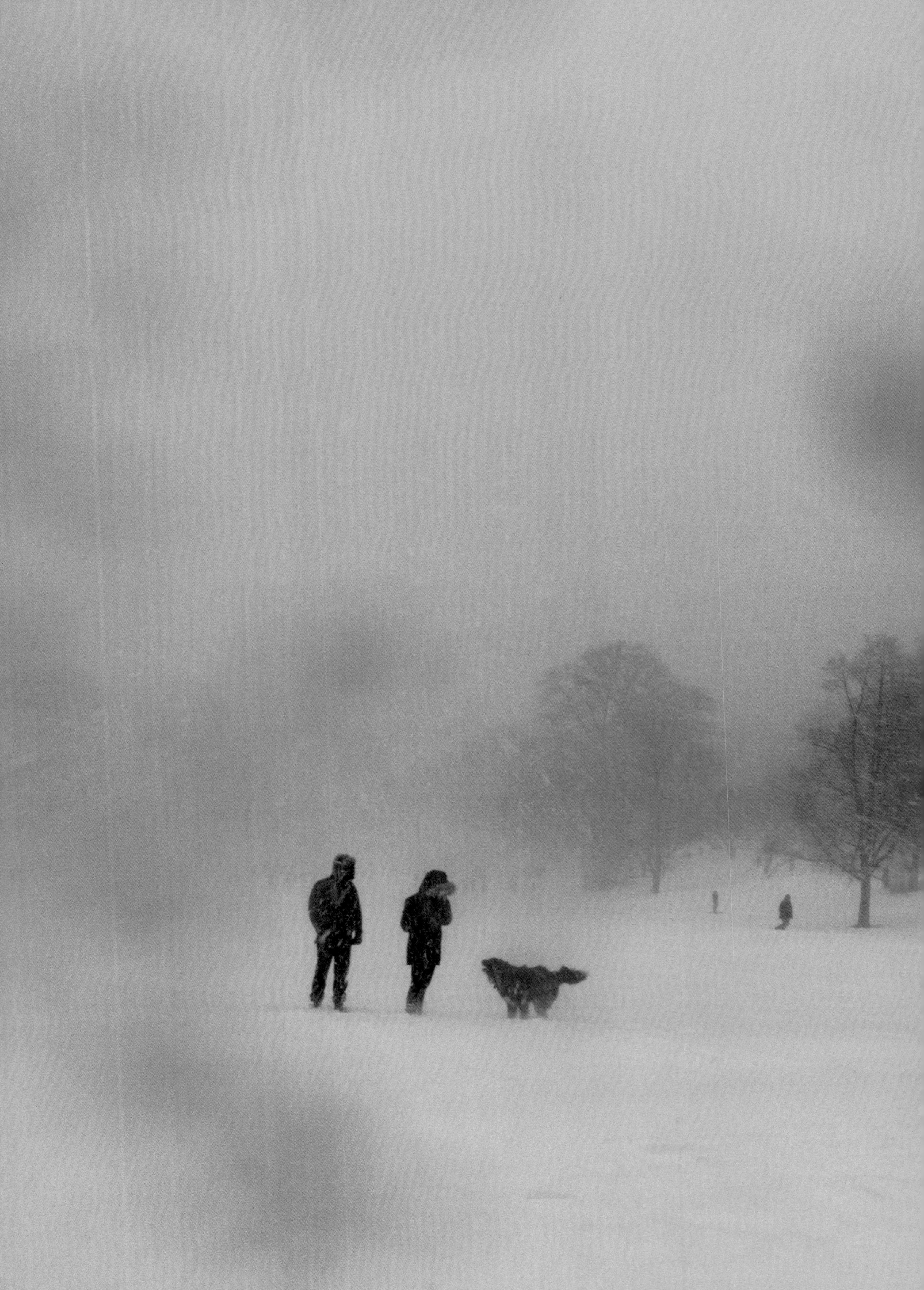

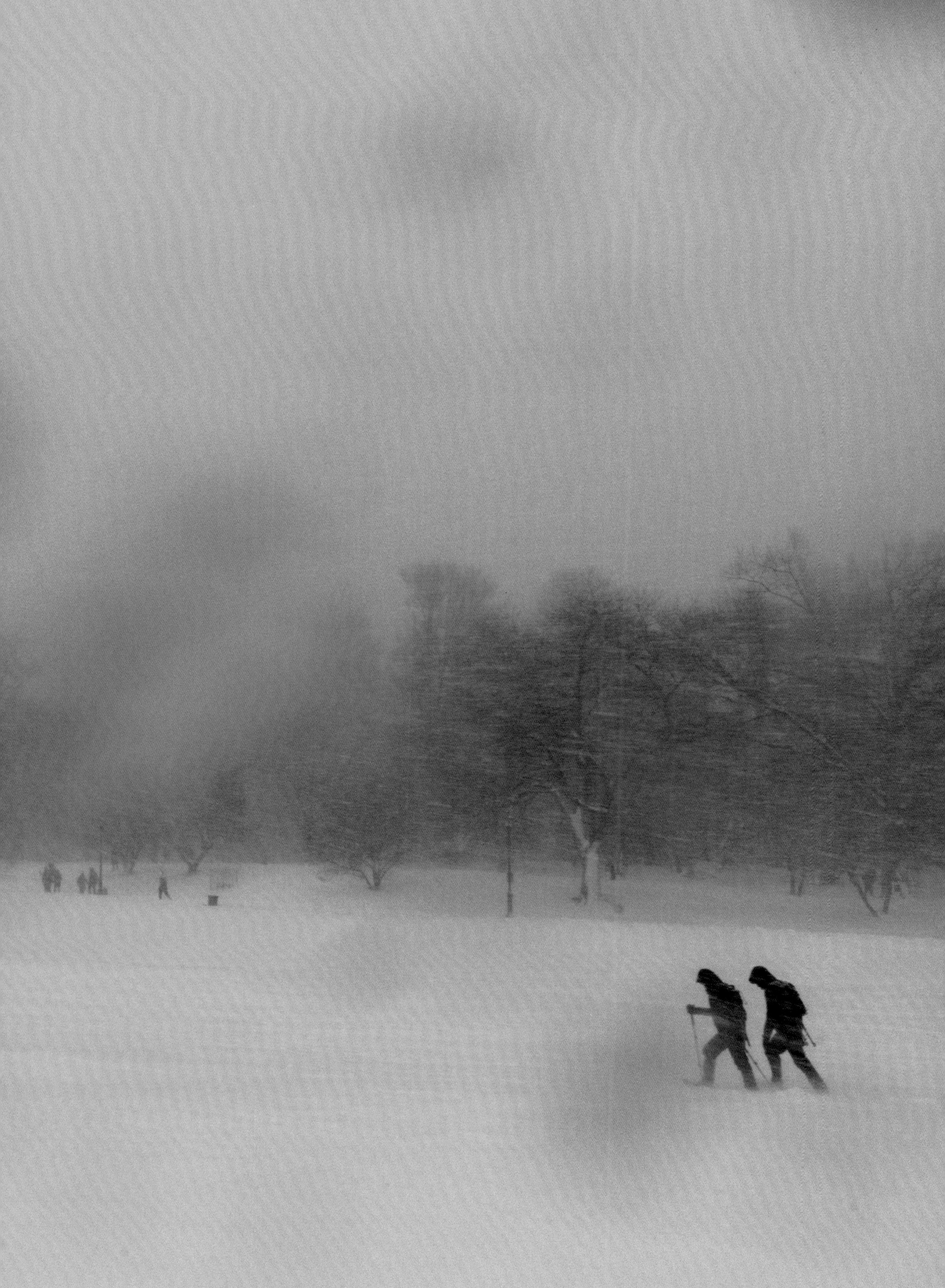

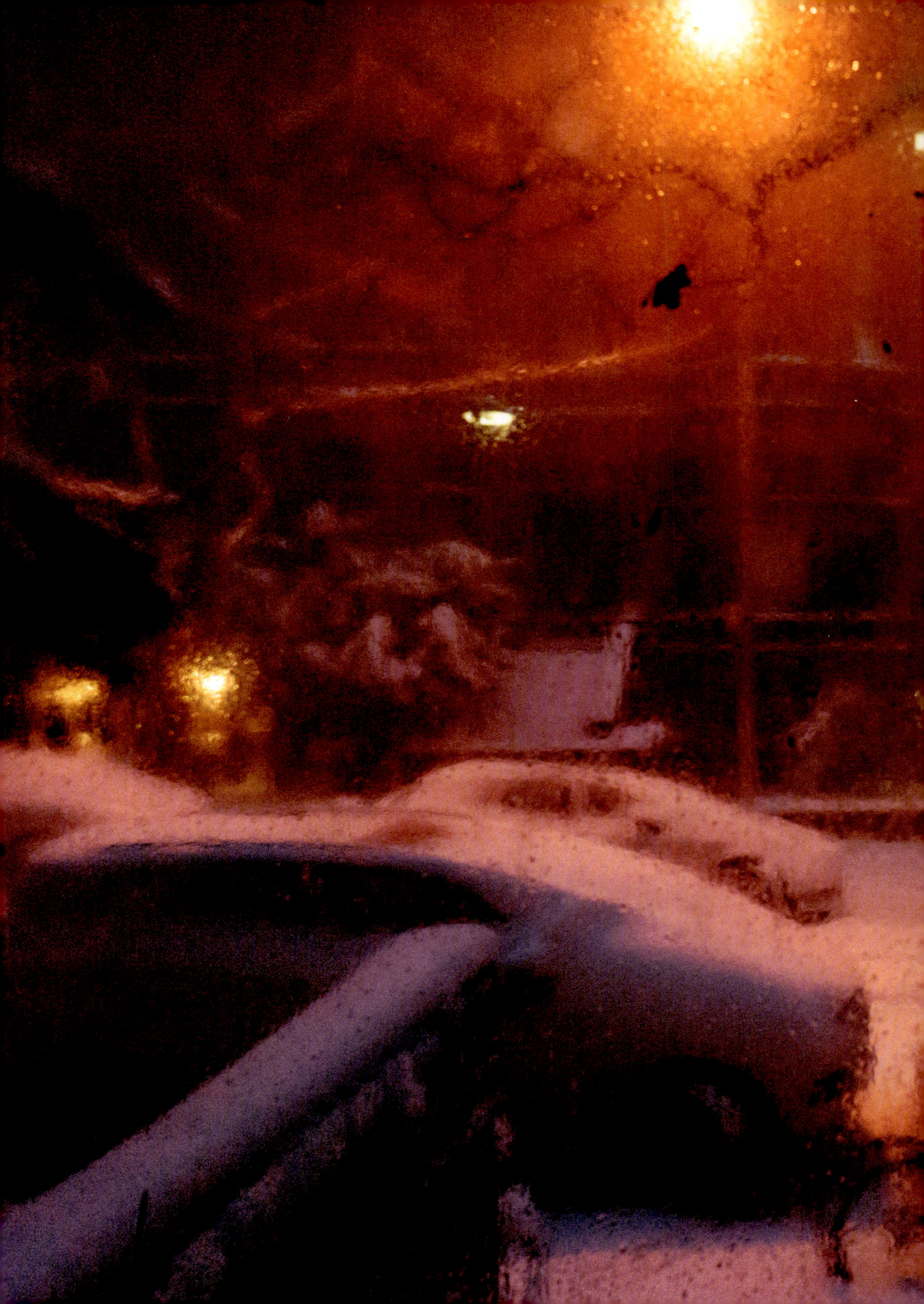

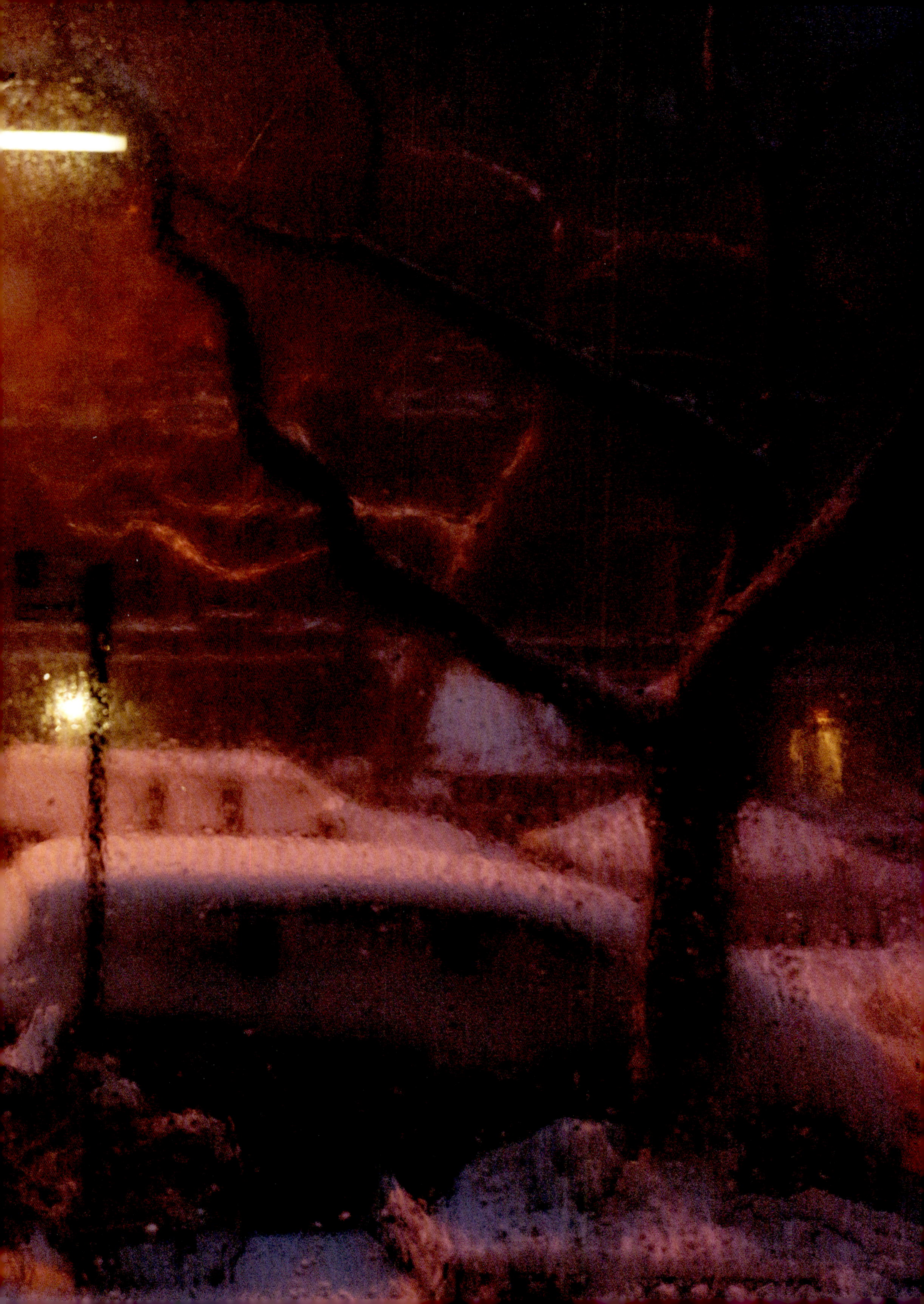

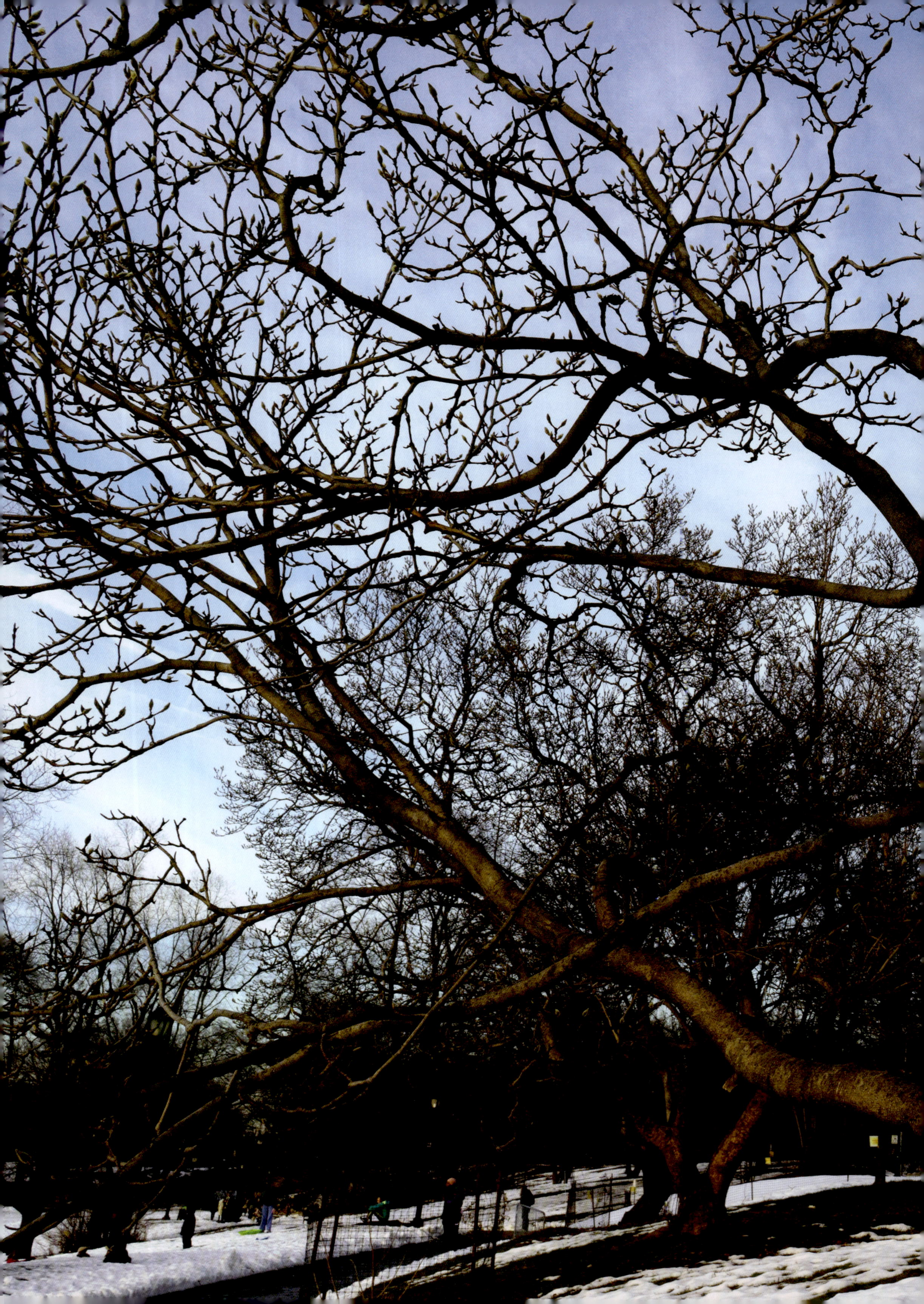

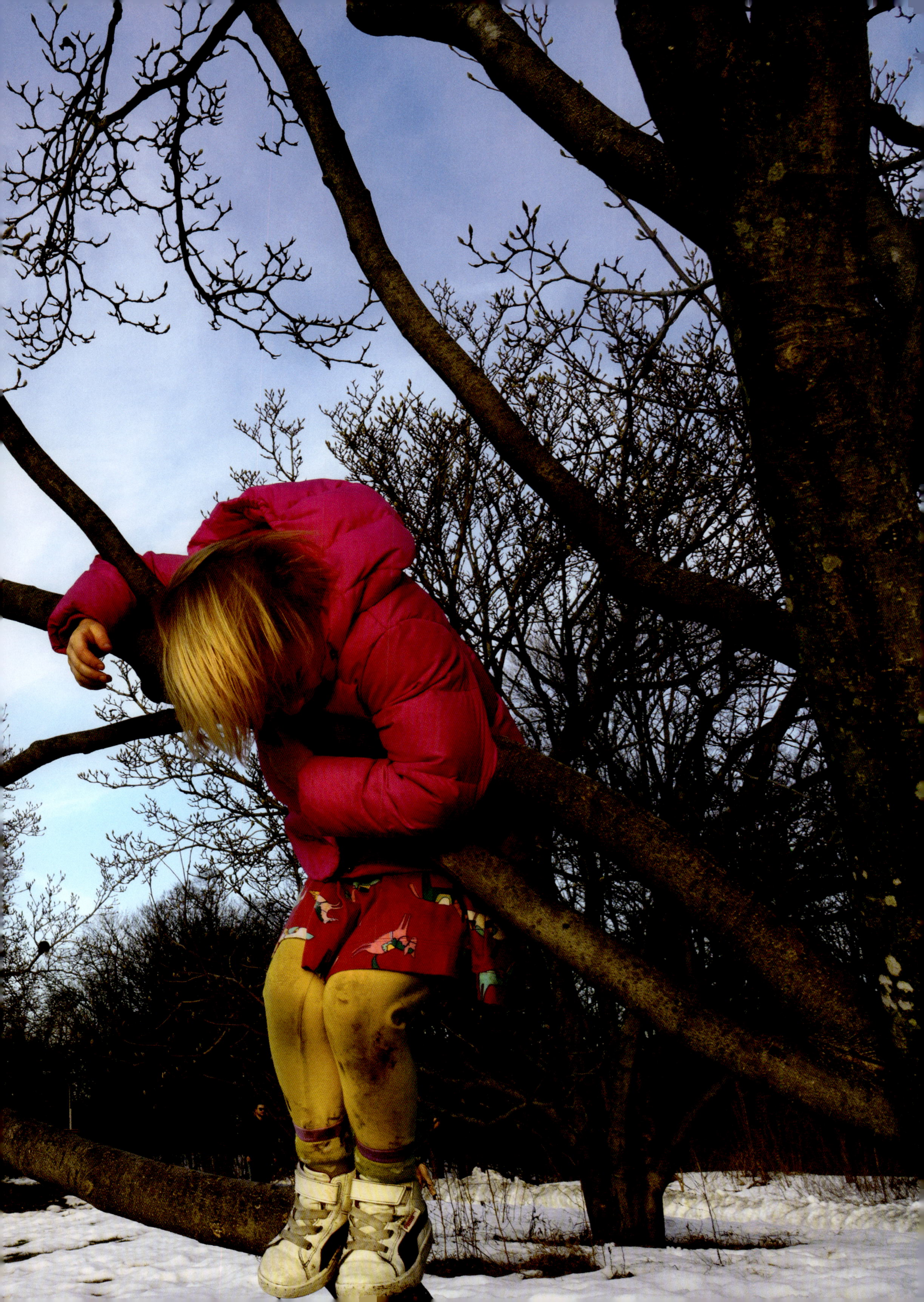

One by one, the streetlights come on again, ringing Long Meadow like a broken halo. It's the hour when green leaves fade to gray, when *we are no longer quite ourselves*. We haunt the evening hour with all those others who prefer reverie to safety—or who, perhaps, simply lost track of time. (For what does the attentive eye care of time, after all?) Marianne Moore heading to the Camperdown elm that she saved with a poem. Helen Levitt meandering home to Bensonhurst. We wander past the brides and the suicides. Past the wild geese taken in the night. Past the fear we women feel, walking so late in the park. I work in the dark, until the shining eyes of a raccoon rhyme with the glowing of the streetlights in the distance. For a moment, why not linger in all this shimmering?

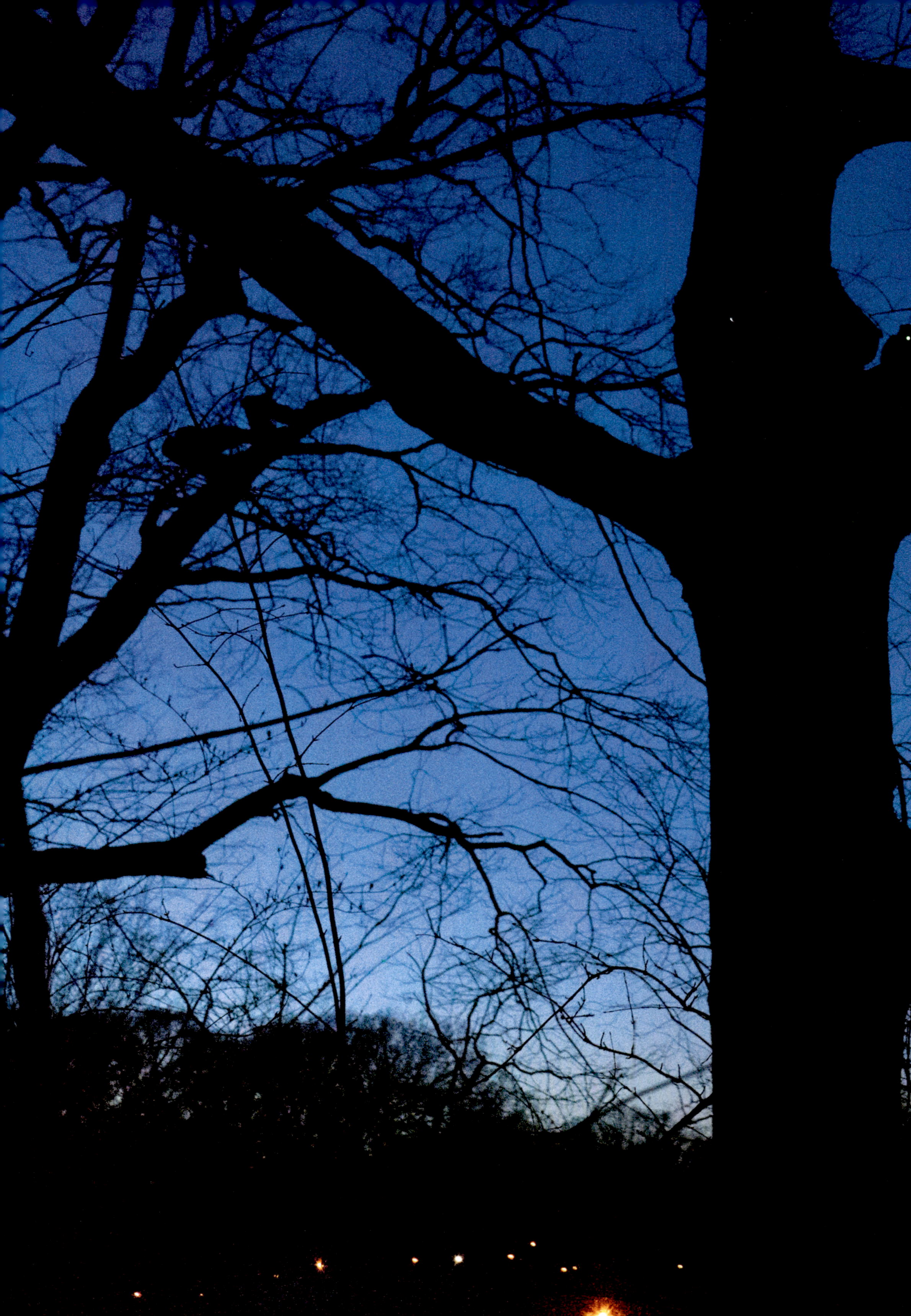

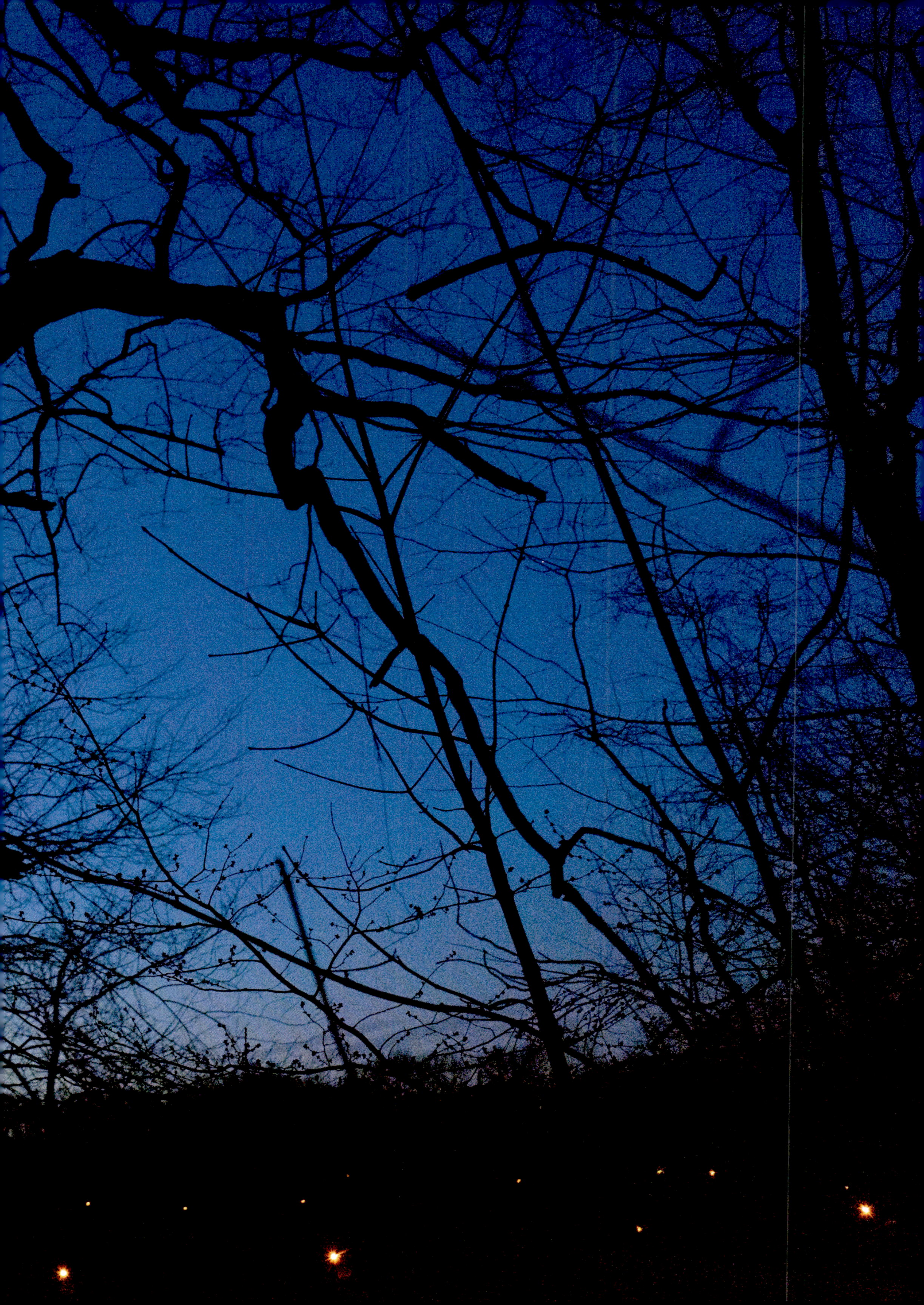

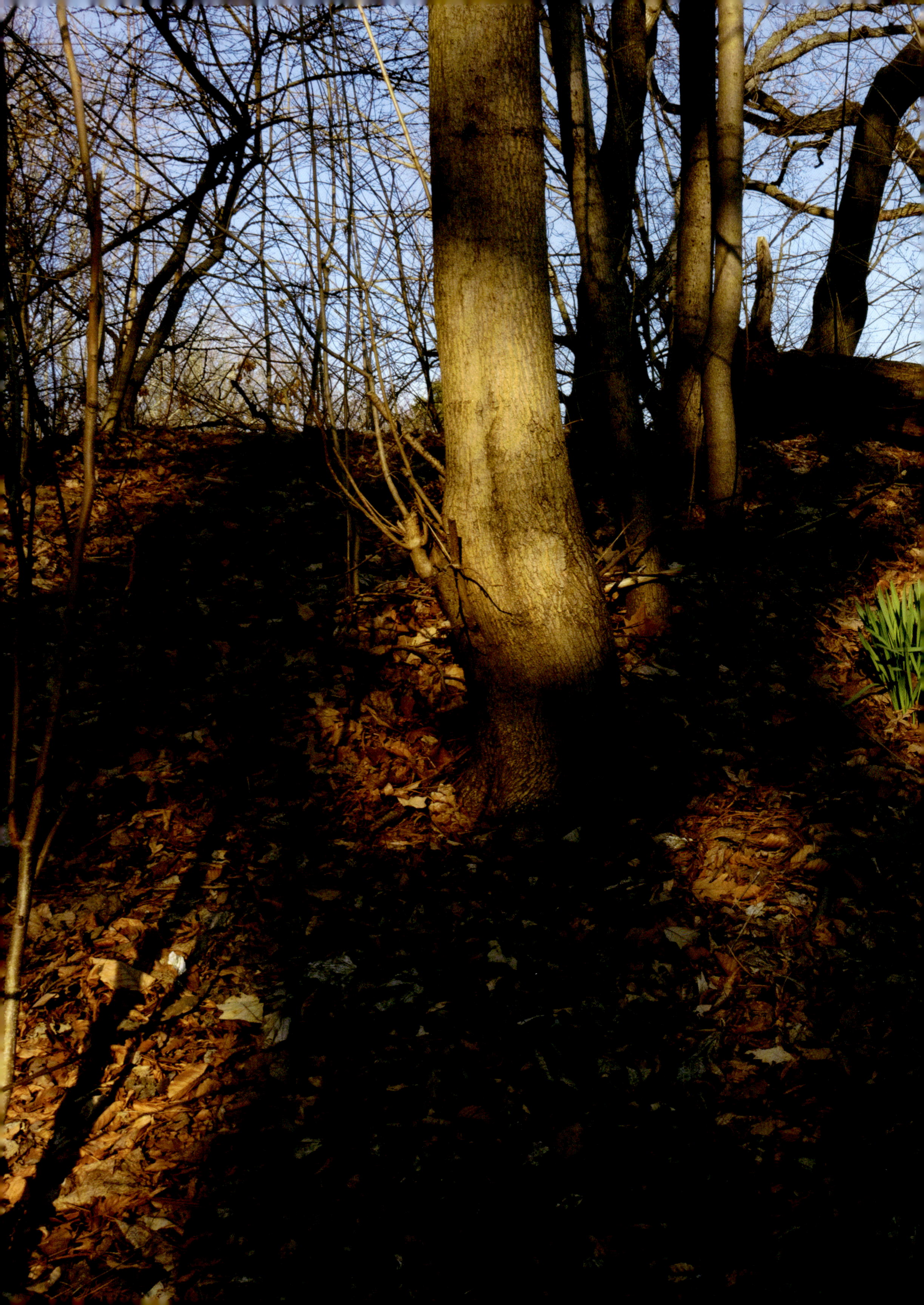

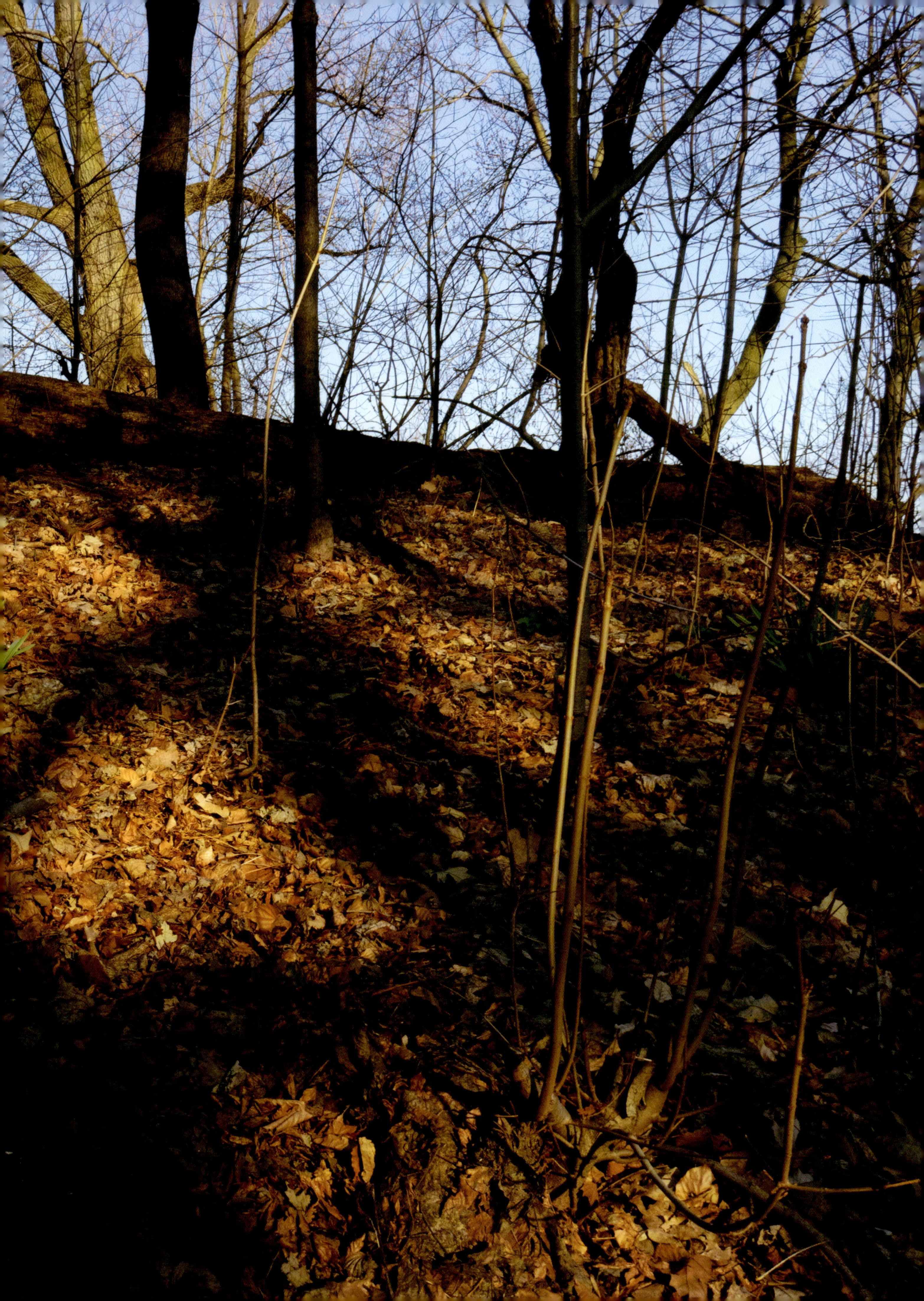

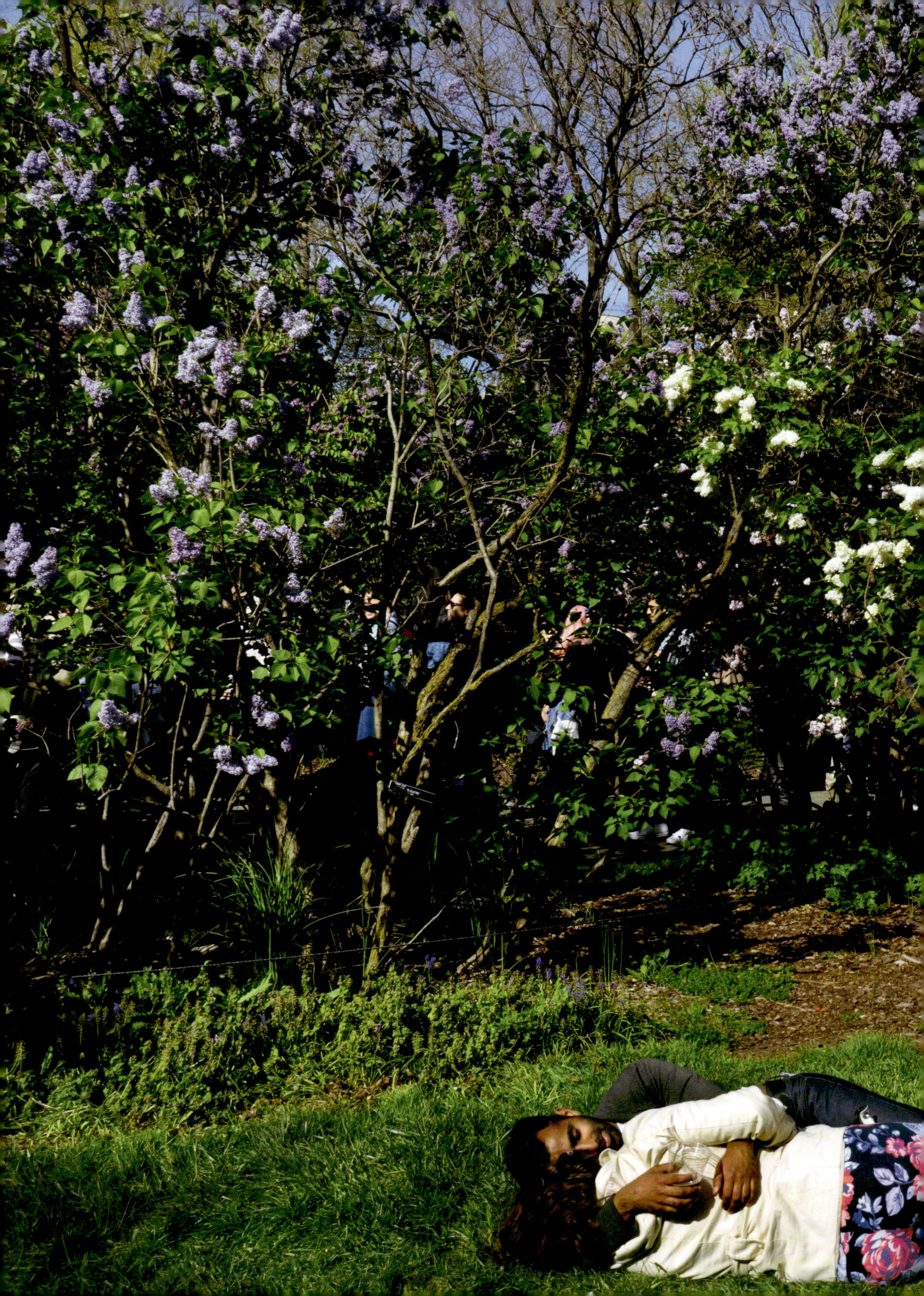

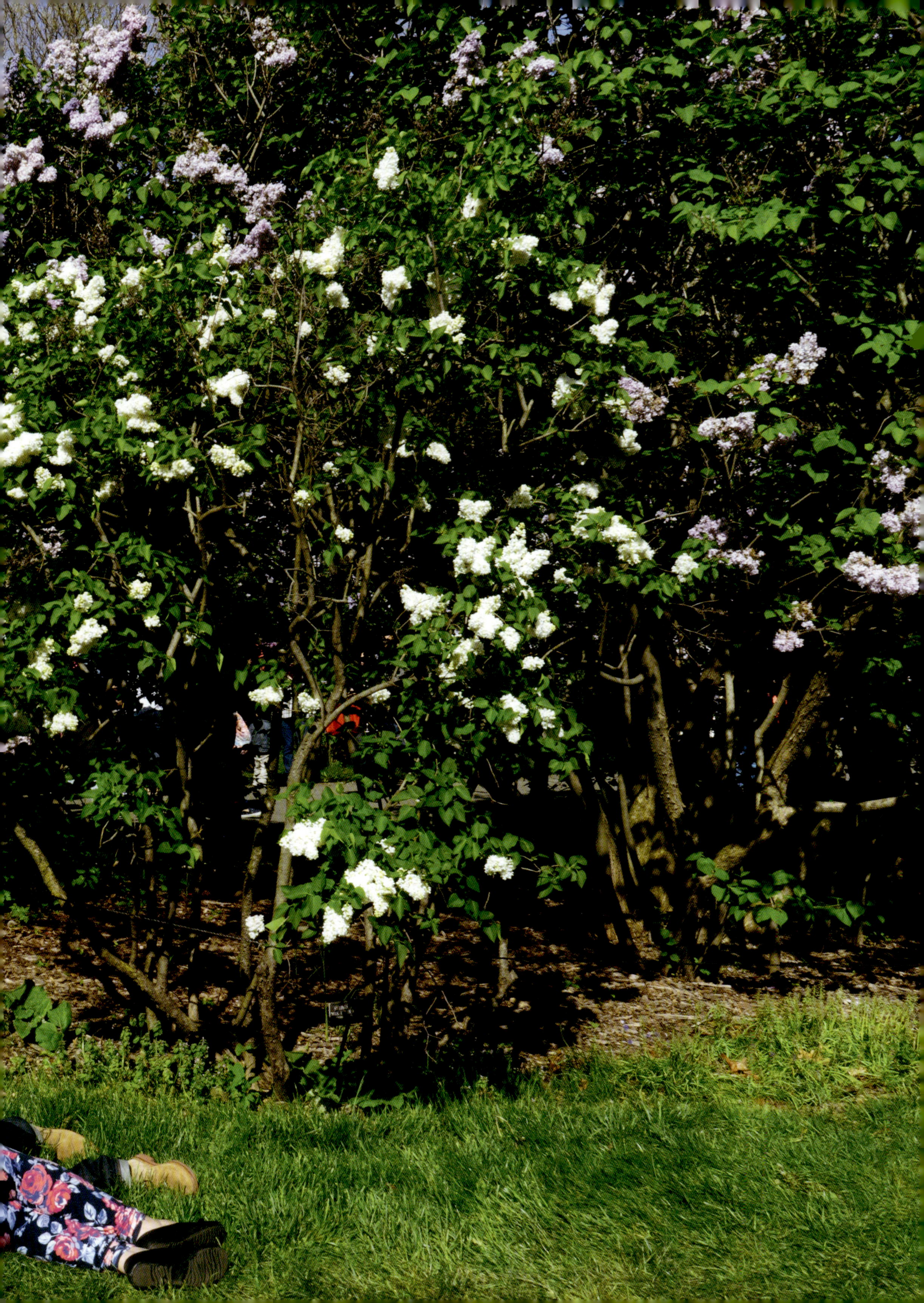

BROOKLYN BOTANIC GARDEN

Our ordeal is over for now.

We were uprooted
because of something falling, something rising,
because of rumors of paradise,
because of violence,
because of dumb luck, right breeze.

And here, now, somewhere
deep in our core, we are still
there, tethered to all those others,
left behind or lost
because of happenstance, wrong turn.

New World, you say? Second chance?
I say: I have been inside the greenest green—
teeming with transplants
from around the world—
and it is, truly, our garden.

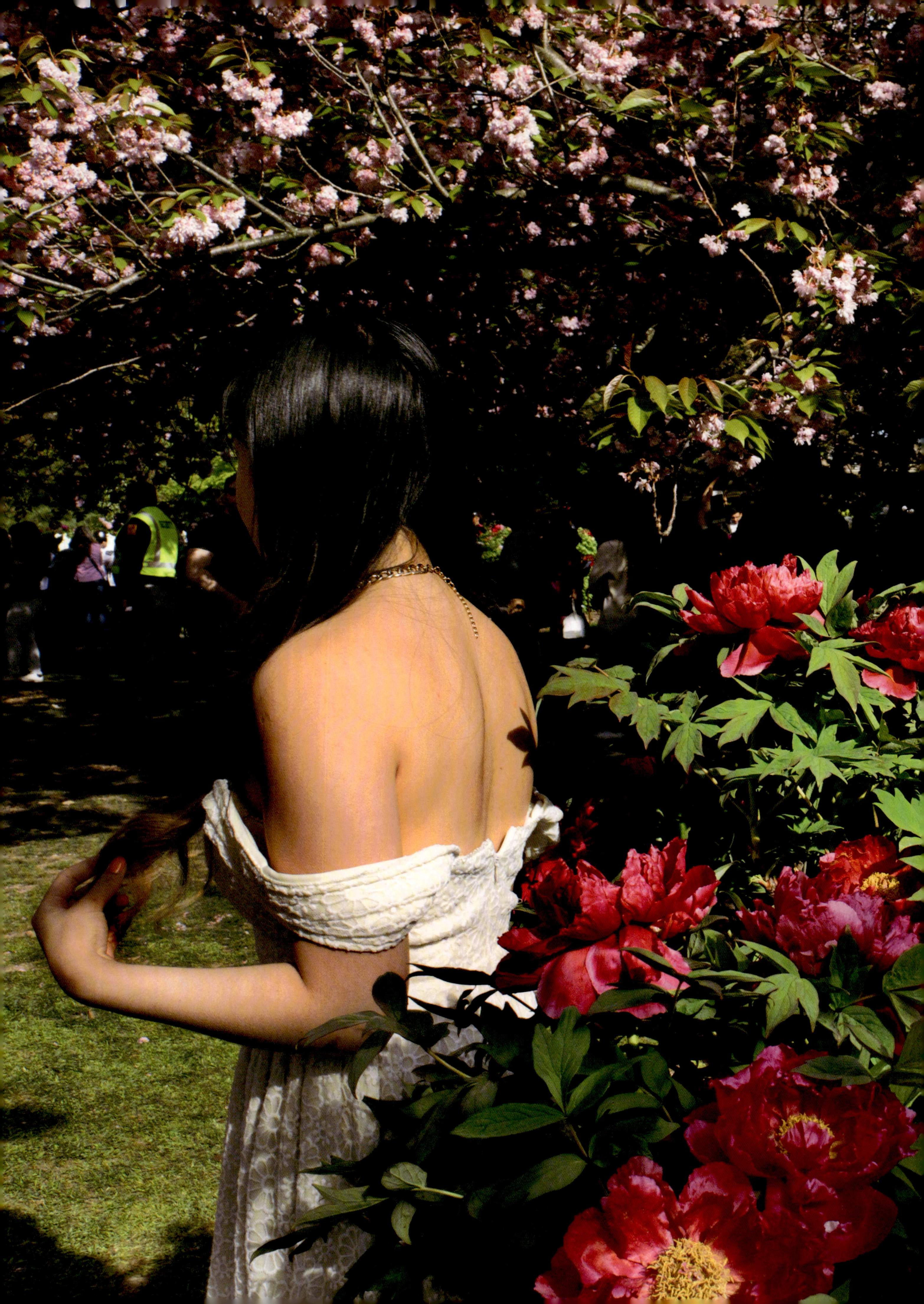

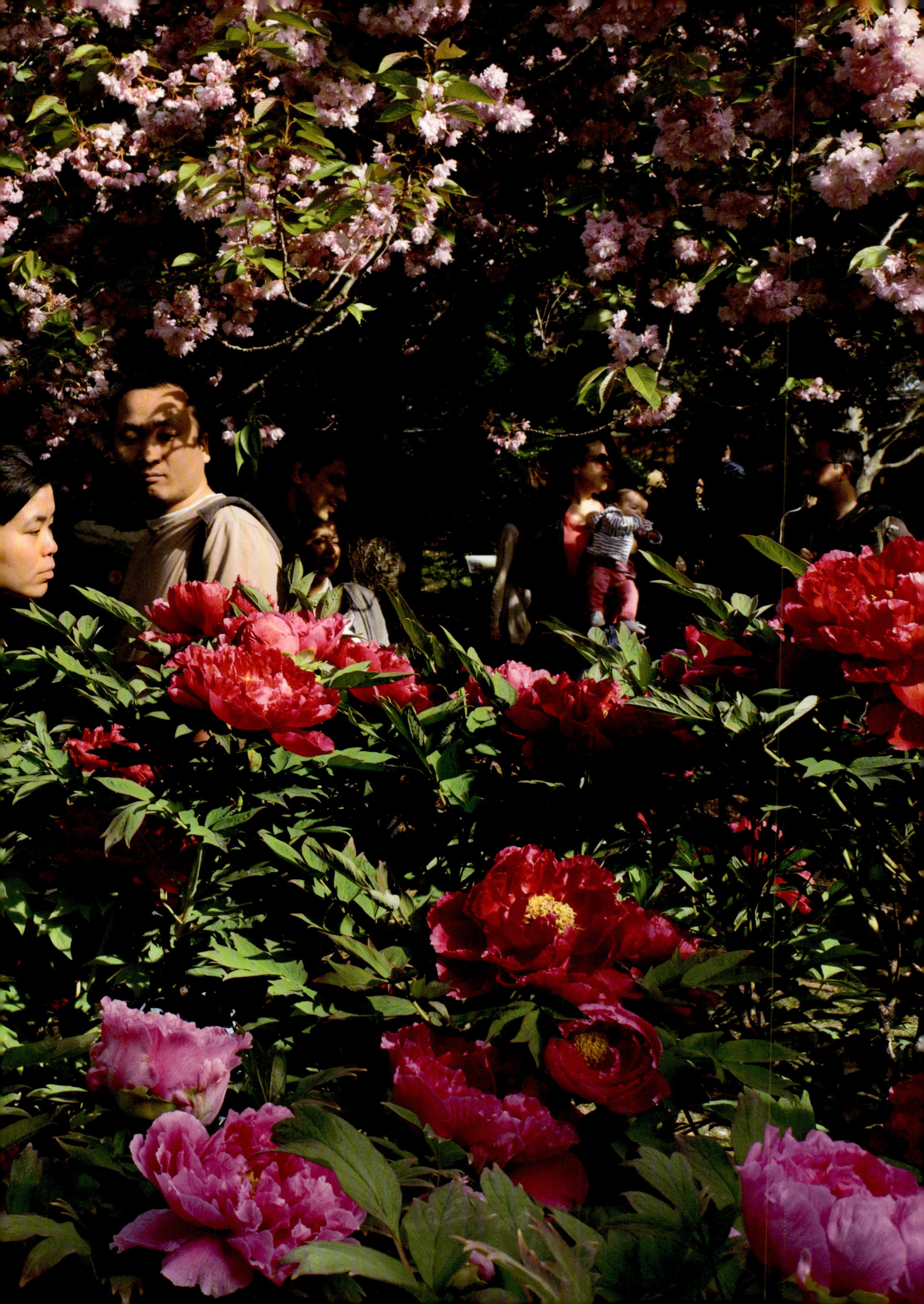

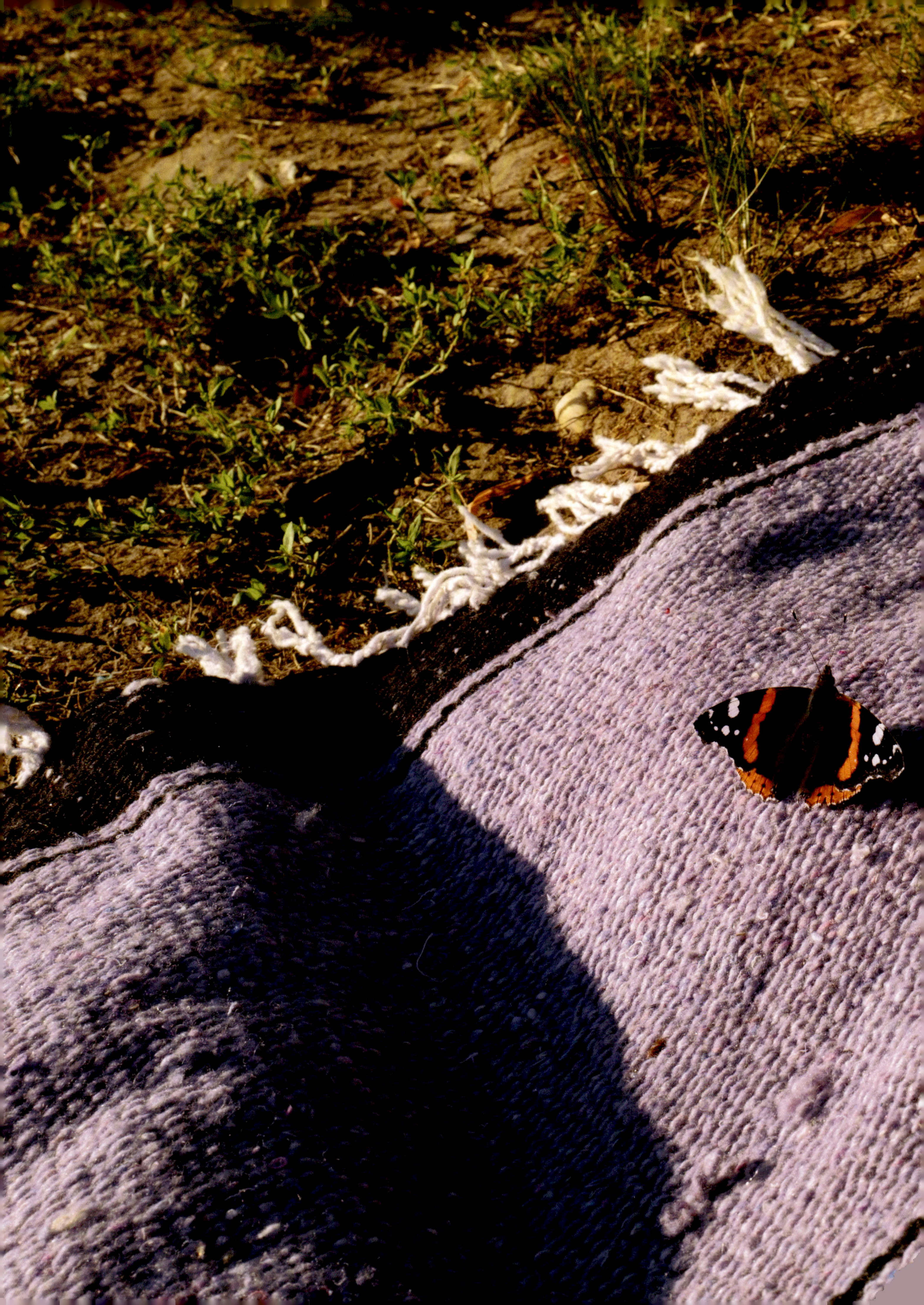

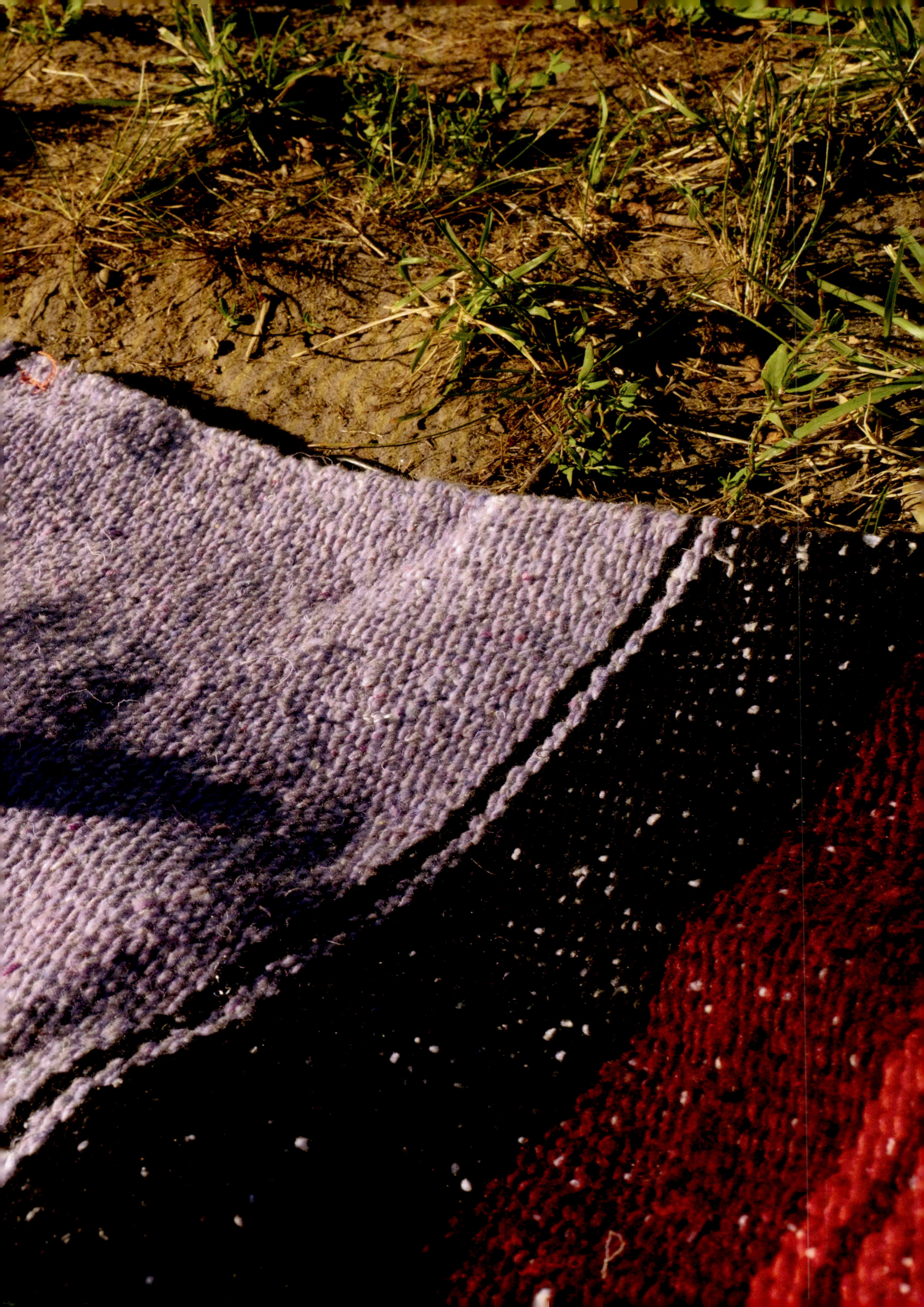

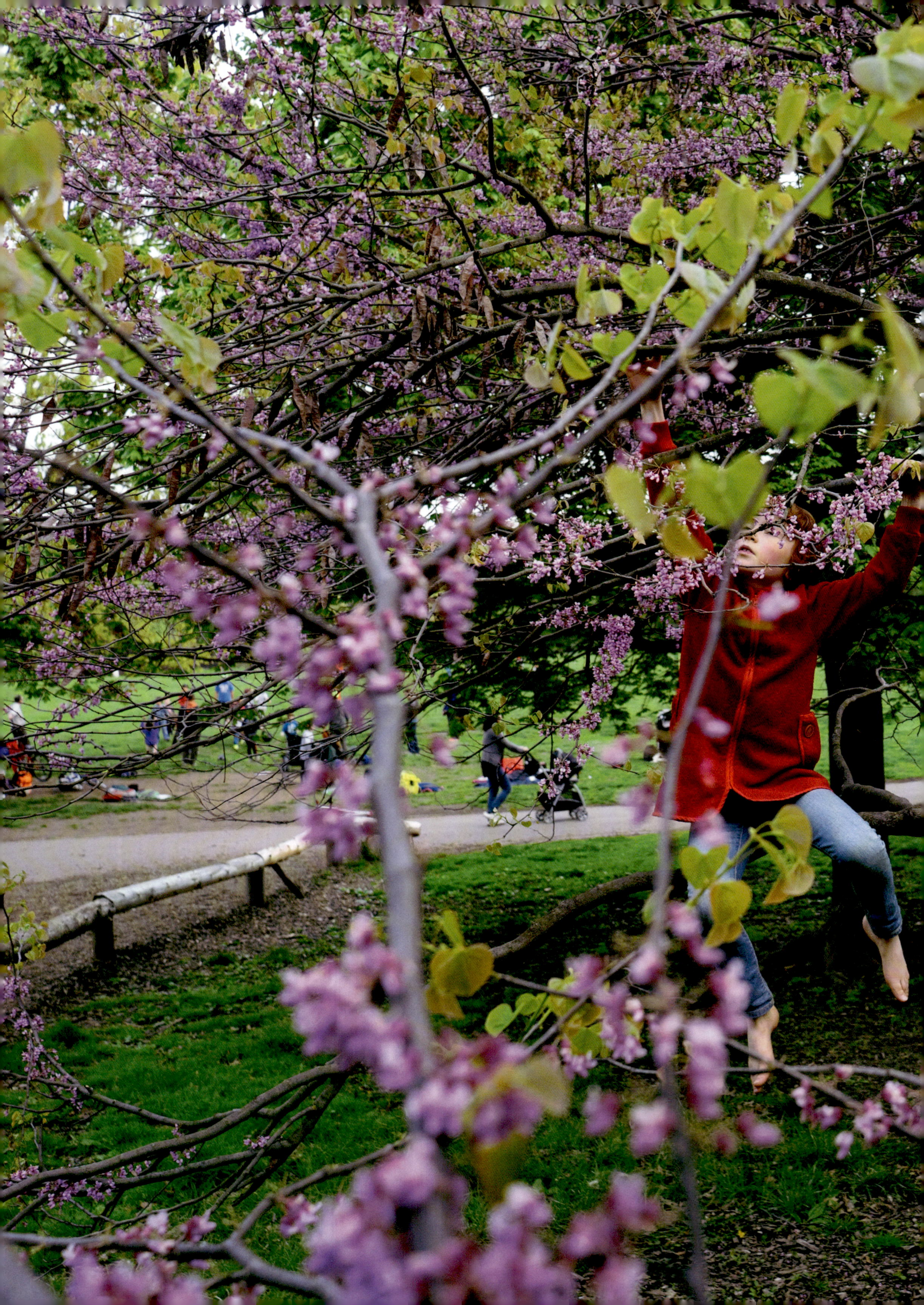

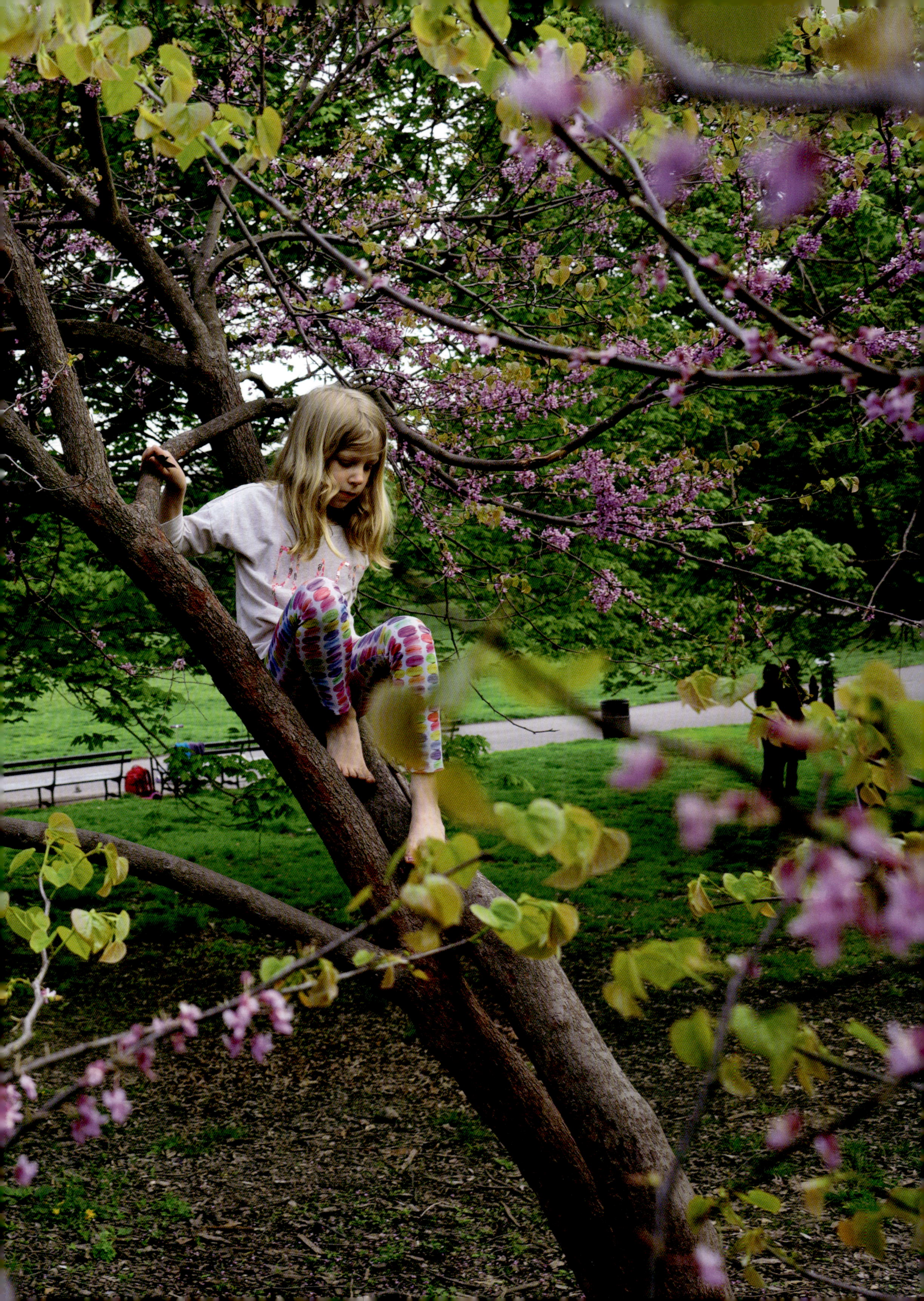

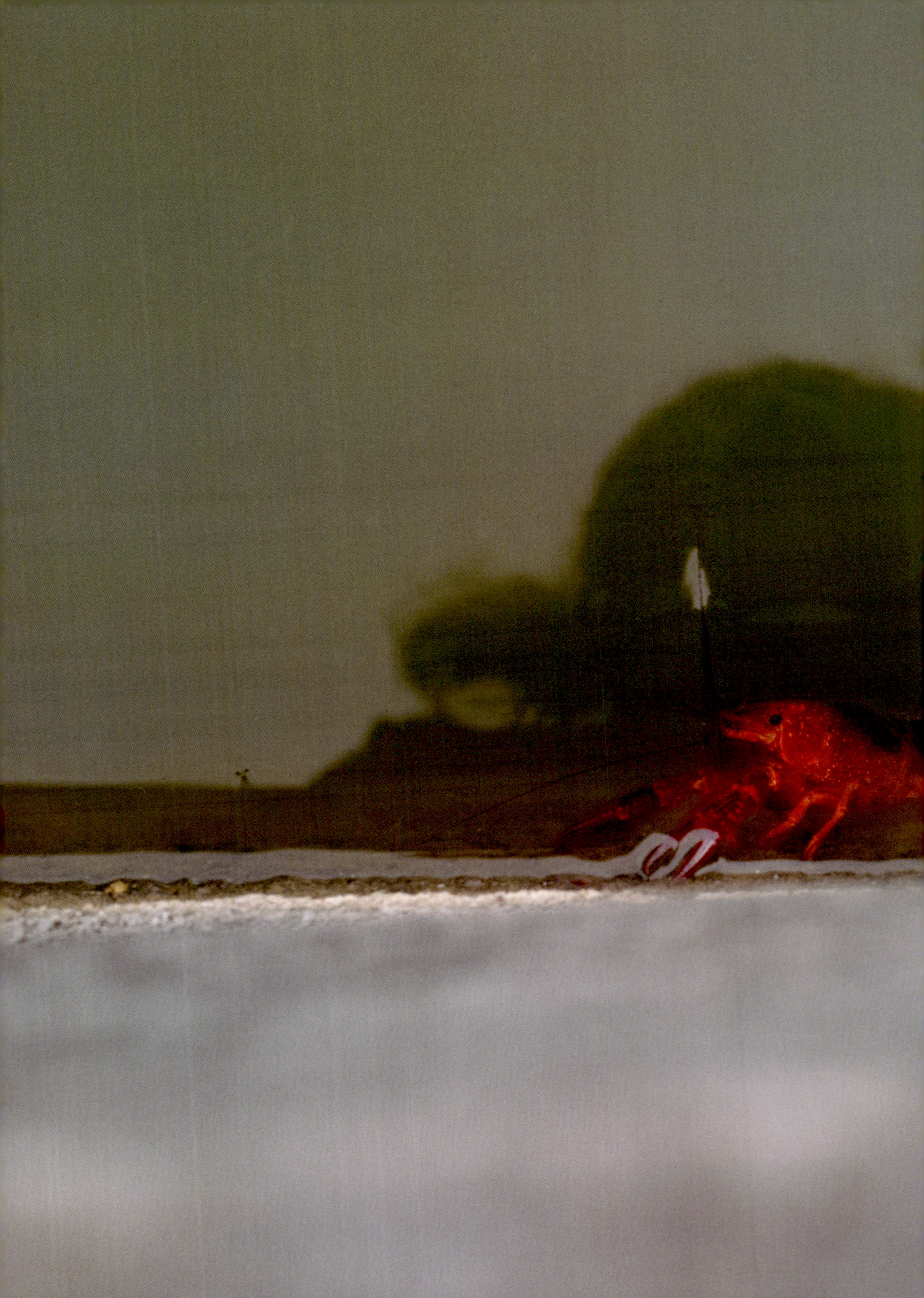

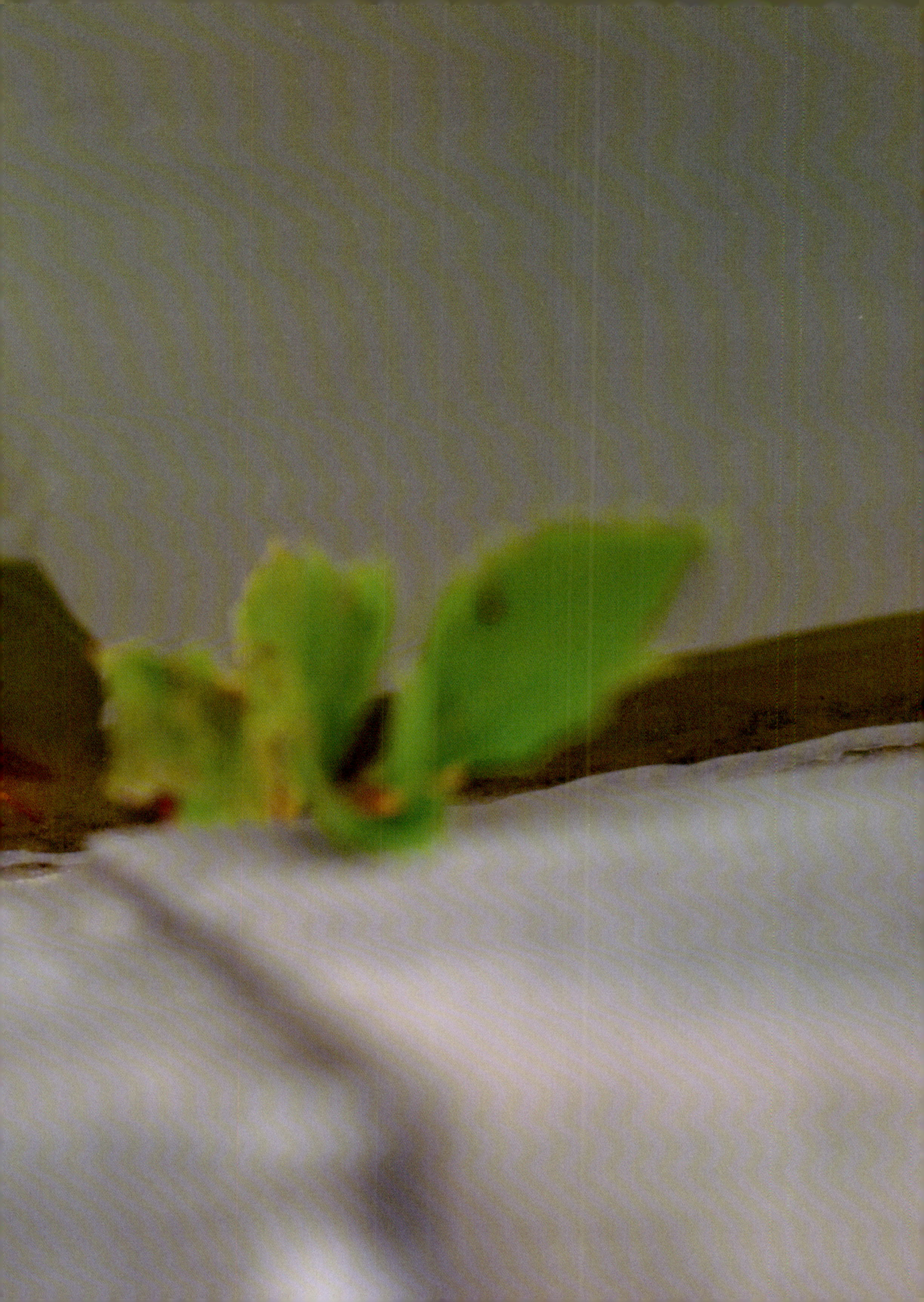

IN THE RAIN

Why do I feel most myself in the rain? As Prospect Park empties out, is it the
scent of solitude? Or the way the brim of a hat makes one invisible? And why,
at the zoo, are there more peacocks than usual? Can the rain multiply anything
that's blue? Or is the equation far simpler? In a downpour, do we see as the rain
sees, the world at a slant? On that slippery slope, do we slide into fluidity? Do we
seep into Long Meadow, where sheep used to graze? Do we turn into water
catching light in another's eye? Or do we float free, biding our sweet time,
before we rise?

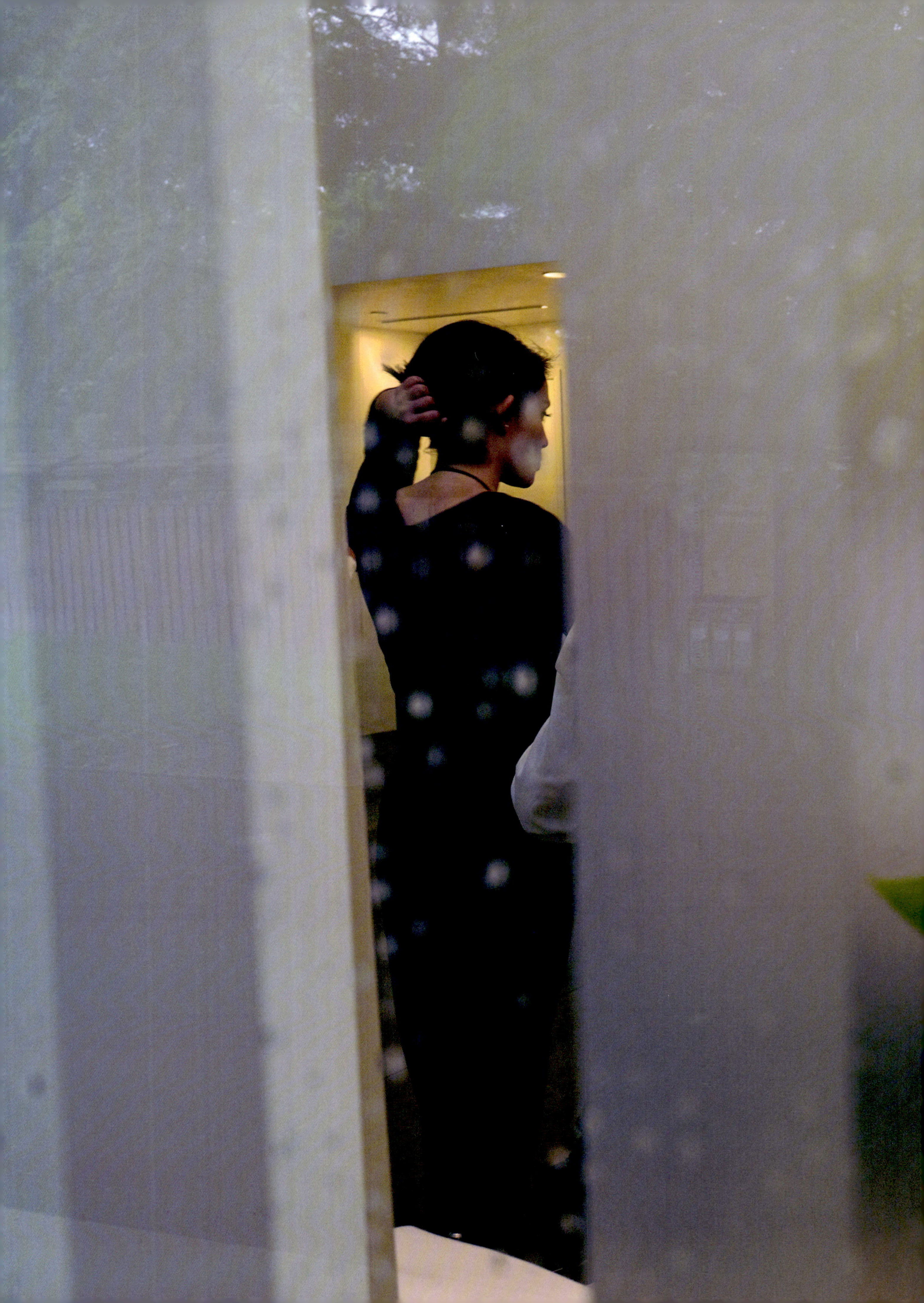

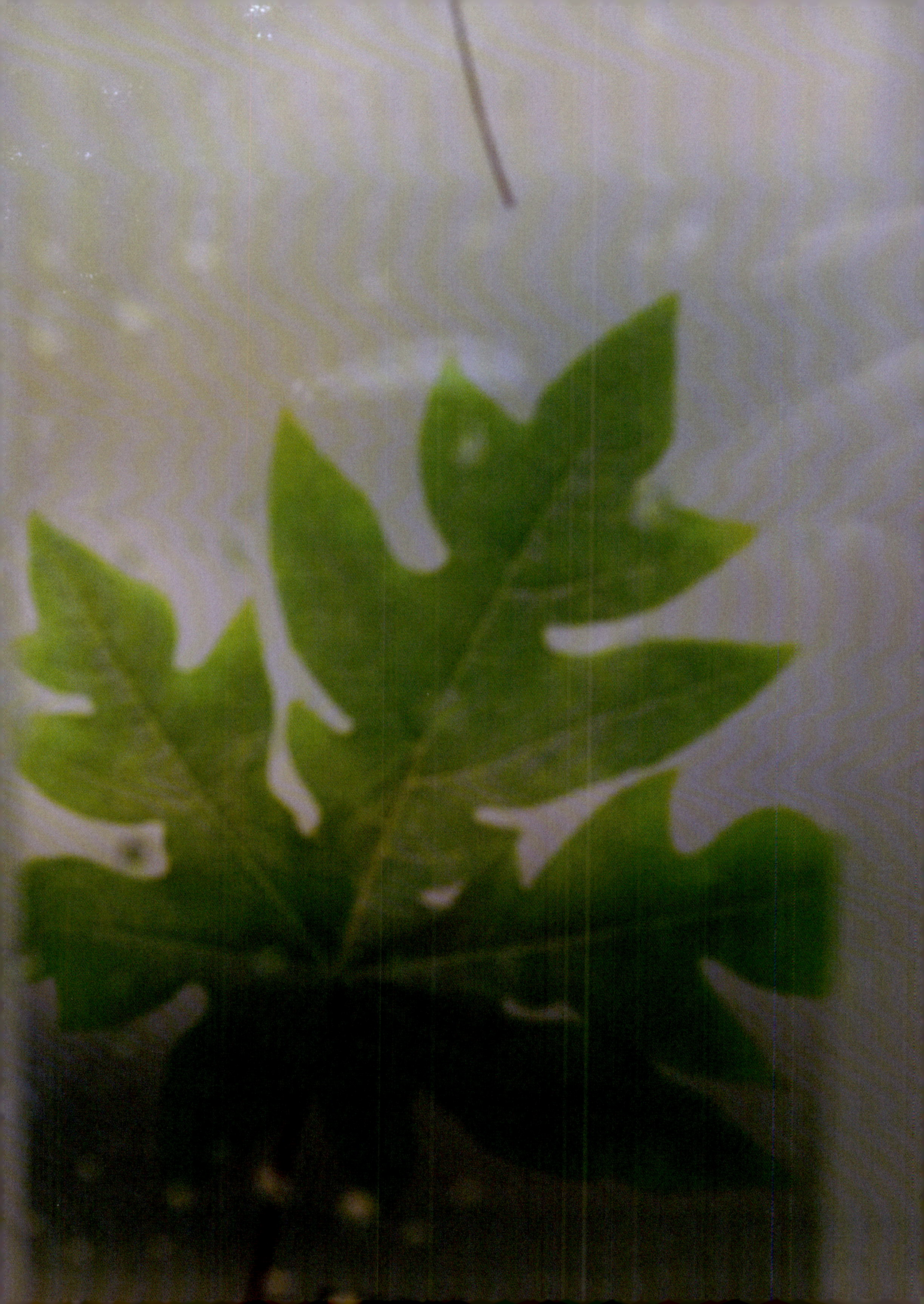

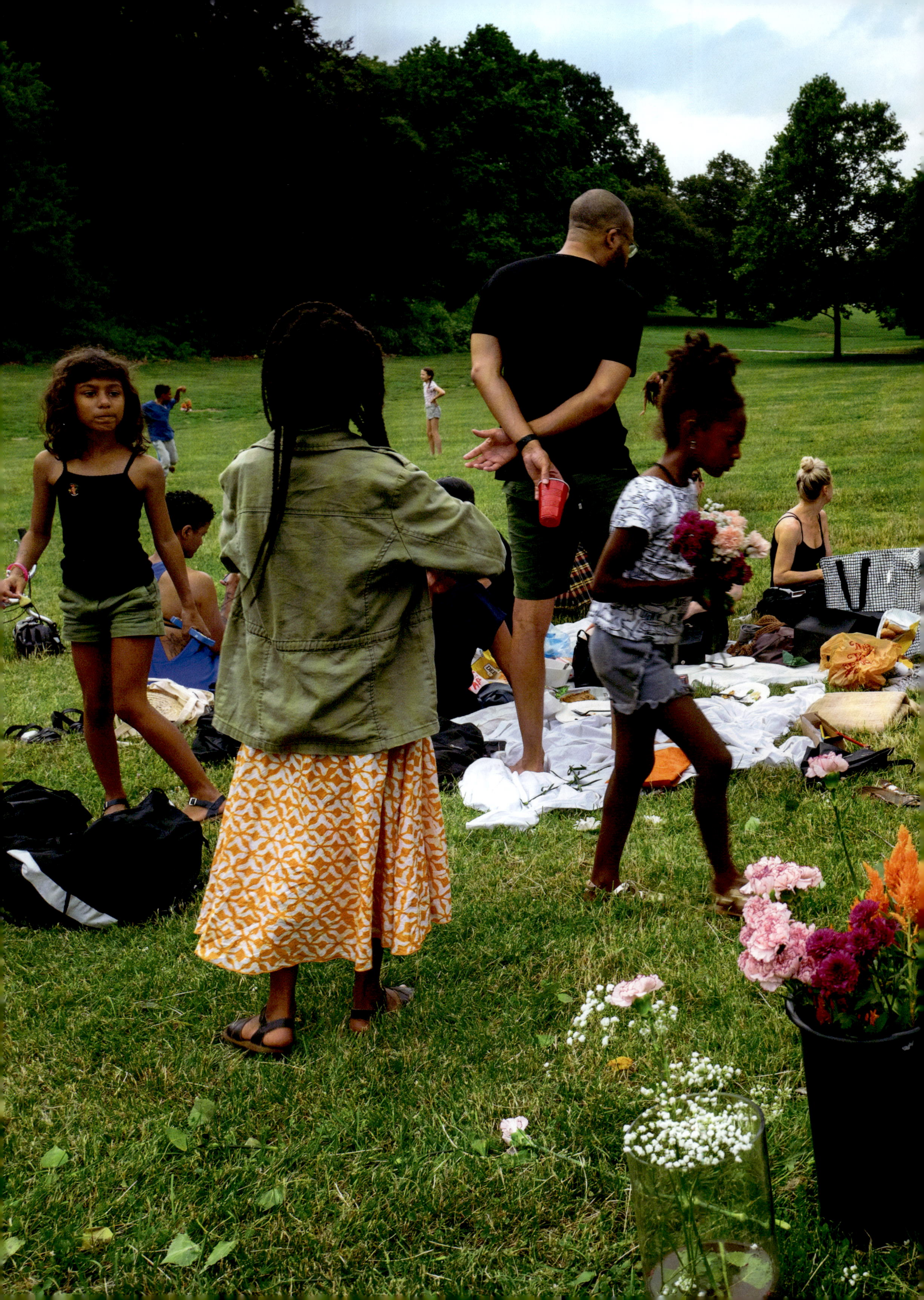

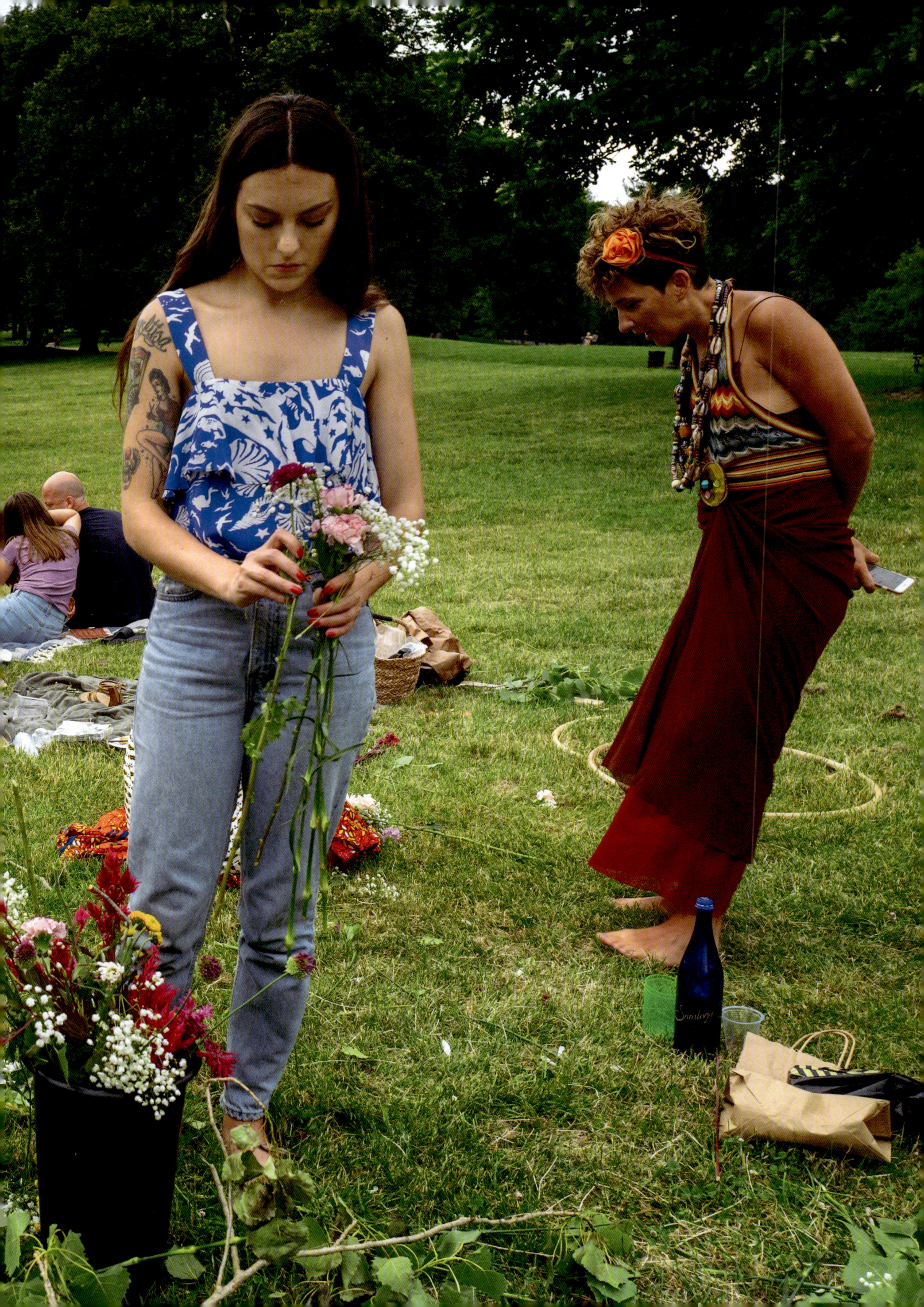

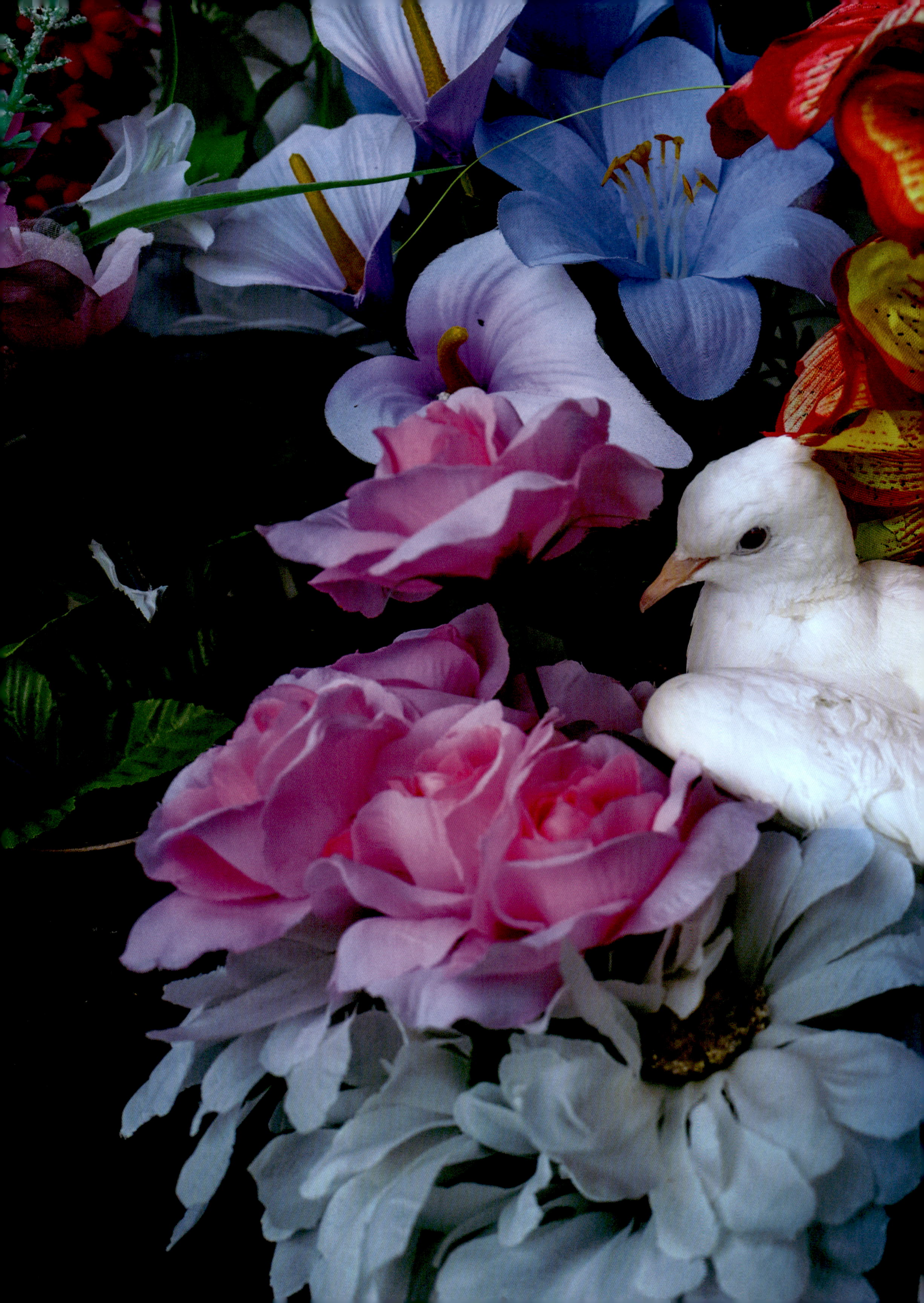

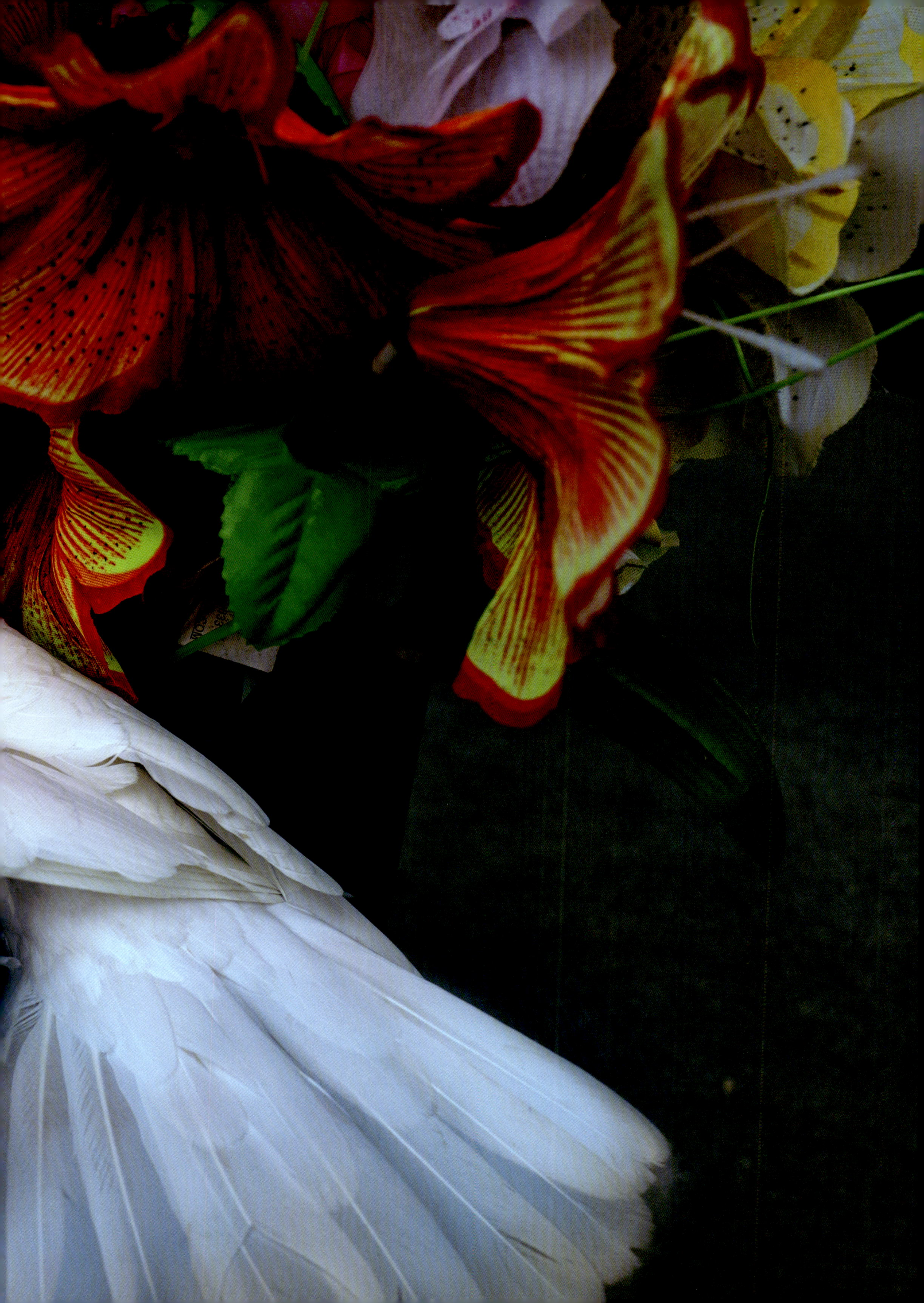

Falling calls to us: Green-Wood Cemetery—second only
to Niagara Falls as America's favorite tourist site—
this city beneath the city of Brooklyn.

Fallen soldiers call to us, some half a million souls: Is this war
to end what divides us ever over, if so many never return?
That's why we keep the living near, and our ghosts even closer.

Let shadows fall where they may. We're called to gather,
we, the quick, and our dead, to picnic with only a blanket
between us—and that moth-eaten linen, memory.

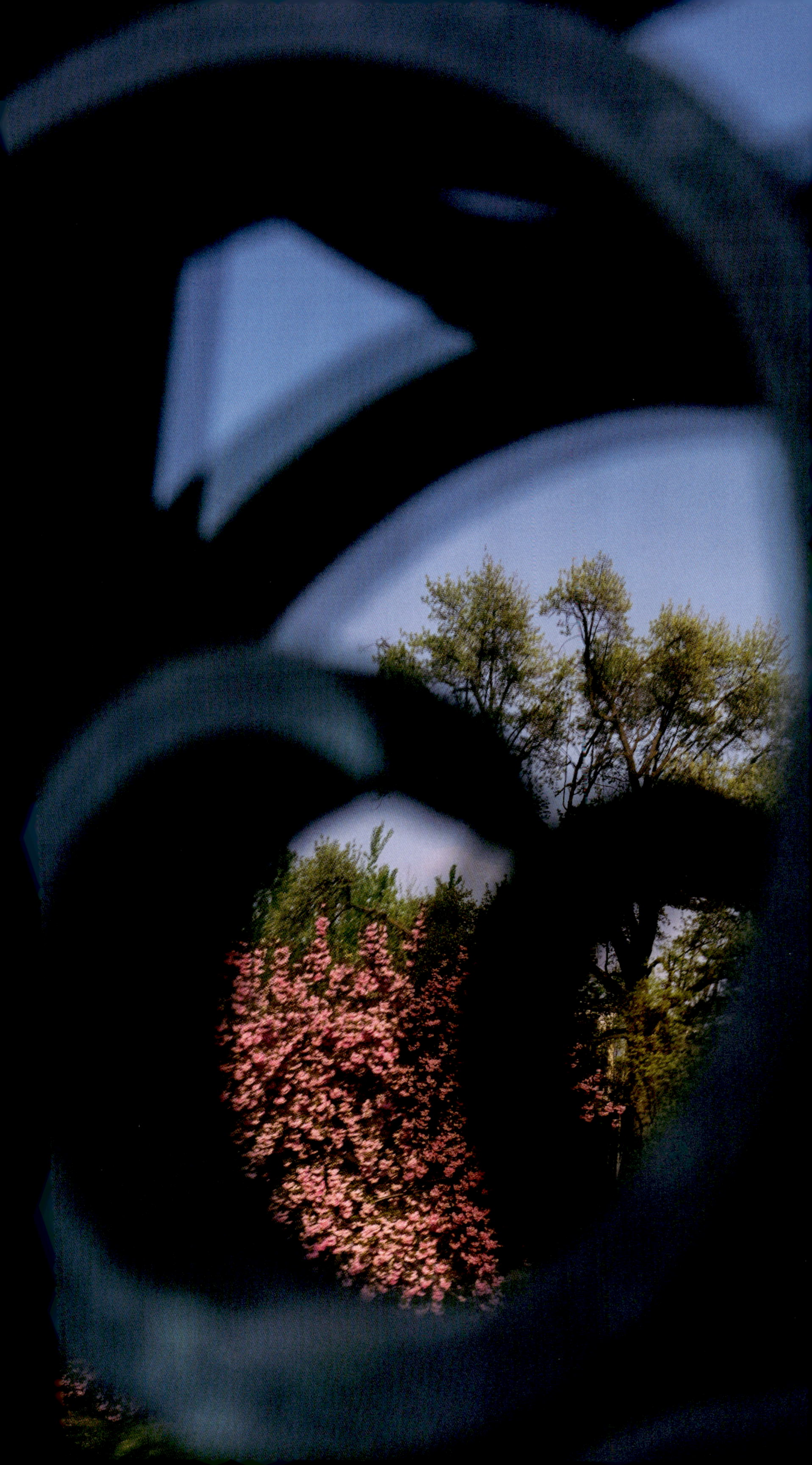

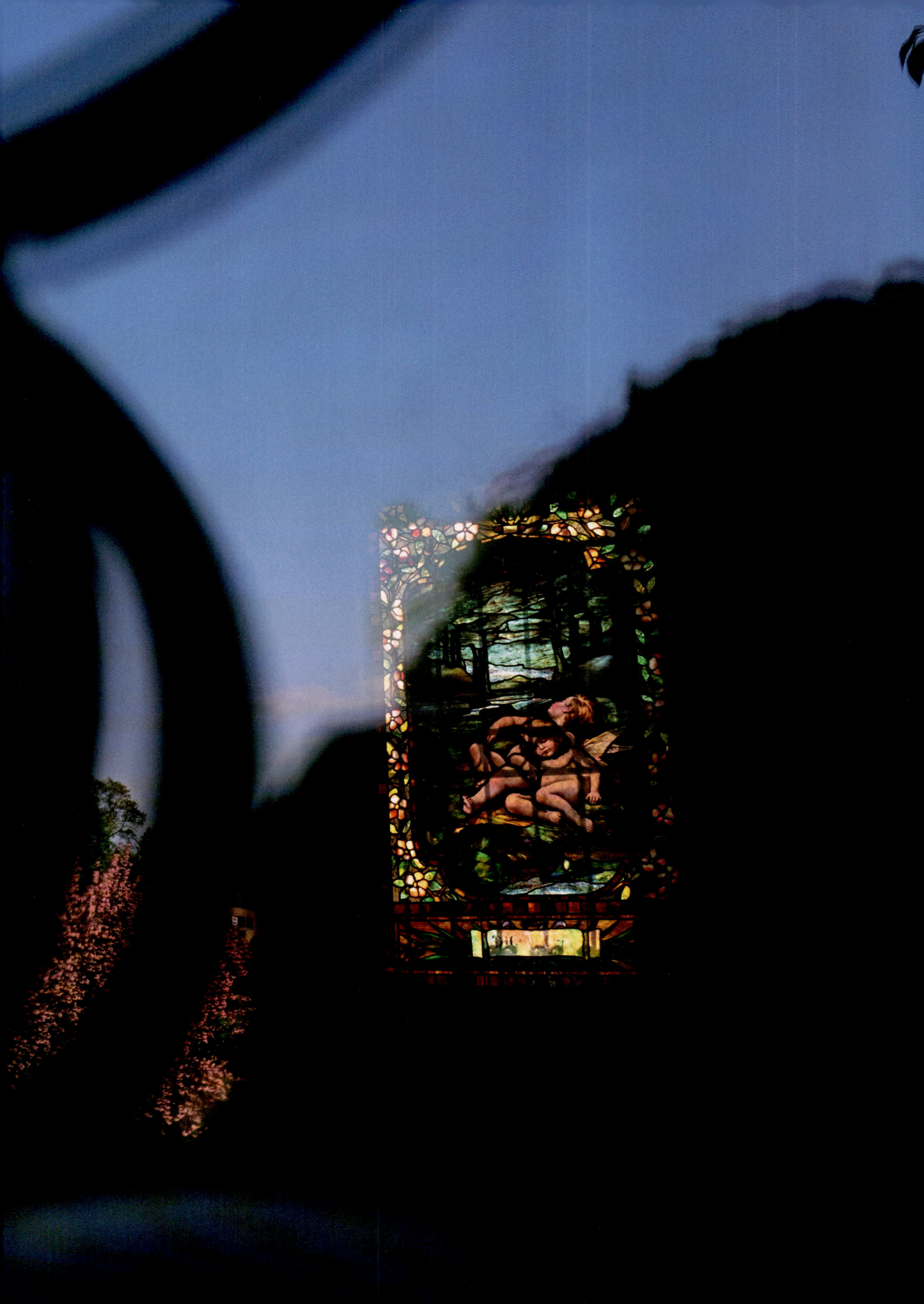

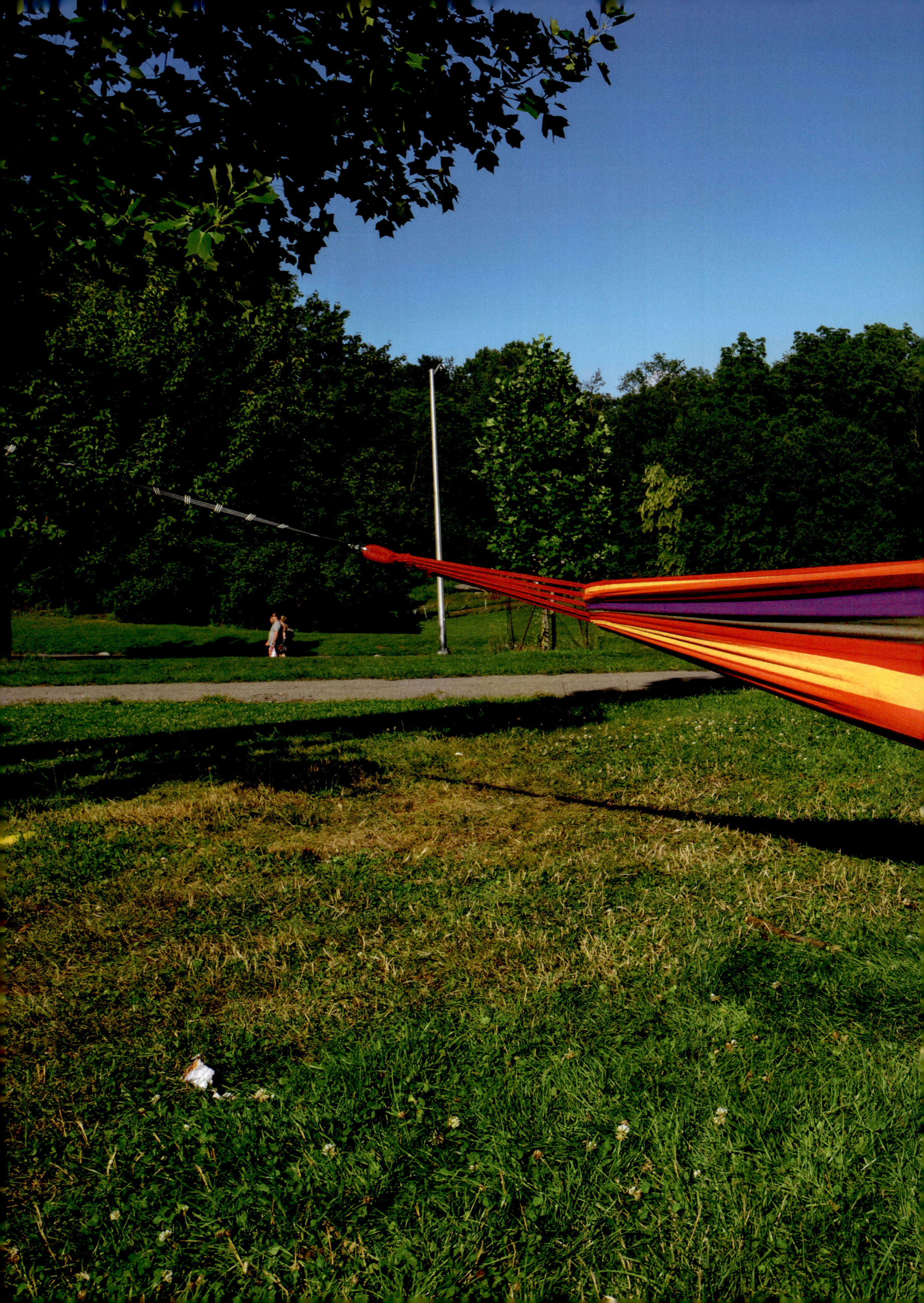

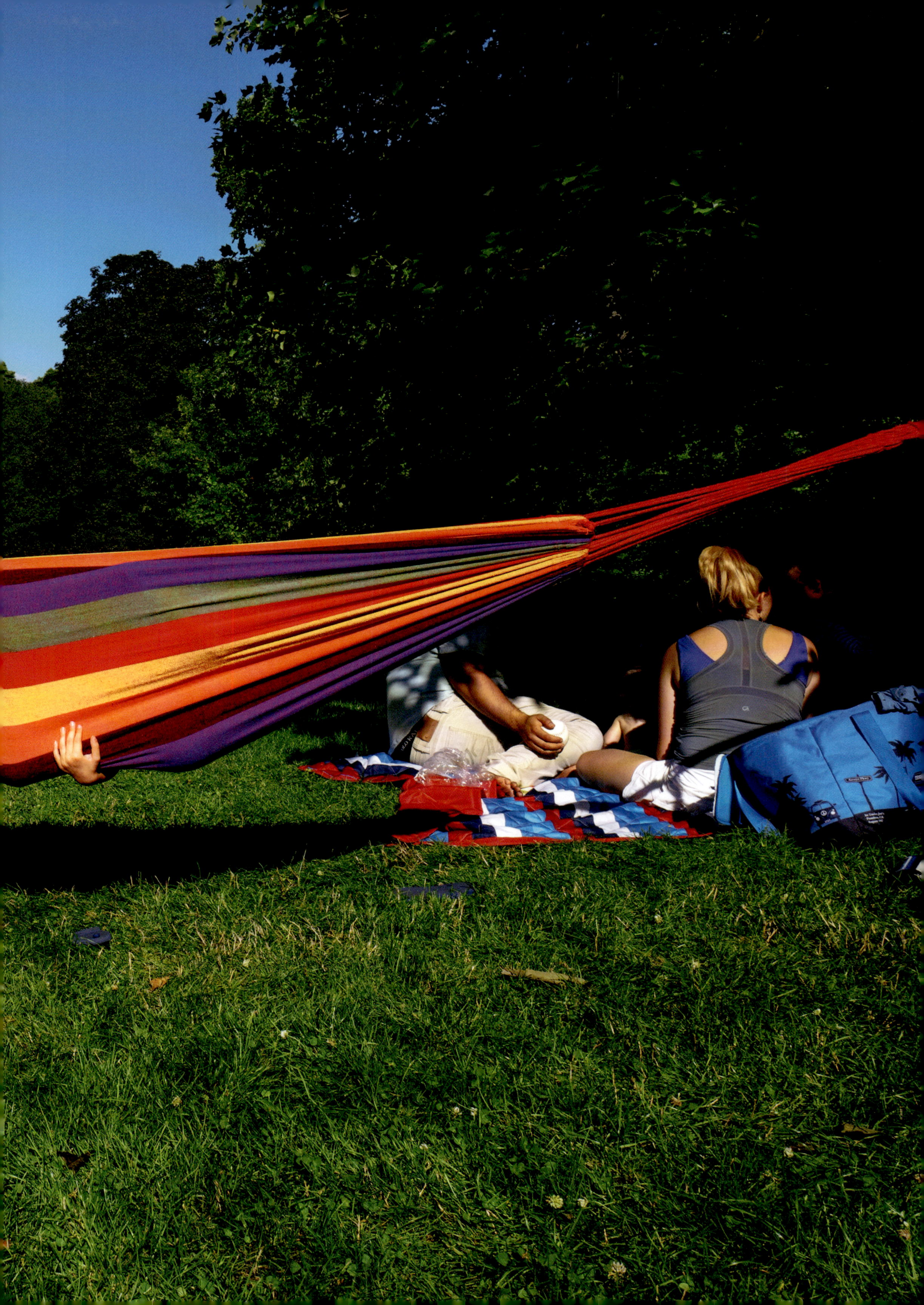

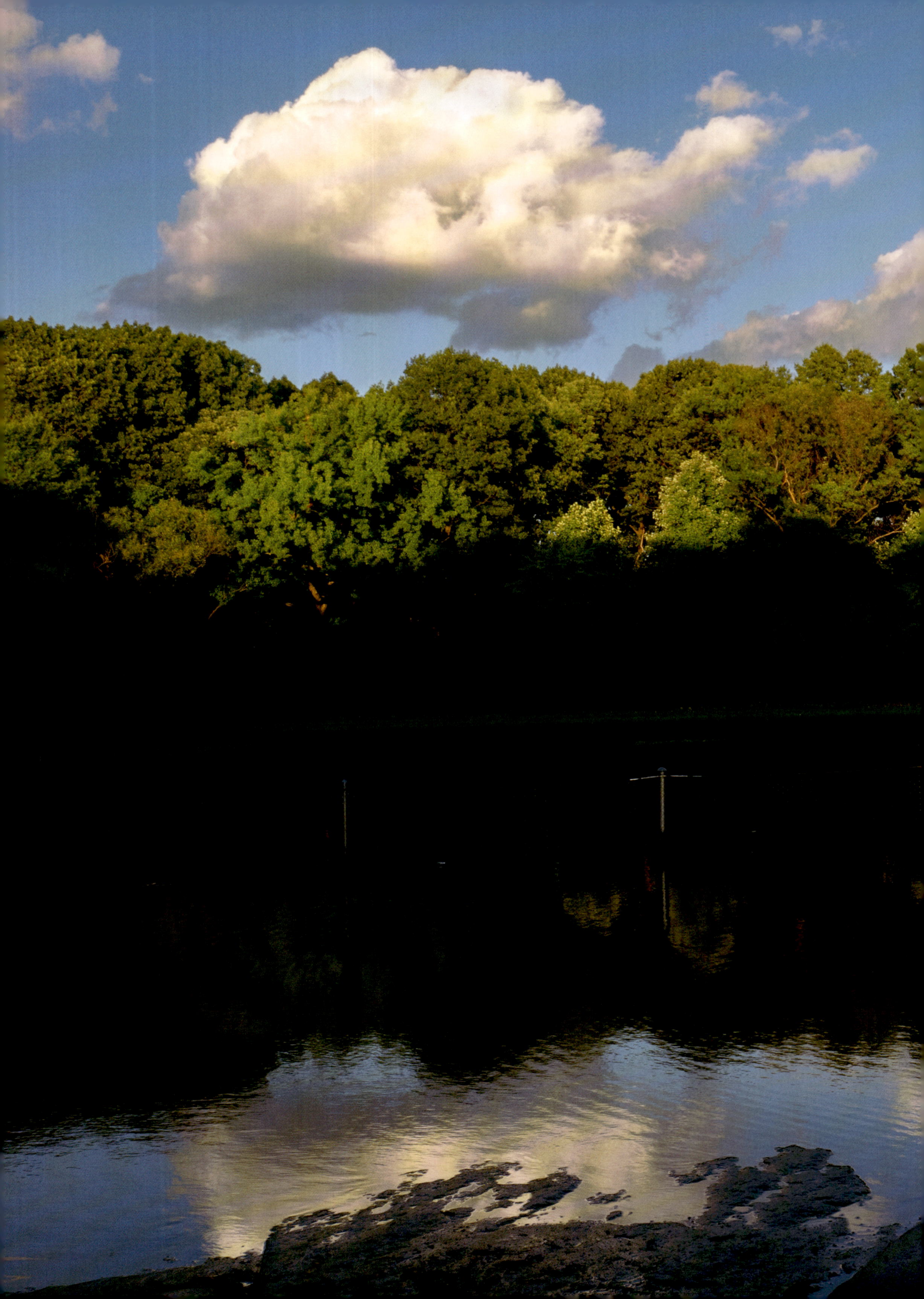

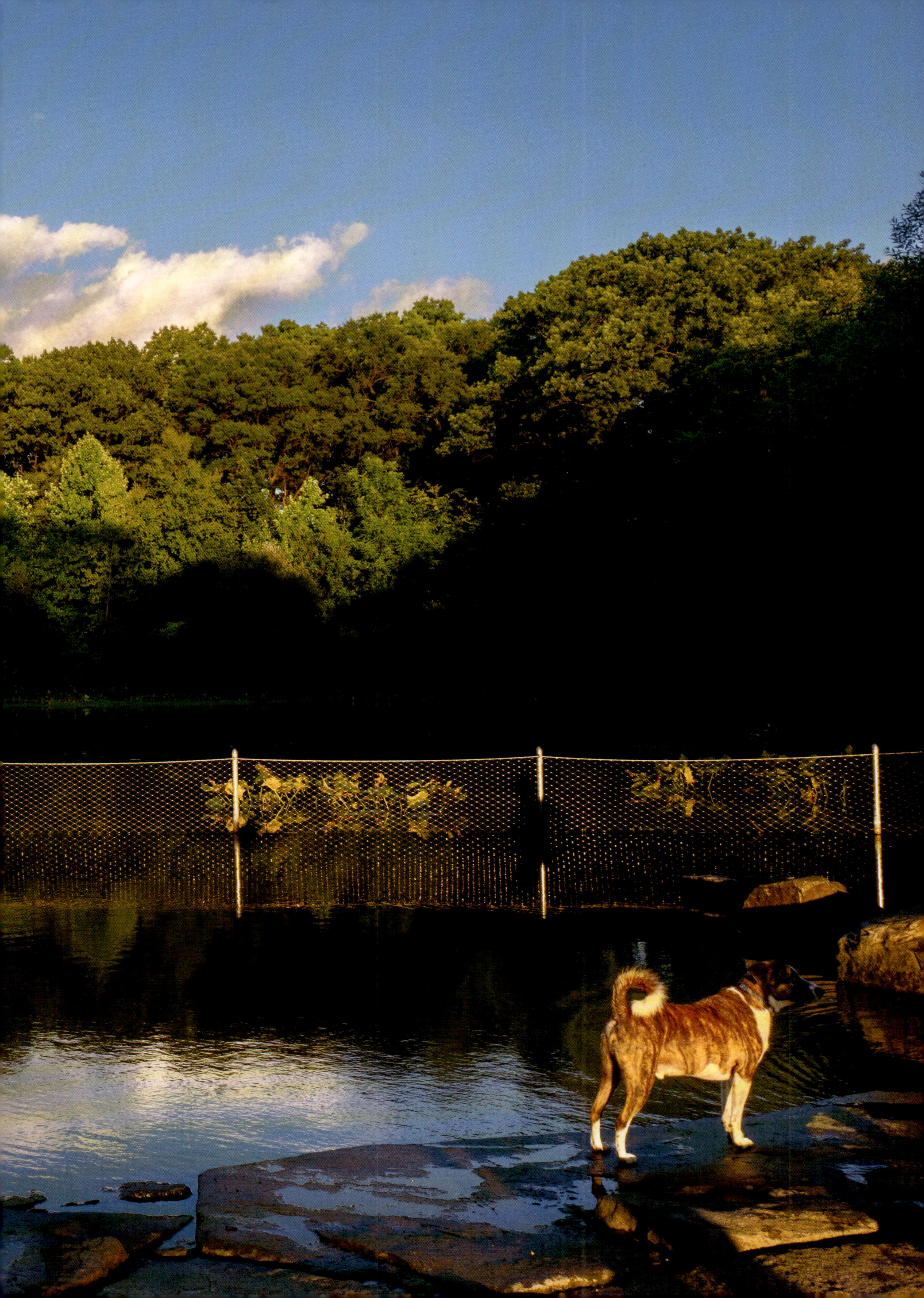

BATTLE PASS, PROSPECT PARK

Thank you, Frederick Law Olmsted, for creating a memorial to a lost battle in the
shape of a park. For inviting us to walk across our losses like water, more a matter
of buoyancy than miracle—for doesn't loss help hold us up, like those dead soldiers
beneath our feet? And lastly, thank you for Long Meadow, your prize. It is part
daydream, part grassland, designed to seem borderless—for aren't the dead here
with us?—like one great green undulating we.

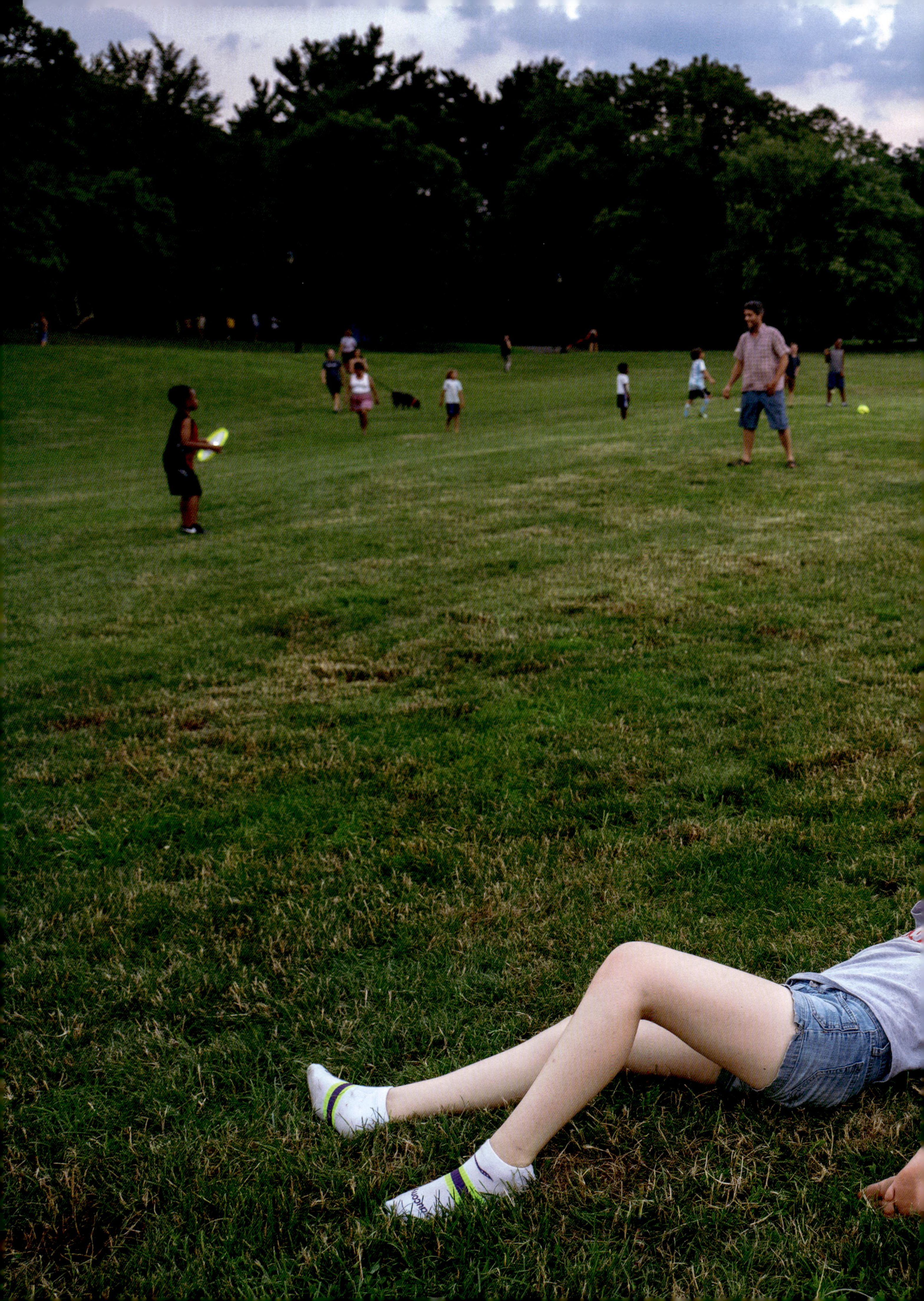

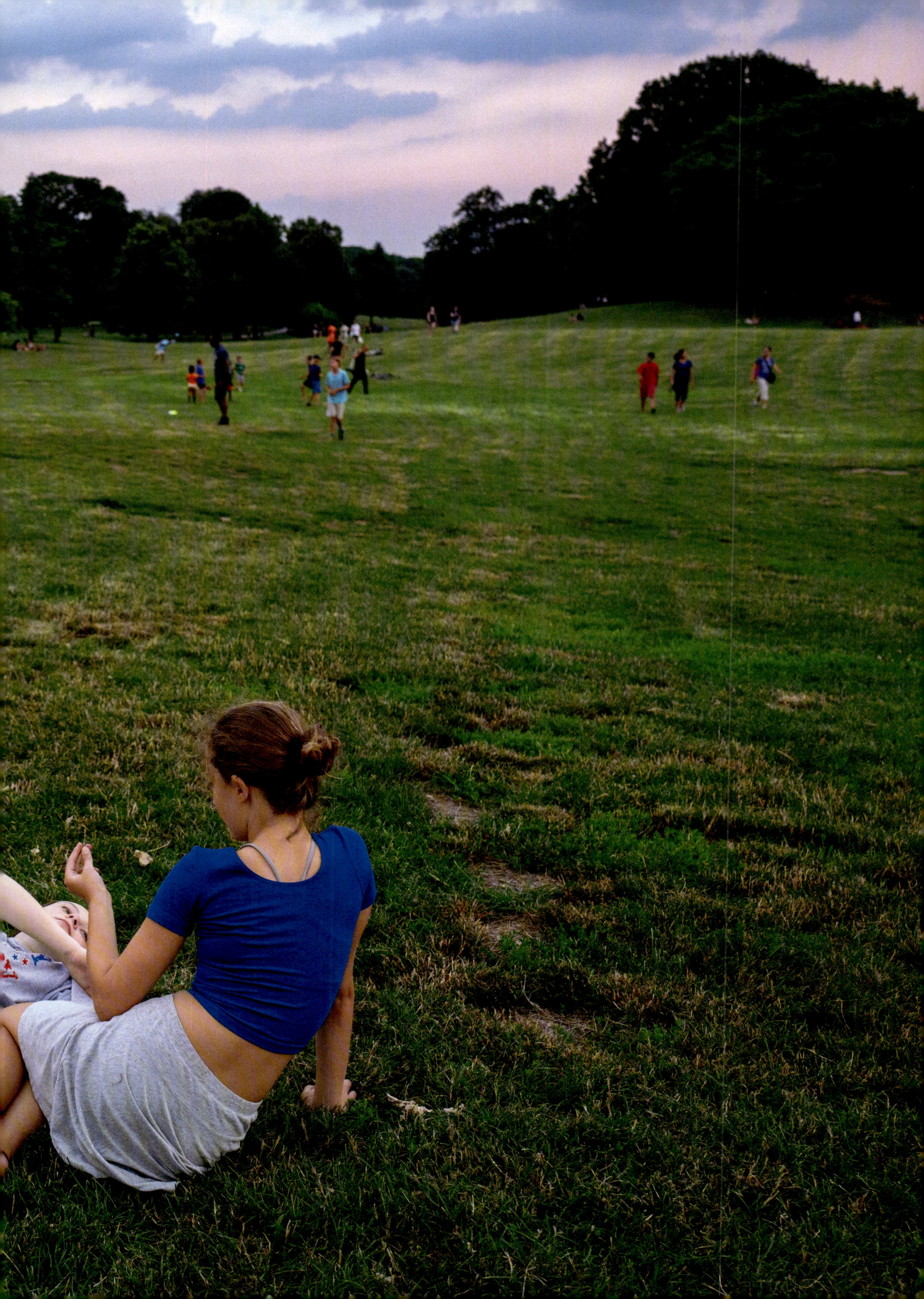

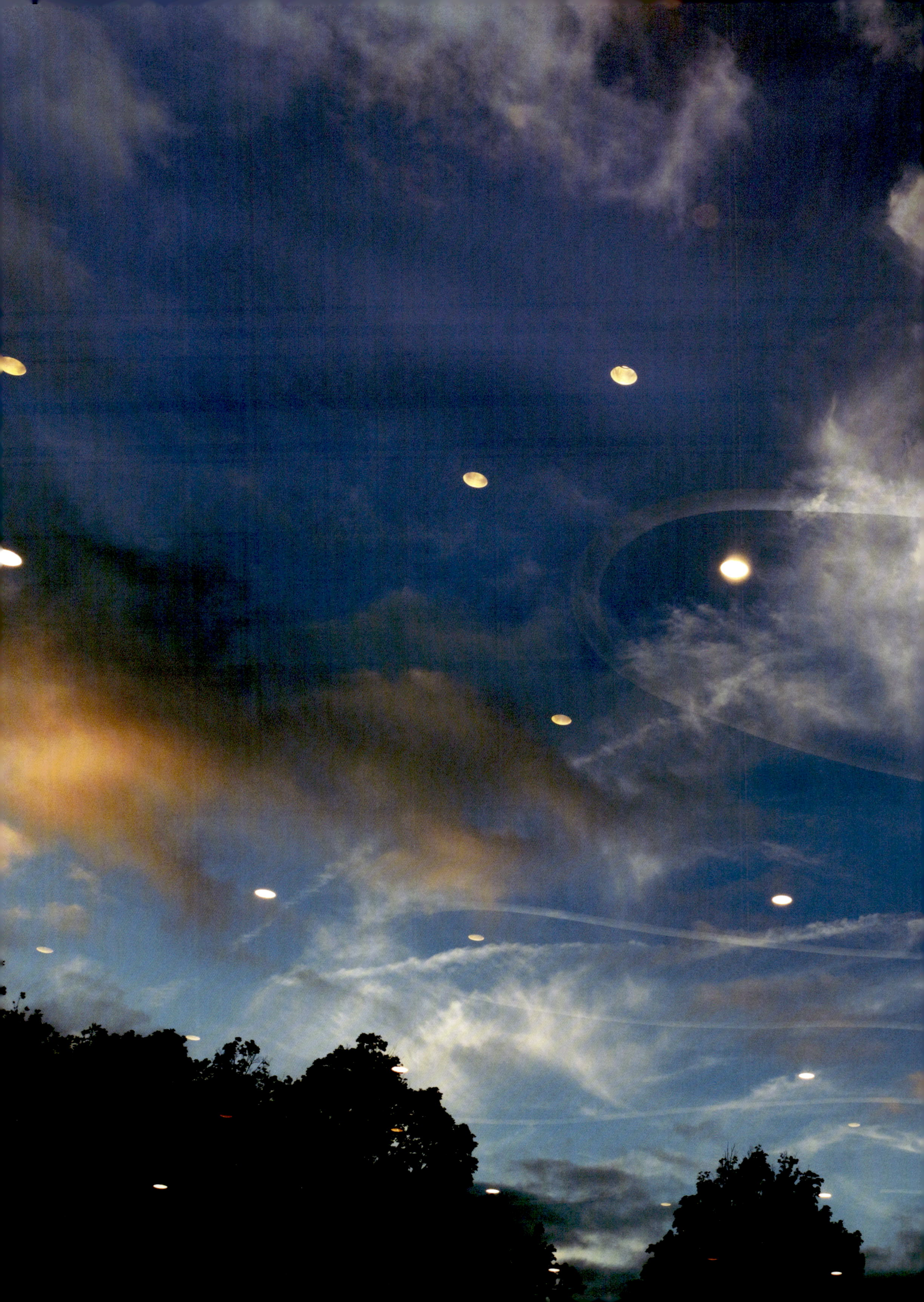

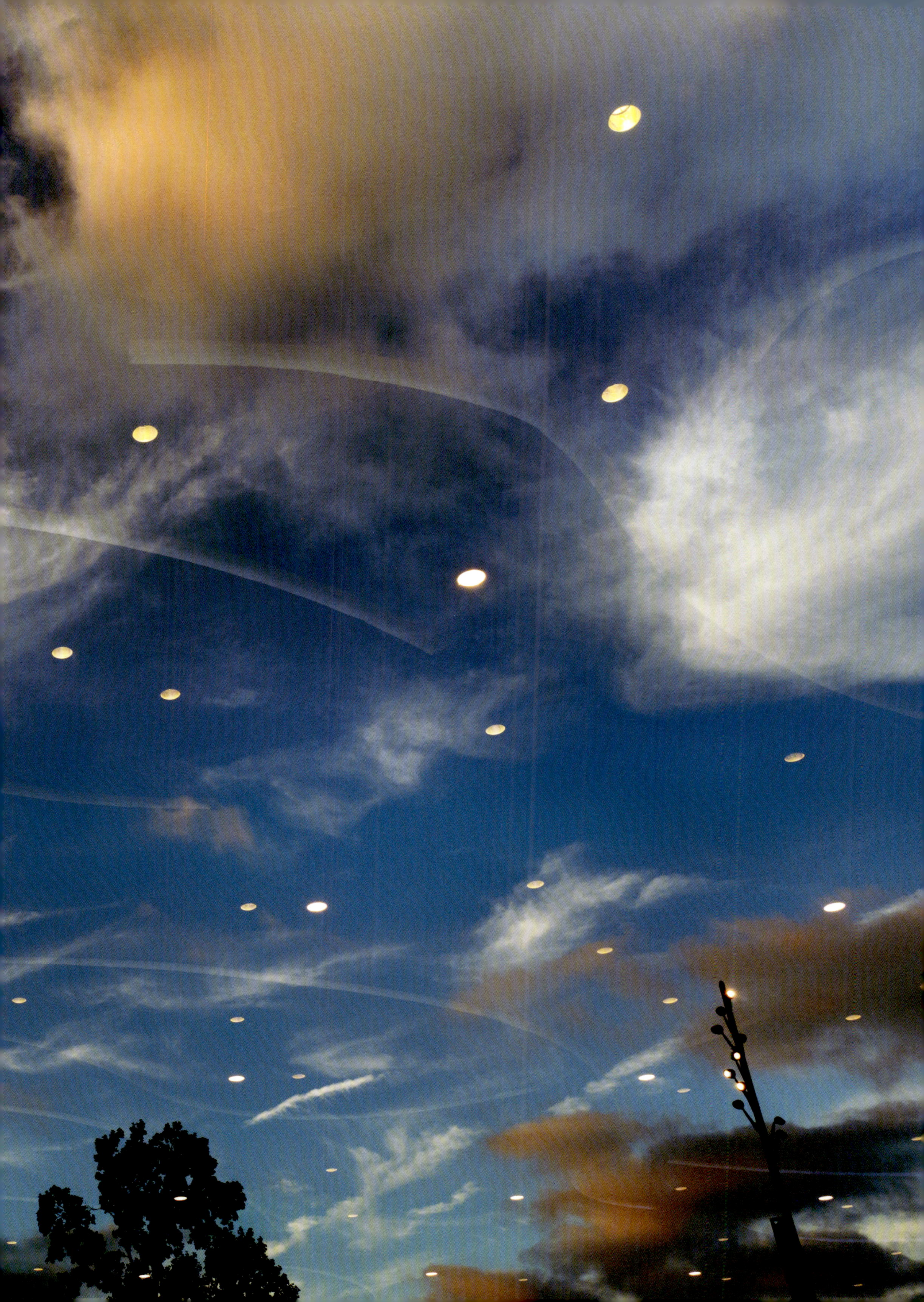

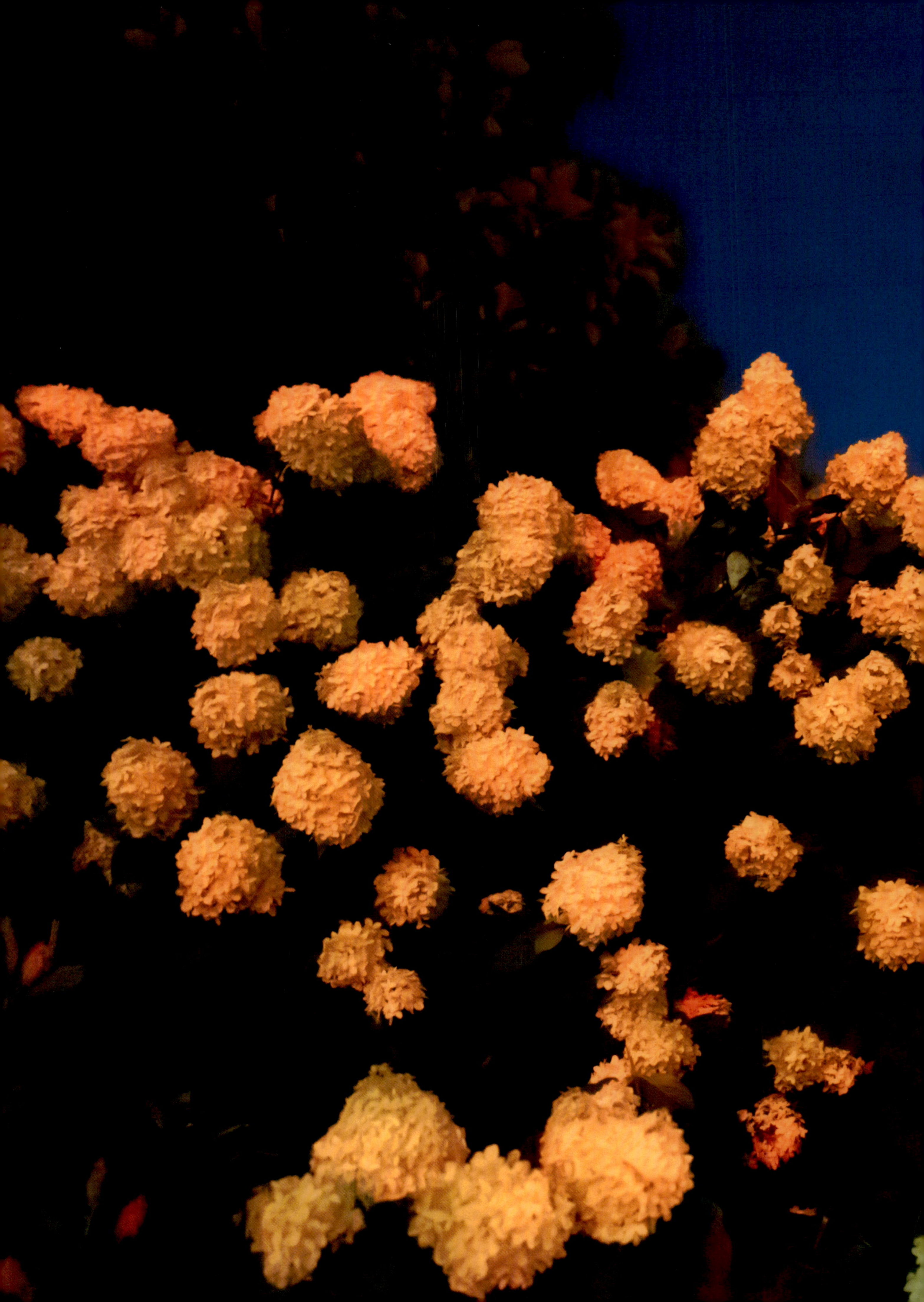

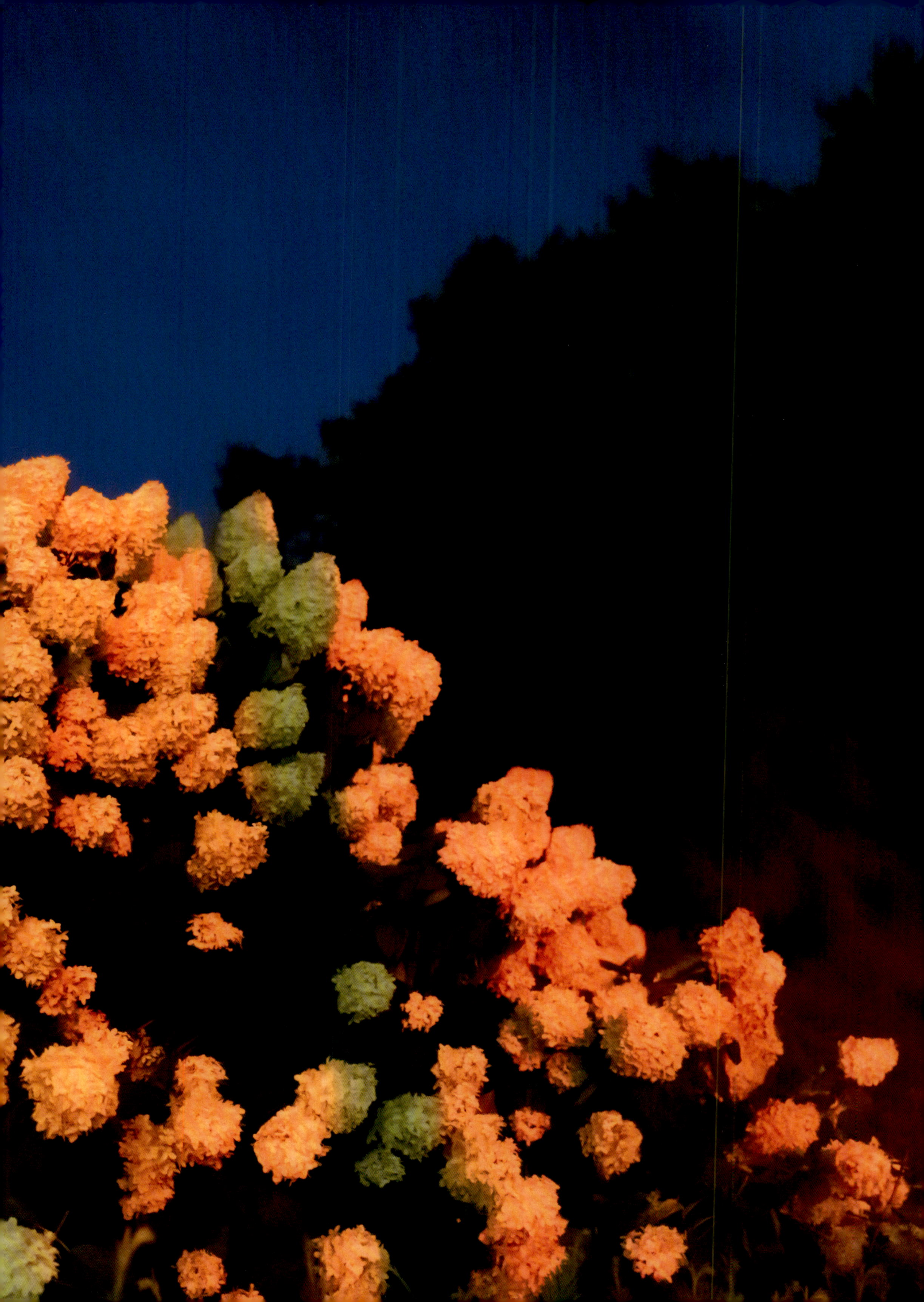

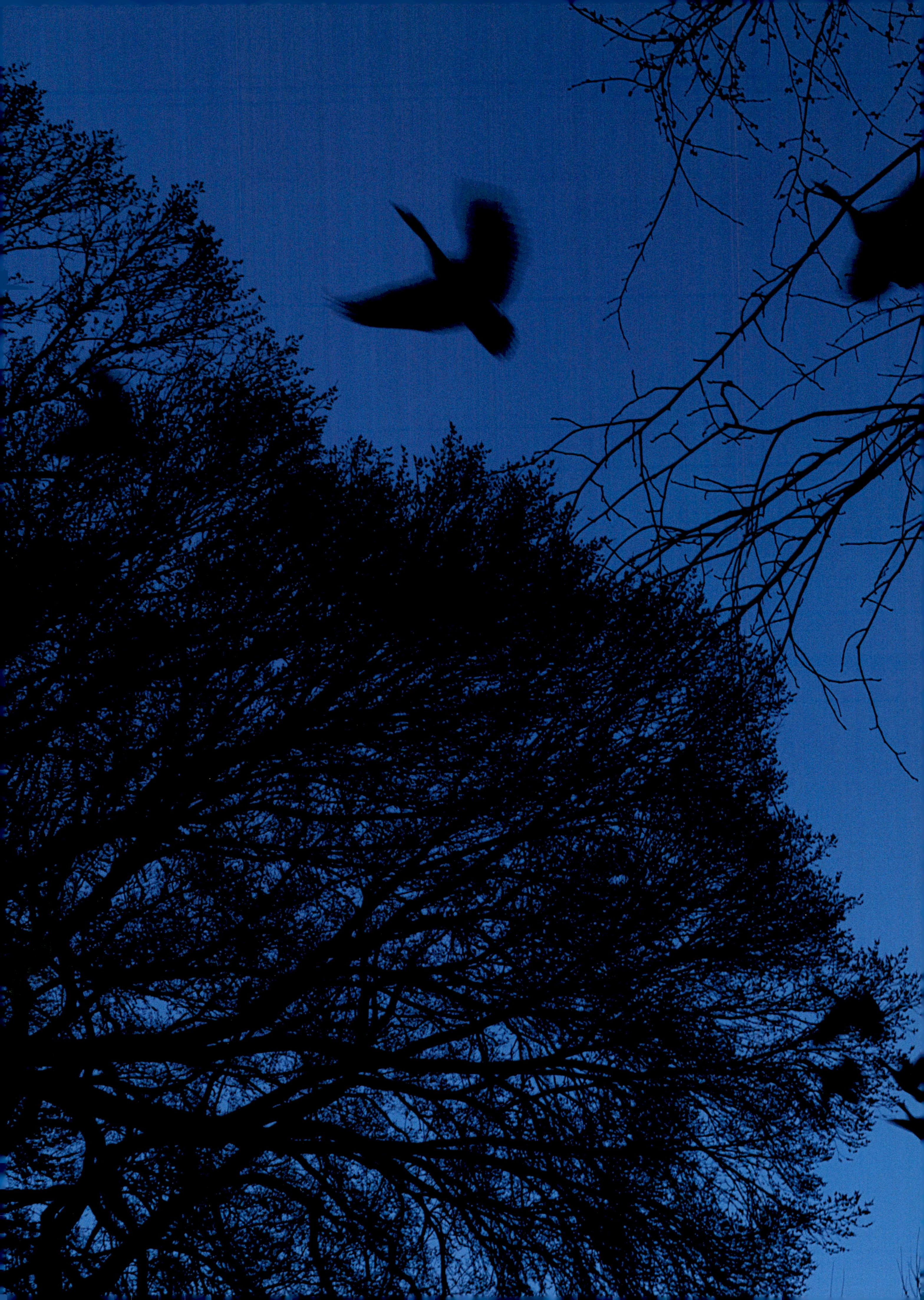

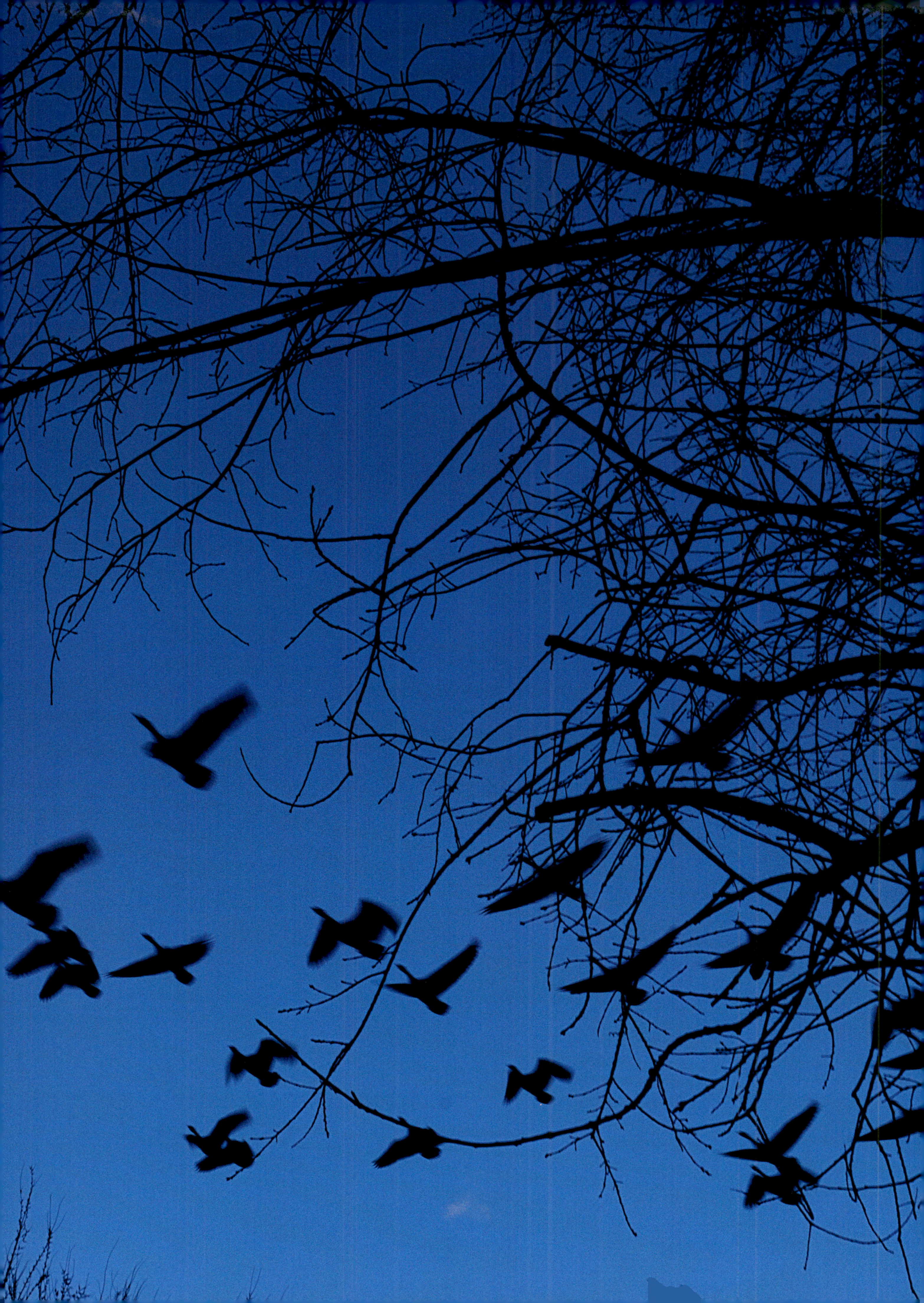

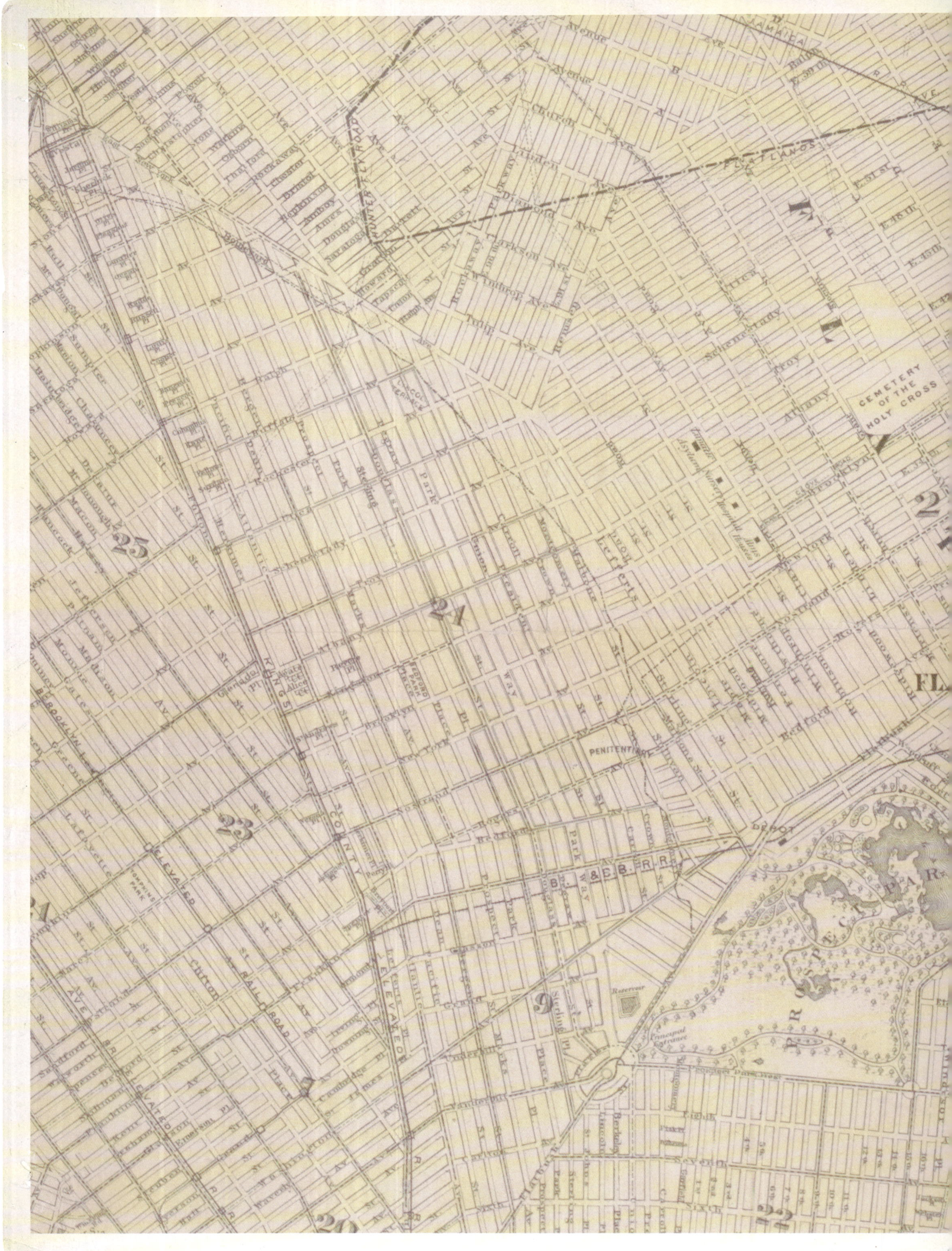

FLATLANDS
CEMETERY OF THE HOLY CROSS
CEMETERY OF THE HOLY CROSS
25
24
23
9
PENITENTIARY
PROSPECT PARK
Reservoir
Principal Entrance
CONEY
KING'S
ELEVATED
RAILROAD
ELEVATED
ATLANTIC AVE
JAMAICA
B. J. & B. B. R. R.
DEPOT
Sterling Pl.
Park Way
BROOKLYN AV.
20
22
21
21

III

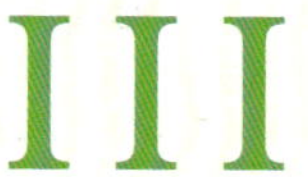

ALEX WEBB

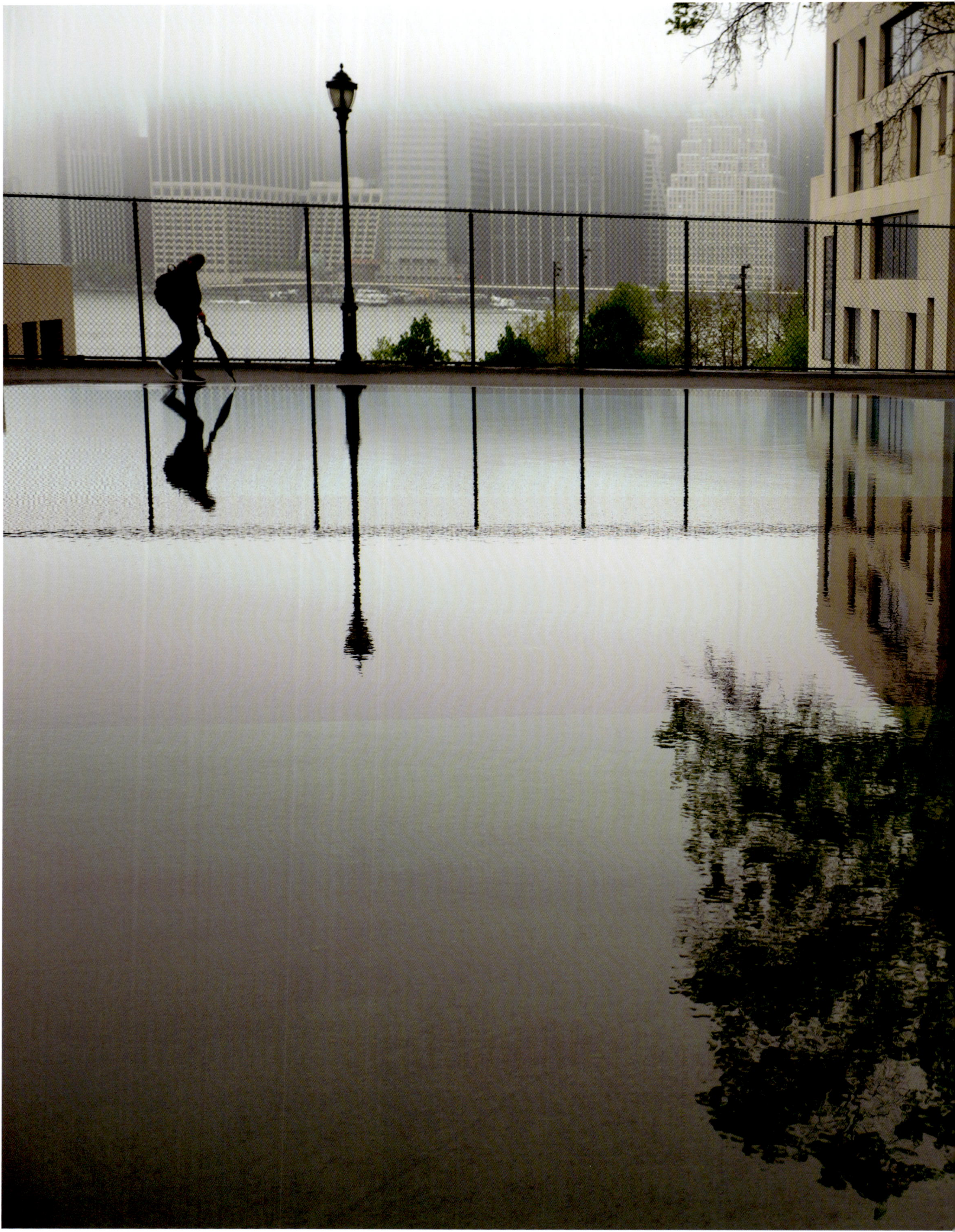

BROOKLYN HEIGHTS, 2017

SUNSET PARK, 2018

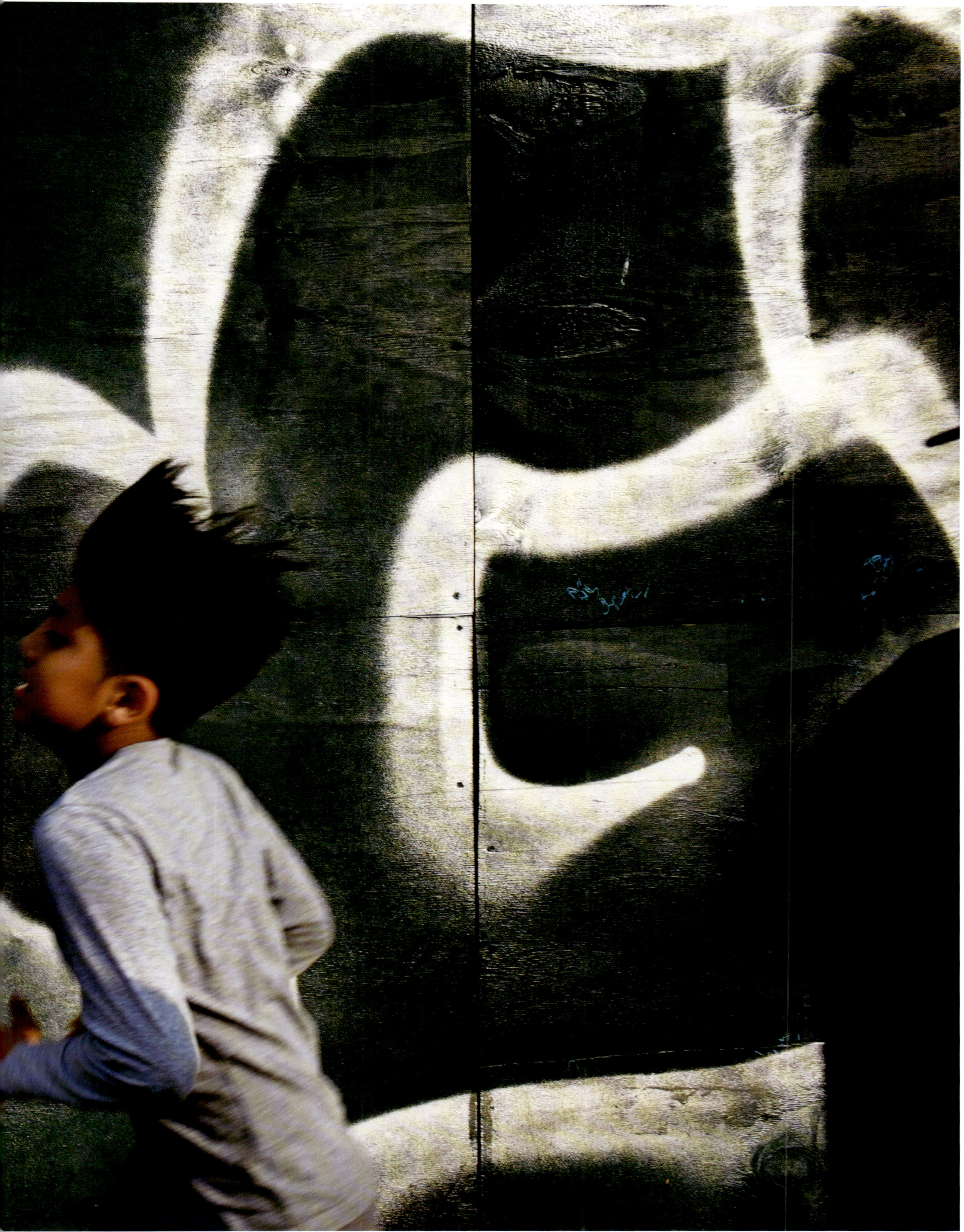

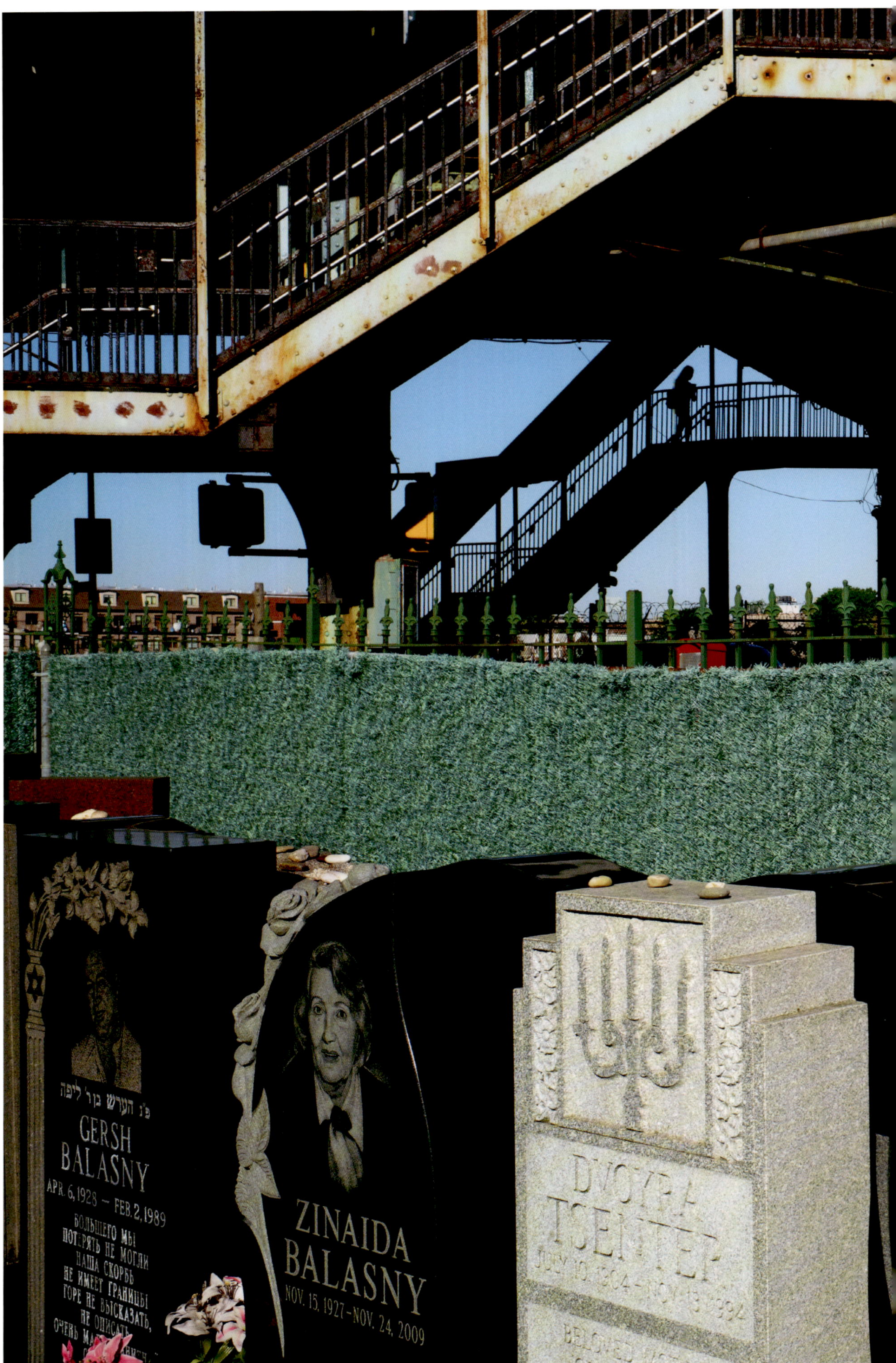

MAPLETON, 2015

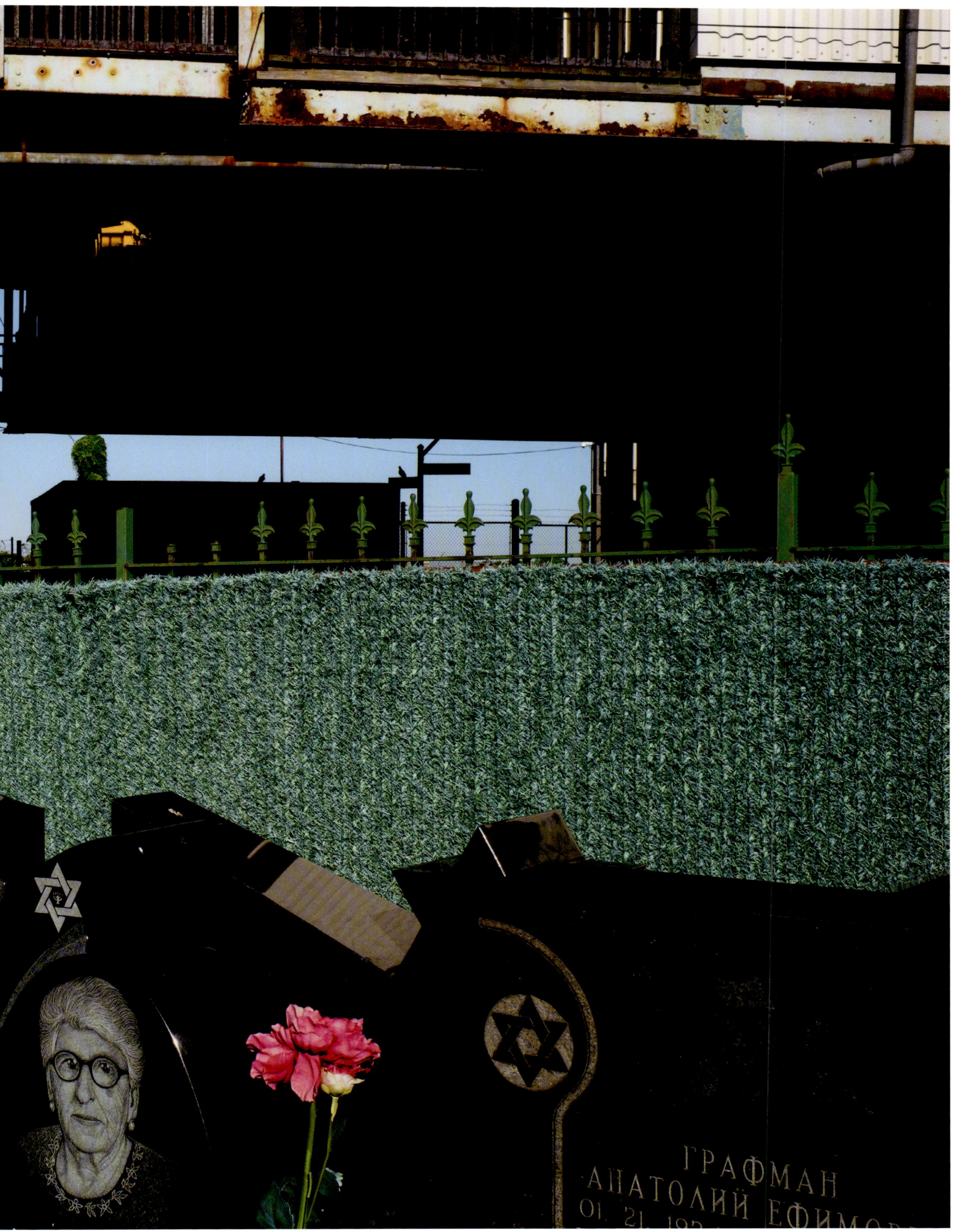
ГРАФМАН
АНАТОЛИЙ ЕФИМОВ
01 21 193

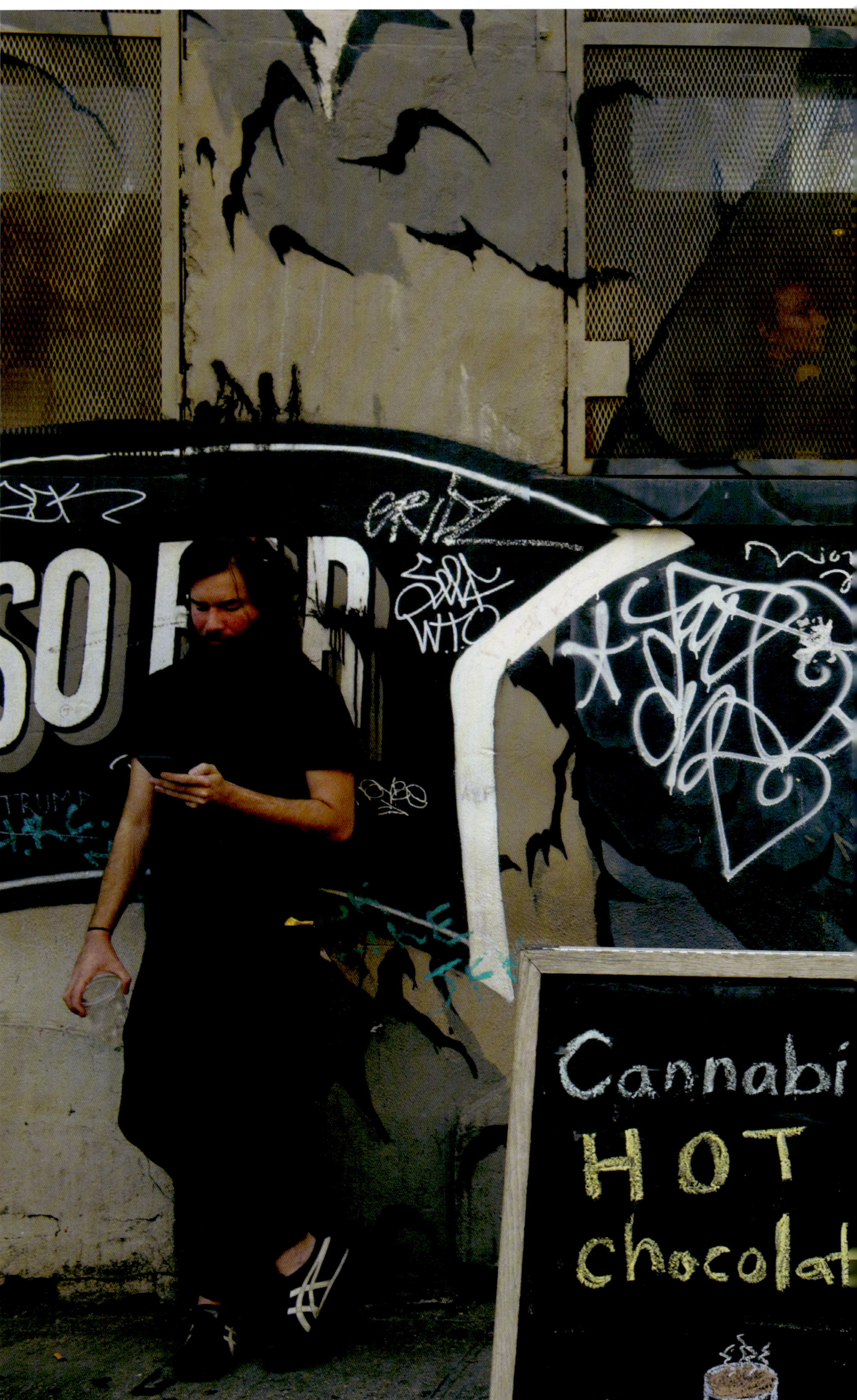

BUSHWICK, 2018

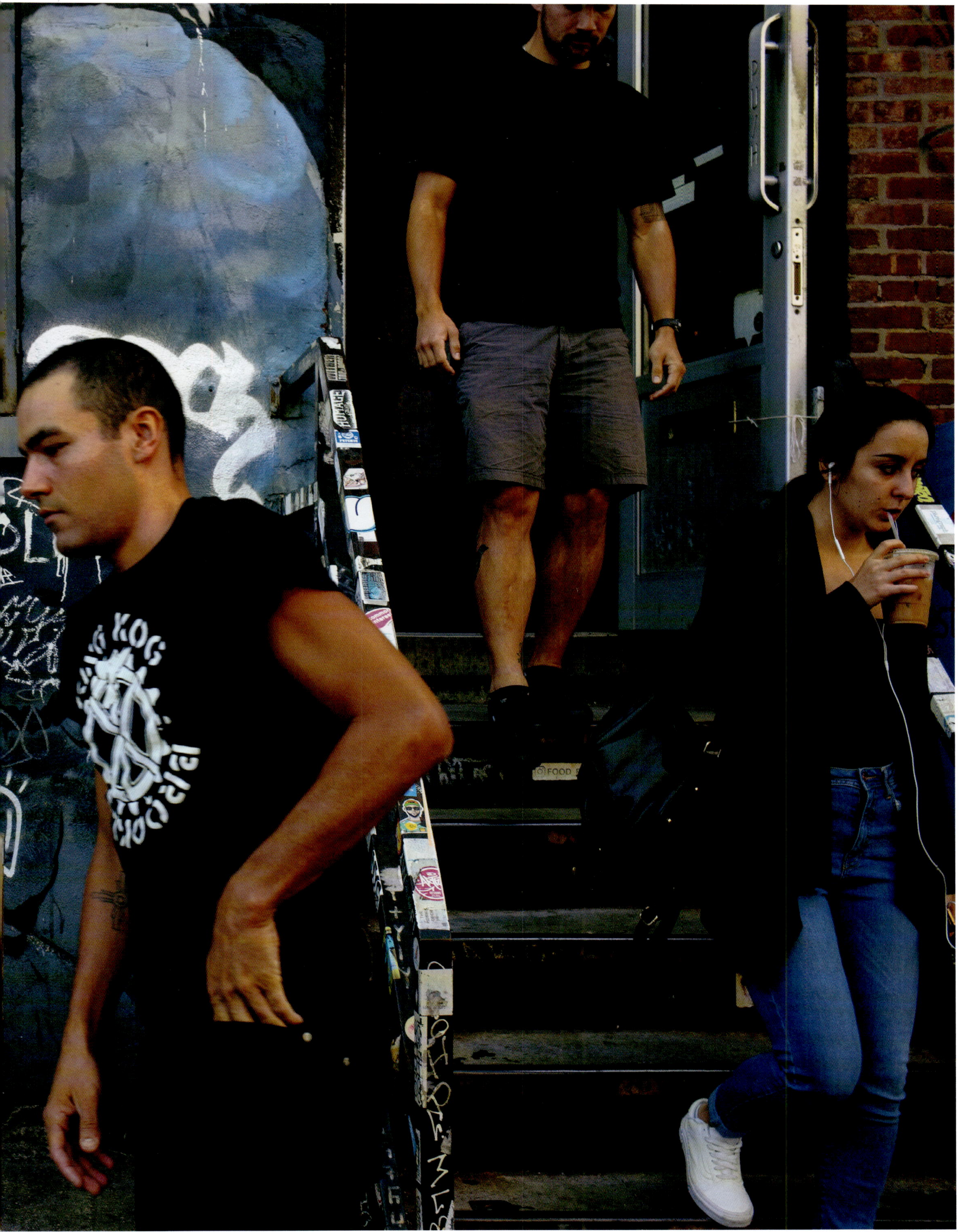

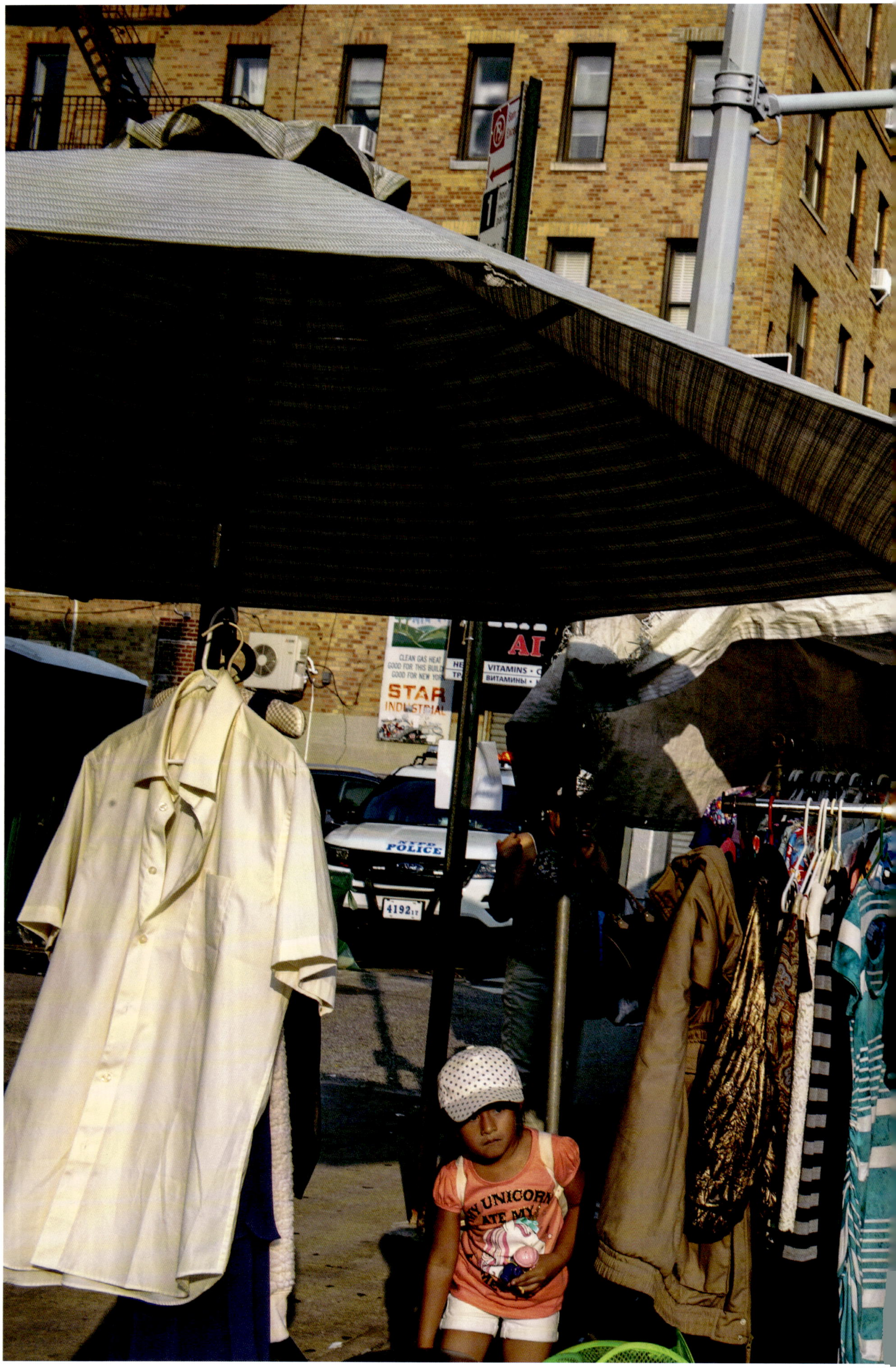

BRIGHTON BEACH, 2018

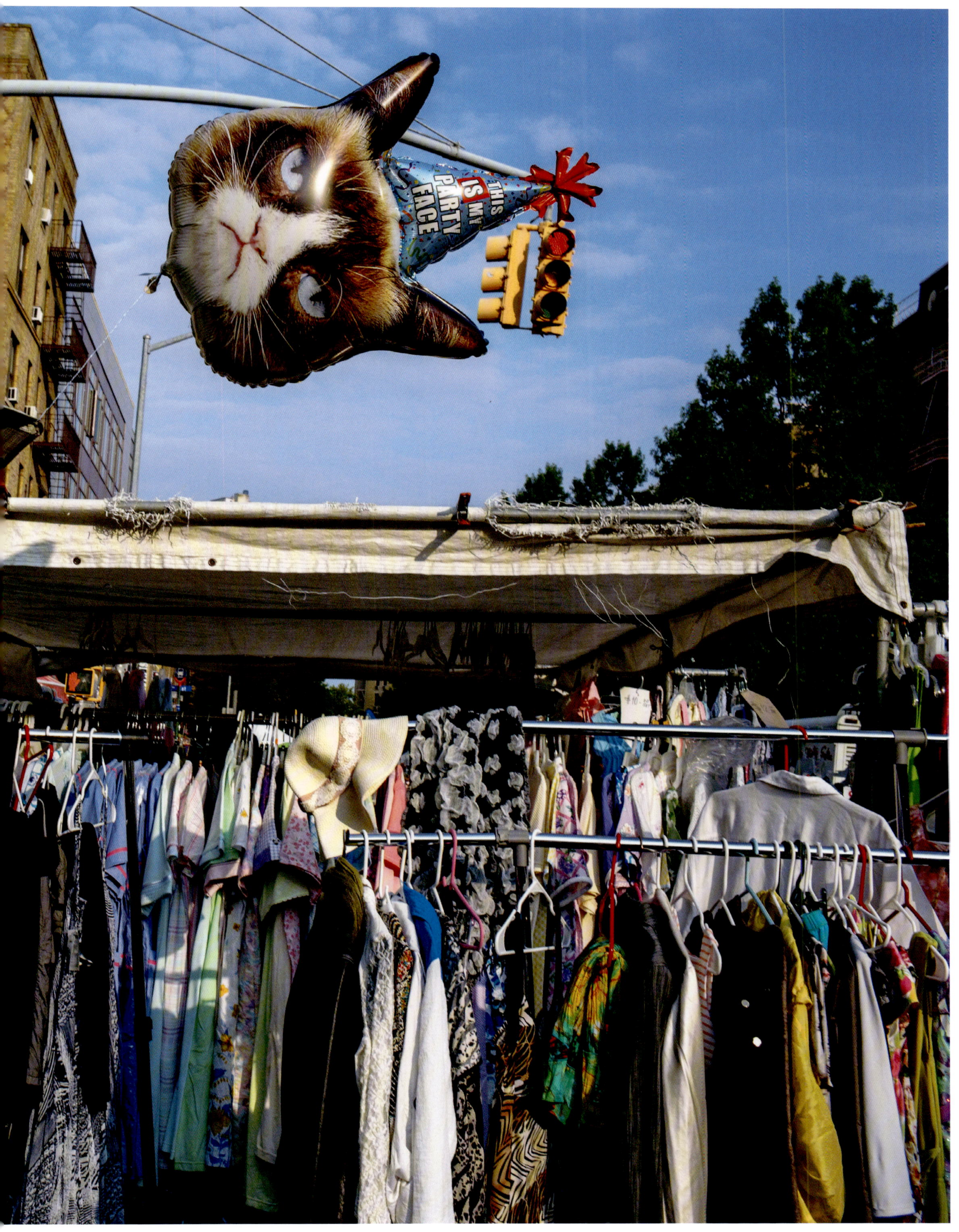

THIS
IS MY
PARTY
FACE

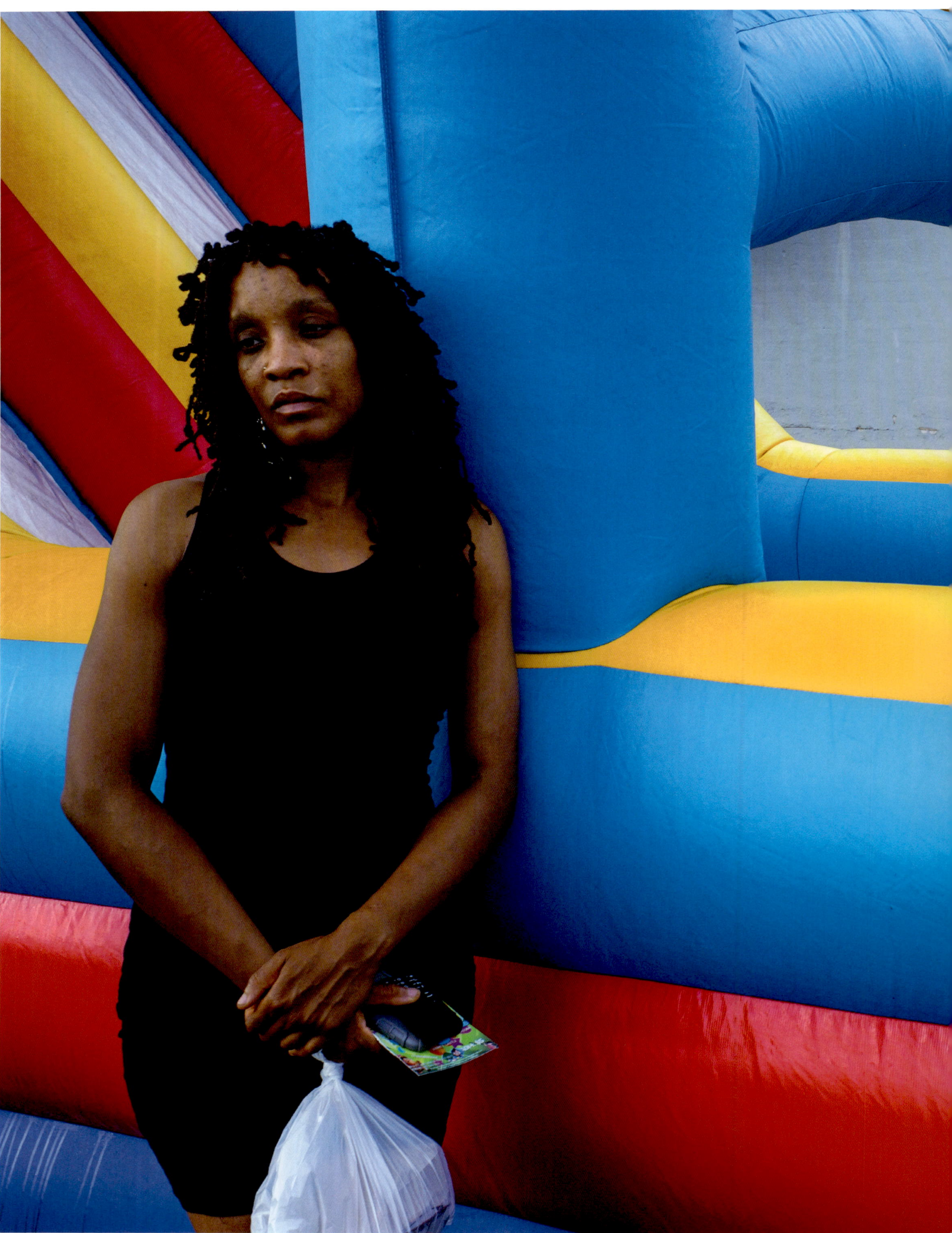

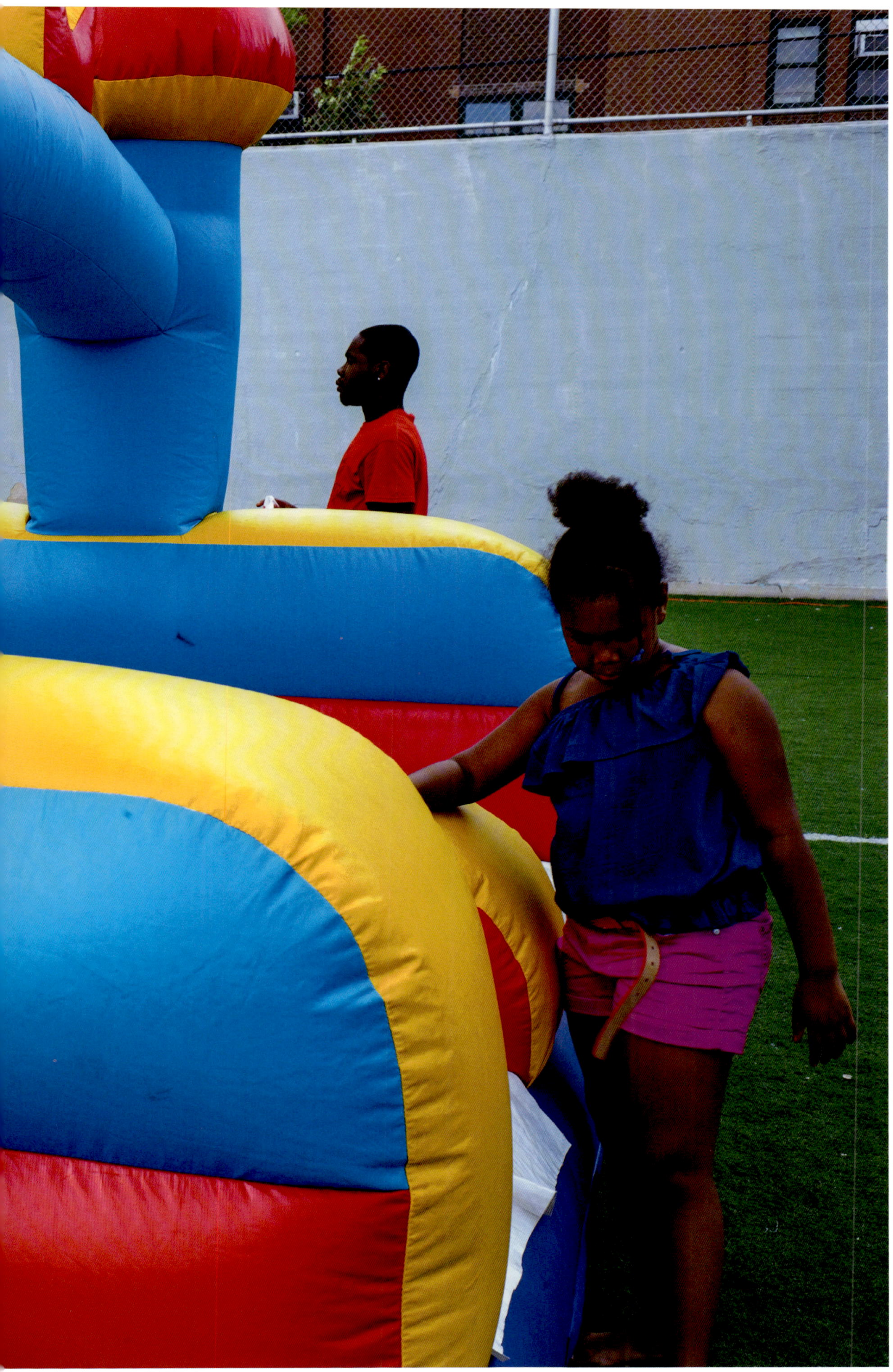

CROWN HEIGHTS, 2015

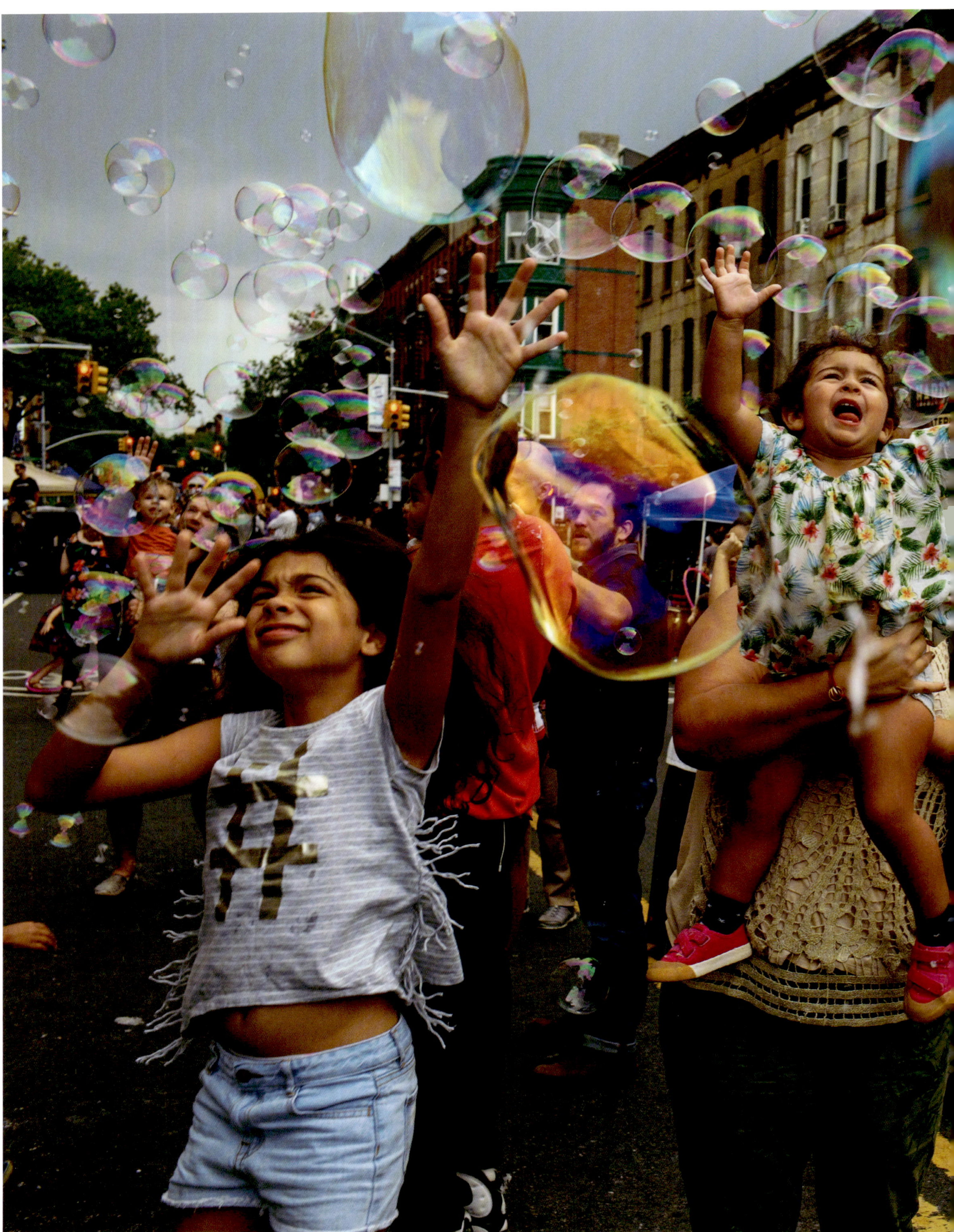

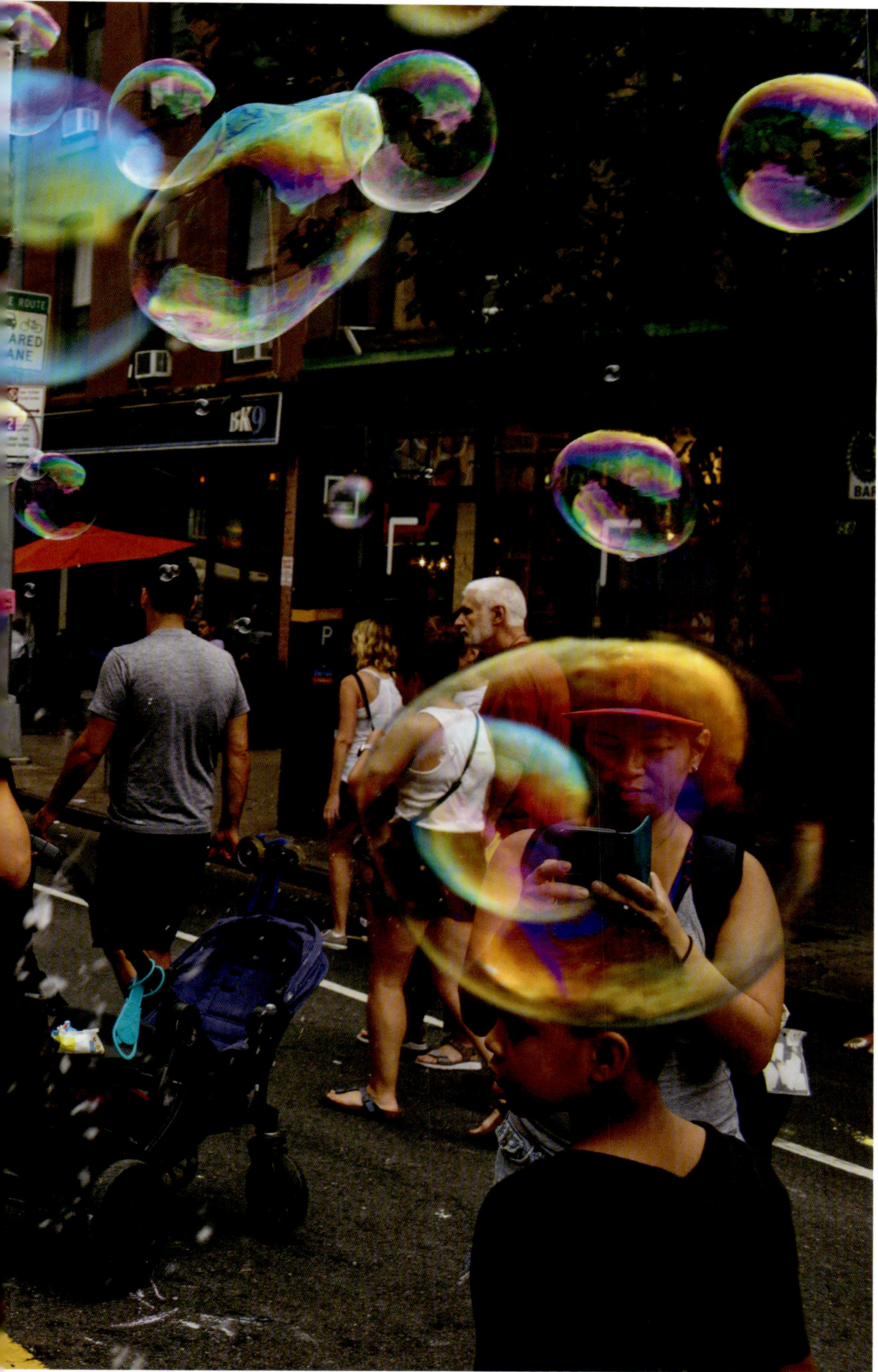

PARK SLOPE, 2018

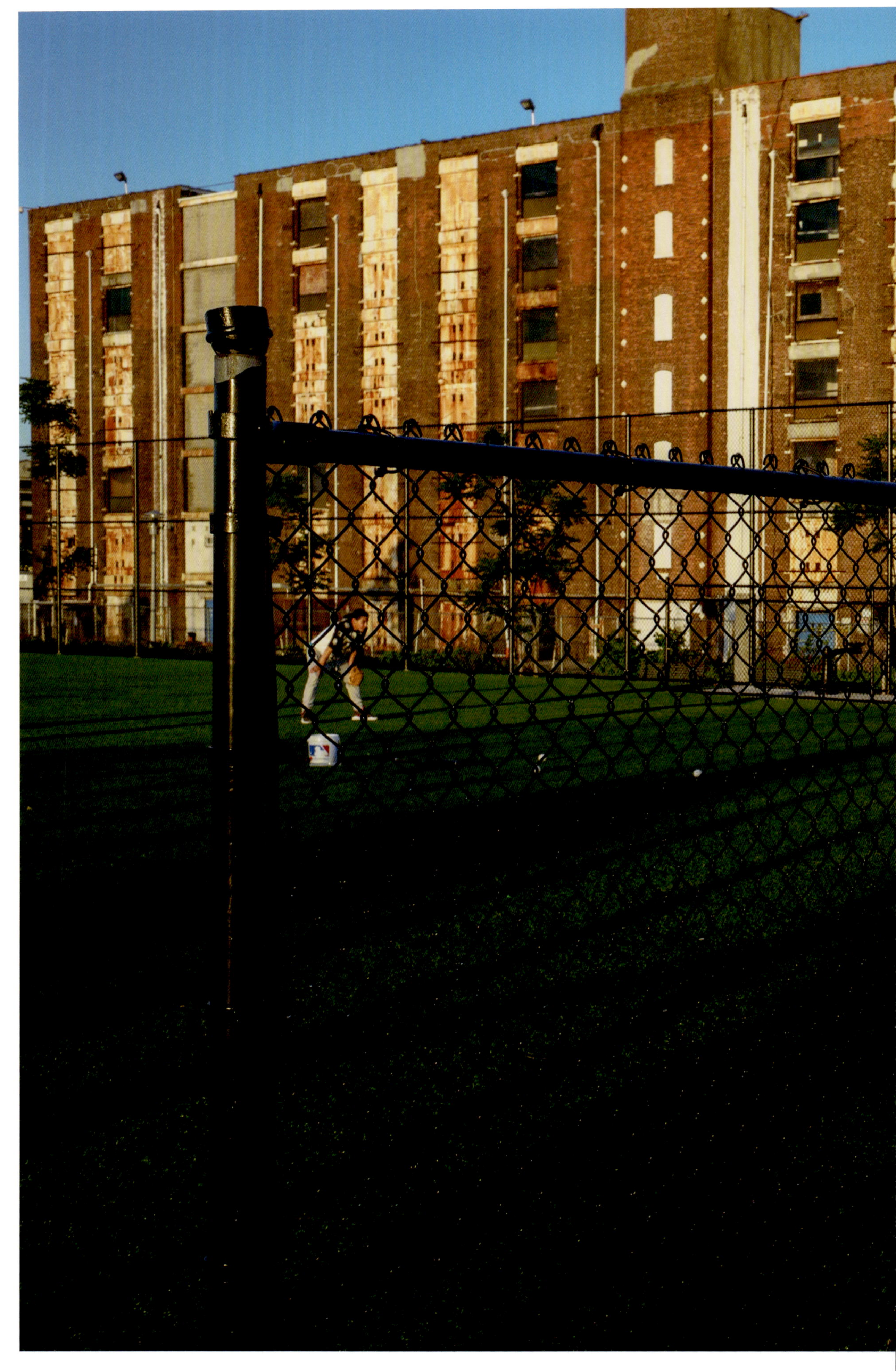

SUNSET PARK, 2015

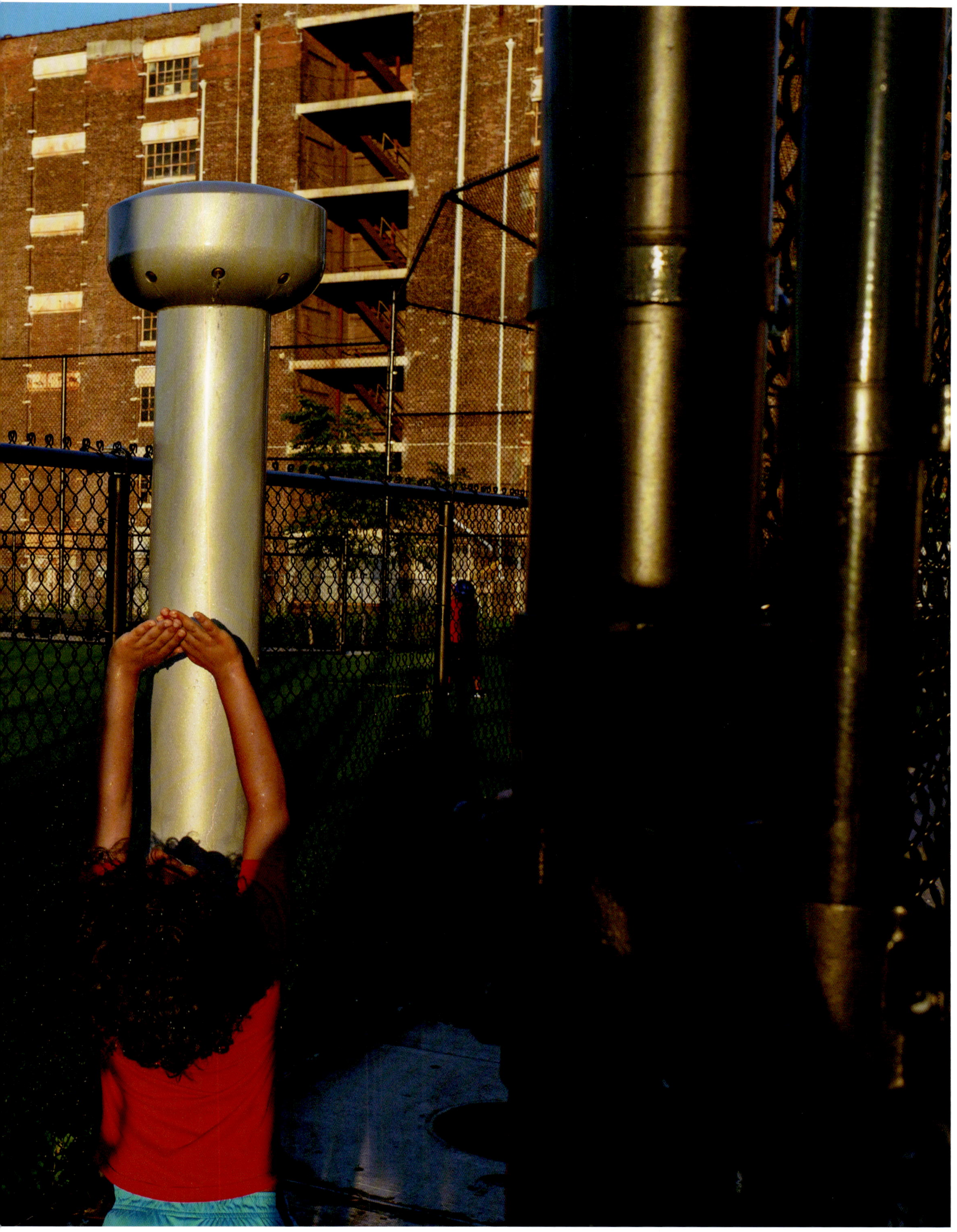

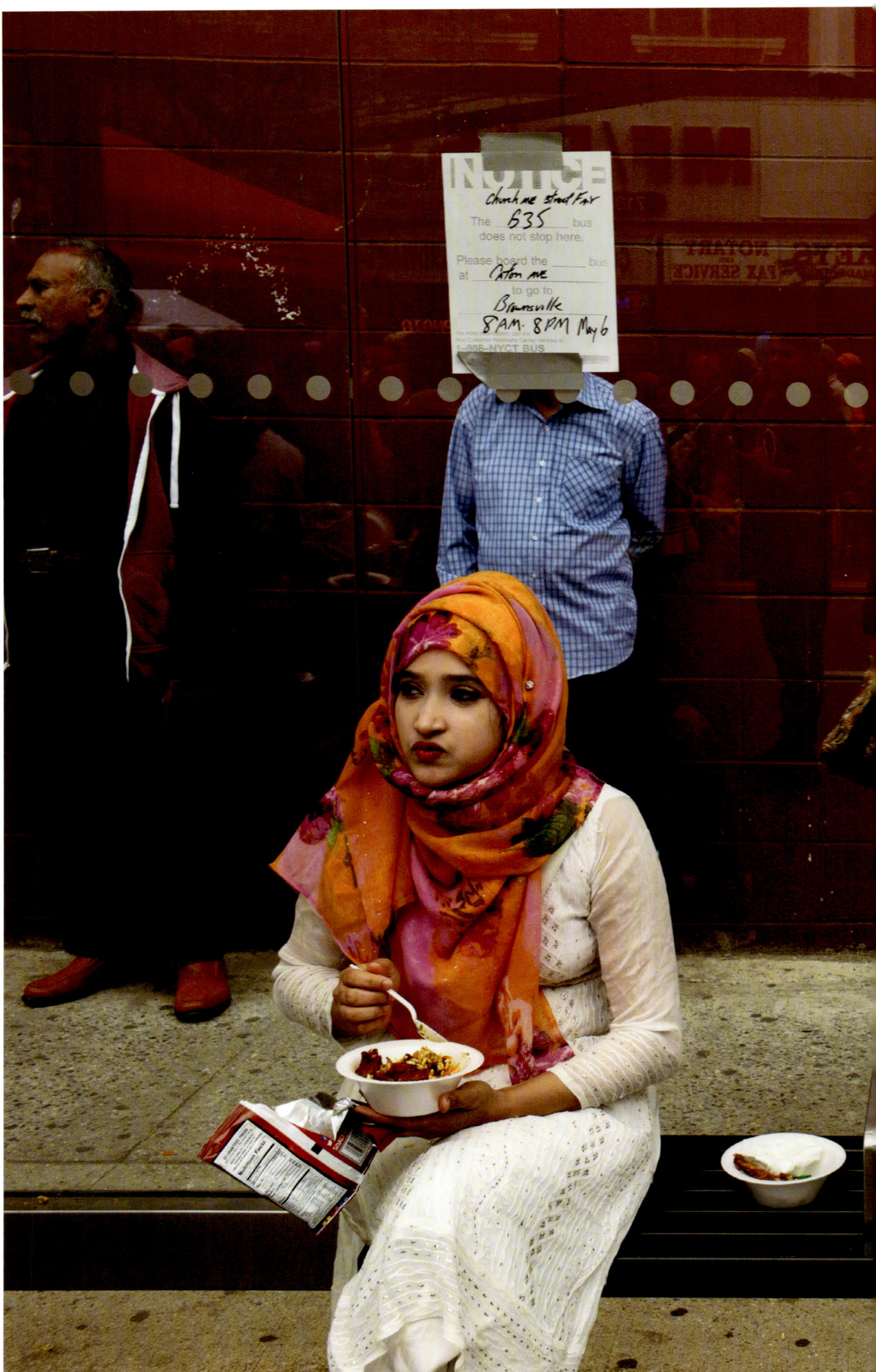

NOTICE
Church ave stad Far
The 635 bus
does not stop here.
Please board the ______ bus
at Cxton ave
to go to
Brownsville
8 AM - 8 PM May 6
1-888-NYCT BUS

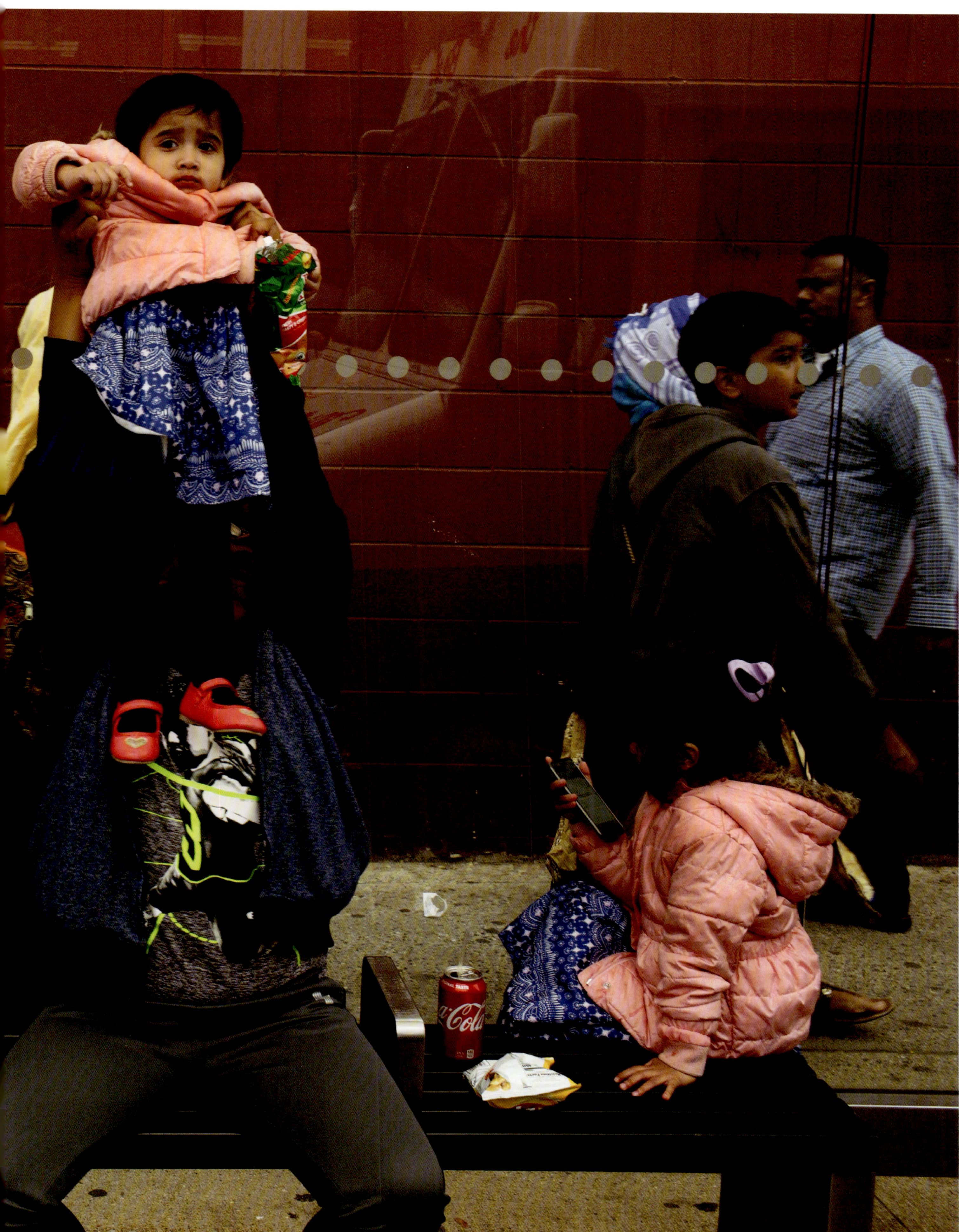

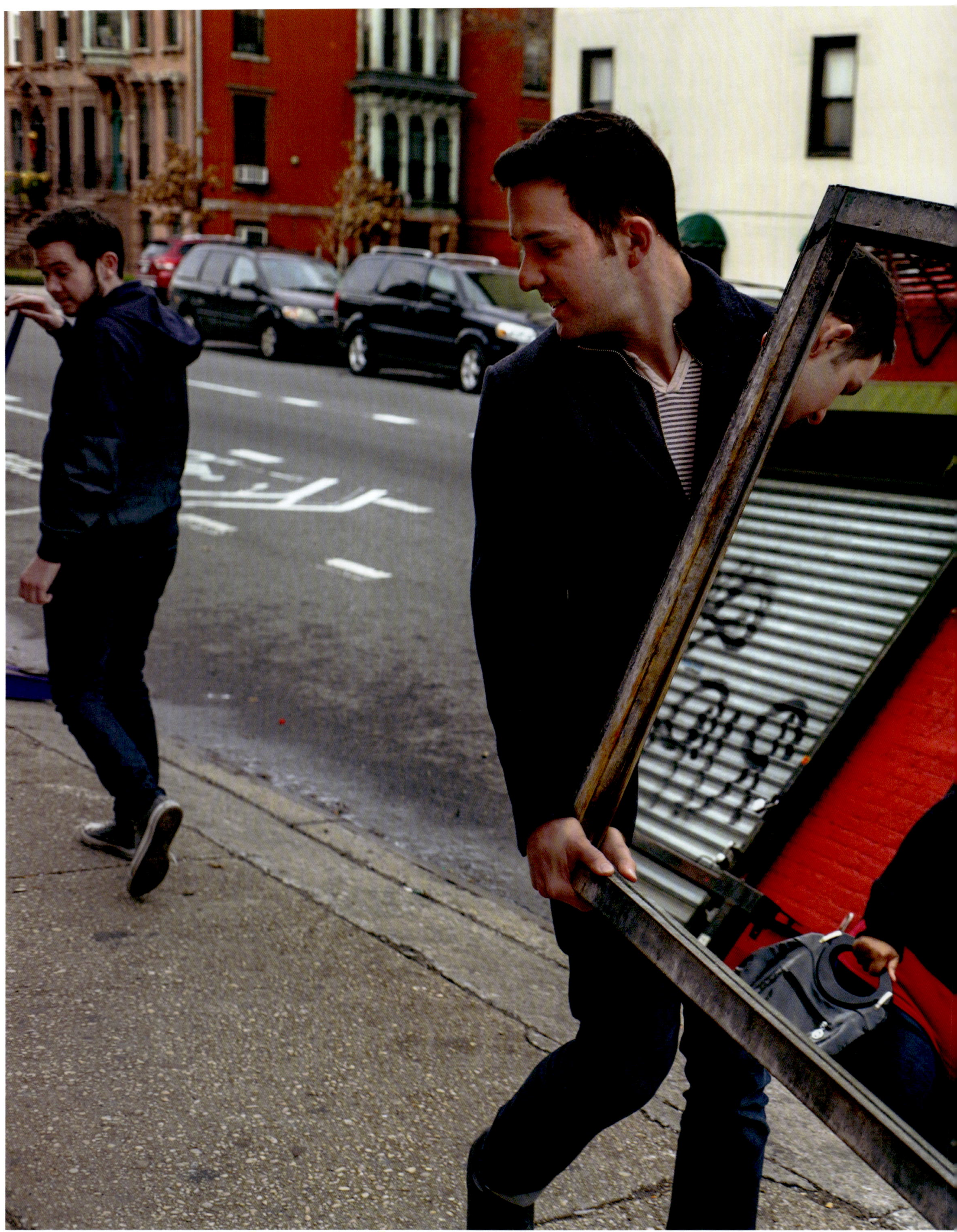

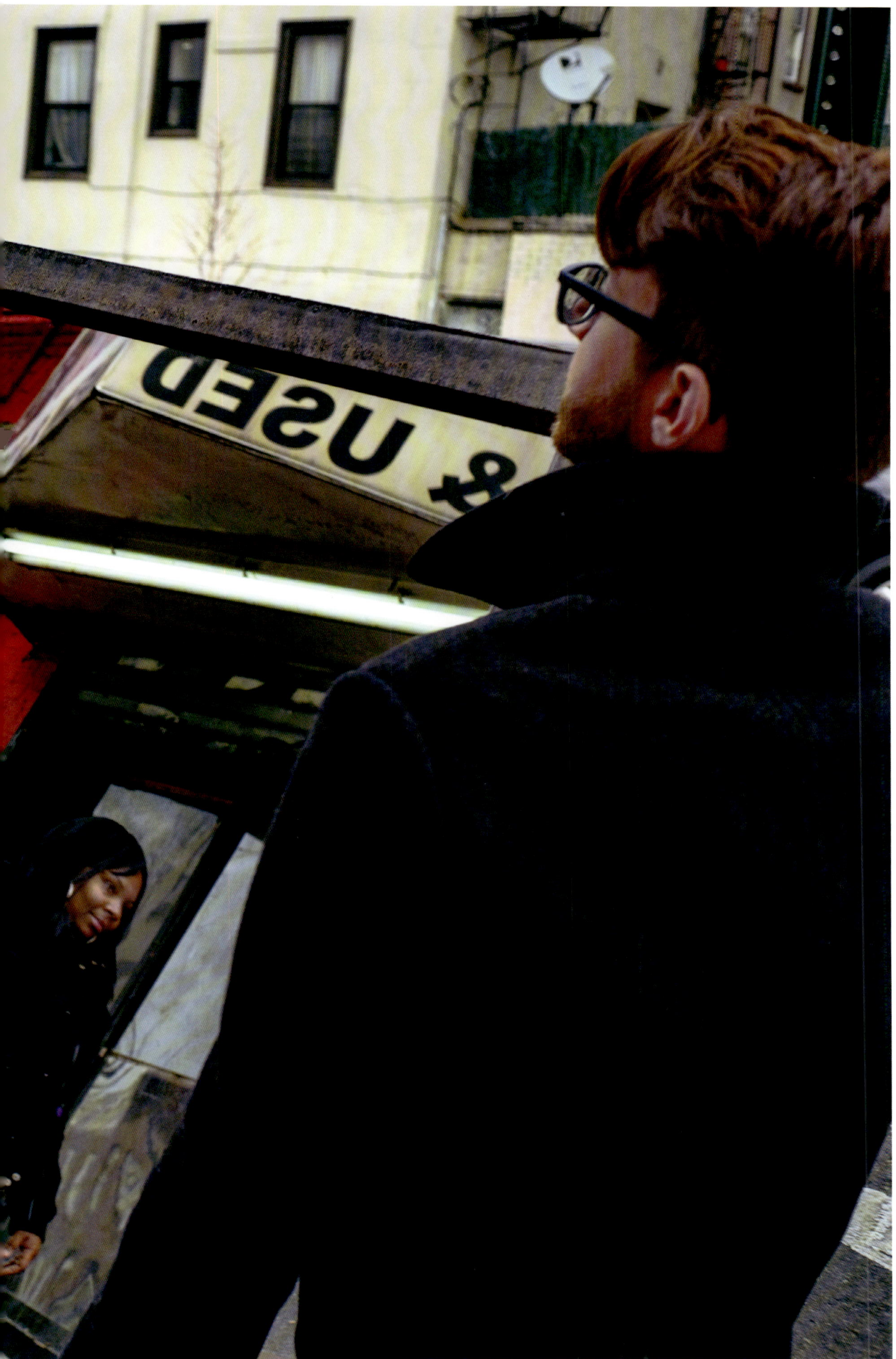

BEDFORD-STUYVESANT, 2014

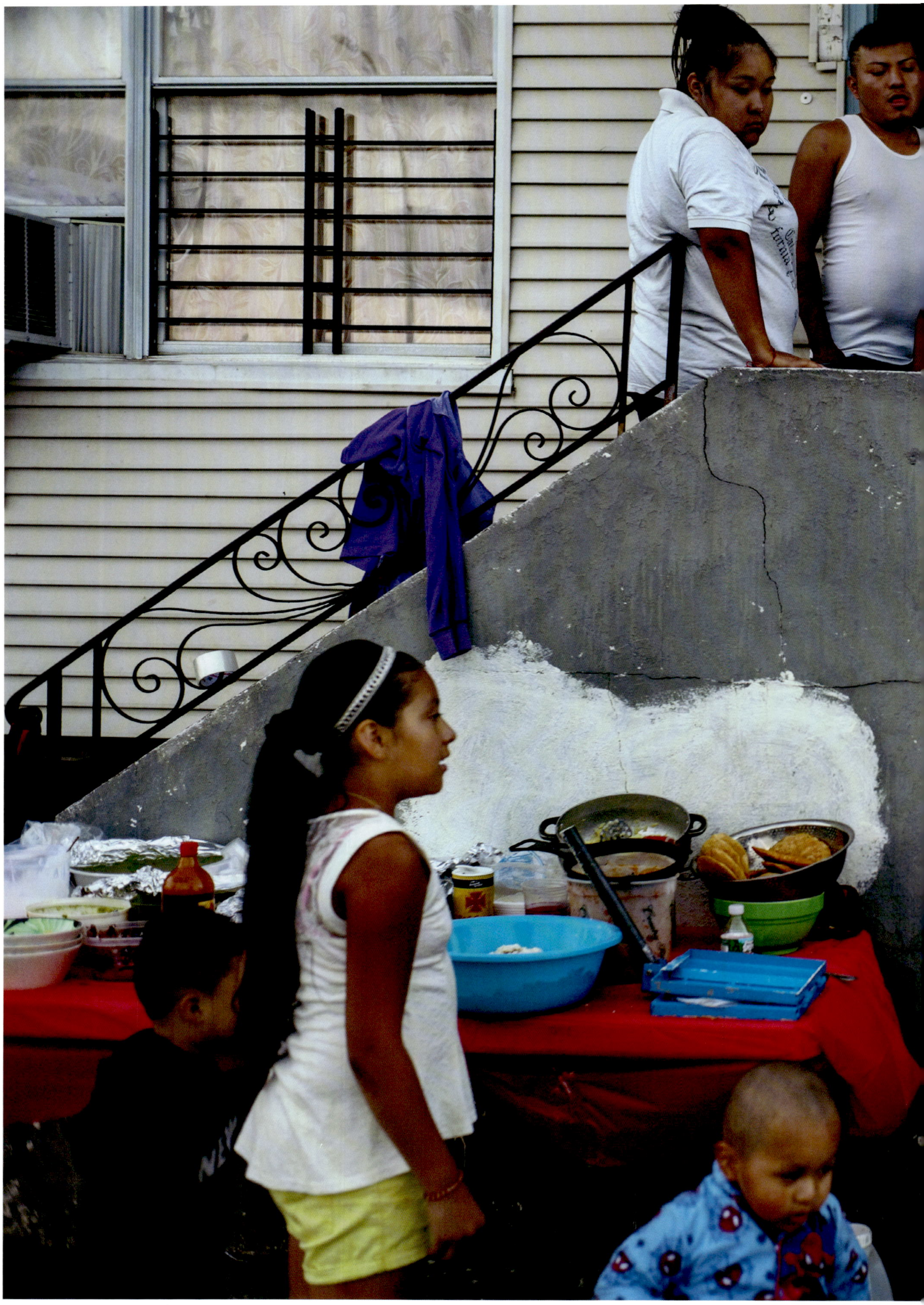

CONEY ISLAND, 2015

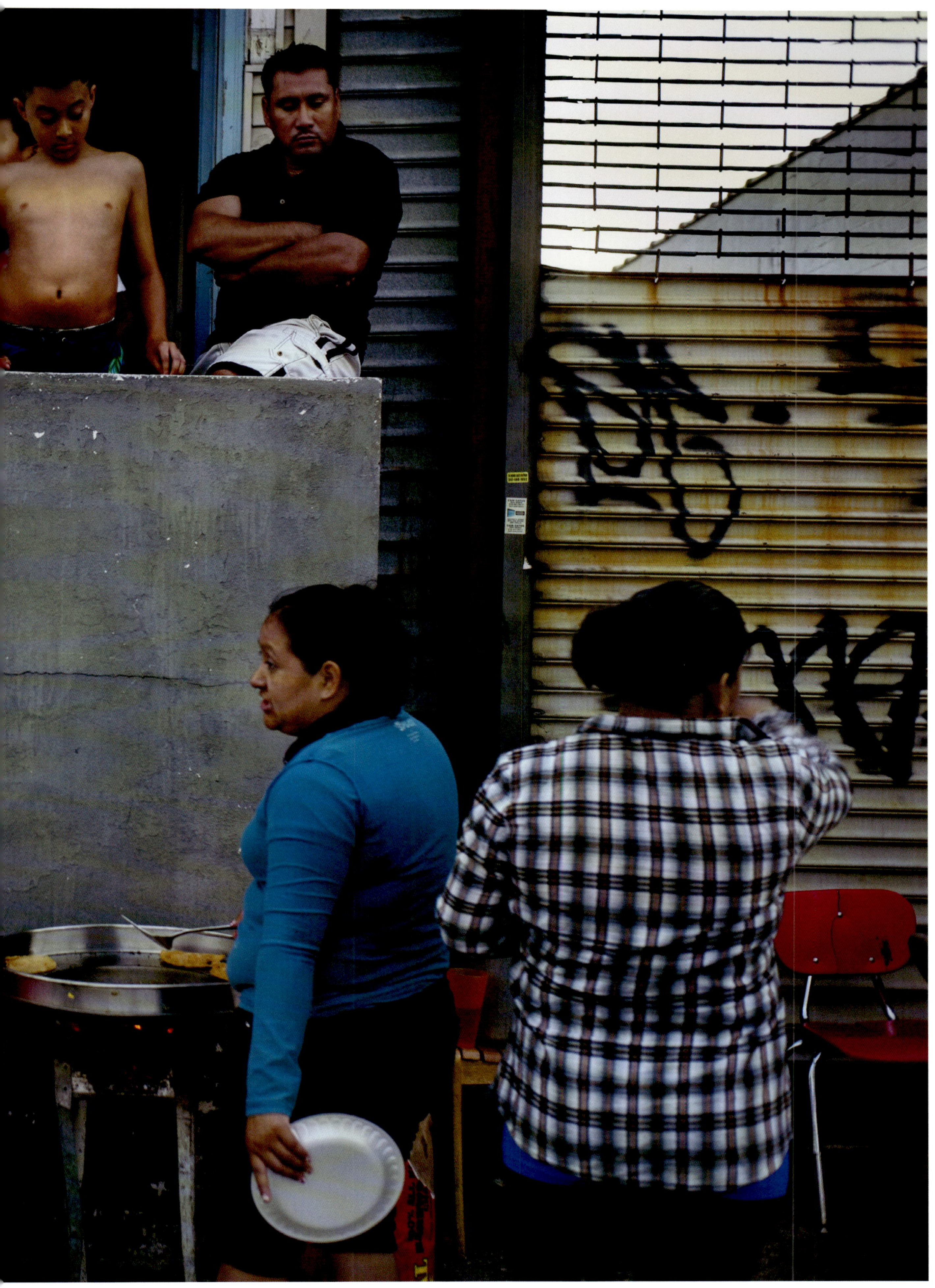

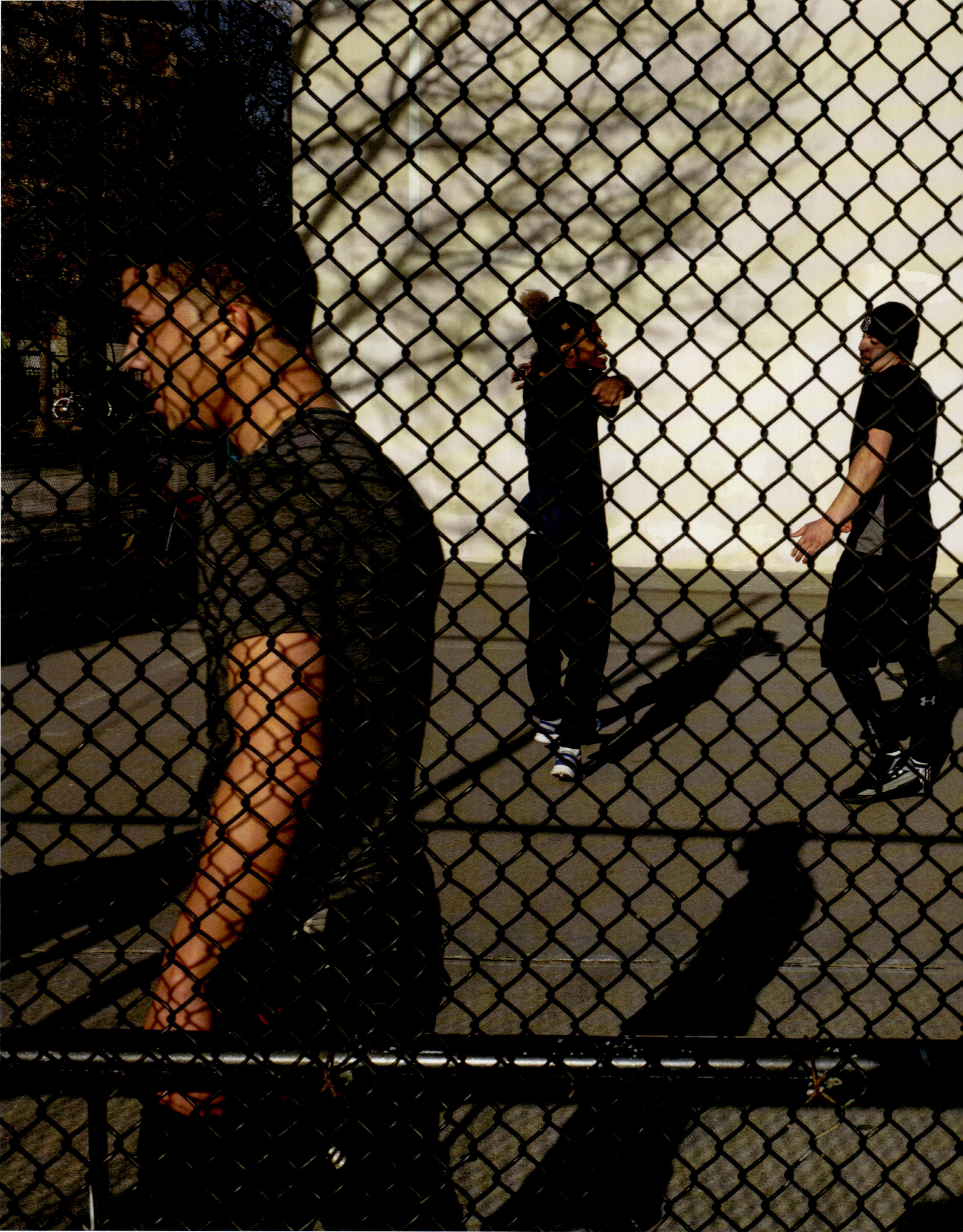

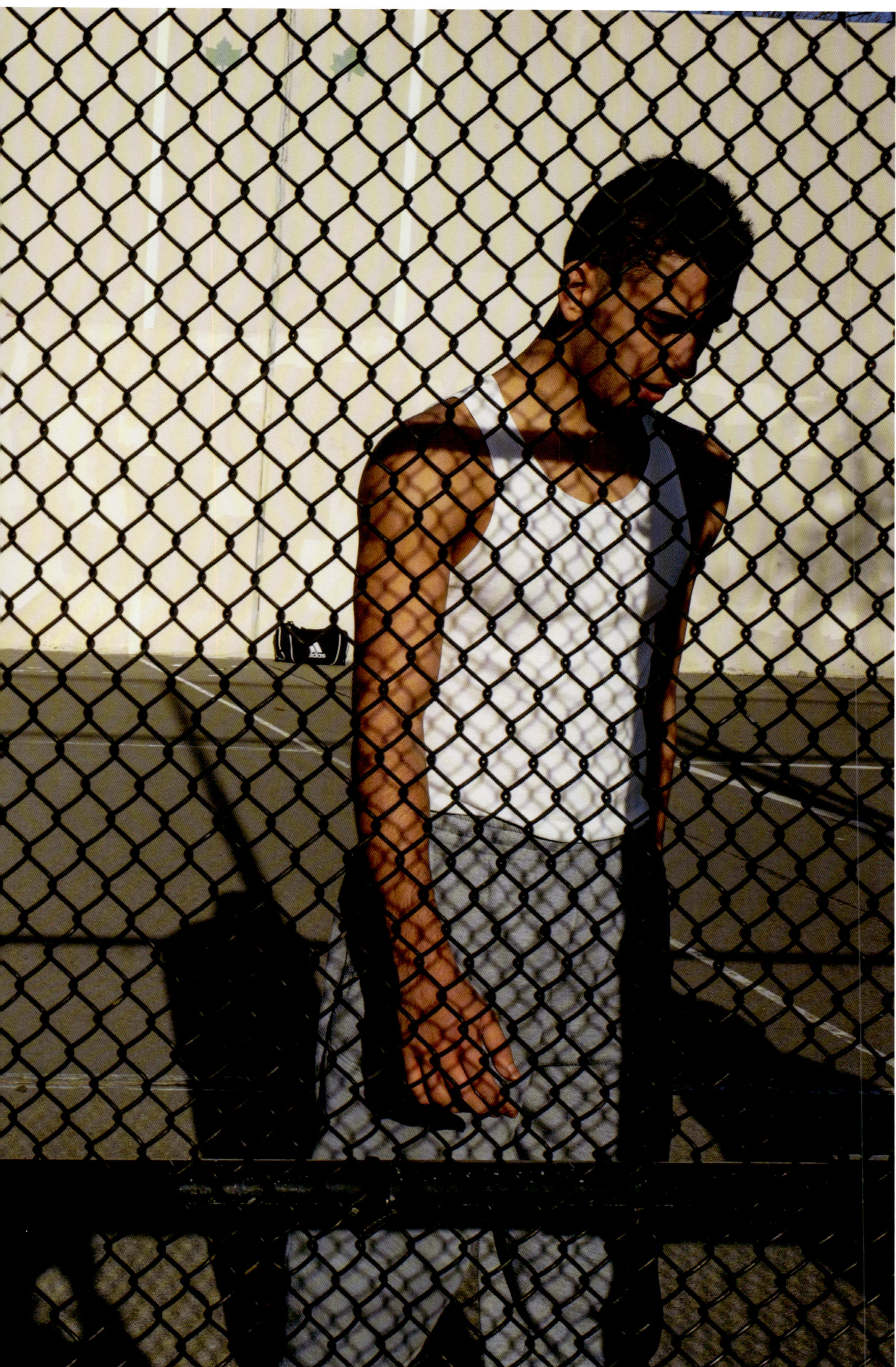

BUSHWICK, 2017

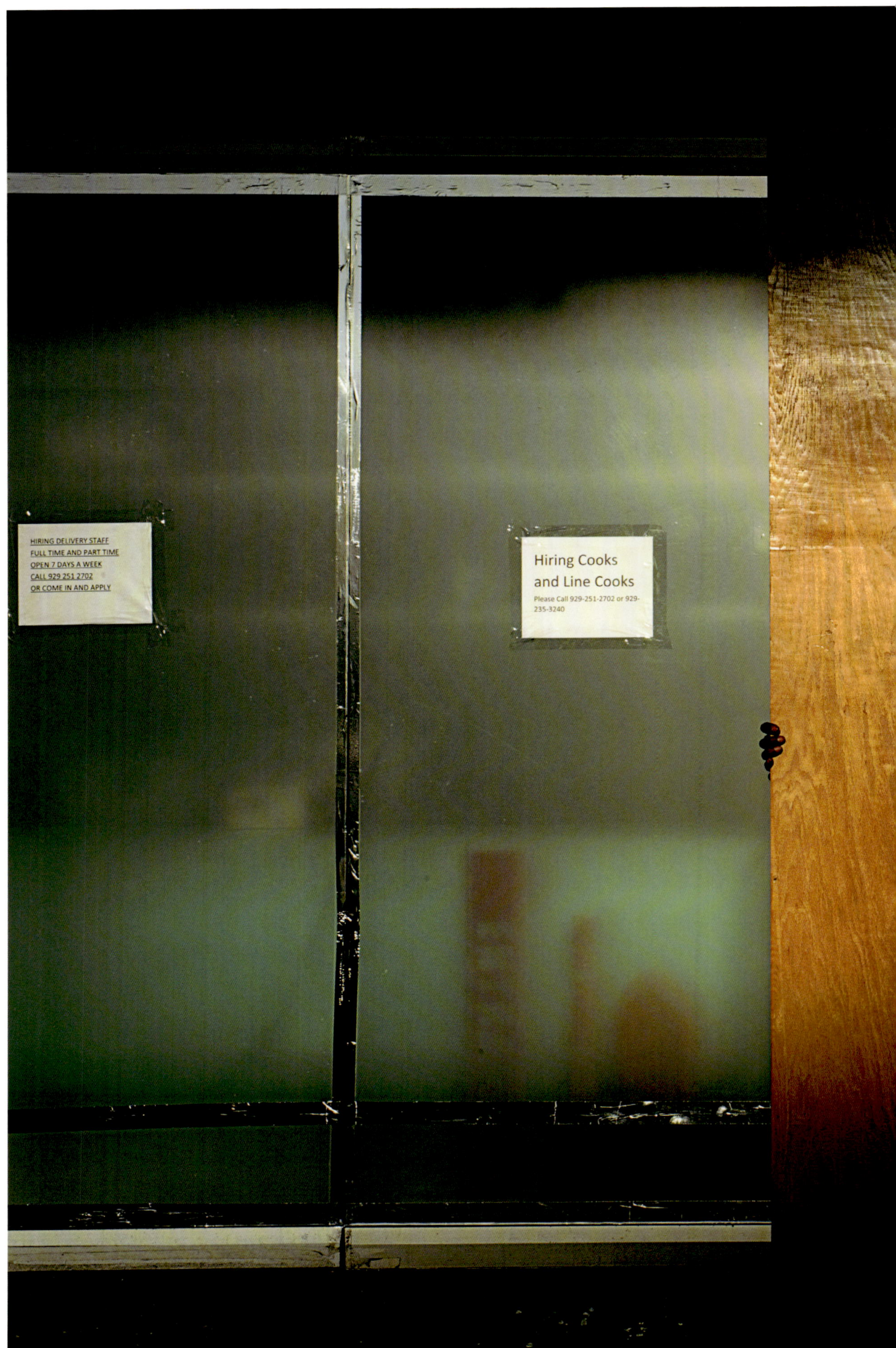
HIRING DELIVERY STAFF
FULL TIME AND PART TIME
OPEN 7 DAYS A WEEK
CALL 929 251 2702
OR COME IN AND APPLY
Hiring Cooks
and Line Cooks
Please Call 929-251-2702 or 929-
235-3240

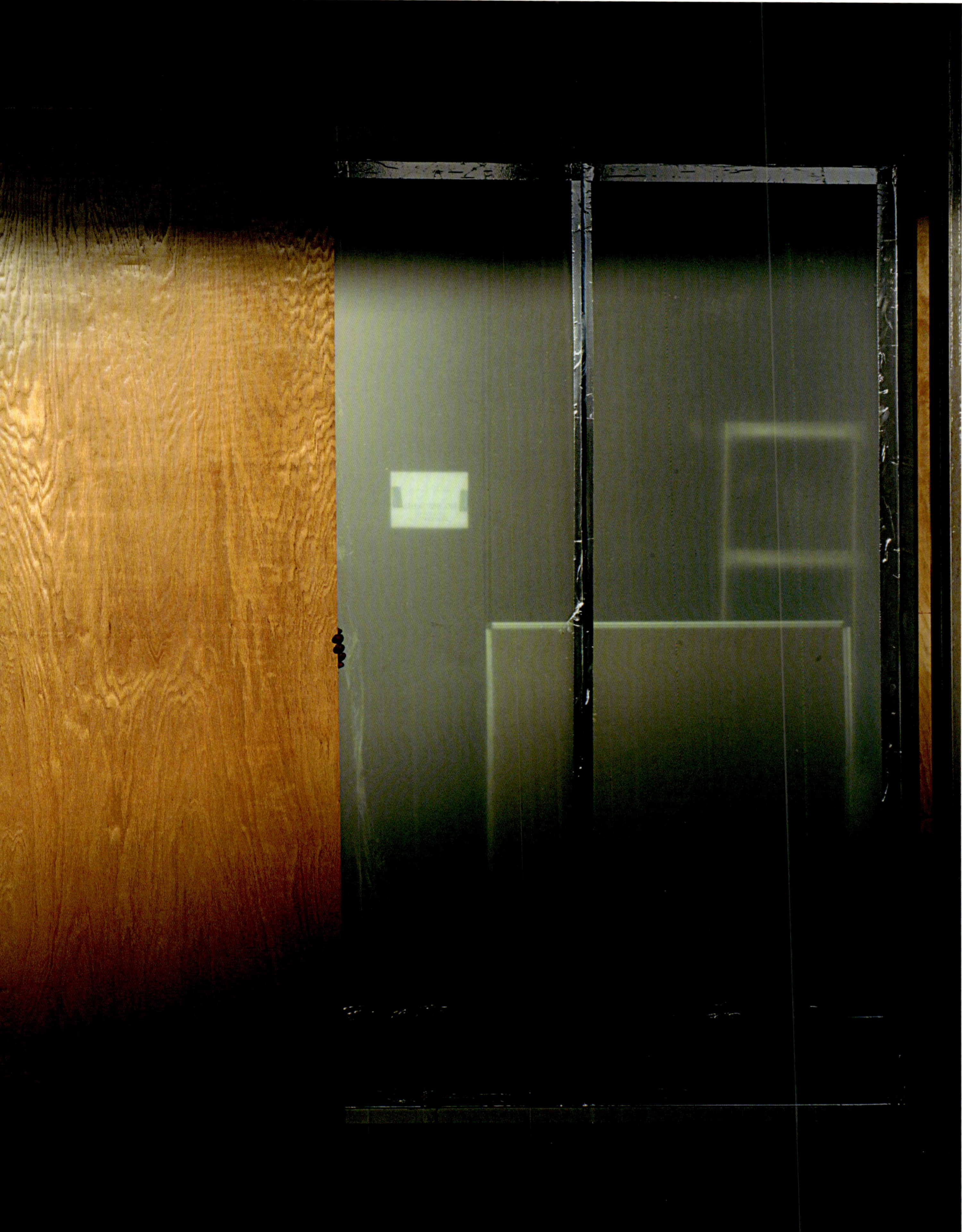

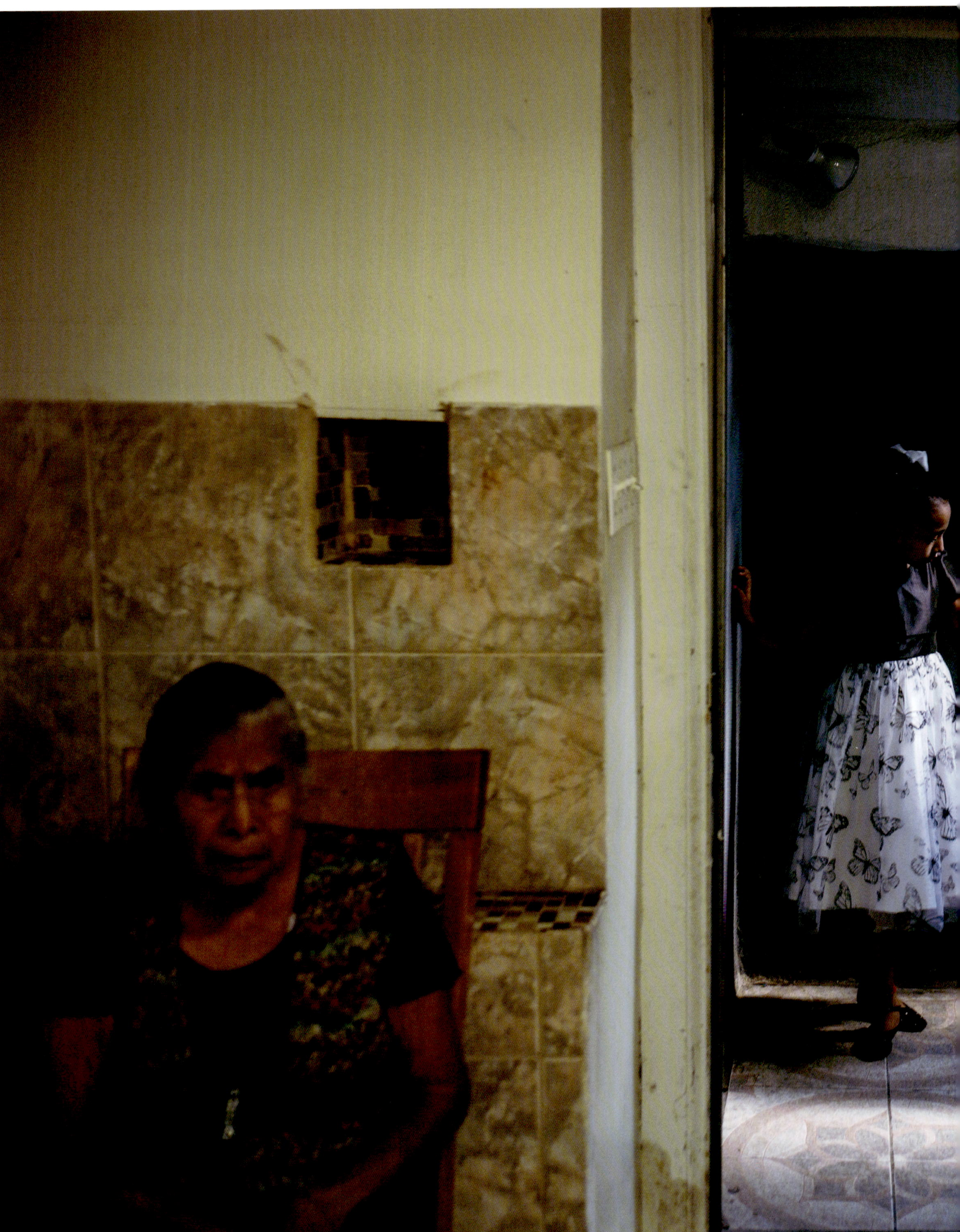

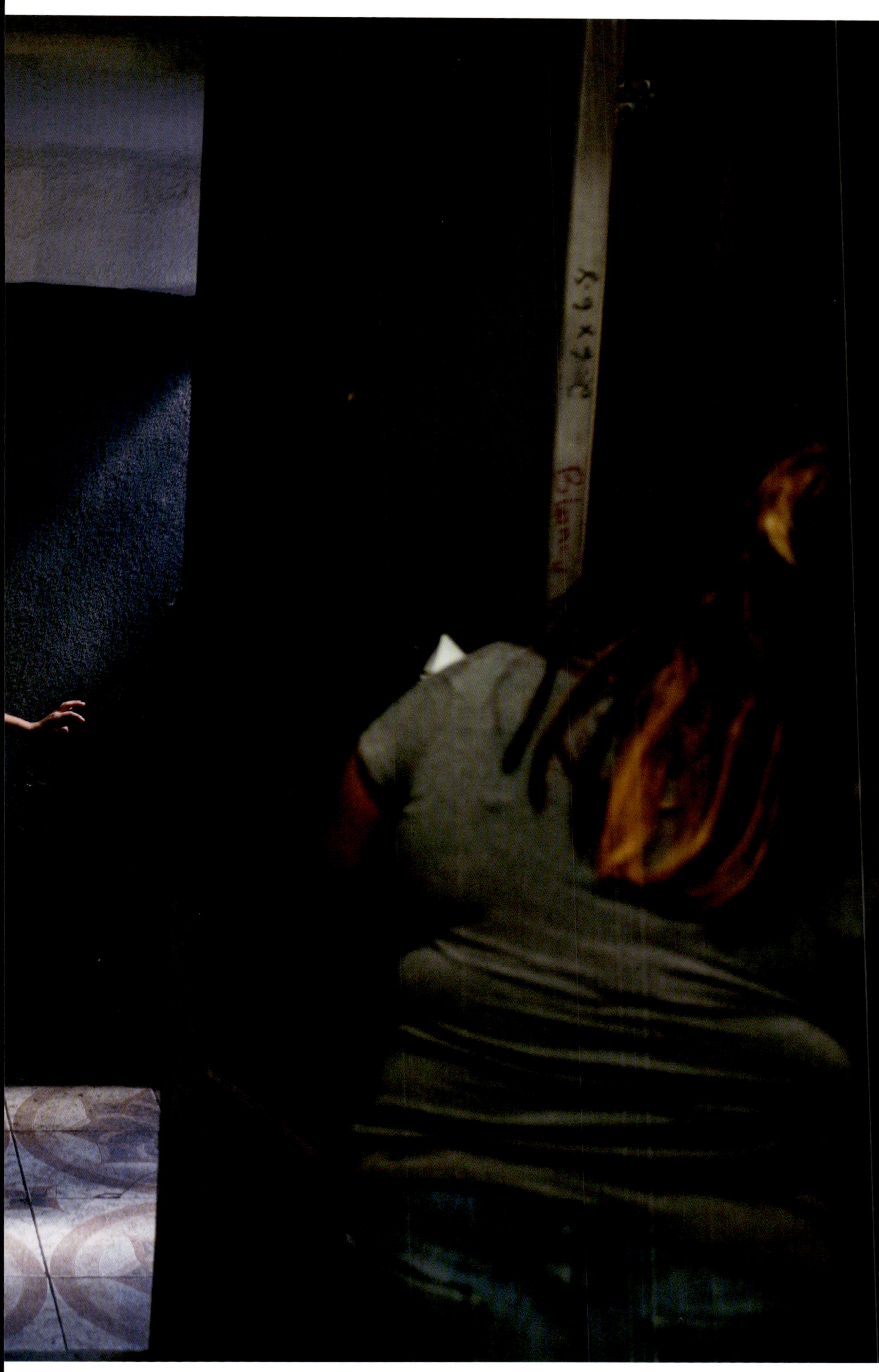

B U S H W I C K , 2 0 1 5

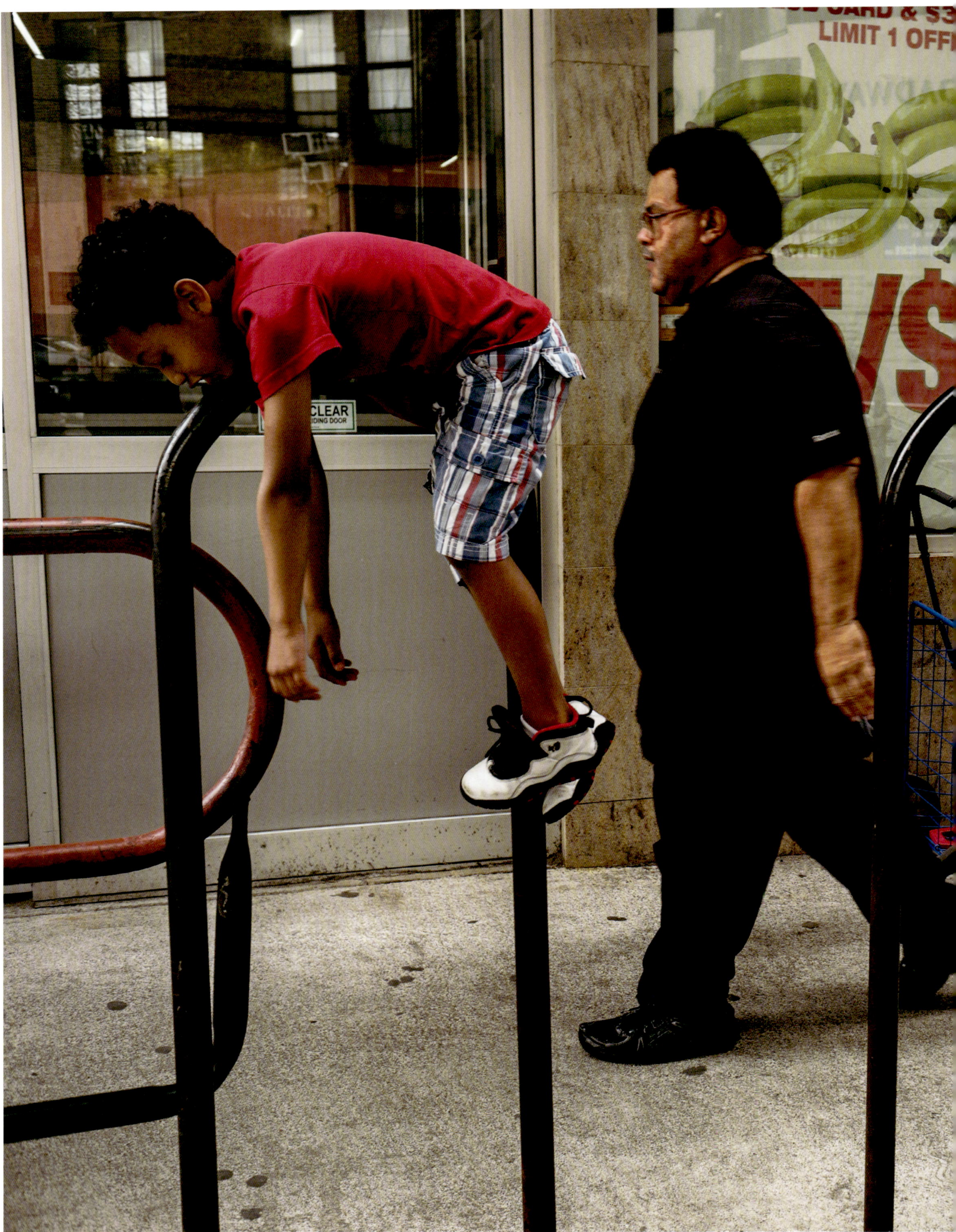
CLEAR
ING DOOR
& S3
LIMIT 1 OFF

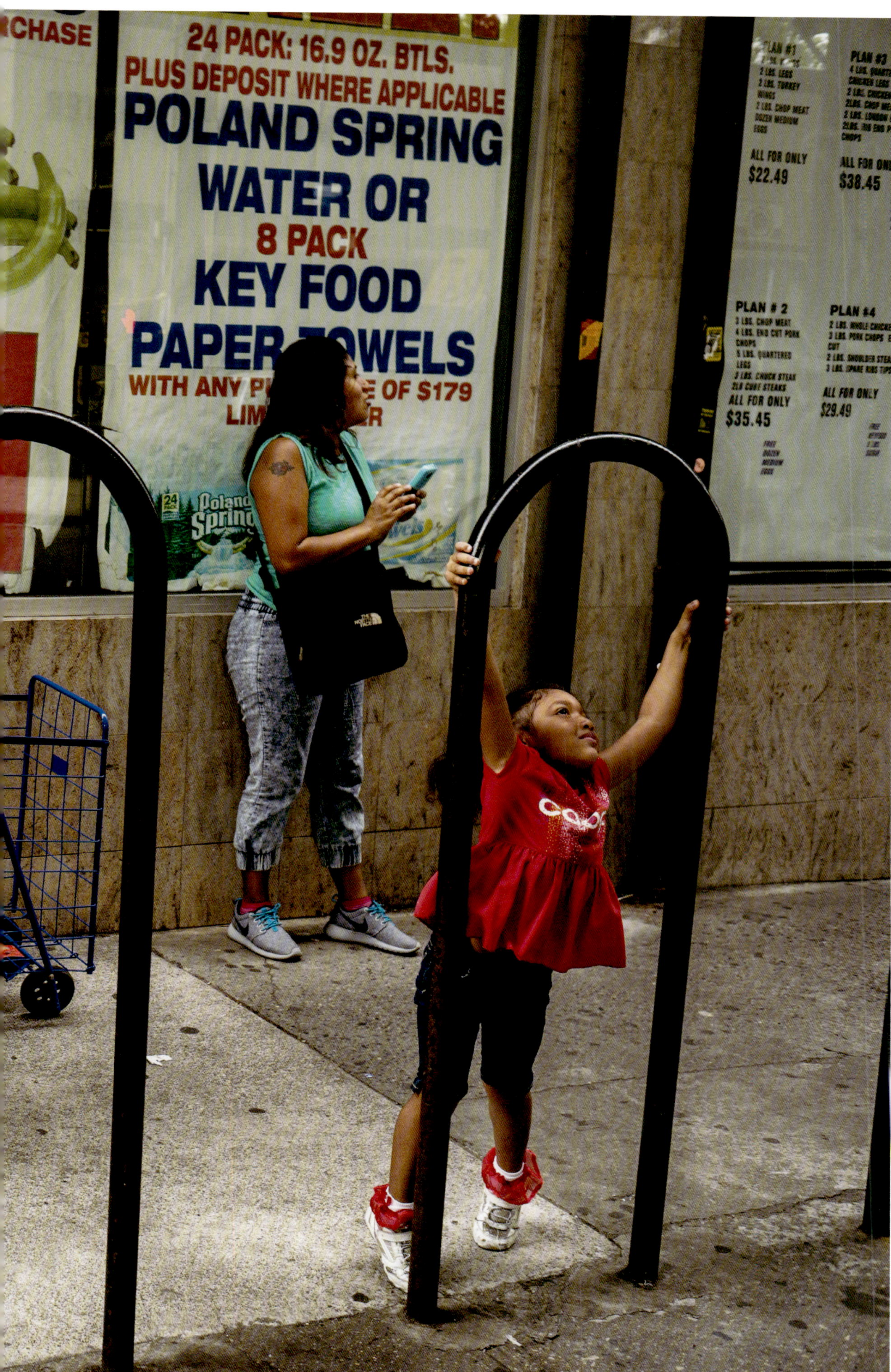
24 PACK: 16.9 OZ. BTLS.
PLUS DEPOSIT WHERE APPLICABLE
POLAND SPRING
WATER OR
8 PACK
KEY FOOD
PAPER TOWELS
WITH ANY PURCHASE OF $179
PLAN #1
2 LBS. LEGS
3 LBS. TURKEY
WINGS
2 LBS. CHOP MEAT
DOZEN MEDIUM
EGGS
ALL FOR ONLY
$22.49
PLAN #3
4 LBS. QUARTERED
CHICKEN LEGS
2 LBS. CHICKEN
2 LBS. CHOP MEAT
2 LBS. LONDON B
2 LBS. RIB END PO
CHOPS
ALL FOR ONLY
$38.45
PLAN # 2
3 LBS. CHOP MEAT
4 LBS. END CUT PORK
CHOPS
5 LBS. QUARTERED
LEGS
3 LBS. CHUCK STEAK
2LB CUBE STEAKS
ALL FOR ONLY
$35.45
PLAN #4
2 LBS. WHOLE CHICKEN
3 LBS. PORK CHOPS E
CUT
2 LBS. SHOULDER STEA
3 LBS. SPARE RIBS TIPS
ALL FOR ONLY
$29.49
CODO

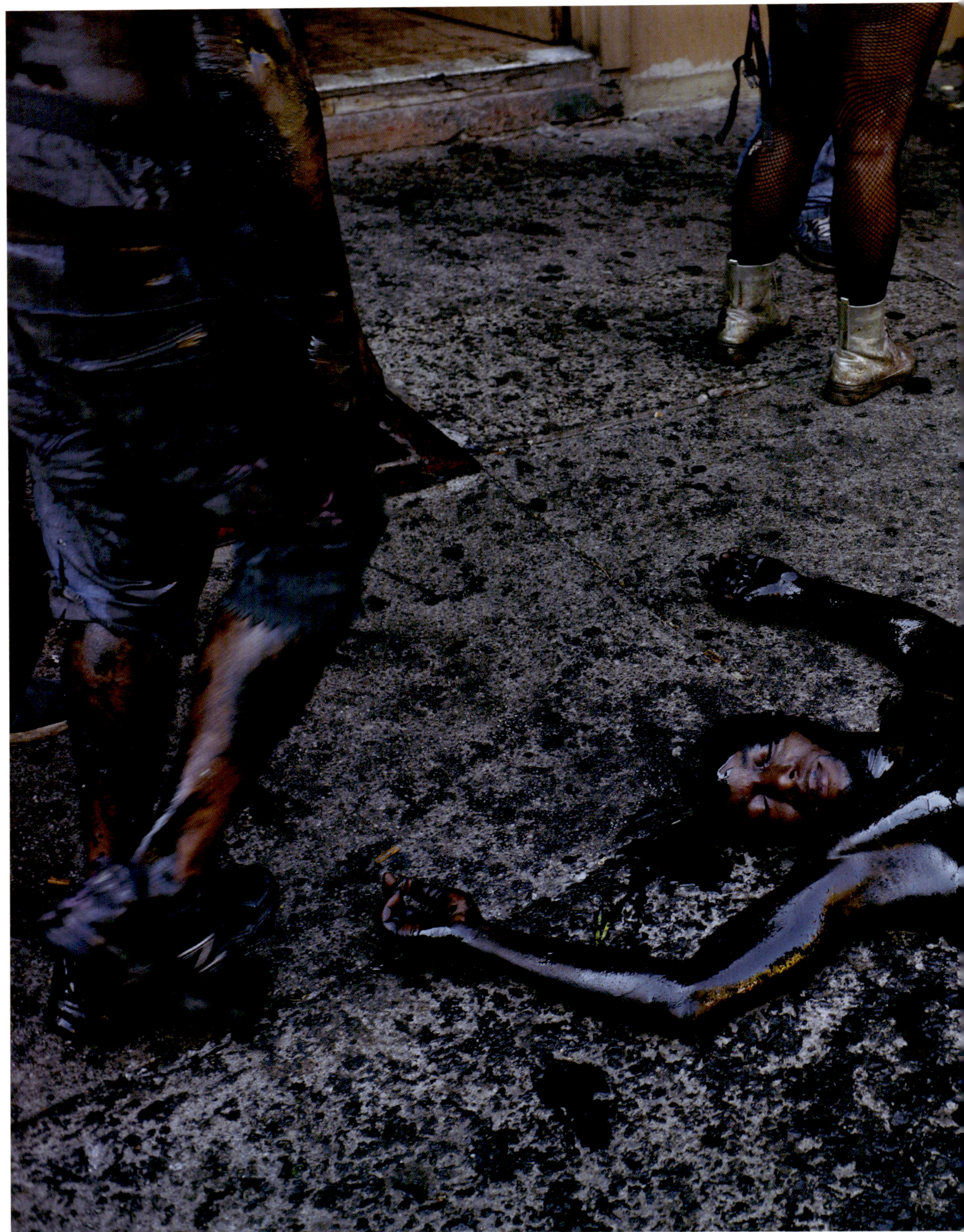

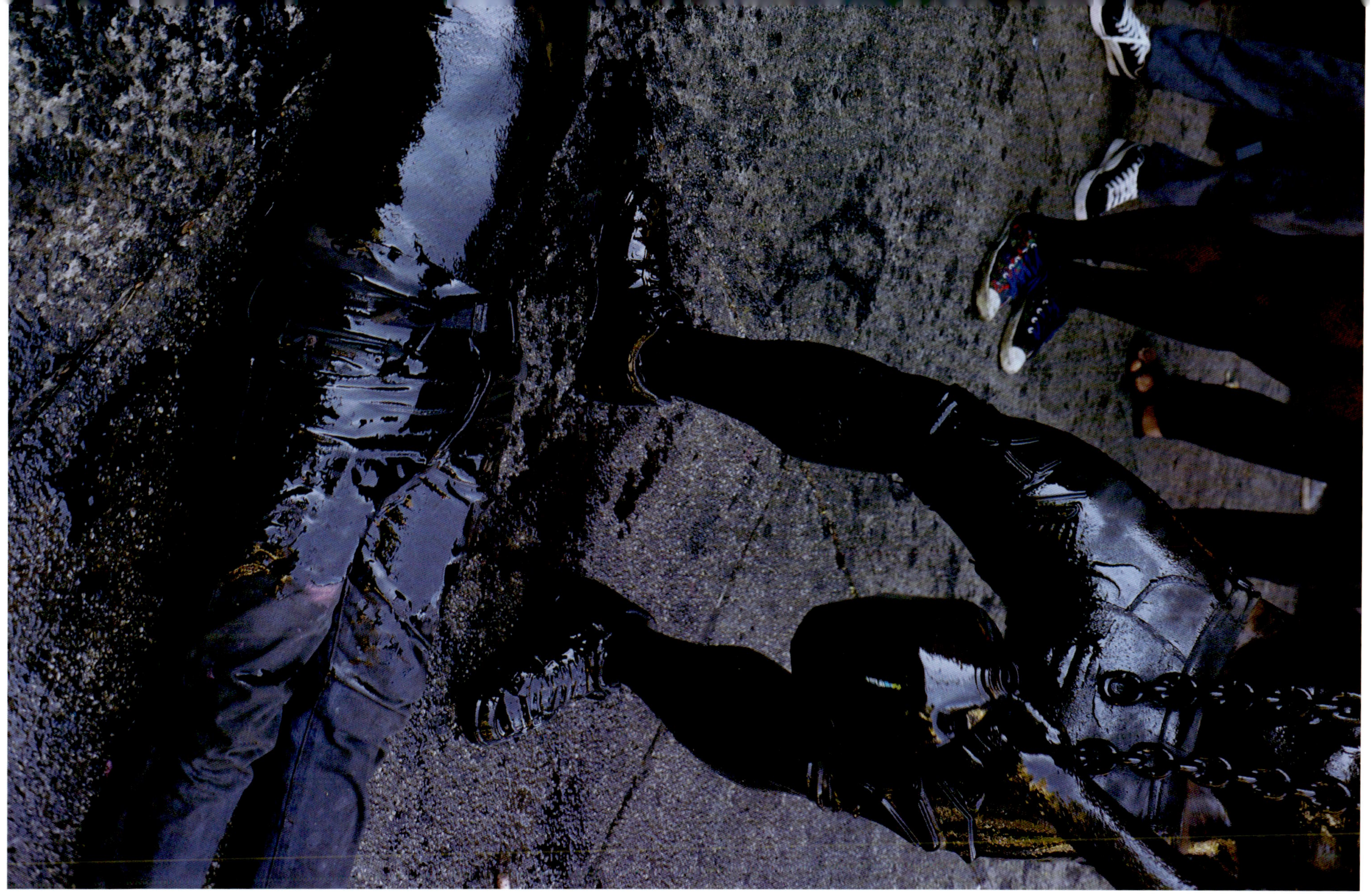

CROWN HEIGHTS, J'OUVERT, 2015

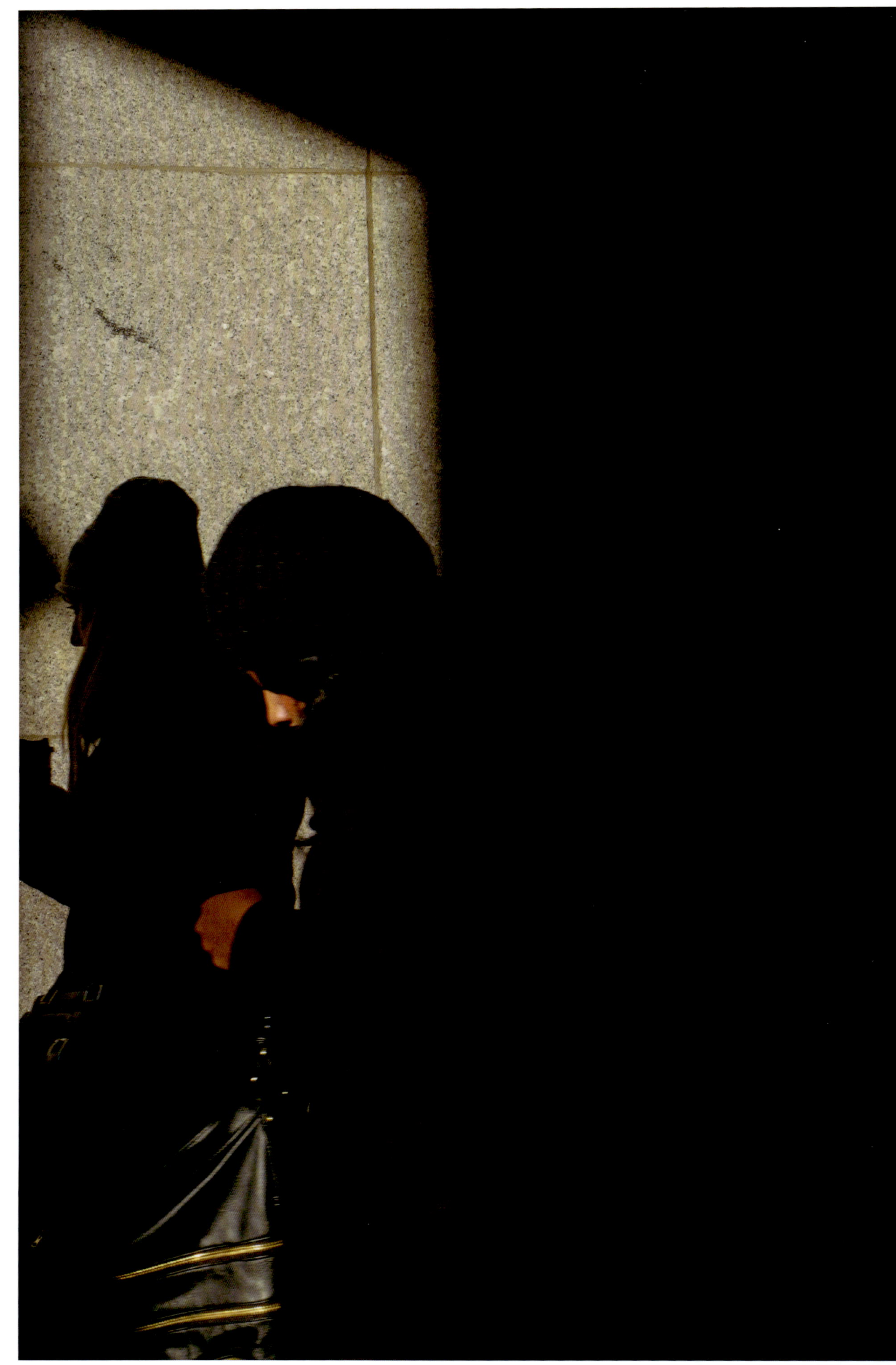

DOWNTOWN BROOKLYN, 2014

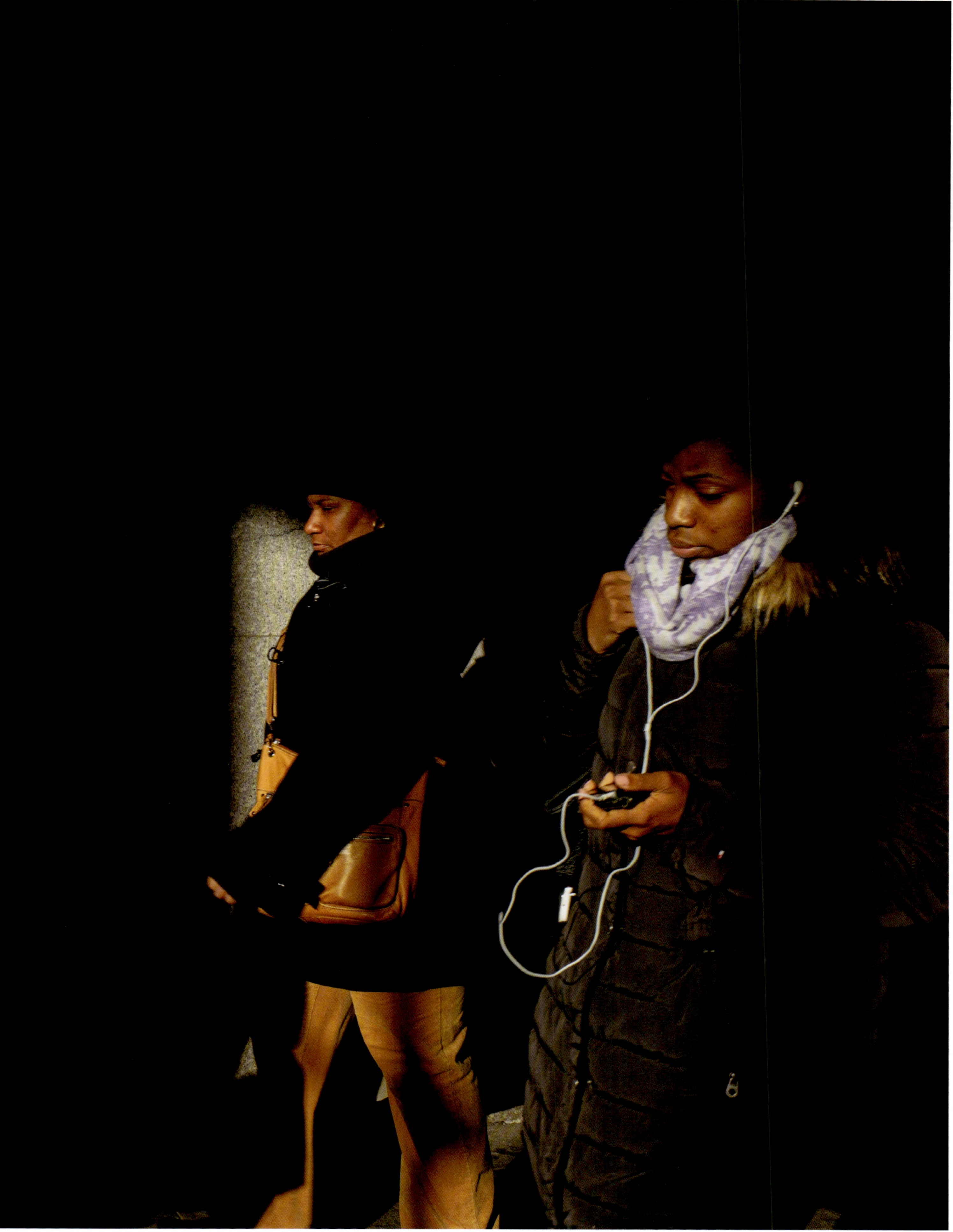

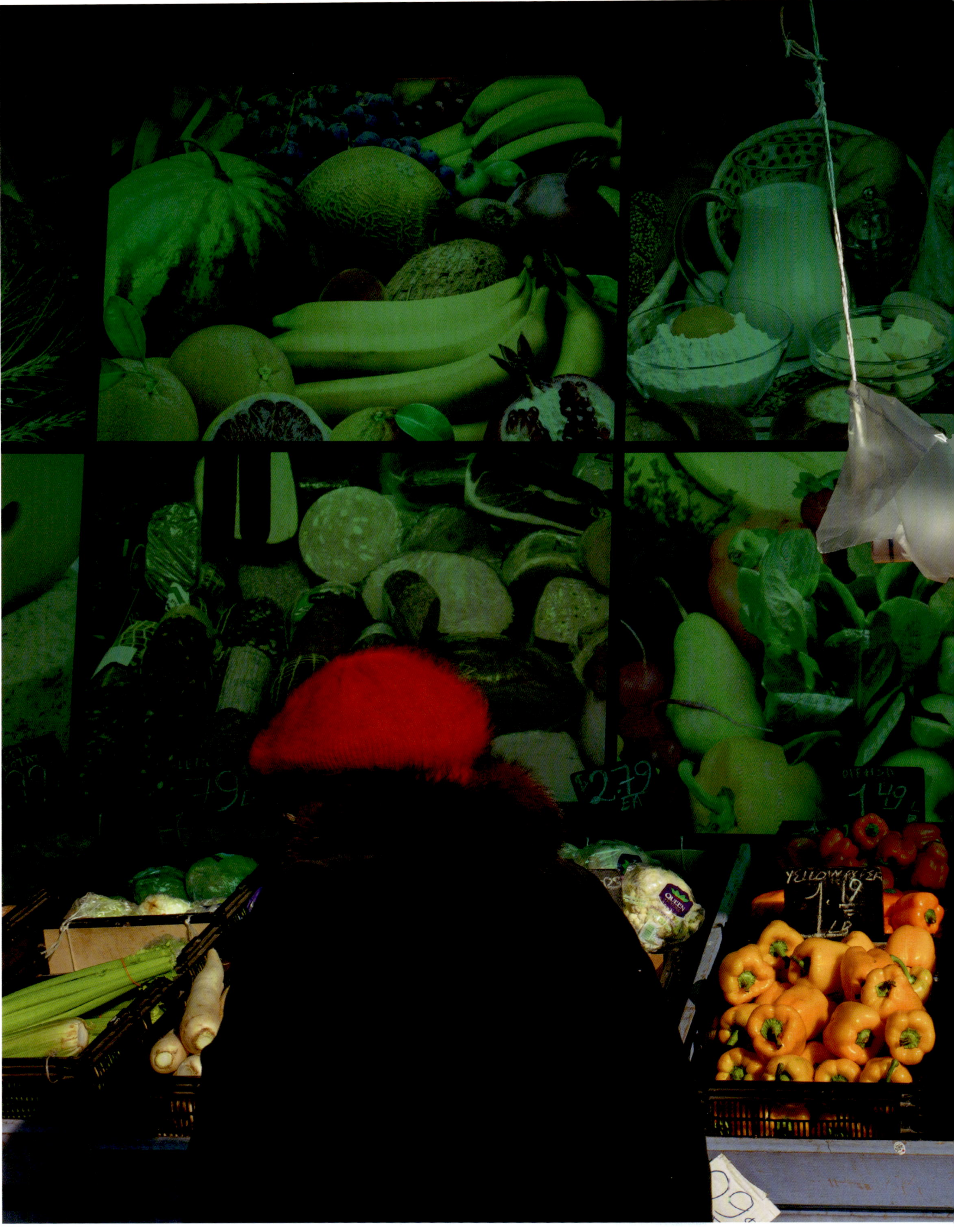

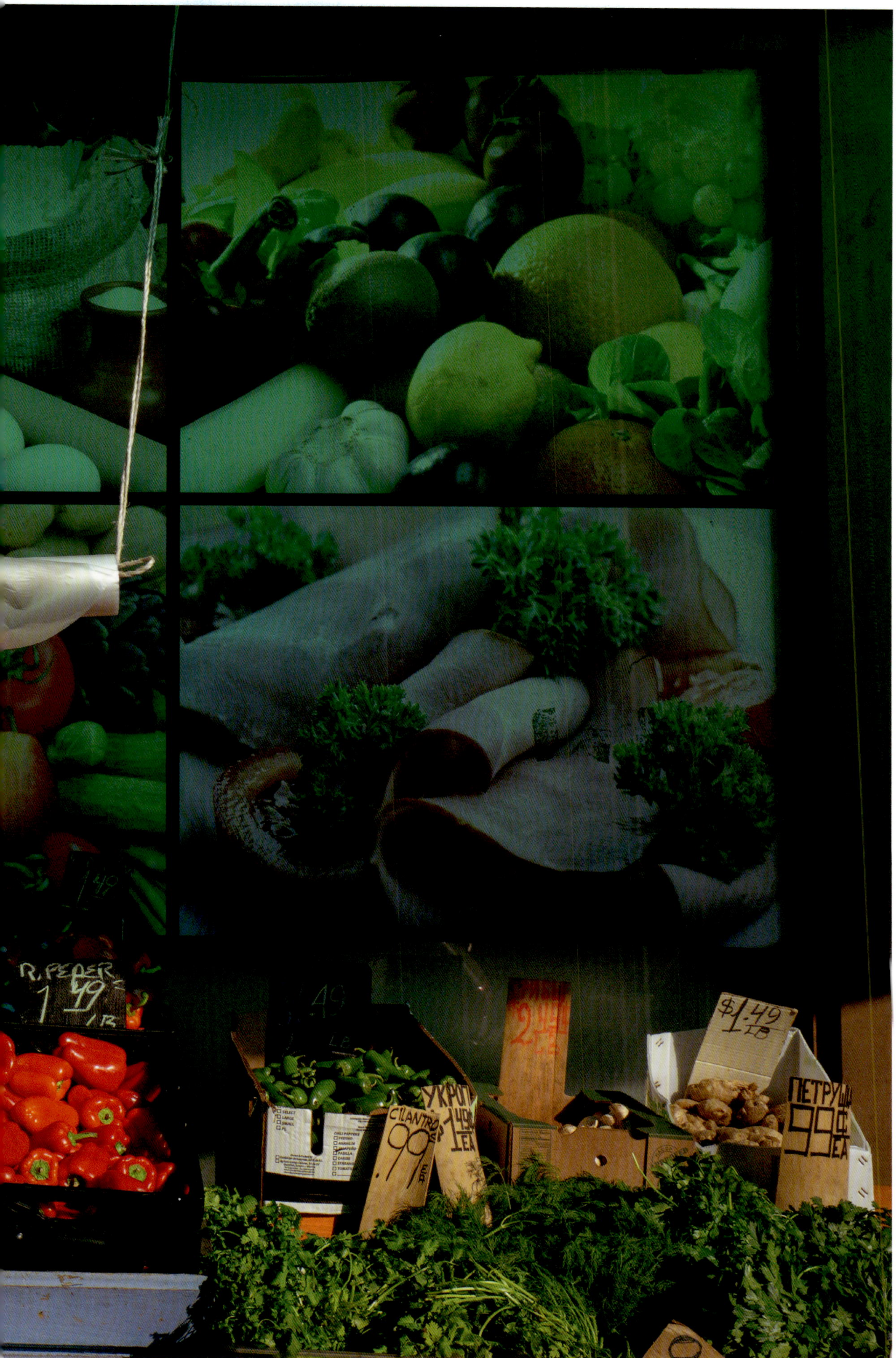

R. PEPER
1.49
/ LB
$1.49 LB
ПЕТРУШ
99 EA
CILANTRO
99 EA
УКРОП
1.49 EA

BRIGHTON BEACH, 2016

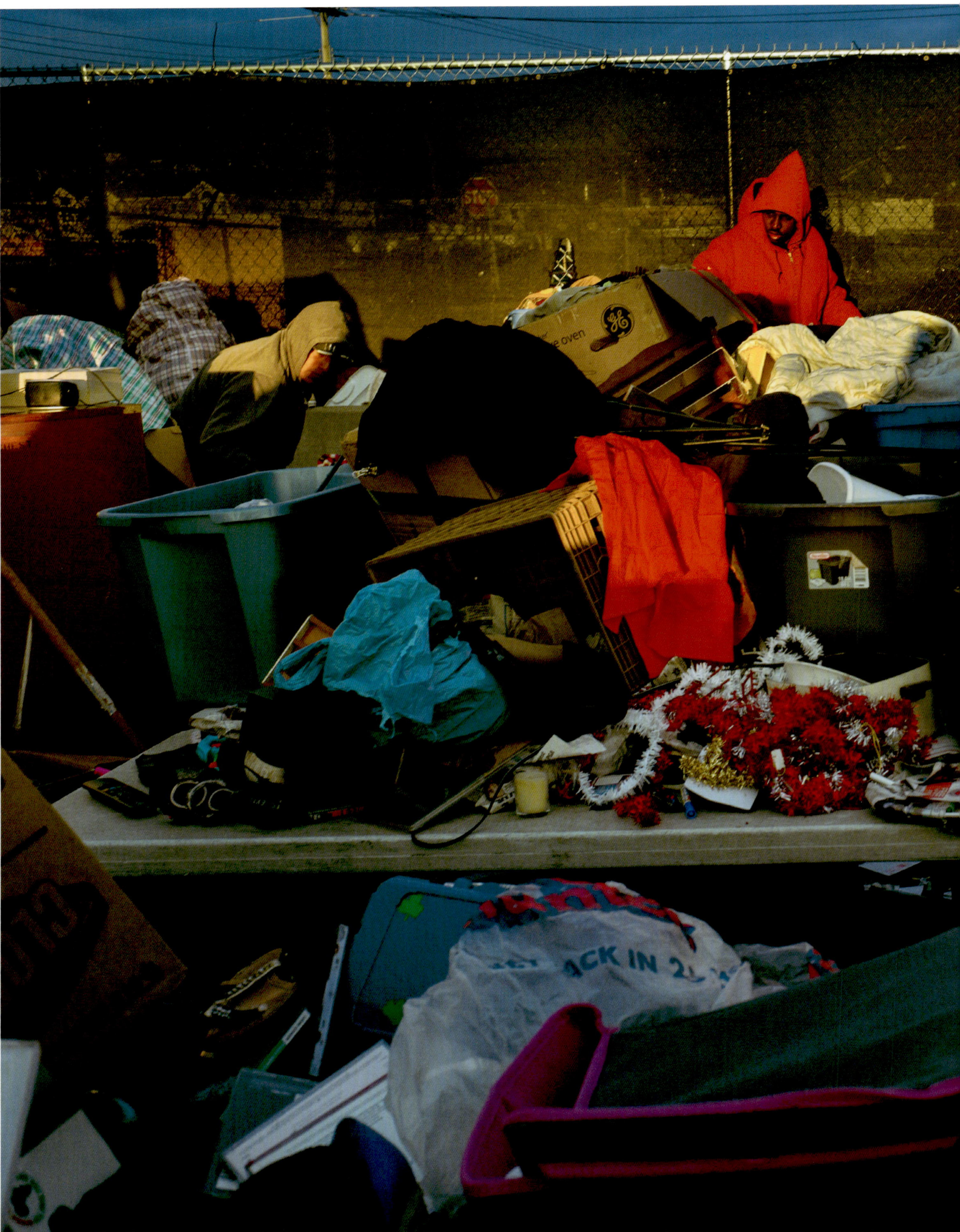

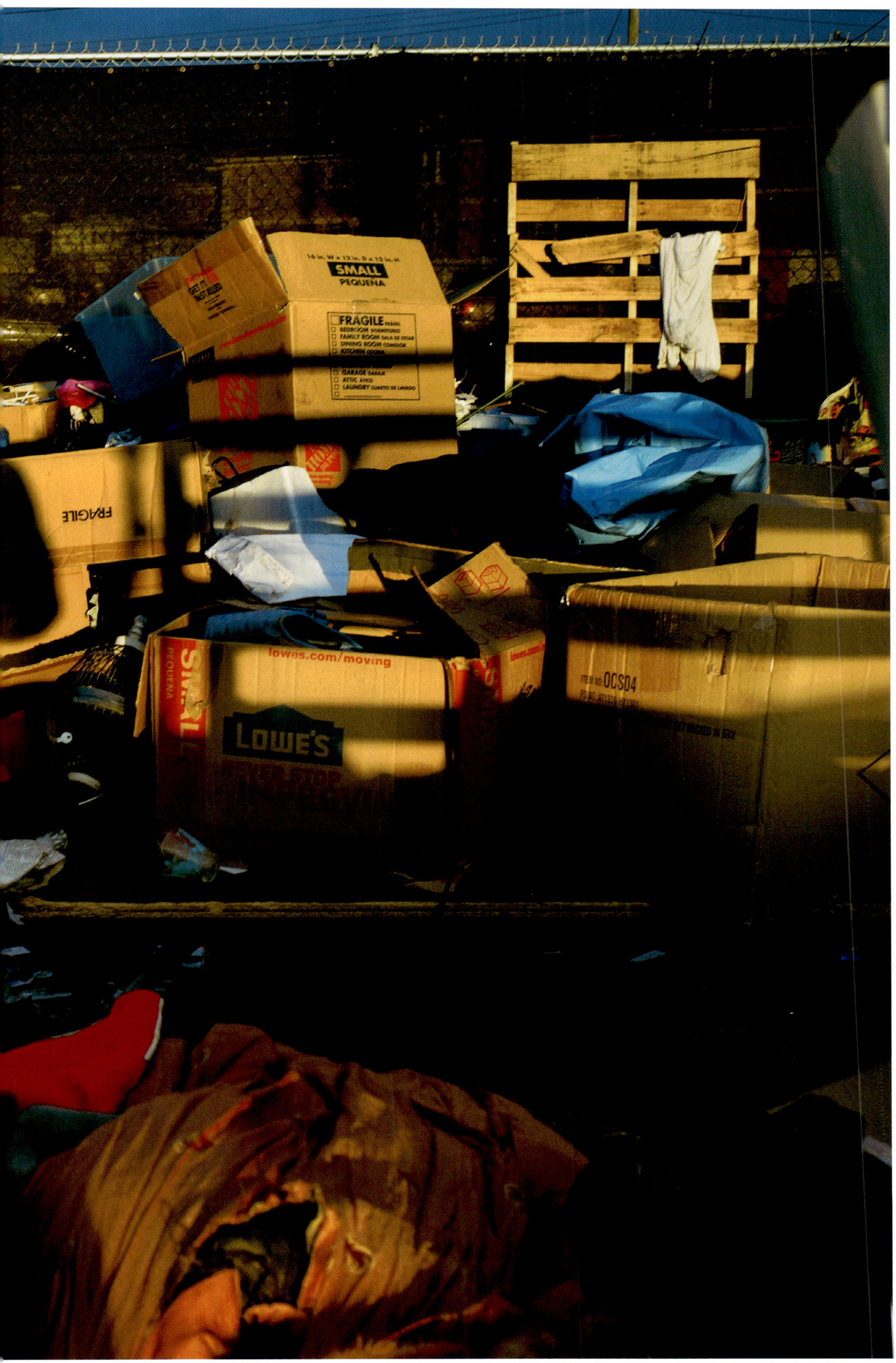

EAST NEW YORK, 2014

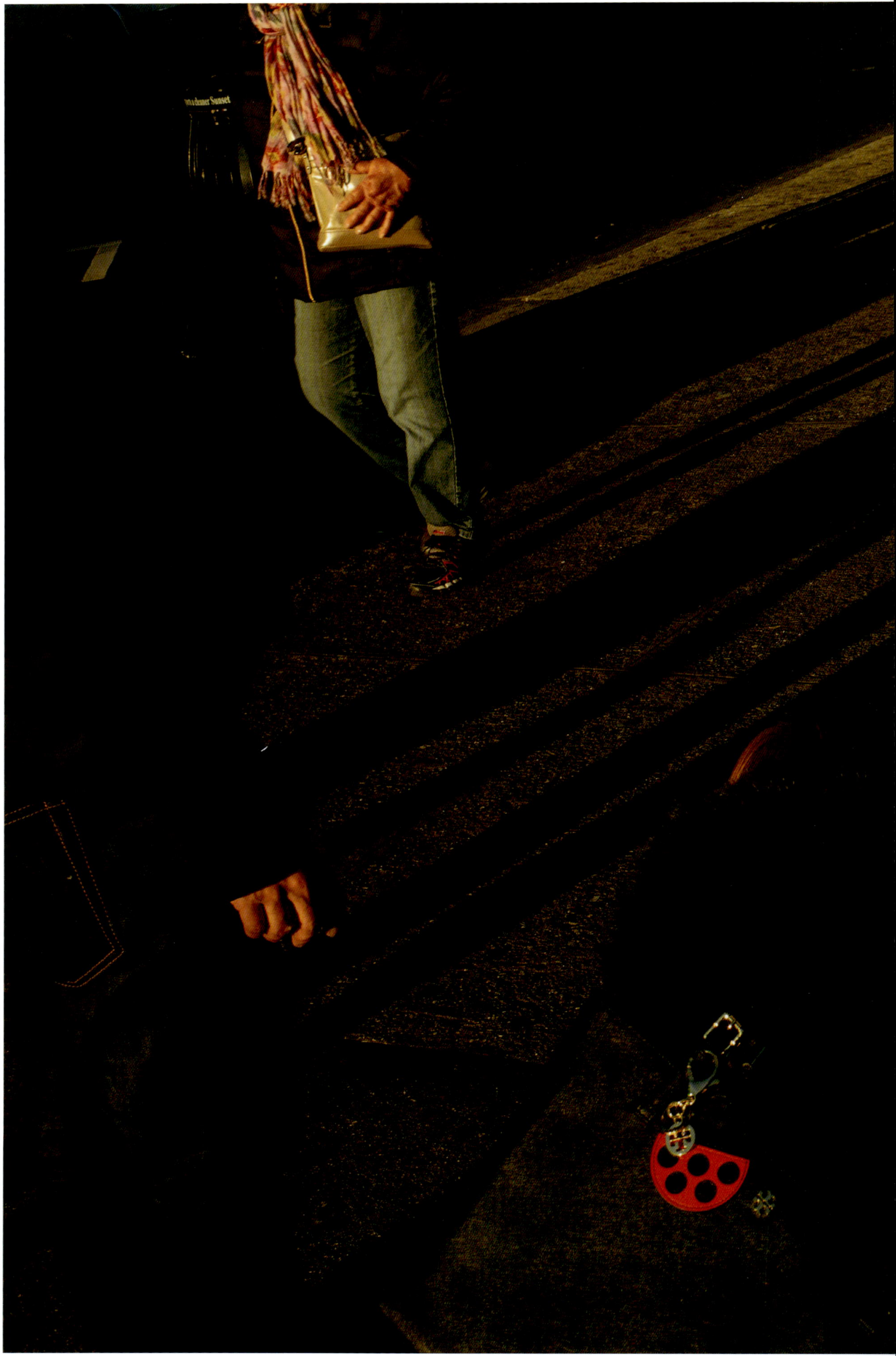

SUNSET PARK, 2014

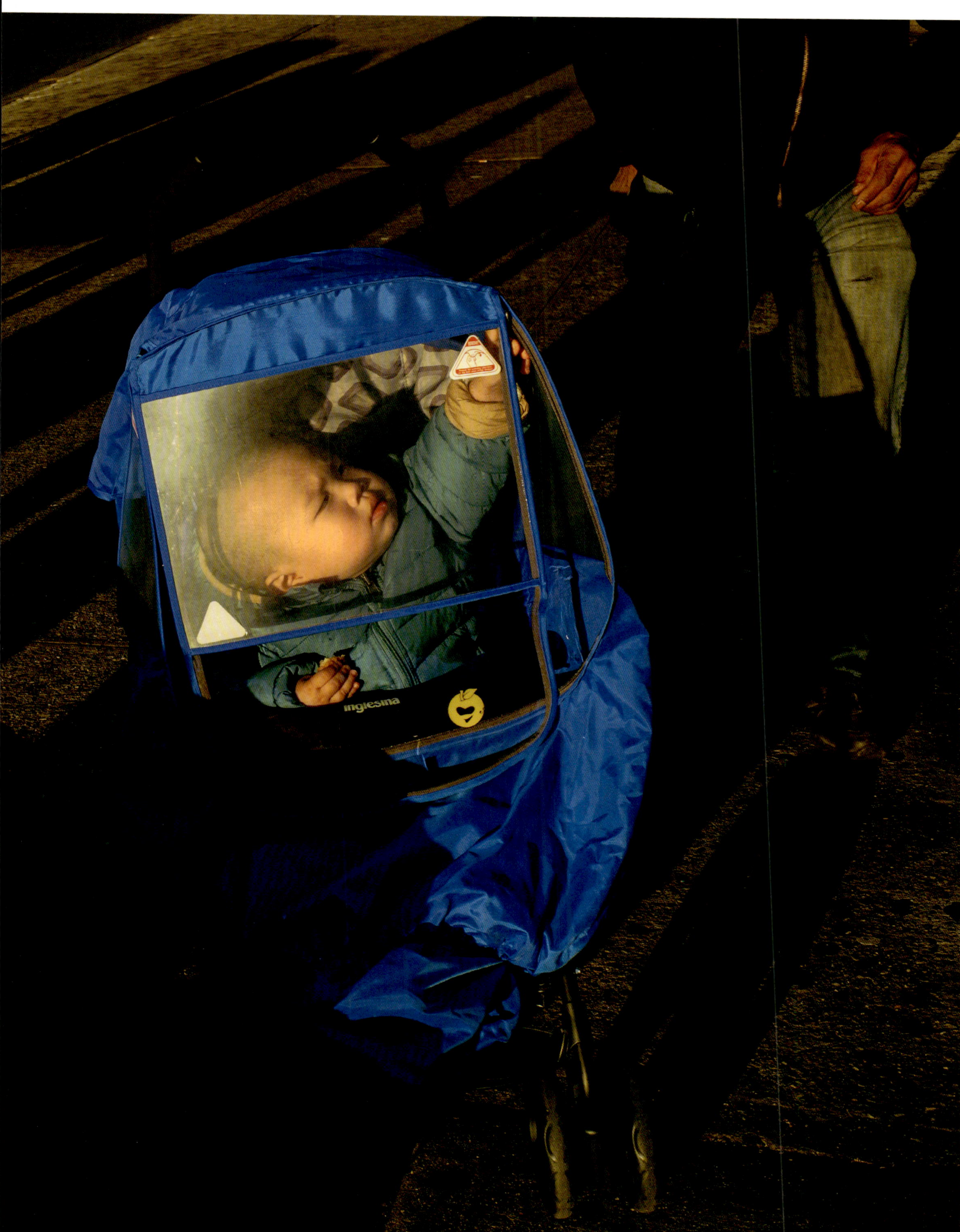

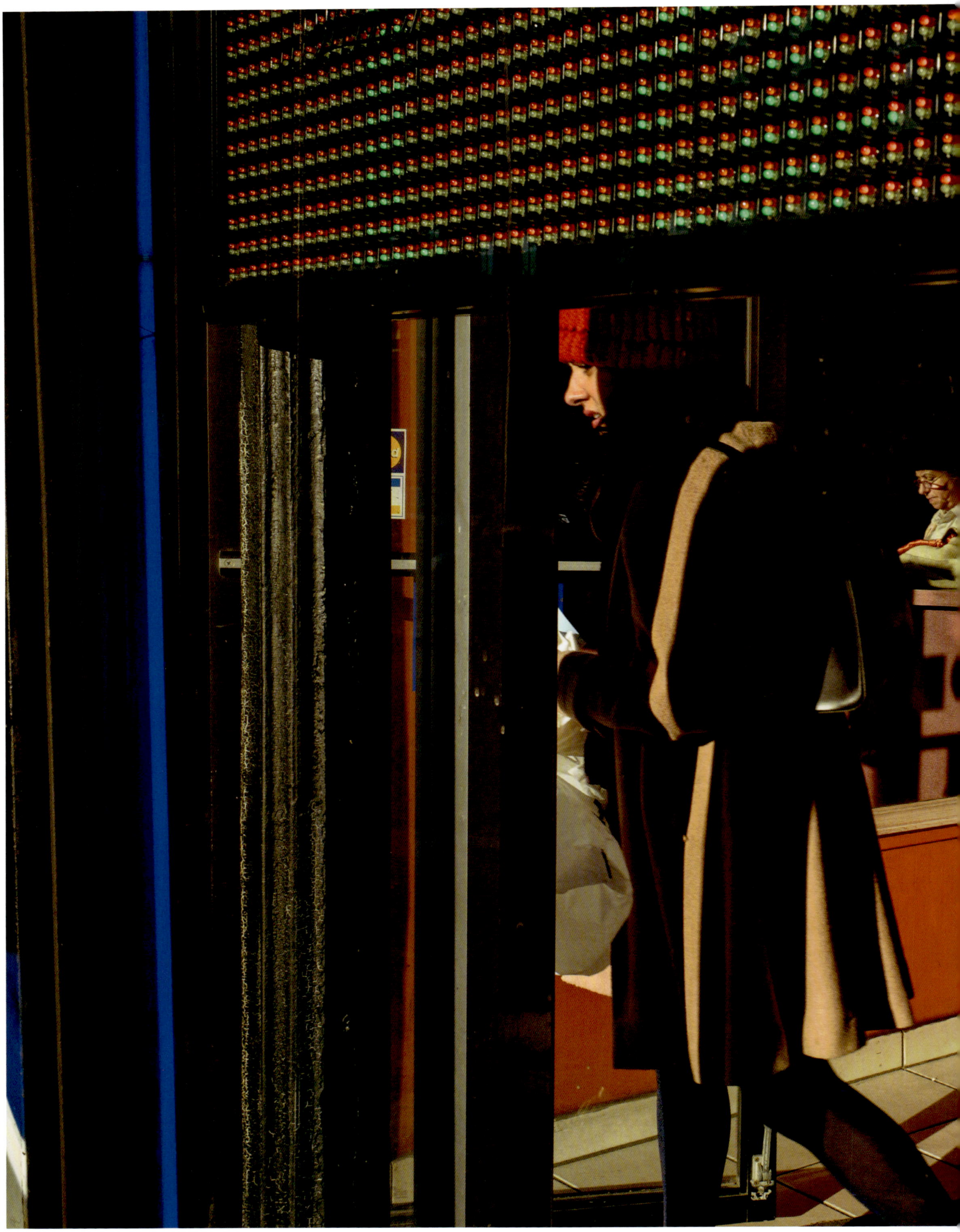

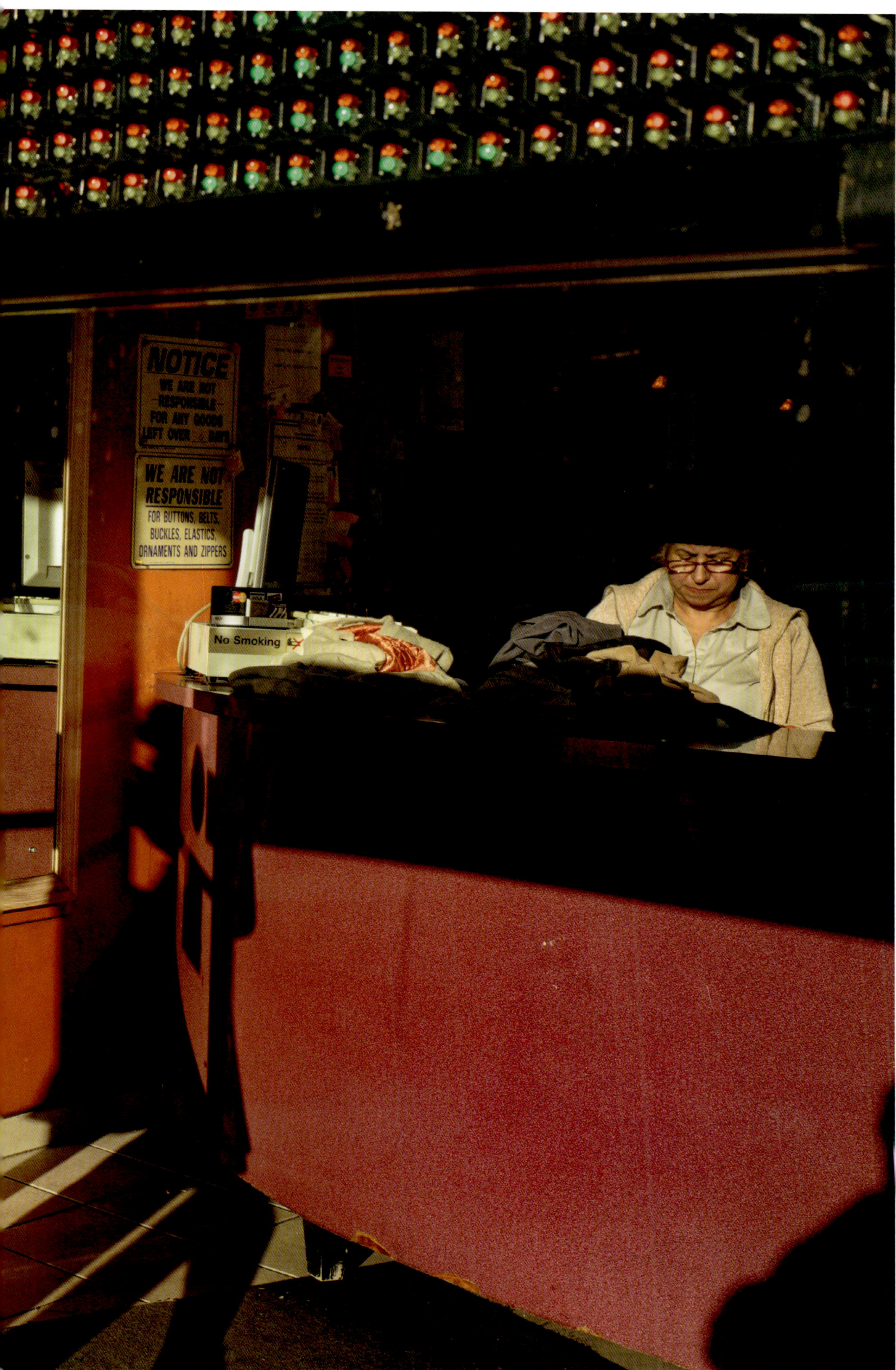
NOTICE
WE ARE NOT
RESPONSIBLE
FOR ANY GOODS
LEFT OVER 30 DAYS
WE ARE NOT
RESPONSIBLE
FOR BUTTONS, BELTS,
BUCKLES, ELASTICS,
ORNAMENTS AND ZIPPERS
No Smoking

WILLIAMSBURG, 2016

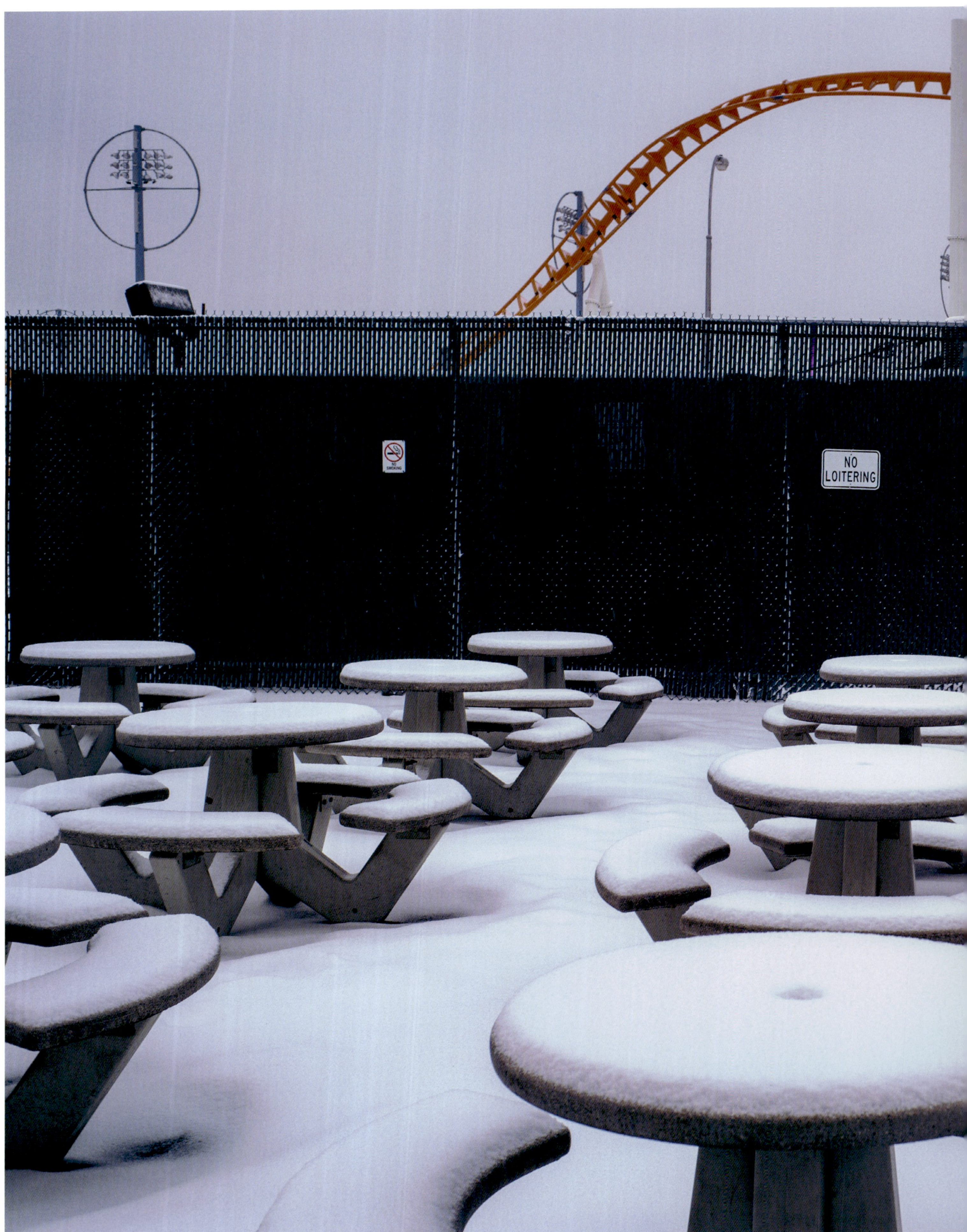
NO
SMOKING
NO
LOITERING

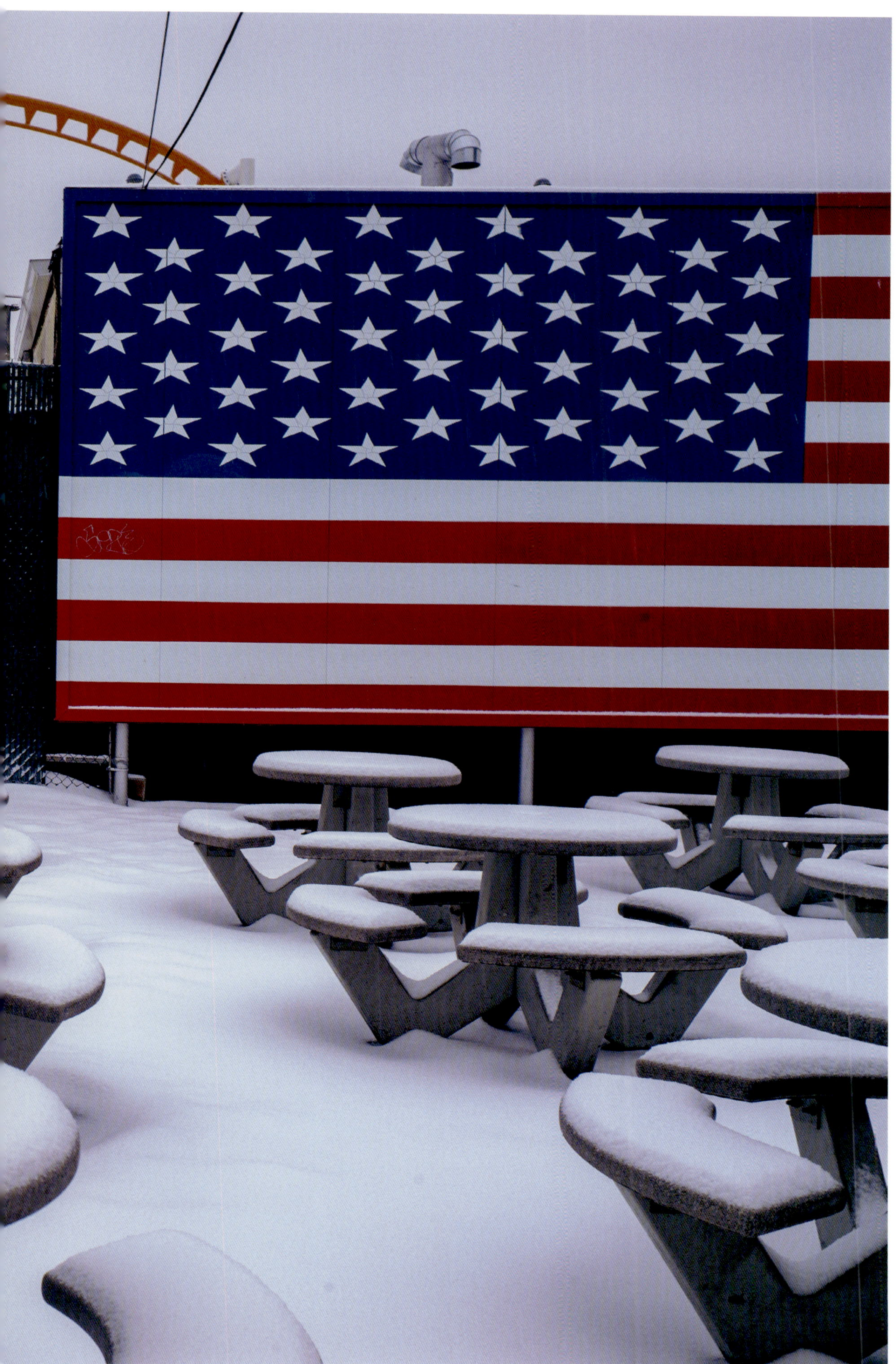

CONEY ISLAND, 2015

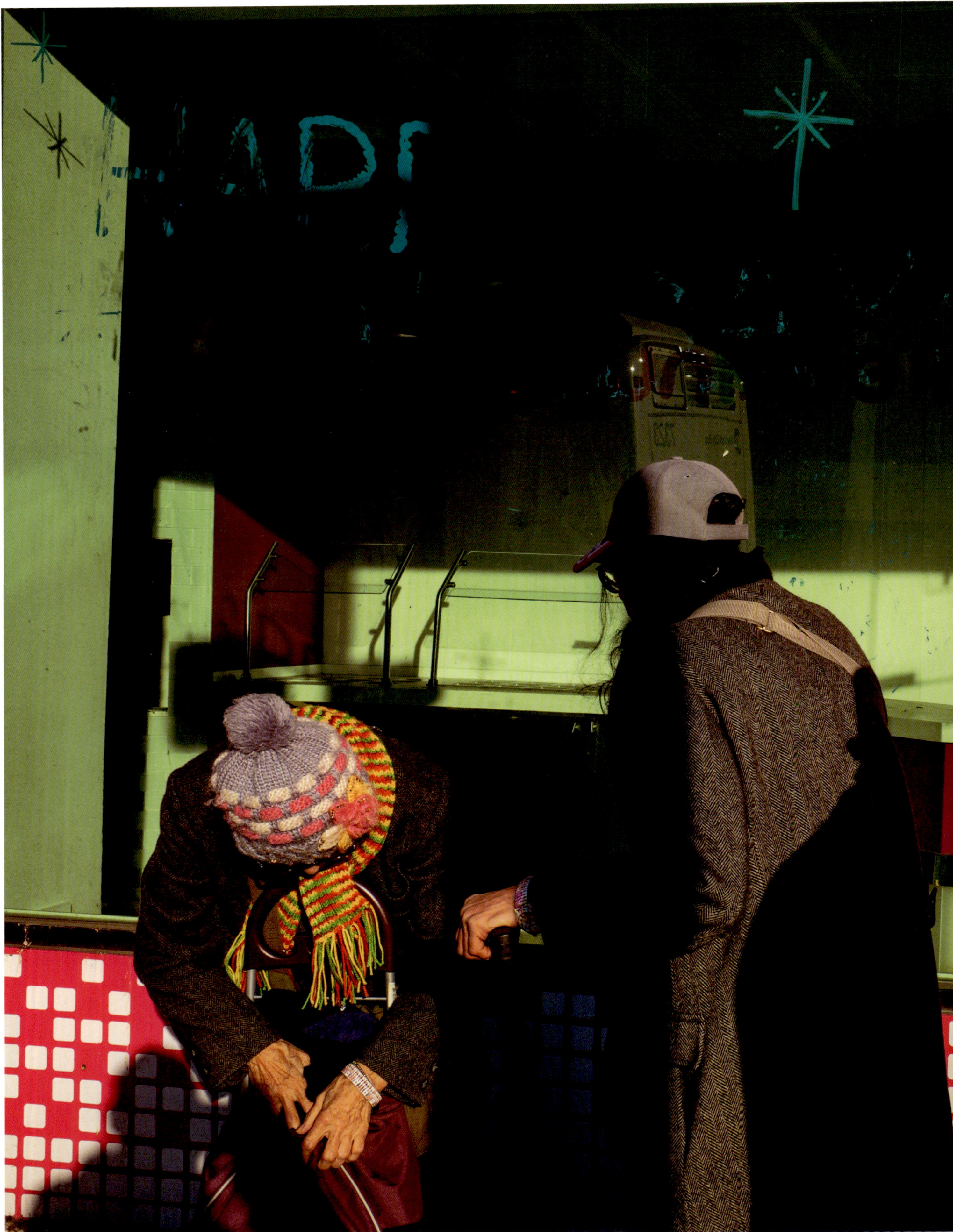

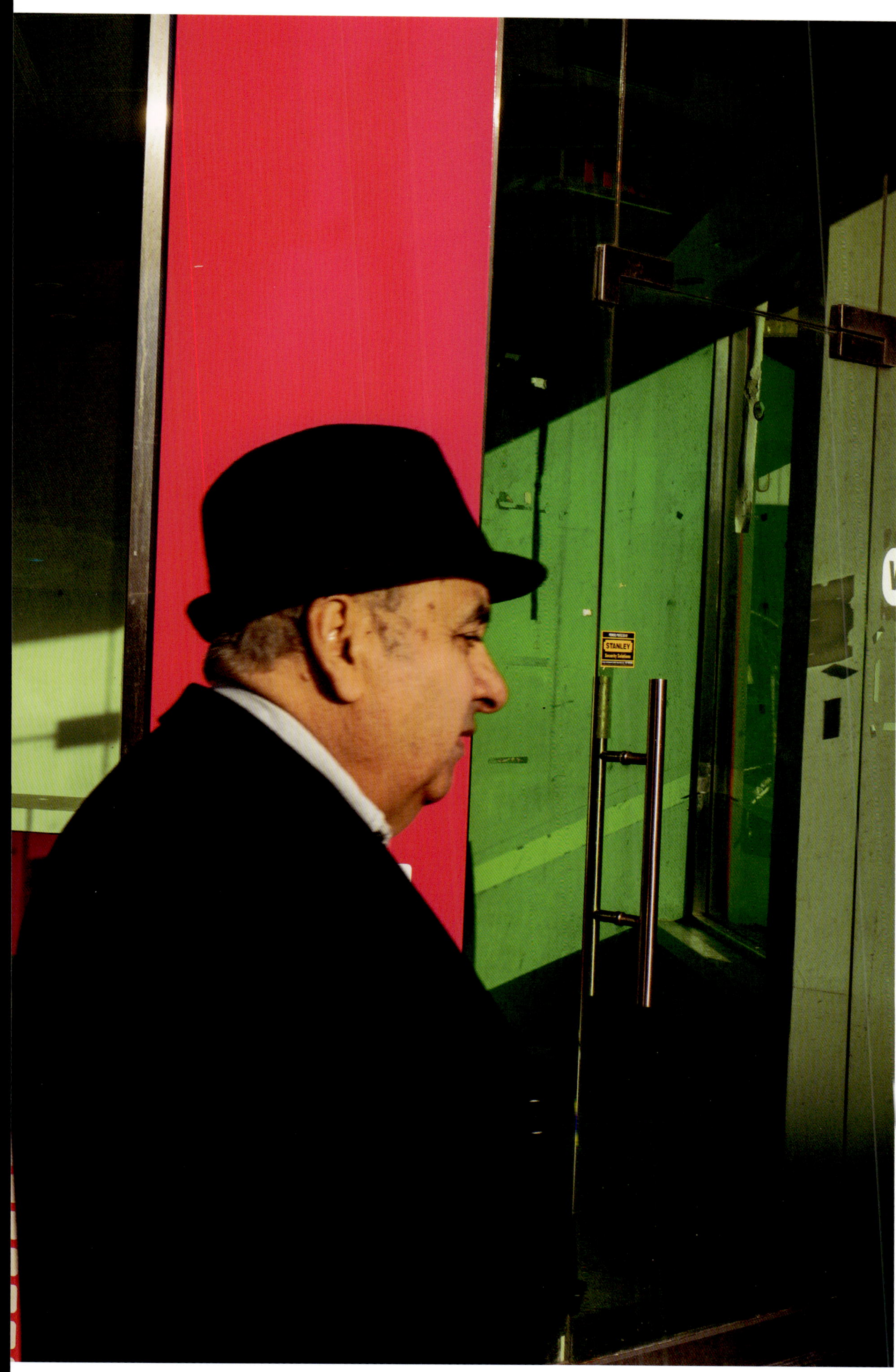

SHEEPSHEAD BAY, 2016

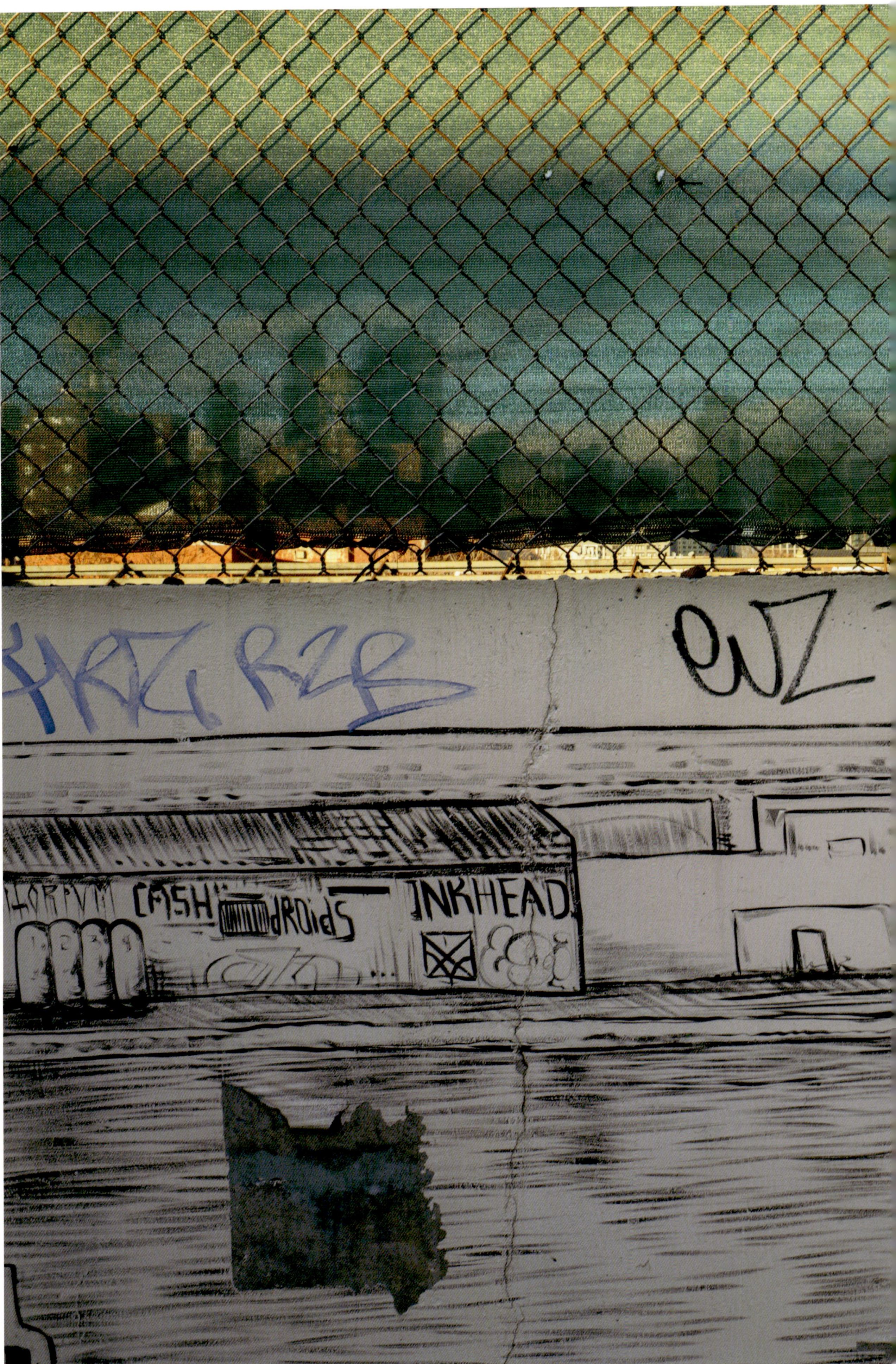

BARTGIRZB
OVZ
HORPVN CASH DROIDS INKHEAD

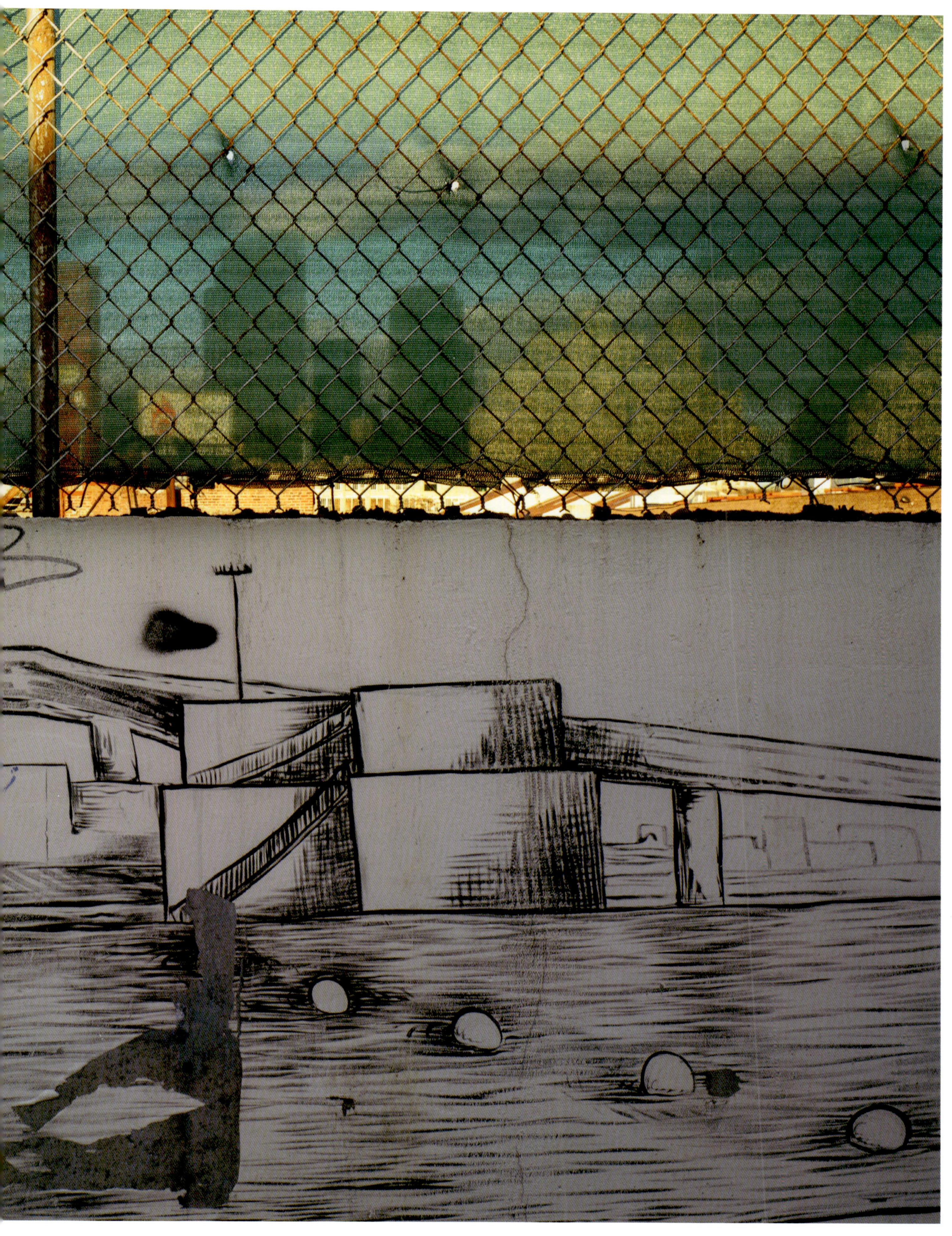

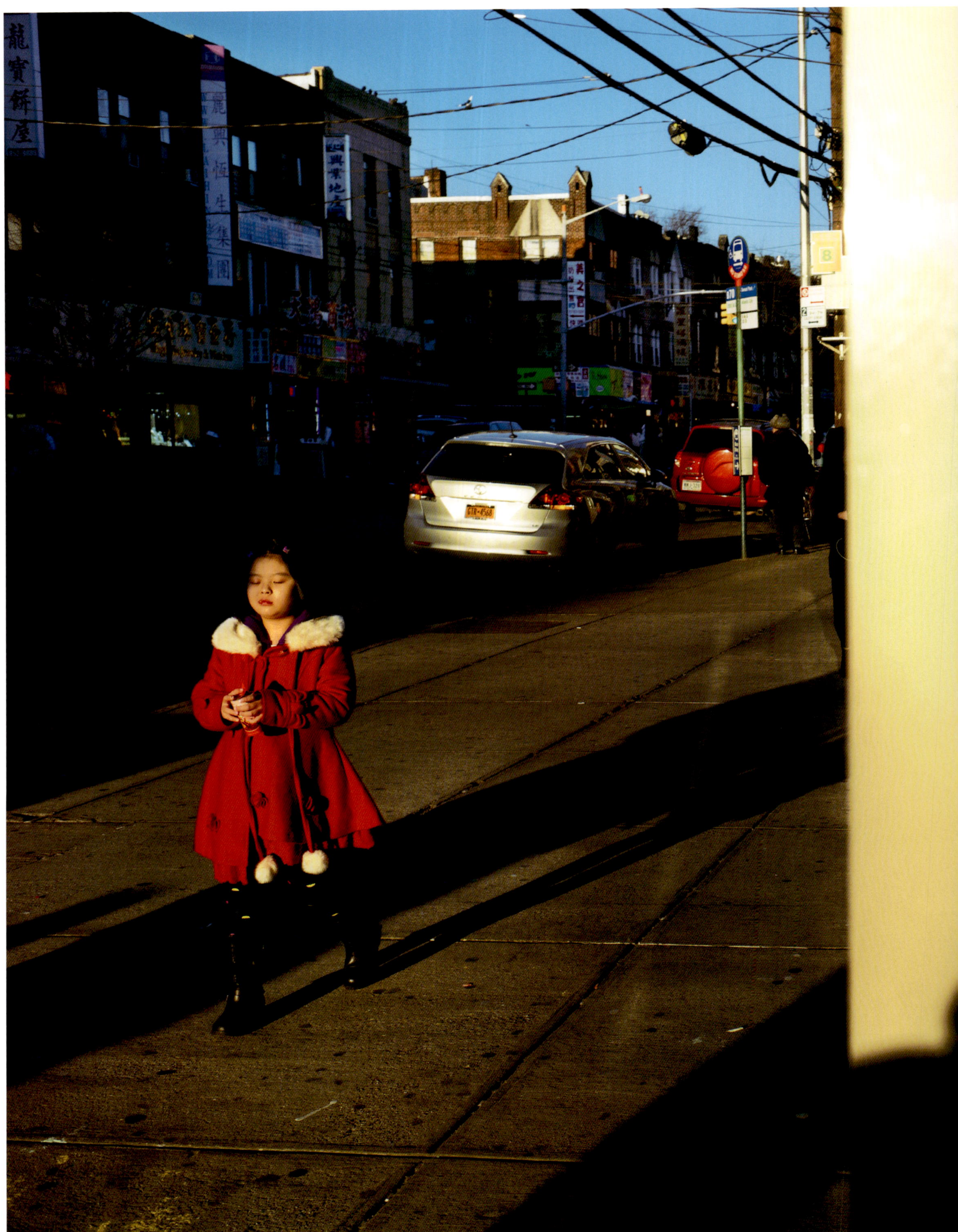

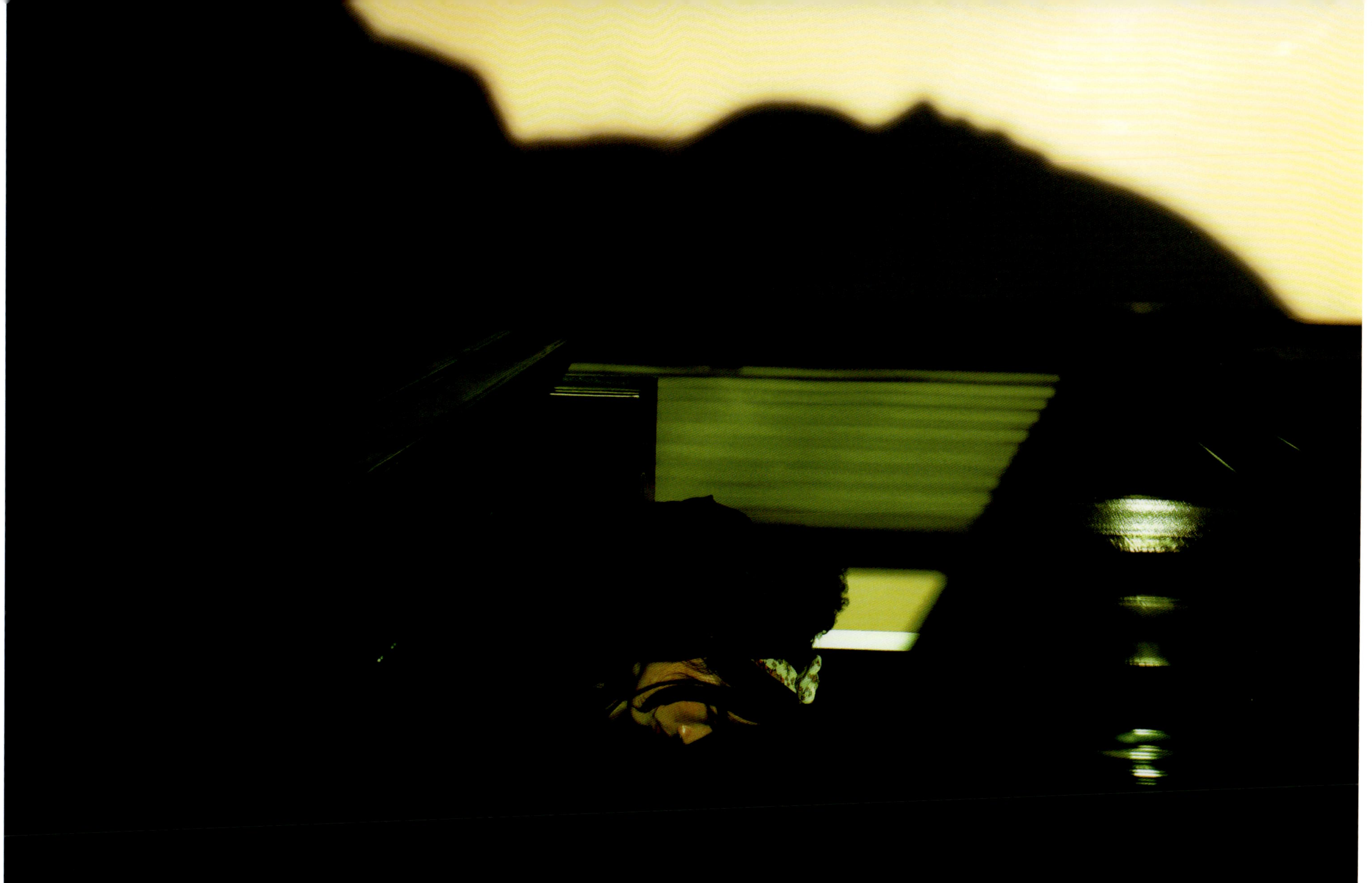

SUNSET PARK, 2014

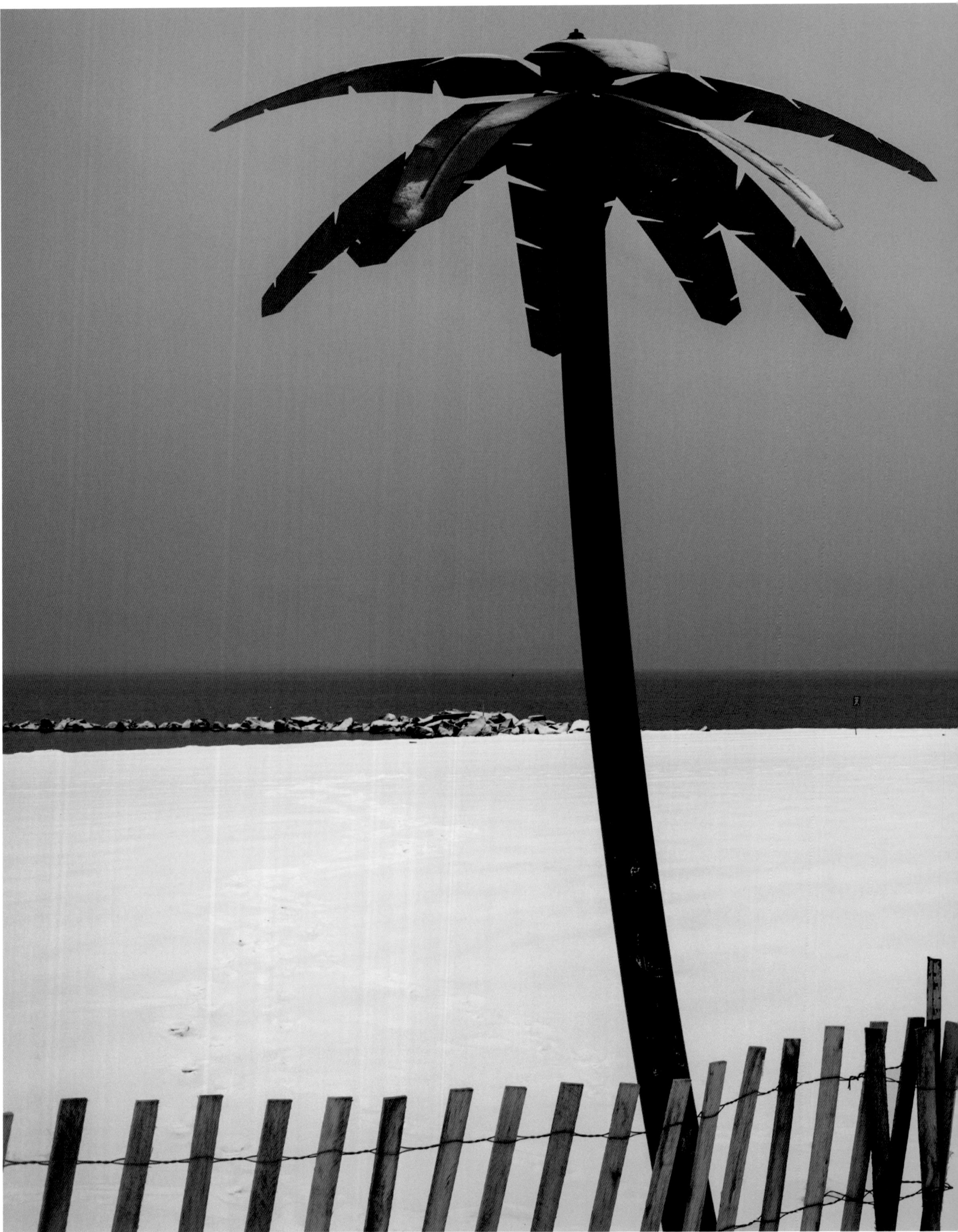

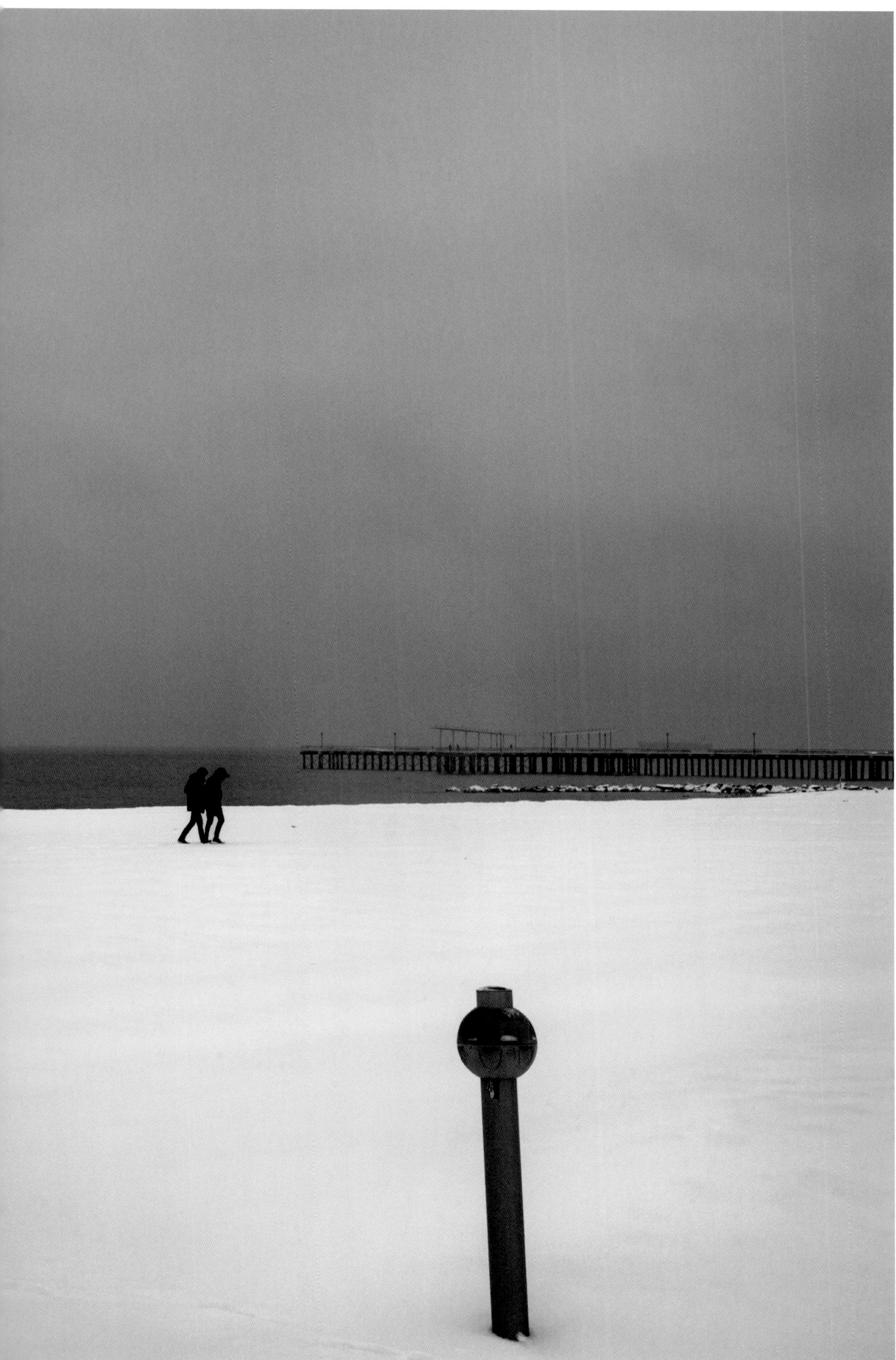

CONEY ISLAND, 2015

PLATE LIST

Rebecca Norris Webb

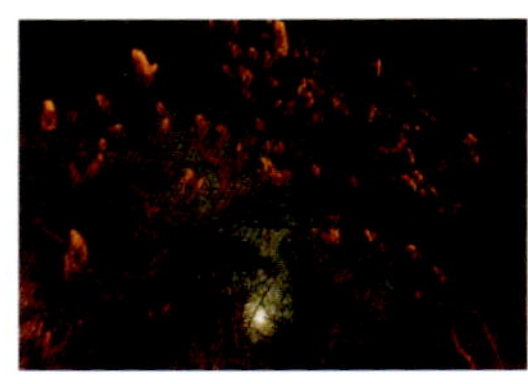

Flying at Night
Prospect Park, 2015

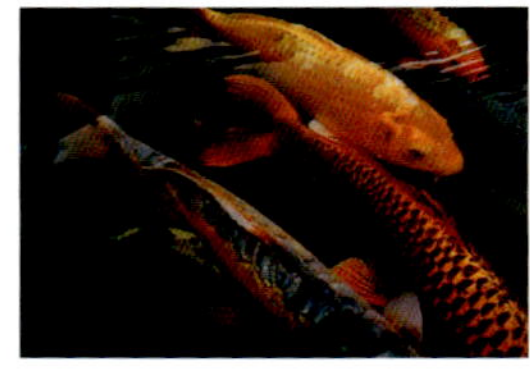

Koi
Green-Wood Cemetery, 2017

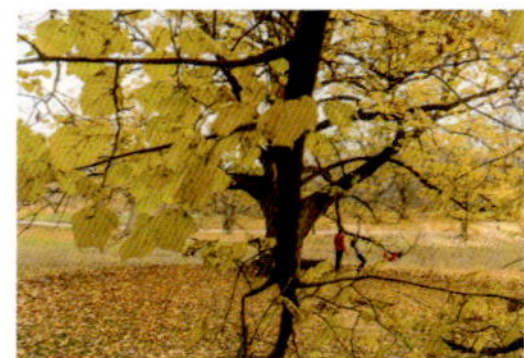

Family Tree
Prospect Park, 2015

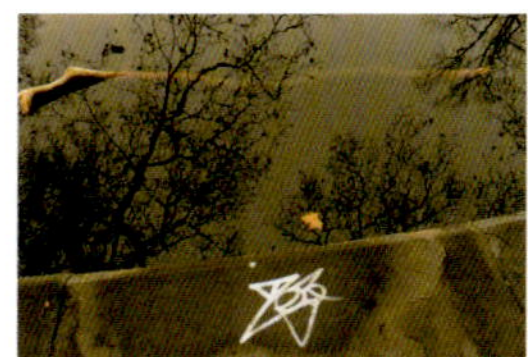

Star
Prospect Park, 2015

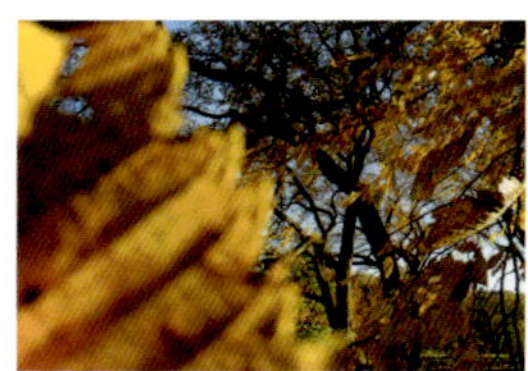

Stand of Elm
Prospect Park, 2018

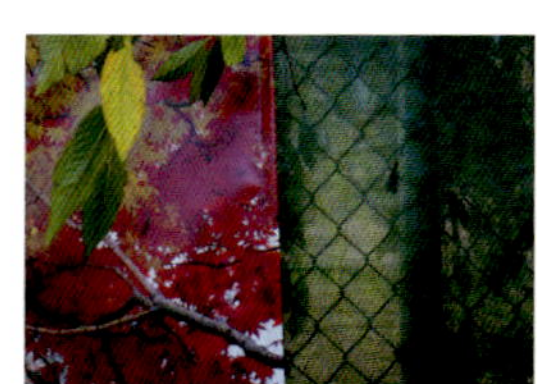

Fall and Fall
Brooklyn Botanic Garden, 2018

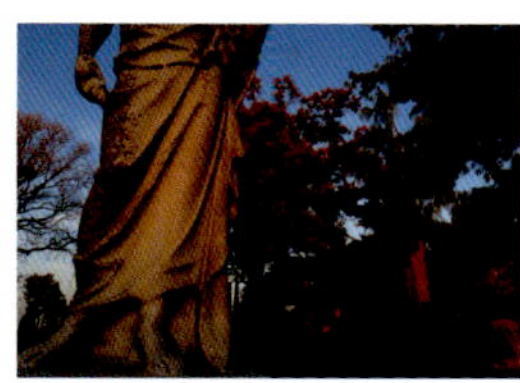

Last Light
Green-Wood Cemetery, 2018

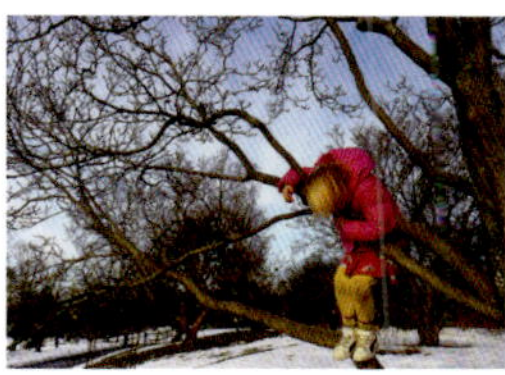

Reverie
Prospect Park, 2016

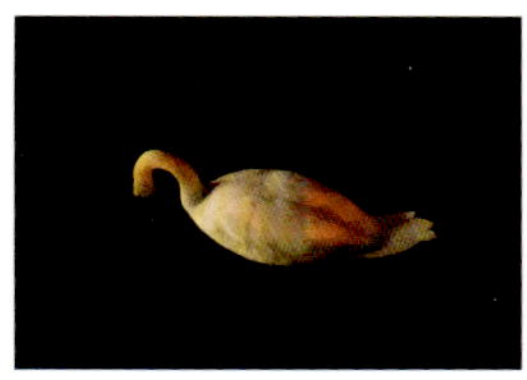

Mute Swan
Prospect Park, 2016

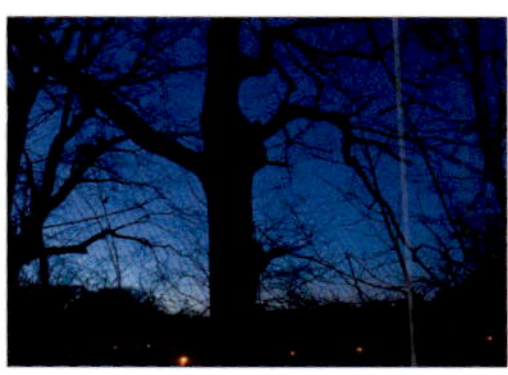

Night Park with Raccoon
Prospect Park, 2017

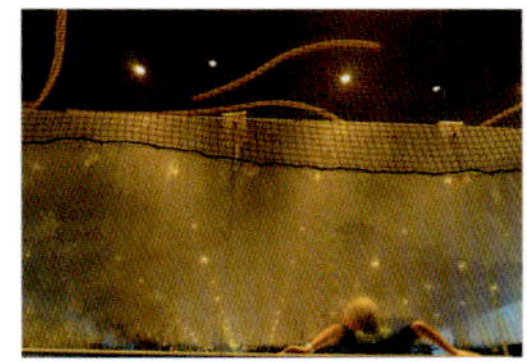

Skater
Prospect Park, 2016

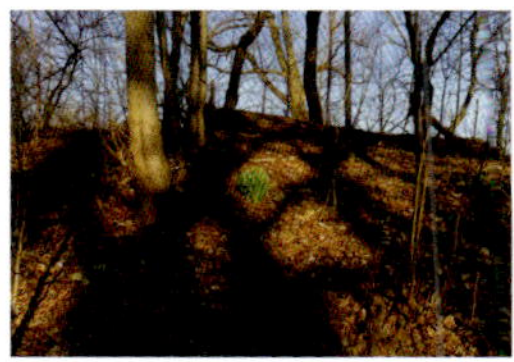

First Daffodils
Prospect Park, 2016

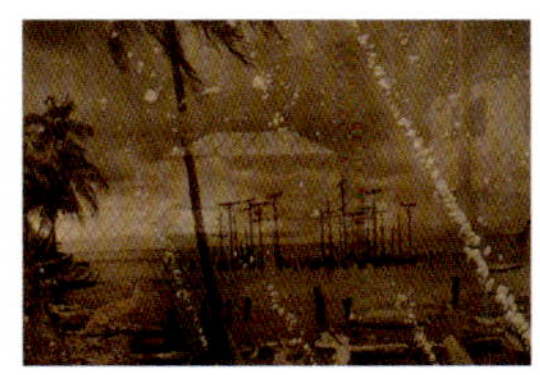

Two Worlds
Prospect Park, 2016

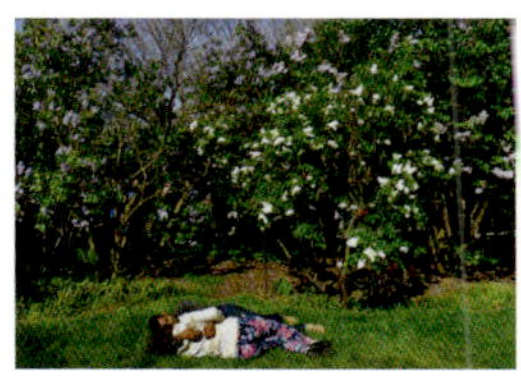

Under the Lilacs
Brooklyn Botanic Garden, 2016

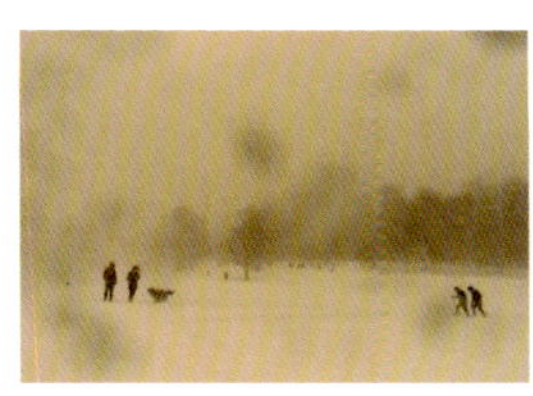

Winter Storm
Prospect Park, 2016

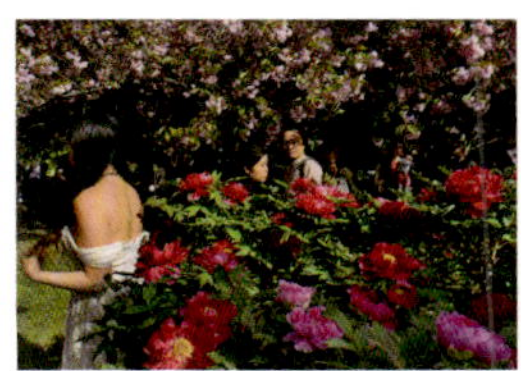

Our Garden
Brooklyn Botanic Garden, 2016

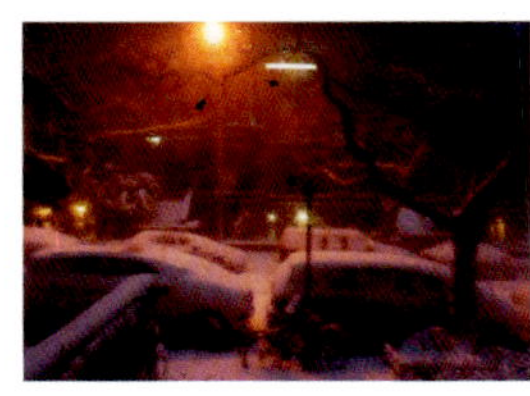

Our Window
near Prospect Park, 2016

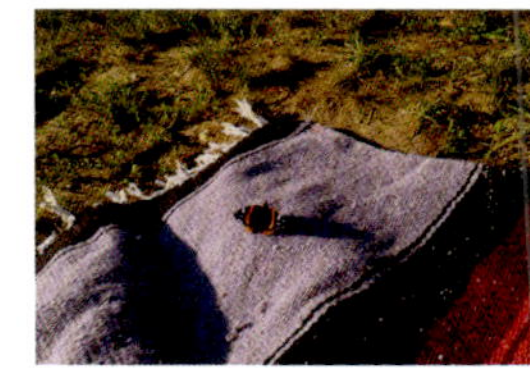

Red Admiral Butterfly
Prospect Park, 2017

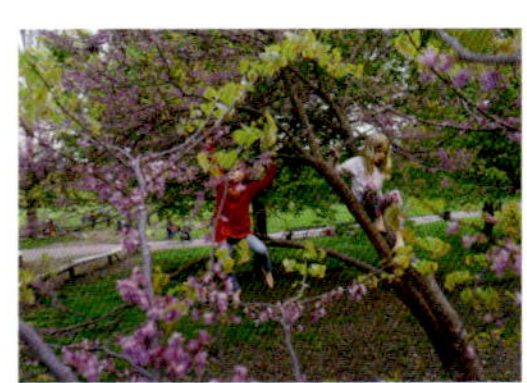

Redbud
Prospect Park, 2017

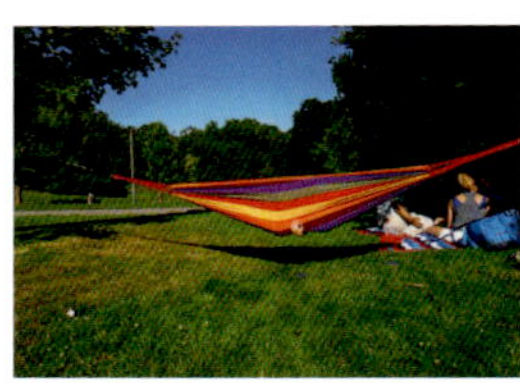

Near Battle Pass
Prospect Park, 2017

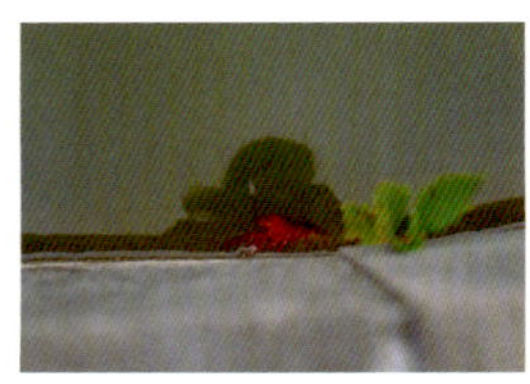

Crayfish
Brooklyn Botanic Garden, 2018

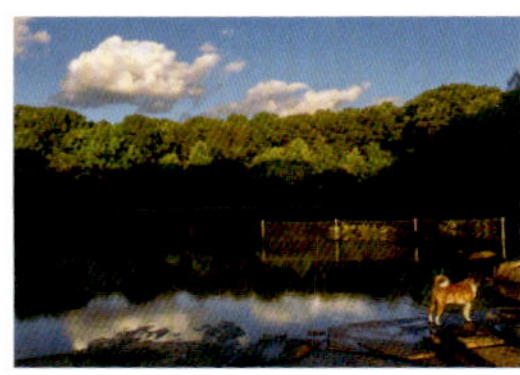

Dog Beach
Prospect Park, 2018

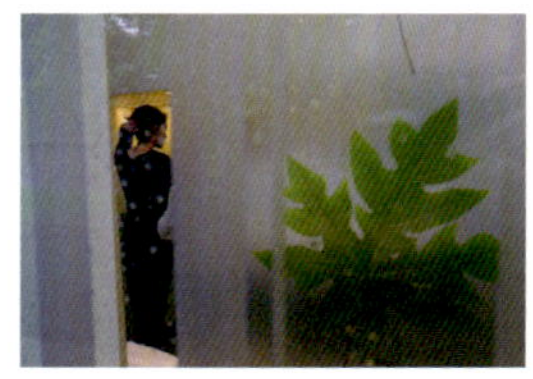

In the Rain
Brooklyn Botanic Garden, 2017

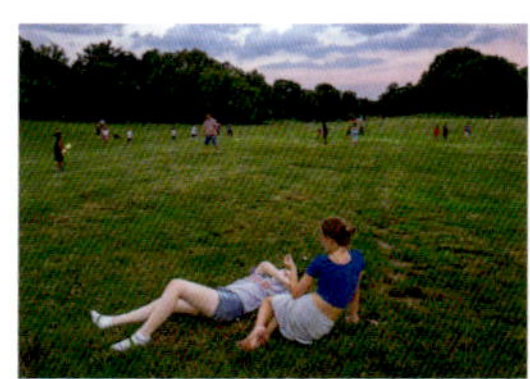

Long Meadow
Prospect Park, 2017

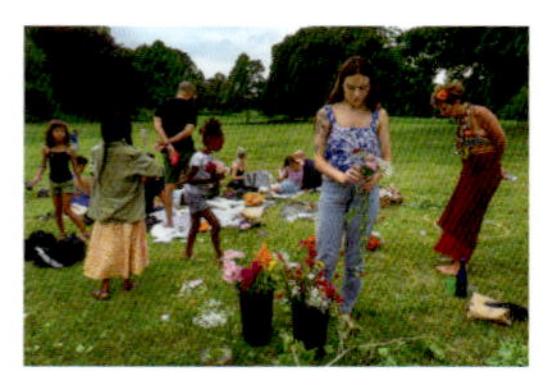

Midsummer Festival
Prospect Park, 2017

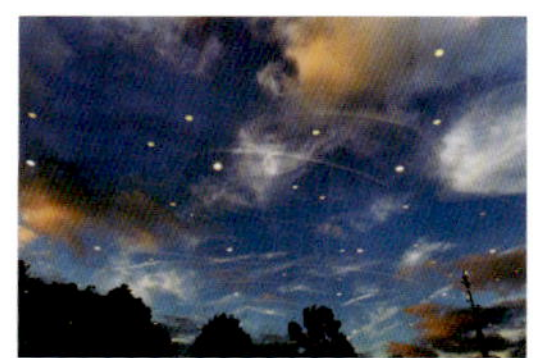

Shimmering
Prospect Park, 2018

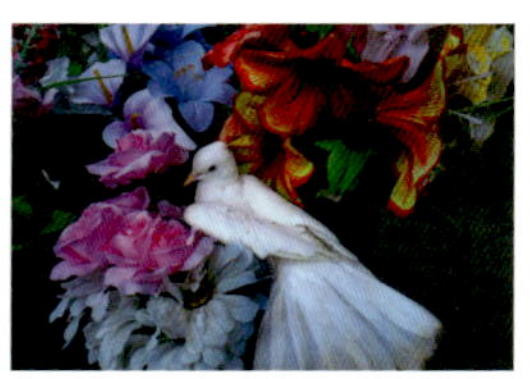

Diana's Dove
Green-Wood Cemetery, 2018

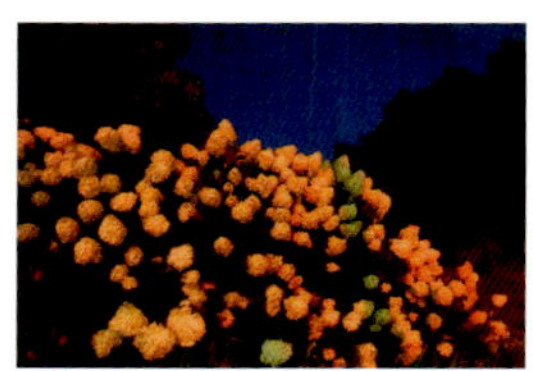

Night Before Aretha Died
Brooklyn Botanic Garden, 2018

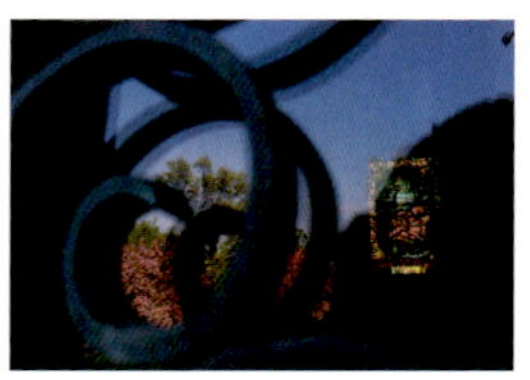

Falling Calls to Us
Green-Wood Cemetery, 2017

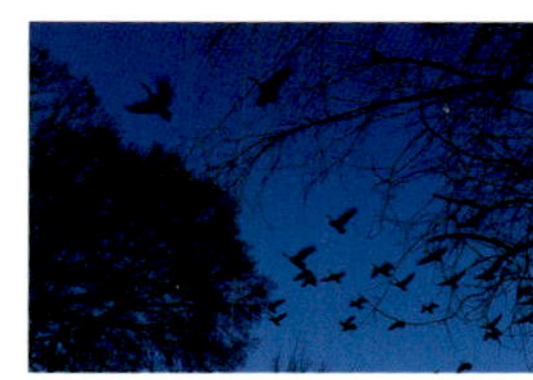

Wild Geese
Prospect Park, 2017

NOTES ON WORDS & IMAGES

Rebecca Norris Webb

"Flying at Night" references the following excerpt from George Oppen's civic poem about the people and the streets of New York City, *Of Being Numerous* (New Directions, 1968): "Obsessed, bewildered / By the shipwreck / Of the singular / We have chosen the meaning / Of being numerous." Additionally, "Flying at Night" is in dialogue with Tomas Tranströmer's "Schubertiana," about looking at New York City at night from a distance: "a spiral galaxy seen from the side," translated by Robert Bly in *The Half-Finished Heaven* (Graywolf Press, 2001, reissued 2017).

"Stand of Elm" is a creative conversation with Adrienne Rich's "What Kind of Times Are These," which begins "There's a place between two stands of trees . . ." and ends with the lines: ". . . because in times like these / to have you listen at all, it's necessary / to talk about trees." The poem is from *Collected Poems: 1950–2012* (W. W. Norton, 2016). Marie Beatrice "Bea" Schol-Schwarz (1898–1969) was the Dutch phytopathologist who discovered the fungus that causes Dutch elm disease. The elm tree *Ulmus x hollandica* "Bea Schwarz" was named in her honor.

"Night Park" is in dialogue with Virginia Woolf's "Street Haunting," an essay about walking at night through the streets of London, which was published in *The Death of the Moth and Other Essays* (Hogarth Press, 1942). It includes the line, "We are no longer quite ourselves." "The Camperdown Elm," the poem Marianne Moore wrote to save Prospect Park's rare tree of the same name, was first published in the *New Yorker*, September 23, 1967.

The form of "Brooklyn Botanic Garden" was inspired by Wisława Szymborska's "Could Have," translated by Clare Cavanagh and Stanisław Baranczak in *View with a Grain of Sand* (Harcourt, 1995).

"In the Rain" was inspired by a conversation with Wah-Ming Chang in Brooklyn in 2018. It is dedicated to Mary Witherell (1961–2019), who once lived across the street from Prospect Park with the love of her life, the artist Gayle Mahoney.

"Diana's Dove" is dedicated to Diana Willensky Thompson (1965–2018). Diana, the first Brooklynite I ever befriended, grew up not far from where I live now in Park Slope. I met her in 1990, the year her father, Elliot Willensky, the former Borough Historian of Brooklyn, died unexpectedly.

THE CITY WITHIN

Interview with Sean Corcoran
Curator of Prints and Photographs, Museum of the City of New York
Winter 2019

Brooklyn was once a city of its own, and was only incorporated into New York City in 1898. It was once farmland, and as the city on Manhattan grew, Brooklyn became its bedroom community, but also the place where stevedores unloaded cargo ships, sailors and shipbuilders worked the Navy Yard, factory workers toiled, breweries worked to satiate the masses, and beach resorts entertained them. It was the place many of the working-class immigrants who passed through Ellis Island called home. Thanks to popular media today, much of the world (and many Americans, for that matter) associates Brooklyn with hipster slackers and vegan trust-fund artists, but in fact it is an archipelago of neighborhoods, and may be even more multicultural than it was over a century ago. It is New York's most populous borough, with well over two and a half million people, and is three times the size of Manhattan.

SEAN CORCORAN: Although it has been historically treated as the "second city" to Manhattan, there is also something of a mythology for Brooklyn that has been created in the words put to page by historical literary titans, including Walt Whitman, Hart Crane, James Agee, Marianne Moore, and Richard Wright (and contemporary authors like Jonathan Lethem, Jhumpa Lahiri, and Hilton Als). You both have a deep background in literature; did this color your approach to this project?

ALEX WEBB: When I began walking the streets of Brooklyn for this project, two literary works in particular initially spoke to me. One was James Agee's *Brooklyn Is*, an extended essay that Agee wrote on commission for *Fortune* in 1939 that, ironically, like *Let Us Now Praise Famous Men* [with Walker Evans, 1941], was not published by the magazine. Equally fascinating was Brooklyn-born Phillip Lopate's 2009 essay "Brooklyn the Unknowable." While both suggest the notion of Brooklyn as an infinitude of streets, Lopate's piece embraces not only the vastness, but also the chaos and the contradictions of Brooklyn.

Vastness, chaos, contradiction: these are all notions that lie close to my heart as a photographer intrigued by the mystery of the streets. Wandering from neighborhood to neighborhood, I have simply responded to the quotidian, yet sometimes enigmatic, world around me. "The magic of the streets is the mingling of the errand and the epiphany," as Rebecca Solnit wrote.

REBECCA NORRIS WEBB: When I first moved to Brooklyn twenty years ago, these lines of George Oppen struck a chord in me: "Obsessed, bewildered / By the shipwreck / Of the singular / We have chosen the meaning / Of being numerous." And what better way to respond to the multiplicity that is Brooklyn than through artist collaborations and other kinds of creative conversations? I think of Walker Evans, whose monumental black-and-white photographs of the Brooklyn Bridge illustrate the epic poem *The Bridge* by his neighbor, Hart Crane. And there's the decades-long friendship between Marianne Moore and Elizabeth Bishop, who first met near another famous literary pair, Patience and Fortitude, the marble lions in front of the New York Public Library. "It seems to me that Marianne talked to me steadily for the next thirty-five years," Bishop wrote about her poetry conversations with her mentor, whom she often met in Moore's apartment near Fort Greene Park in Brooklyn. The younger poet would later memorialize Moore, a striking figure with her red hair and black cape fluttering behind her:

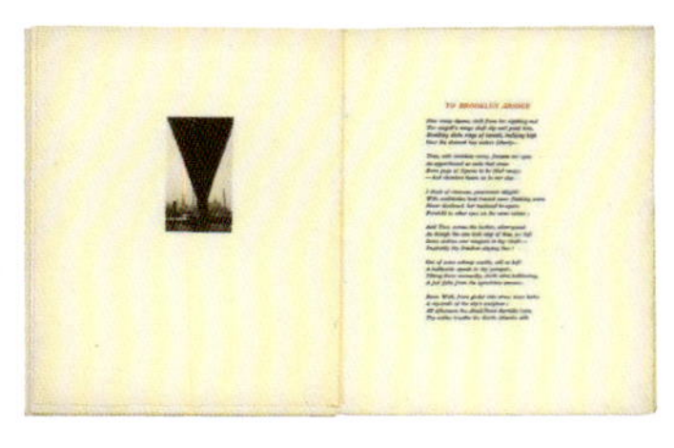

Walker Evans, pages from
The Bridge: A Poem by Hart Crane. 1930

Come like a light in the white mackerel sky . . .
over the Brooklyn Bridge . . .
please come flying.

SC: Similarly, there is a rich tradition of imagery by Brooklyn-born photographers, such as Helen Levitt, Morris Engle, Harold Feinstein, Leonard Freed, and countless others. How did you confront this cultural / historical legacy while recording your own perceptions of the borough today?

AW: As a young photographer, I remember responding to certain images of Brooklyn, most of them from Coney Island: Robert Frank's Fourth of July sleepers on the beach, Bruce Davidson's young woman fixing her hair in a cigarette machine mirror, and Garry Winogrand's surreal image of a man's body—seemingly headless—beneath the boardwalk. More recently, I think of Eugene Richards's sidewalk image of a family playing in a plastic swimming pool, some of Bruce Gilden's edgy Coney Island pictures, or Thomas Roma's *Sunset Park* [1998] and other projects from Brooklyn. However, all these images I recall from the borough were taken in black and white. Photographing Brooklyn in color—especially on those clear fall and winter afternoons when golden shafts of light permeate the streets of the borough—I often feel I'm exploring a kind of unknown territory.

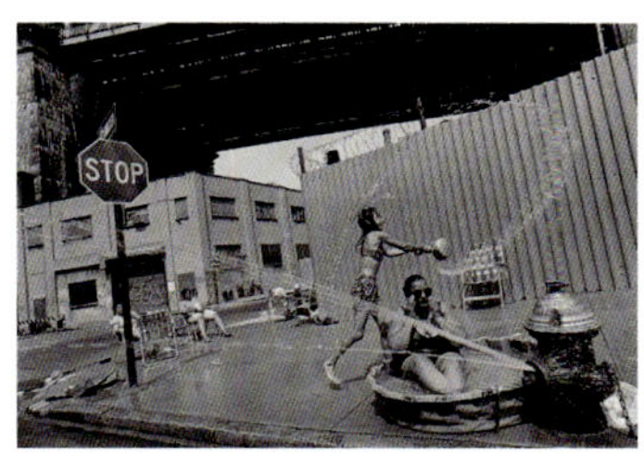

Eugene Richards, *Grandmother,
Brooklyn*, 1993

R N W : Walking and photographing in the Brooklyn Botanic Garden, Green-Wood Cemetery, and Prospect Park, I feel I'm returning to my street photography roots, particularly the work of Helen Levitt. In 1988, her lyrical images spoke to the young photographer I was then, moving to New York from the Great Plains to study photography at the International Center of Photography and, hopefully, to find my way back to writing the poetry that had been eluding me. Levitt's work encouraged me to

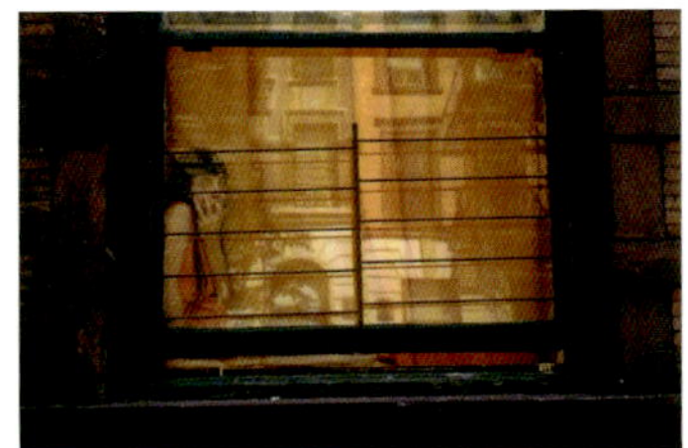

Helen Levitt, *New York*, 1972

try my hand at spontaneous street photography, focusing my camera on those inhabiting this cacophonous, often overwhelming place who were, perhaps, even shyer than I was: children. And ever since I learned that Levitt grew up in Brooklyn, I've often wondered whether she walked through the same green spaces where I've walked—and what would have caught her eye. No surprise that Levitt showed up in one of my text pieces, "Night Park," whose first line arose from the rhythm of walking in Prospect Park's Long Meadow past twilight, as I watched the streetlights flickering on again.

S C : Rebecca, your work often deals with the interconnection between people and the natural world. Can you expand on this notion in regard to working in Brooklyn?

R N W : Around twenty years ago, I took a pivotal photograph in Brooklyn. Late one afternoon in 1998, I decided to visit Coney Island's aquarium near closing time. Turning a corner, I came upon a beluga whale, whose white body seemed to float

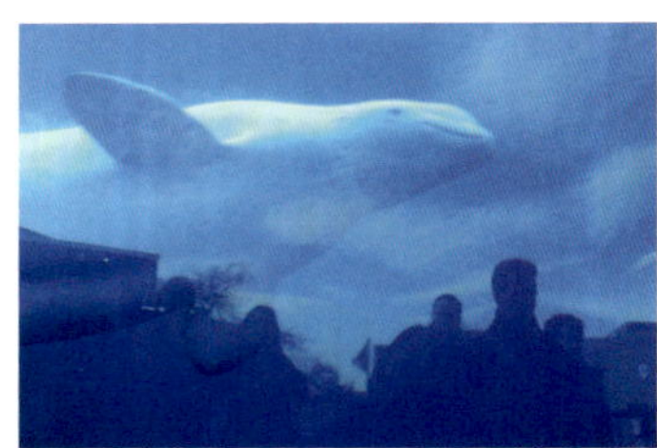

Rebecca Norris Webb,
Beluga Whale, Brooklyn, 1998

high over the heads of the few remaining aquarium visitors, whose faces were reflected in the glass tank. I thought to myself—I'll get rid of that reflection. Then I realized that there was something intriguing about the relationship between the watchers and the watched. That led to my seven-year project *The Glass Between Us* [2006], in which I photographed and wrote about the relationship between people and animals in twenty-five cities around the world.

Because this Coney Island photograph led me to my first book, I consider Brooklyn my creative home. It's where I became the bookmaker I am today, working in a hybrid personal-documentary form, which weaves together my photographs and spare text to explore our complicated relationship with the natural world. I tend to work deeply in landscapes where I've lived or spent considerable time, as I did for my third book, *My Dakota* [2012], which is a kind of road trip of my grief for my brother through the badlands and prairies of South Dakota, where I came of age. With *Brooklyn* I hope that, taken together, my words and images expand on the notion of green space, to include not only the shifting light illuminating a particular elm tree or mute swan or young woman's face, but also the deep shadows of history falling across Prospect Park—once the site of a former [Revolutionary War] battlefield—and the reverie and memory flowing through it.

S C : Alex, for more than two decades you've lived in Brooklyn, but during that time New York City has rarely been the subject of your camera. Is there a reason for this?

A W : Until I was twenty-three, I photographed largely where I lived: in the Boston area, where I grew up, and later in New York, where I moved in 1974 as a young photographer. Then in 1975, I made two photographic trips that changed me fundamentally—as a photographer and as a human being—to Haiti and the US-Mexico border. Those journeys led to my working deeper into Latin America and the Caribbean, and ultimately resulted in my photographing in color—a huge transformation for a photographer who had consistently only embraced black and white. That obsession for photographing outside of my own culture, especially in the so-called tropics, fueled my work for over thirty-five years.

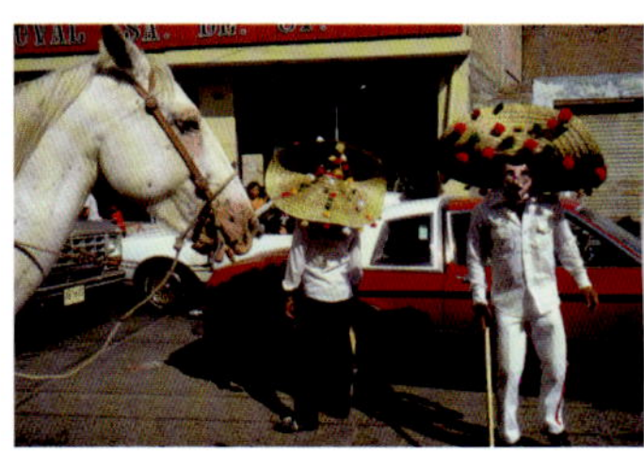

Alex Webb, *Aguascalientes,*
Mexico, 1985

However, while photographing in a variety of Brooklyn neighborhoods for this project, I began to realize that I was passing through many of the same cultures I'd photographed in the 1980s and 1990s. The oil-drenched J'Ouvert revelers in Crown Heights, celebrating in the early morning hours before the West Indian Day Parade, transported me back to the streets of Grenada during carnival. Photographing an Assumption Day celebration in Bushwick—and being invited into a cellar apartment for tamales—reminded me of Assumption Day in Aguascalientes, Mexico, in 1985. Some thirty years later while photographing this Brooklyn fiesta, I felt as if I'd entered a Mexican village, since most of the celebrants hailed from the small town of Piaxtla, in the south-central state of Puebla, Mexico.

S C : *Brooklyn: The City Within* is your fifth collaborative project, so you are clearly comfortable working as a team. Could you talk a little more about working together over the past decade?

A W : With our first collaboration, *Violet Isle: A Duet of Photographs from Cuba* [2009], Rebecca and I discovered that by bringing together our two linked but distinct visions, we could create a more multilayered portrait of a place than either of us could do individually. Brooklyn—the richly diverse and complicated borough that we've called home for so long—seemed to call out for collaboration. Moreover, it seemed particularly fitting for us, because collaborative bookmaking is the creative home we share.

R N W : That said, no one book of photographs could ever capture all the worlds that make up Brooklyn. At best, it's just one more voice—or in our case, two voices—added to the chorus that is Brooklyn.

S C : Sometimes things that are familiar are the most difficult things to photograph. Did this project make you reexamine or alter your perceptions of Brooklyn?

A W : I'm not sure we could have done this book without the impetus of our eventual departure from Brooklyn. The vantage point of our leaving enabled us to see our home borough with fresh eyes. This allowed each of us to say farewell creatively in our own ways—me by photographing the streets, Rebecca by photographing and writing about the green spaces near where we live.

R N W : While working on this book, Alex and I were reminded that Brooklyn is part of our heritage. For Alex, it was his grandfather, Ernest Webb, born in Shanghai to a seafaring family, who moved to Brooklyn as a child in the late nineteenth century. For me, it was my Montenegrin grandmother, Mary Raisovich. At six years old, in 1910, she first saw Whitman's "Brooklyn of ample hills" from the deck of a ship heading to Ellis Island, a view that she'd never forget.

Could it be "the city within" is that place inhabiting us, no matter how long ago we passed through?

ACKNOWLEDGMENTS

We'd like to thank Aperture's Senior Editor Denise Wolff for helping us create this unique book, David Chickey and Montana Currie for making such a beautiful design, and Esteban Mauchi of Laumont Photographics for his luminous prints. We'd also like to thank the rest of the Aperture team, in particular Chris Boot, Kellie McLaughlin, Sally Knapp, Susan Ciccotti, True Sims, and Nelson Chan. And we're grateful to curator Sean Corcoran for his perceptive questions and his curation of our *Brooklyn* exhibition at the Museum of the City of New York. In addition, Rebecca would like to give a special thanks to Wah-Ming Chang for her insights about the text, and we'd like to thank Tom Bollier for accompanying us on press. We're deeply grateful for the support of Anne Stark Locher and Kurt Locher, Melissa and James O'Shaughnessy, and Maria Eduarda and Ricardo Brito S. Pereira.

Finally, we dedicate this book to the people of Brooklyn, including our friends and neighbors, our fellow photographers and writers, and all those others we've shared this borough with for the past twenty years.

BIOS

ALEX WEBB (born in San Francisco, 1952) has published more than fifteen books, including *Memory City* (2014, with Rebecca Norris Webb), *La Calle: Photographs from Mexico* (Aperture, 2016), as well as a survey of his color work, *The Suffering of Light* (Aperture, 2011). Webb became a full member of Magnum Photos in 1979. His work has been shown widely, and he has received numerous awards, including a Guggenheim Fellowship in 2007.

REBECCA NORRIS WEBB (born in Rushville, Indiana, 1956), originally a poet, often explores the complicated relationship between people and the natural world in her seven books, including *The Glass Between Us* (2006), *Violet Isle: A Duet of Photographs from Cuba* (2009, with Alex Webb), and *My Dakota* (2012). A 2019 NEA grant recipient, she has exhibited at the Museum of Fine Arts, Boston, and the Cleveland Museum of Art, among other museums.

SEAN CORCORAN (interview) is the curator of prints and photographs at the Museum of the City of New York and has written extensively on photography, including essays for *Elliott Erwitt: At Home and Around the World* (Aperture, 2016), and *I See a City: Todd Webb's New York* (2017).

BROOKLYN: THE CITY WITHIN
by Alex Webb and Rebecca Norris Webb
Interview by Sean Corcoran

Front cover: Alex Webb, *Williamsburg*, 2016
Back cover: Rebecca Norris Webb, *Night Before Aretha Died*, Brooklyn Botanic Garden, 2018

Editor: Denise Wolff
Designer: David Chickey
Senior Production Manager: True Sims
Production Manager: Nelson Chan
Senior Text Editor: Susan Ciccotti
Editorial Assistant: Charlotte Chudy
Copy Editor: Sally Knapp
Work Scholars: Bowen Fernie, Rachel Kober, Charis Morgan

Additional staff of the Aperture book program includes:
Sarah Meister, Executive Director; Michael Famighetti, Editor in Chief; Emily Patten,
Managing Editor, Books; Noa Lin, Assistant Editor, Books; Caroline Foulke, Editorial Assistant;
Iesha E. Coppin-Forde, Editorial Assistant, Books; Karina Eckmeier, Designer and Project
Manager; Minjee Cho, Production Director; Andrea Chlad, Production Manager; Thomas Bollier,
Production Consultant; Kellie McLaughlin, Director of Sales and Outreach; Richard Gregg,
Director of Book Sales and Operations

Special thanks:
Brooklyn: The City Within was made possible, in part, with generous support from Anne Stark
Locher and Kurt Locher, Melissa and James O'Shaughnessy, and Maria Eduarda and Ricardo Brito
S. Pereira.

Interview image credits:
Eugene Richards: Courtesy of the artist; Helen Levitt: © Helen Levitt Film Documents LLC, all
rights reserved, courtesy of Thomas Zander Gallery

First edition, 2019
Printed in China
10 9 8 7 6 5 4 3 2

Library of Congress Control Number: 2019904137
ISBN 978-1-59711-456-1

To order Aperture books, contact:
orders@aperture.org

For information about Aperture trade distribution worldwide, visit:
aperture.org/distribution

aperture

548 West 28th Street, 4th Floor
New York, NY 10001
aperture.org

Aperture is a nonprofit publisher dedicated to creating insight, community, and understanding
through photography.